THE ARDEN SHAKESPEARE

THIRD SERIES

General Editors: Richard Proudfoot, Ann Thompson,
David Scott Kastan and H. R. Woudhuysen

OTHELLO

REVISED EDITION

THE ARDEN SHAKESPEARE

ALL'S WELL THAT ENDS WELL	edited by G. K. Hunter*
ANTONY AND CLEOPATRA	edited by John Wilders
AS YOU LIKE IT	edited by Juliet Dusinberre
THE COMEDY OF ERRORS	edited by R. A. Foakes*
CORIOLANUS	edited by Peter Holland
CYMBELINE	edited by J. M. Nosworthy*
DOUBLE FALSEHOOD	edited by Brean Hammond
HAMLET, Revised	edited by Ann Thompson and Neil Taylor
JULIUS CAESAR	edited by David Daniell
KING HENRY IV PART 1	edited by David Scott Kastan
KING HENRY IV PART 2	edited by James C. Bulman
KING HENRY V	edited by T. W. Craik
KING HENRY VI PART 1	edited by Edward Burns
KING HENRY VI PART 2	edited by Ronald Knowles
KING HENRY VI PART 3	edited by John D. Cox and Eric Rasmussen
KING HENRY VIII	edited by Gordon McMullan
KING JOHN	edited by E. A. J. Honigmann*
KING LEAR	edited by R. A. Foakes
KING RICHARD II	edited by Charles Forker
KING RICHARD III	edited by James R. Siemon
LOVE'S LABOUR'S LOST	edited by H. R. Woudhuysen
MACBETH	edited by Sandra Clark and Pamela Mason
MEASURE FOR MEASURE	edited by J. W. Lever*
THE MERCHANT OF VENICE	edited by John Drakakis
THE MERRY WIVES OF WINDSOR	edited by Giorgio Melchiori
A MIDSUMMER NIGHT'S DREAM	edited by Harold F. Brooks*
MUCH ADO ABOUT NOTHING, Revised	edited by Claire McEachern
OTHELLO, Revised	edited by E. A. J. Honigmann, with a new introduction by Ayanna Thompson
PERICLES	edited by Suzanne Gossett
ROMEO AND JULIET	edited by René Weis
SHAKESPEARE'S POEMS	edited by Katherine Duncan-Jones and H. R. Woudhuysen
SHAKESPEARE'S SONNETS, Revised	edited by Katherine Duncan-Jones
THE TAMING OF THE SHREW	edited by Barbara Hodgdon
THE TEMPEST, Revised	edited by Virginia Mason Vaughan and Alden T. Vaughan
TIMON OF ATHENS	edited by Anthony B. Dawson and Gretchen E. Minton
TITUS ANDRONICUS	edited by Jonathan Bate
TROILUS AND CRESSIDA, Revised	edited by David Bevington
TWELFTH NIGHT	edited by Keir Elam
THE TWO GENTLEMEN OF VERONA	edited by William C. Carroll
THE TWO NOBLE KINSMEN, Revised	edited by Lois Potter
THE WINTER'S TALE	edited by John Pitcher

* Second series

THE ARDEN SHAKESPEARE

OTHELLO

Edited by
E. A. J. HONIGMANN

With a new introduction by
AYANNA THOMPSON

Bloomsbury Arden Shakespeare
An imprint of Bloomsbury Publishing PLC

B L O O M S B U R Y
LONDON • OXFORD • NEW YORK • NEW DELHI • SYDNEY

Bloomsbury Arden Shakespeare
An imprint of Bloomsbury Publishing Plc

50 Bedford Square
London
WC1B 3DP
UK

1385 Broadway
New York
NY 10018
USA

www.bloomsbury.com

Bloomsbury is a registered trade mark of Bloomsbury Publishing Plc

This edition of *Othello*, edited by E. A. J. Honigmann, 1997

Revised Edition with a new introduction by Ayanna Thompson, published 2016 by the Arden Shakespeare

The general editors of the Arden Shakespeare have been
W. J. Craig and R. H. Case (first series 1899–1944)
Una Ellis-Fermor, Harold F. Brooks, Harold Jenkins and
Brian Morris (second series 1946–82)

Present general editors (third series)
Richard Proudfoot, Ann Thompson, David Scott Kastan and H. R. Woudhuysen

British Library Cataloguing-in-Publication Data
A catalogue record for this book is available from the British Library.

ISBN: HB: 9781472571779
PB: 9781472571762
ePDF: 9781472571793
ePub: 9781472571786

Library of Congress Cataloging-in-Publication Data
A catalog record for this book is available from the Library of Congress.

Typeset by RefineCatch Limited, Bungay, Suffolk
Printed and bound in India

The Editors

E. A. J. Honigmann was the author of more than a dozen books on Shakespeare and his contemporaries, including *Shakespeare; Seven Tragedies; the Dramatist's Manipulation of Response* (1976, 2002) and *Myriad-Minded Shakespeare* (1989, 1998). He taught as a lecturer at Glasgow University, as a Fellow of the Shakespeare Institute in Stratford-upon-Avon (Birmingham University), as Joseph Cowen Professor of English Literature in the University of Newcastle-upon-Tyne, and in Canada and the USA. His *The Texts of Othello and Shakespearian Revision* is a companion volume to his Arden edition.

Ayanna Thompson is Professor of English at George Washington University, and she specializes in Renaissance drama and issues of race in/as performance. She is the author of *Teaching Shakespeare with Purpose: A Student-Centred Approach* (2016), *Passing Strange: Shakespeare, Race, and Contemporary America* (2011), and *Performing Race and Torture on the Early Modern Stage* (2008). She is the editor of *Weyward Macbeth: Intersections of Race and Performance* (2010) and *Colorblind Shakespeare: New Perspectives on Race and Performance* (2006). Professor Thompson has served as a Trustee of the Shakespeare Association of America and a member of the Board of Directors for the Association of Marshall Scholars.

For
Elsie McConnachie Honigmann
(née Packman)
10.7.1919–6.12.1994

Only a sweet and virtuous soul
Like seasoned timber, never gives:
But, though the whole world turn to coal,
Then chiefly lives.
(George Herbert)

CONTENTS

LIST OF ILLUSTRATIONS

GENERAL EDITORS' PREFACE

The earliest volume in the first Arden series, Edward Dowden's *Hamlet*, was published in 1899. Since then the Arden Shakespeare has been widely acknowledged as the pre-eminent Shakespeare edition, valued by scholars, students, actors and 'the great variety of readers' alike for its clearly presented and reliable texts, its full annotation and its richly informative introductions.

In the third Arden series we seek to maintain these well-established qualities and general characteristics, preserving our predecessors' commitment to presenting the play as it has been shaped in history. Each volume necessarily has its own particular emphasis which reflects the unique possibilities and problems posed by the work in question, and the series as a whole seeks to maintain the highest standards of scholarship, combined with attractive and accessible presentation.

Newly edited from the original documents, texts are presented in fully modernized form, with a textual apparatus that records all substantial divergences from those early printings. The notes and introductions focus on the conditions and possibilities of meaning that editors, critics and performers (on stage and screen) have discovered in the play. While building upon the rich history of scholarly activity that has long shaped our understanding of Shakespeare's works, this third series of the Arden Shakespeare is enlivened by a new generation's encounter with Shakespeare.

THE TEXT

On each page of the play itself, readers will find a passage of text supported by commentary and textual notes. Act and scene divisions (seldom present in the early editions and often the product of eighteenth-century or later scholarship) have been retained for ease of reference, but have been given less prominence than in previous series. Editorial indications of location of the action have been removed to the textual notes or commentary.

In the text itself, elided forms in the early texts are spelt out in full in verse lines wherever they indicate a usual late twentieth-century pronunciation that requires no special indication and wherever they occur in prose (except where they indicate nonstandard pronunciation). In verse speeches, marks of elision are retained where they are necessary guides to the scansion and pronunciation of the line. Final -ed in past tense and participial forms of verbs is always printed as -ed, without accent, never as -'d, but wherever the required pronunciation diverges from modern usage a note in the commentary draws attention to the fact. Where the final -ed should be given syllabic value contrary to modern usage, e.g.

> Doth Silvia know that I am banished?
>
> (*TGV* 3.1.214)

the note will take the form

> 214 **banished** banishèd

Conventional lineation of divided verse lines shared by two or more speakers has been reconsidered and sometimes rearranged. Except for the familiar *Exit* and *Exeunt*, Latin forms in stage directions and speech prefixes have been translated into English and the original Latin forms recorded in the textual notes.

COMMENTARY AND TEXTUAL NOTES

Notes in the commentary, for which a major source will be the *Oxford English Dictionary*, offer glossarial and other explication of verbal difficulties; they may also include discussion of points of interpretation and, in relevant cases, substantial extracts from Shakespeare's source material. Editors will not usually offer glossarial notes for words adequately defined in the latest edition of *The Concise Oxford Dictionary* or *Merriam-Webster's Collegiate Dictionary*, but in cases of doubt they will include notes. Attention, however, will be drawn to places where more than one likely interpretation can be proposed and to significant verbal and syntactic complexity. Notes preceded by * discuss editorial emendations or variant readings.

Headnotes to acts or scenes discuss, where appropriate, questions of scene location, the play's treatment of source materials, and major difficulties of staging. The list of roles (so headed to emphasize the play's status as a text for performance) is also considered in the commentary notes. These may include comment on plausible patterns of casting with the resources of an Elizabethan or Jacobean acting company and also on any variation in the description of roles in their speech prefixes in the early editions.

The textual notes are designed to let readers know when the edited text diverges from the early edition(s) or manuscript sources on which it is based. Wherever this happens the note will record the rejected reading of the early edition(s) or manuscript, in original spelling, and the source of the reading adopted in this edition. Other forms from the early edition(s) or manuscript recorded in these notes will include some spellings of particular interest or significance and original forms of translated stage directions. Where two or more early editions are involved, for instance with *Othello*, the notes also record all important differences between them. The textual notes take a form that has been in use since the nineteenth century. This comprises, first: line reference, reading adopted in the text and closing square bracket; then: abbreviated reference, in italic, to the earliest edition to adopt the accepted reading, italic semicolon and noteworthy alternative reading(s), each with abbreviated italic reference to its source.

Conventions used in these textual notes include the following. The solidus / is used, in notes quoting verse or discussing verse lining, to indicate line endings. Distinctive spellings of the base text follow the square bracket without indication of source and are enclosed in italic brackets. Names enclosed in italic brackets indicate originators of conjectural emendations when these did not originate in an edition of the text, or when the named edition records a conjecture not accepted into its text. Stage directions (SDs) are referred to by the number of the line within or immediately after which they are placed. Line numbers with a decimal point relate to centred entry SDs not falling within a verse line and to SDs more than one line long, with the number after the point indicating the line within the SD: e.g. 78.4 refers to the fourth line of the SD following line 78. Lines of SDs at the start of a scene are numbered 0.1, 0.2, etc. Where only a line number precedes a square bracket, e.g. 128], the note relates to the whole line; where SD is added to the number, it relates to the whole of a SD within or immediately following the line. Speech prefixes (SPs) follow similar conventions, 203 SP] referring to the speaker's name for line 203. Where a SP reference takes the form e.g. 38+ SP, it relates to all subsequent speeches assigned to that speaker in the scene in question.

Where, as with *King Henry V*, one of the early editions is a so-called 'bad quarto' (that is, a text either heavily adapted, or reconstructed from memory, or both), the divergences from the present edition are too great to be recorded in full in the notes. In these cases, with the exception of *Hamlet*, which prints an edited text of the quarto of 1603, the editions will include a reduced photographic facsimile of the 'bad quarto' in an appendix.

INTRODUCTION

Both the introduction and the commentary are designed to present the plays as texts for performance, and make appropriate reference to stage, film and television versions, as well as introducing the reader to the range of critical approaches to the plays. They discuss the history of the reception of the texts within the theatre and scholarship and beyond, investigating the interdependency of the literary text and the surrounding 'cultural text' both at the time of the original production of Shakespeare's works and during their long and rich afterlife.

PREFACE TO THE FIRST EDITION

'What I would now like to propose to you', the General Editor of the Arden Shakespeare wrote to me on 17 August 1982, 'is that you consider taking on the editing of the next Arden *Othello*.' He suggested 1988 as the completion date. I was tempted, but did I really want to give five or six years to a single play? After some soul-searching I signed a contract with Methuen & Co. to deliver the edition in 1988 in a form 'acceptable to the General Editor', with 'sufficient appendices' (whatever that means: is five sufficient?). I knew, of course, that *Othello* had received much less detailed editorial attention than *Hamlet* or *King Lear*, though not that so much editorial work still remained to be done. Five or six years have stretched to somewhat more, the Arden Shakespeare is no longer published by Methuen, its General Editor has been joined by two other General Editors, the edition of *Othello* needed a companion volume on *The Texts of 'Othello'* (Routledge, 1996) – much has changed, yet my gratitude to Richard Proudfoot has remained constant (or rather, has grown with the years). He chose the editor, he read through my drafts and always commented encouragingly (and, to my great advantage, critically). On almost every page I am indebted to him, and I gladly acknowledge this. At a later stage, in the last year or so, a second General Editor (David Scott Kastan) checked through the edition: I am grateful to him as well for many helpful comments.

Over the years innumerable offprints of articles on *Othello* have reached me, some from old friends, others from complete strangers. It was not possible to refer to all of them, the list of publications on the play being now so huge, but I hope that the edition has benefited, directly or indirectly. Other friends and colleagues have helped in different ways – sending books that were unobtainable in Britain, inviting me to give lectures or to write papers on *Othello*, or simply answering my questions: David Bevington, Helen Boden, Susan Brock, T. W. Craik, Katherine Duncan-Jones, R. A. Foakes, the late Charlton Hinman, Harold Jenkins, Holger Klein, Giorgio Melchiori, Sylvia Morris, Barbara Mowat, Elisabeth Orsten, Edward Pechter, Willem Schrickx, the late Terence Spencer, Marvin Spevack, Rosamond Kent Sprague and Stanley Wells. Mairi McDonald, Marian Pringle and Robert Smallwood of the Shakespeare Centre, Stratford-upon-Avon, were efficient and helpful in locating books, manuscripts and illustrations. In addition I am grateful to the librarians and officials of the Bodleian Library, the British Film Institute, the British Library, Cambridge University Library and Trinity College, Cambridge, Durham University Library, the Public Record Office, the Theatre Museum (London) and, last but not least, Newcastle University Library (the Robinson Library). To all, my sincere thanks: without their generous cooperation this edition would have had many more gaps and faults.

Jane Armstrong, a friend from the Methuen years and Arden 2, who took charge of the third Arden Shakespeare for the publisher, has been, as usual, understanding and supportive. Her colleagues, Penny Wheeler and Judith Ravenscroft, were equally tactful and efficient in dealing with the unforeseen quirks of an edition of Shakespeare – or should I say, of an editor of Shakespeare?

My greatest debt – for putting up with *Othello* uncomplainingly for so long, and for having so much else in common with the gentle Desdemona – is acknowledged in my dedication.

E. A. J. Honigmann
Newcastle upon Tyne

INTRODUCTION

How and where to begin? An introduction like this one serves not only to frame William Shakespeare's *Othello* but also to prioritize its themes, topics and contexts. While there are differences of opinion about how best to frame *Romeo and Juliet* (should one foreground early modern concepts of love before contextualizing certain literary forms, like the sonnet), the debates are rarely heated or political, and unsurprisingly they rarely replicate themselves in the court of public opinion. For *Othello*, however, the debates get extremely heated and traverse the terrain between the academic and the public.

For instance, when *The Guardian* announced that the Royal Shakespeare Company was casting its first black actor to play Iago in its 2015 production, the readers reacted with impassioned comments about how *Othello* should be framed – that is, what histories, social contexts and themes should be foregrounded. Some readers decried the article's claim that Iago 'is usually interpreted as being a deeply malignant racist' because they argued this misinterprets the play's historical context: 'it was never really a play "about" racism anyway (not exactly a hot button social issue of Shakespeare's day)'; and 'Whatever else happens it won't be Shakespeare's vision'. Other commentators responded by providing a different contextualization altogether, one that did not rely on Shakespeare's time period: 'Casting a black actor as Iago is not a new thing – it's been done by at least one director who wanted to make the point that racism is not just a black/white issue and can manifest itself in all kinds of subtle and insidious ways'; and 'Maybe this explains why some critics were hostile when Ira Aldridge played Othello because having an actual black actor play the role wasn't Shakespeare's vision'. And others wanted to frame the discussion outside of the context of the play by addressing contemporary casting practices: 'Dear RSC – Just cast more black actors across more roles across your season and then we would cease to have news "stories" like this.'[1]

So is *Othello* a play about race? Or maybe it is a play about religion and ethnicity? Or maybe it is a play about jealousy in general? Perhaps it is really a domestic tragedy framed within a military narrative? Or is it the exact opposite: a military tragedy framed in a domestic drama? Or possibly it is simply an experiment in transforming a comedy into a tragedy? Or maybe *Othello* is about the nature of evil? Or the nature of man? Or the nature of woman? Or the nature of the family? Or the changing nature of the family in an increasingly global world?

The way we frame the story of *Othello* will impact the way the play will be understood and performed, and students, scholars, performers and audience members have long debated the best way to crystallize the story of the play. Of course, the idea that stories are crafted – that they are not innate or natural – is another way to frame *Othello*: it is a play about storytellers, their tall-tales and their effects on gullible listeners. After all, Othello won Desdemona's heart by telling her 'the story of my life / From year to year – the battles, sieges, fortunes / That I have passed' (1.3.130–2). The story was so compellingly crafted that the Duke admits, 'I think this tale would win my daughter too' (1.3.172). Moreover, Othello's dying words are a request for the way his story should be framed in the future: 'When you shall these unlucky deeds relate, / Speak of me as I am. Nothing extenuate, / Nor set down aught in malice' (5.2.339–41). Othello dies worrying about the way his life will be framed so he narrates exactly how he thinks, believes and hopes it should be told ('Set you down this' 5.2.349).

Storytelling matters in very explicit and tangible ways in *Othello*, and Othello is not the only character who is attentive to this fact. While Iago suggests that Othello duped Desdemona with lies ('she first loved the Moor, but for bragging and telling

1 All quotations come from online comments to Brown.

her fantastical lies' 2.1.220–1), he himself is a master story crafter. After all, from the beginning of the play Iago recognizes that the best way to exact revenge is to 'abuse Othello's ear' (1.3.394). Iago realizes that once a person is characterized or pigeonholed within a certain narrative structure (Desdemona as a 'super-subtle Venetian', Othello as an 'erring Barbarian' and Cassio as 'a finder out of occasions') it can prove difficult-to-near impossible to escape that plot, or to recast oneself (or others) into alternative narrative structures. He who controls the storytelling controls the world in *Othello*.

It is clear, then, that while any introduction to *Othello* will be interpreted as an argument about the play's meaning, the play teaches us to be sceptical of adhering to one frame, or one story: the act of framing something narrowly often makes it impossible to accept other narratives and other perspectives. Keeping this in mind, it is instructive to note that *Othello* does not exist in one historical moment, or one historical context, alone. It does not merely come out of and reflect the early-seventeenth century; rather, it is a play whose stagings, readings and meanings have mutated and evolved over time. The *Othello* that we read or see in the twenty-first century is not the same that Shakespeare's audience read or saw in early modern England, or that slave owners saw in nineteenth-century America, or that Afrikaners saw in Apartheid South Africa. Many eras reframe the story of the Moor of Venice. Nonetheless, while these various *Othello*s are obviously discrete historical events reflecting and commenting upon the time in which they were produced, they are never entirely isolated or separate; they comment upon each other; they revise each other; and they invite readers and audience members to see both the connections and fissures between them. If we learn anything from *Othello* it should be that there are benefits to accepting multiple stories, frames and narratives.

Some might argue that we experience multiple frames when reading or seeing any, and all, of Shakespeare's plays – that

Shakespeare's plays are both timely and untimely all at once. While this is true to a certain extent, there is something different about the ways history and context get framed for Shakespeare's Venetian plays, *The Merchant of Venice* and *Othello*. The violent histories that occurred towards Jews and Africans since the early modern period render history and context more fraught and complex when approaching the constructions and presentations of religion and race in Shakespeare's plays. For instance, in various historic moments *Merchant* and *Othello* have been employed to promote anti-Semitic and racist beliefs: the Nazis considered staging *Merchant* to vilify the Jews, and blackface minstrel shows were first staged alongside performances of *Othello* to mock blacks. Of course, the obverse is also true with both *Merchant* and *Othello* employed in efforts to combat anti-Semitism and racism: Jewish actors/directors have proudly claimed Shylock as their own, and black actors have identified performing in *Othello* as a 'rite of passage'. When staging either play now, directors must decide which historical construction of the 'Jew' or the 'Moor' they will employ. And, of course, they must also be cognizant of the various historical constructions their audience members will bring with them to the theatre – and whether those constructions are in harmony with or at odds against the production's intended constructions.

This is all to suggest that reading, seeing and/or discussing *Othello* in our post-slavery and post-Civil Rights Era moment is both a rewarding and a challenging experience. It is useful to learn and discuss the historical moment in which *Othello* was composed, but it is just as important to review the historical moments *Othello* has passed through, affected and been affected by. The play is not an inanimate object that never changes. Instead *Othello* is a dynamic organism that is affected by every hand that touches it – from the actors who perform the role, the visual artists who re-imagine and re-animate the character, the creative writers who rewrite the plot, to the scholars who contextualize its various, disparate and interconnected histories.

Othello, then, exists in history (multiple time periods) and through history (the stories and frames we use to recreate it). We constantly create new stories in which to frame *Othello* because it is a play that interrogates stories, frames and contexts; it is a play that invites revision.

Therefore, this introduction is not limited to early modern English history. While I will spend time laying out the historical context in which *Othello* was created, paying particular attention to Shakespeare's source materials and the evidence about early modern constructions of racial and religious difference, I will also spend time discussing the life of the play in different historical moments, demonstrating how meanings develop, accrue and metamorphose over time. In essence I will be writing about multiple *Othello*s, inviting you to imagine if, when and how different readers and audience members were affected by these histories, contexts and performances. Moreover, the dynamic nature of the play will be presented in a global context with attention paid to non-Western approaches to and performances of *Othello*.

This is an unusual Arden edition because I am writing a new introduction to the play while maintaining E. A. J. Honigmann's editorial work. In other words, this is not the Arden4 *Othello*, but rather a type of Arden3b. While Honigmann's editorial decisions remain both useful and admirable, the birth of early modern race studies changed critical approaches to *Othello* since Honigmann's introduction was published in 1997 (for more on this topic see p. 62ff). This introduction, then, is written for a new generation of readers, readers who expect a contemporary view of *Othello* that was not widely available critically when Honigmann prepared his introduction. This introduction is heavily informed by early modern race studies, performance studies and global Shakespeare studies, fields that have grown exponentially since the turn of the millennium and have, in turn, changed the ways we read, produce and see *Othello*. Like the critical revolution that occurred with the birth of new historicism in the 1980s, the

1 *A Moor Offering a Parrot to a Lady* (c. 1660–70) by Nicolaes Berchem (courtesy of The Ella Gallup Sumner and Mary Catlin Sumner Collection Fund, 1961.29, Wadsworth Atheneum Museum of Art, Hartford, CT)

impacts of early modern race studies and global Shakespeare studies on the ways we experience *Othello* cannot be underestimated. A seismic change has occurred.

In practical terms, the revised Arden3 *Othello* contains the new introduction, Honigmann's excellent edition of the play, commentary notes, longer notes and appendices. All references to the introduction have been updated to reflect the new introduction, but the bulk of the notes and appendice. those created by Honigmann for the 1997 edition because t. remain instructive and constructive.

What is *Othello*?: Genre

While both the folio and quarto label the play as a tragedy, *Othello* is related to several other generic forms that might not at first seem readily apparent to the modern reader. First is the morality play, a medieval allegorical theatrical form in which moral lessons were taught through characters who personify moral qualities, like charity or vice. The genre thrived in fifteenth- and sixteenth-century Europe and helped establish vernacular drama, which in turn helped set the stage for the secular drama that thrived in early modern England. The anonymous play *Mankind* (c. 1465) provides a good example. Characters who represent the enticements of earthly pleasures (Newguise, Nowadays and Nought), try to tempt Mankind, a farmer, away from Mercy. Essential to the morality play tradition is the moral conundrum the central character – the mankind figure – must face when tempted by figures who actively endeavour to lure him to commit vices such as avarice, lust and gluttony.

Although originating from popular folk performances, the Vice is a character in the morality play. A temptation figure who performs the blithe spirit of worldly pleasures (as opposed to spiritual ones), 'The Vice was a favorite with the audience' and the Vice's role was 'almost invariably the longest single part' in the performance (Mares, 13). The Vice 'is on intimate terms with the audience and cracks jokes with individual members of it' and does not appear to be 'subject to the limitations of the other characters' (Mares, 14). In one scene in *Mankind*, for instance, Titivillus, the Vice figure, is visible to the audience but is invisible to Mankind, and he addresses the audience directly as he plays tricks on Mankind. Furthermore, the Vice is frequently depicted as a worldly figure who frequently 'give[s] an account of extraordinary travels' (Mares, 19). And the Vice even performs his worldliness by dressing as an Egyptian or a Turk with the aid of blackface and red-face makeup (Mares, 19–20).

Shakespeare was clearly aware of and interested in the structure of morality plays and the figure of the Vice. In a famous metadramatic moment, Richard III willingly adopts the tempter's role: 'Thus, like the formal Vice, Iniquity, / I moralize two meanings in one word' (*R3* 3.1.82–3). And Aaron, the Moor, in *Titus Andronicus*, Shakespeare's first tragedy, is clearly related to the worldly corrupting figure of the Vice. Like Richard III, Aaron is afforded more direct addresses to the audience than other character, and he also seems preternaturally aware of the plot structure into which he has been scripted. 'If there be devils, would I were a devil, / To live and burn in everlasting fire, / So I might have your company in hell / But to torment you with my bitter tongue' (*Tit* 5.1.147–50). Likewise, in the *Henry IV* plays, Shakespeare adopts the morality play structure in which a type of psychomachia, that is the battle for the soul of man, is set up for the young Prince Hal. Despite the fact that Hal announces early in the first play that he is only pretending to enjoy the debauchery of the tavern, his father, the king, and his quasi-step-father, Falstaff, are set up to represent the decision he must make between virtue and vice.

Shakespeare's employment of elements from the morality play within *Othello*, then, is not that surprising. By the end of the play, Othello seems to interpret the events through the lens of the morality play, even identifying Iago as a Vice figure or devil. Looking for Iago's cloven foot, Othello says, 'I look down towards his feet, but that's a fable' (5.2.283). Yet Shakespeare's alterations to the genre demonstrate the experimental nature of his work. First, the Vice figure is not the racialized character in *Othello*; rather the mankind figure is explicitly racialized (Othello) and the Vice figure is the native,

2 William Haviland as Iago (late nineteenth century or early twentieth century), photograph by J. and L. Caswall Smith (used by permission of the Folger Shakespeare Library under a Creative Commons Attribution-ShareAlike 4.0 International Licence). Haviland's portrait picks up on the Vice tradition.

a Venetian (Iago). Furthermore, while Iago makes it clear that he has served abroad in battle with Othello ('And I, of whom his eyes had seen the proof / At Rhodes, at Cyprus and on other grounds, / Christian and heathen' 1.1.27–9), Othello, the mankind figure, is nonetheless the character associated with extraordinary travels ('an extravagant and wheeling stranger / Of here and everywhere' 1.1.134–5). Thus, Shakespeare seems to employ familiar aspects of the morality play, tempting audience members to believe they understand how the play will progress based on its generic form and structure only to have those expectations thwarted, disrupted and subverted.

Shakespeare was not content to borrow from merely one generic tradition though; rather, he blended several unlikely generic bedfellows together almost as if placing the audience in Othello's position – that is, as one who feels as if he is always misreading events, customs and characters. For instance, several comedic motifs get folded into *Othello*'s web. First, there is the plotline of the father who cannot control his wily daughter. Because a daughter's obedience was prized in early modern English society, plots capitalized on the humour that can ensue when daughters intentionally deceive their fathers. *A Midsummer Night's Dream* after all begins with a father's complaint about his daughter's unwillingness to marry the man he intends for her. Not unlike Brabantio's claims about Othello's courtship of his daughter Desdemona, Egeus complains to the Duke that Lysander has tricked his daughter into loving him: 'With cunning hast thou filched my daughter's heart, / Turned her obedience (which is due to me) / To stubborn harshness' (*MND* 1.1.37–9). In fact, the rhetorical similarities between Egeus's complaint and Brabantio's are stark with both men concerned with the effects of 'cunning', a word which implies both run-of-the-mill trickery and devilish witchcraft on a daughter's 'obedience'. Brabantio declares that they must 'find out the practices of cunning hell' (1.3.103) to discover why Desdemona would marry Othello, and then pointedly asks her, 'Do you perceive, in all this noble company, / Where most you owe obedience?' (1.3.179–80). Brabantio's language provides a clear rhetorical echo to Shakespeare's earlier use of this plotline for comic effect. Of course, a daughter's disobedience can also be the stuff of tragedy as Shakespeare thoroughly explored when he created two generically disparate plays based on the same source material, the story of Pyramus and Thisbe: *Romeo and Juliet* and *A Midsummer Night's Dream*.

Yet Shakespeare adds to the generic comic expectations by also weaving in the familiar plotline of the older husband who is cuckolded by his younger wife. Chaucer helped to popularize the comedic structure of the so-called January–May romance genre in 'The Merchant's Tale' in *The Canterbury Tales*, in which January, a man of sixty years, marries the youthful May so that he can beget an heir. Because she is so young and wild, May has sex with a young squire in a pear tree. Likewise, in 'The Miller's Tale,' the young wife Alisoun cuckolds her old and uxorious husband John. Thus, when Othello declares to the Duke and the Venetian senators that he is too old to be motivated primarily by a physical desire for Desdemona ('I therefore beg it not / To please the palate of my appetite, / Nor to comply with heat, the young effects / In me defunct' 1.3.262–5), the audience could hear echoes of other familiar January–May plots. By pointing out the comic plotlines that Shakespeare embeds in *Othello*, I am not suggesting that the play is any less tragic than it is. Rather, I want to emphasize the way Shakespeare cannibalized and transformed familiar structures, plots and character types, thereby subverting audience expectations.

Othello also taps into the popularity of the romance narrative. The early modern prose romance was indebted to the medieval chivalric romance, in which knights went on marvel-filled adventures to fulfill fairy-tale like quests. Othello's personal narrative, the one that Desdemona would 'Devour up' with her 'greedy ear' (1.3.151, 150), borrows liberally from popular romances of the time, including John Mandeville's travels (for more, see p. 17). Those tales were filled with extreme adventure and demonstrations of pure love, and the inclusion of their generic elements in *Othello* serves to highlight the fantastical aspects of those narratives. Even though we hear him described as such, the audience never gets to see Othello as a military leader or heroic adventurer. So the romance genre is invoked to highlight its absence in *Othello*.

Of course, *Othello* is tragic in structure, tone and content. Yet even within tragedy, we see Shakespeare experimenting with multiple sub-genres. The play is set up in a bifurcated fashion with a political tragedy bleeding into a domestic one, and vice versa. The movement of the play from Venice to Cyprus, after all, is governed by the political anxiety that the Turks will seize the important military base and trading island of Cyprus. The Duke and senators of Venice are willing to ignore the complaints of their fellow senator Brabantio precisely because they need the Moor to agree to battle the Turks. This is a political tragedy. But Shakespeare kills the Turks off in a storm so that the military narrative dies a natural death. The comic plot of the rebellious daughter marrying her true love against her father's wishes then transforms into a domestic tragedy (Callaghan, *Women*, 35ff). The genre was popularized by plays like the anonymous *Arden of Faversham* in which a cuckolding wife plots her husband's death with her lover only to be delayed by a series of accidents and chance events. Othello seems to fear that he is the duped victim in a domestic tragedy only to become the villain of one.

Once again, by blending these various tragic generic elements with those from morality plays, domestic comedies and January–May plot structures, Shakespeare seems to be prompting his audience to interrogate the expectations we bring to characters, narratives and encounters with the unfamiliar. *Othello*, in the end, is a play about how well or how difficult it is to integrate disparate people, personal narratives, culture and cultural narratives.

Where is *Othello*?: Early Modern Contexts

1. Sources One can get a better sense of how Shakespeare blended generic elements into *Othello* by understanding the early modern sources and contexts that Shakespeare used to create *Othello*. Scholars tend to agree that Shakespeare must have read and been influenced by the Italian writer Giovanni Battista Giraldi, known by his classical pseudonym Cinthio (1504–1573). *Gli Hecatommithi* (see Appendix 3 for Cinthio's text), Cinthio's suite of 100 interwoven novellas, which are organized in groups of ten according to different topics and themes about love, was first published in Italian in 1565 and then in French in 1583. Although we cannot be certain if Shakespeare read the text in the original Italian, the translated French version, or some lost early modern English translation (the first extant English translation did not appear until 1753), it is clear that he borrowed plots, themes and characters from *Gli Hecatommithi*. While *Measure for Measure* (written around the same time as *Othello*) is influenced by the fifth story in the eighth decade, the group that addresses ingratitude, *Othello* is indebted to the seventh story in the third decade, the group that addresses the infidelity of husbands and wives.

In Cinthio's tale, an unnamed Moor who lives in Venice proves himself 'valiant' and 'skillful' to the Signoria, Venice's governing authority. Disdemona, 'a virtuous Lady of wondrous beauty', whose name in Italian means unlucky or ill-omened, falls in love with the Moor 'impelled not by female appetite but by the Moor's good qualities'. Nonetheless, 'the Lady's relatives did all they could to make her take another husband'. While there is no Turkish threat to Cyprus in *Gli Hecatommithi*, the Signoria send the Moor 'to maintain Cyprus'. The unnamed Ensign who accompanies the Moor to Cyprus, 'fell ardently in love with Disdemona, and bent all his thoughts to see if he could manage to enjoy her'. Because Disdemona remains oblivious to the Ensign's advances, 'the love which he had felt for the Lady now changed to the bitterest hate'. As in Shakespeare's *Othello*, the Ensign chips away at the Moor's confidence by telling him that Disdemona is unfaithful, and yet in Cinthio's version his digs are more pointed racially: 'The woman has come to dislike your blackness'.

Cinthio's Disdemona gives voice to the story's moral when she states, 'I fear greatly that I shall be a warning to young girls not to marry against their parents' wishes; and Italian ladies will learn by my example not to tie themselves to a man whom Nature, Heaven, and manner of life separate from us'. In the end, the Ensign and the Moor kill Disdemona together by bludgeoning her to death with sand-filled socks which leave no marks on her body; and then they fake her death by making it look as if she was killed by a collapsed ceiling. Through complicated plot twists, the faked death is eventually revealed, the Moor is sentenced to exile, and Disdemona's relatives eventually hunt him down and kill him. The Ensign continues enacting his wicked deeds until he dies under torture: 'he was tortured so fiercely that his inner organs were ruptured'. Everything is eventually revealed by the unnamed Ensign's wife, who knew all the facts but was too scared of her husband to reveal them while he was still living.

One of Shakespeare's exceptional talents was his ability to ingest older plots, narratives and stories and then to transform them into new creations. While Cinthio's tale has a didactic purpose – to warn young girls not to marry 'a man whom Nature, Heaven, and manner of life separate' from them – Shakespeare's *Othello* resists this simplistic moral thrust. Desdemona, unlike Disdemona, dies protecting Othello and continuing to pledge her love for him. Desdemona's death, in other words, hardly lends itself to a clear moral narrative. Likewise, the fact that Shakespeare's Othello kills himself instead of being killed by Disdemona's relatives 'as he richly deserved', according to Cinthio's tale, thwarts the moralism inherent in vendetta narratives.

Shakespeare was able to make his Moor more richly textured than Cinthio's by weaving other sources into the play to fill out Othello's backstory. In particular, it seems that Shakespeare used *A Geographical History of Africa*, an influential geographical and ethnographic book about Africa (the first of its kind in early modern Europe). Its author, an Andalusian Muslim who lived in Fez, Hasan ibn Muhammad al-Wazzan (c. 1485–1554), was captured by pirates in the Mediterranean, taken to Rome, and then gifted to Pope Leo X, who christened him Johannes Leo Africanus. First published in Italian in 1550, *A Geographical History of Africa* was held up as the authoritative text on north and west Africa for centuries, and the first English translation was published in 1600 by John Pory. It was subsequently included in many travel narratives published in England.

While scholars debate how much of Africanus's geographical history Shakespeare actually read, it seems clear that Shakespeare found the author's personal narrative a rich one to mine for *Othello*. The idea of a well-born, educated and experienced African who works his way into the upper echelons of white, European power is clearly echoed in *Othello*. Shakespeare's tragic hero, after all, explains that he comes from 'men of royal siege' (1.2.22), and explains that he was 'taken by the insolent foe / And sold to slavery' from which he received 'redemption' (1.3.138–9). Shakespeare's Othello, then, tells a tale that echoes the fascinating reality of Johannes Leo Africanus's life.

Shakespeare also appears to have used bits and pieces from a new early modern English translation of a famous Roman encyclopedia by Pliny the Elder, *The Historie of the Natural World*, translated by Philemon Holland in 1601. While Pliny's text, like Africanus's, provides a wide range of information about botany, zoology and astronomy, the more fabulous parts of the narrative about the 'Nature of Man' seem to be echoed in *Othello*. For example, Pliny includes an interesting section on 'the diversitie of other nations' and focuses on the Scythians, some of whom he calls 'Anthropophagi' (Pliny, 153 and 154).

3 *Portrait of an African Man (Christophle le More?)* (c. 1525–30) by Jan Jansz Mostaert (courtesy of Rijksmuseum, Amsterdam)

Furthermore, Shakespeare may have gotten specific geographical locations like the 'Hellespont' (see commentary note on 3.3.456–9) from Pliny's encyclopedic text (Pliny, 154 and 190).

Yet Othello's narrative of self blends the personal ('my travailous history' 1.3.140) with the fantastical ('cannibals that each other eat, / The Anthropophagi, and men whose heads / Do grow beneath their shoulders' 1.3.144–6), and this narrative structure echoes a different wildly popular text, John Mandeville's *The Book of Marvels and Travels* (c. 1371). Supposedly written by an English Christian pilgrim who travels in and around Jerusalem, *The Book of Marvels and Travels* is a fabricated tale that blends travelogues, fantasy narratives and fiction often in the same moment. Take for example, Mandeville's description of cannibals in India: 'One travels from this country via many lands and islands . . . and after fifty-two days' travel one reaches the land called Lamuri. . . . The land is held in shared ownership, in that one man has it one year, another man another year. . . . They do, however, have one wicked habit: they eat human flesh more enthusiastically than anything else. Merchants bring them their children to sell, and if they are fat they are eaten straightaway' (Mandeville, 78–9). Mixing the guidebook structure ('after fifty-two days' travel') with fantasy (a town of communist cannibals), Mandeville's *Book* seems to provide Shakespeare with an elastic narrative structure that can encompass veracity and fantasy.

Shakespeare also appears to have browsed books about the social and political structure of Venice, texts he used for both *Othello* and his earlier Venetian play, *The Merchant of Venice* (c. 1596). In particular, he seems to have used Sir Lewes Lewkenor's English translation of Gaspar Contarini's *De Magistratibus et Republica Venetorum* (c. 1543), *The Commonwealth and Government of Venice* (1599) when writing *Othello*. Written by Contarini when he was an ambassador to Charles V, *De Magistratibus* romanticizes the Venetian state, explicitly painting a portrait of balance, fortune and evenhandedness. Lewekenor's

English translation was significant because the early modern English were often looking to Venice for models of social, political and economic prosperity. Thus, Lewekenor's text analyses the structures of the political (the Duke and Grand Council), military (generals and commanders of empyreal outposts) and social systems (a two-class system with nobility/gentlemen and commoners). While there is more to say about early modern perceptions of Venice (for more, see p. 22ff), suffice it to say that Shakespeare not only borrowed fictional sources for plots and characters, but also non-fictional sources for information about foreign social and political systems. Iago's attentiveness to issues of class and rank ('Preferment goes by letter and affection / And not by old gradation, where each second / Stood heir to th' first' 1.1.35–7) clearly reflects Shakespeare's intertextual interests.

Theatrically, *Othello* is indebted to dramas that featured 'negro Moor[s]' (*Alcazar* 2.1.3), especially George Peele's *The Battle of Alcazar* (c. 1591), the first early modern English play to do so. A play that relates the true history of the Moroccan defeat of the Portuguese in 1578, including the death of the King of Portugal, *Alcazar* features 'barbarous', 'ambitious', 'lusty' and 'manly' Moors of various different skin colours (*Alcazar* 1.1.6; 3.2.25; 3.3.12; 3.3.20). Muly Mahamet, the play's 'negro Moor', who is the offspring of the former king and his black bond slave, tricks the Portuguese into supporting his bid for power. A chorus figure, who introduces each act, declares of Muly Mahamet:

> And ill betide this foul ambitious Moor
> Whose wily trains with smoothest course of speech
> Hath tied and tangled in a dangerous war,
> The fierce and manly King of Portugal.
>
> (*Alcazar* 5.1.1–5)

With his characterization of the smooth talking negro Moor who manipulates his European friends rhetorically, Peele helped set the stage for Shakespeare's depictions of race, rhetoric and

4 *Mulay Ahmad* (c. 1609) by Peter Paul Rubens (photograph © 2016 Museum of Fine Arts, Boston, USA)

intercultural collisions.[1] While not a stereotypical stage villain, Muly Mahamet is frequently discussed by other characters in terms of his colour, as if his racial difference might provide a reason for his ambitiousness and cunning.

Peele's Muly Mahamet is most closely related to Shakespeare's Aaron, the Moor. It should come as no surprise, then, that critics have argued that Peele may have been a co-author on *Titus Andronicus*.[2] Like Muly Mahamet, Aaron is described as a 'barbarous Moor' who is 'raven-coloured' (*Tit* 2.2.78; 83). And like Muly Mahamet, Aaron is a truly gifted rhetorician who frequently cites classical allusions, translates Latin and puns incessantly. When the Roman army defeats the Goths, Aaron is taken prisoner along with the Goths. Unbeknownst to the Romans, he and the Empress of the Goths, Tamora, have been having an affair. Thus, when Tamora unexpectedly rises in power in Rome, Aaron rises with her and helps to plot her revenge. In *Titus Andronicus*, Aaron represents the creative force of chaos and destruction. He can improvise; he dreams up creative ways to torture the Romans; and he understands the narrative plots into which the Romans script him.

The fascinating theatrical and characterological moves that Shakespeare makes from *Titus Andronicus* to *Othello* effectively divide the devil figure from the 'raven-coloured love'. So Iago embodies the devilish improvisational and rhetorical effectiveness of Muly Mahamet and Aaron, the Moor, while Othello embodies the blackness of them. In Othello, Shakespeare seems to return to a small figure he included in *The Merchant of Venice*, the Prince of Morocco. While a humorous character

1 For more on other early modern racialized characters see Jones, E. For more on race and rhetoric see Smith, *Race*.

2 While Dover Wilson was the first to speculate that *Titus Andronicus* was co-authored with George Peele (Wilson *Titus*), and while Brian Vickers followed up (Vickers, 148–243), Gary Taylor and John Nance have employed sophisticated computer modelling to prove the point (Taylor and Nance).

who attempts to marry the wealthy, white Portia, the Prince of Morocco begins his wooing by telling the 'gentle queen' (*MV* 2.1.12) stories about his adventures:

> By this scimitar,
> That slew the Sophy and a Persian prince,
> That won three fields of Sultan Solyman,
> I would o'erstare the sternest eyes that look,
> Outbrave the heart most daring on the earth,
> Pluck the young sucking cubs from the she-bear,
> Yea, mock the lion when 'a roars for prey,
> To win the lady.
>
> (*MV* 2.1.24–31)

The Prince of Morocco clearly thinks that telling adventure stories from exotic lands will win Portia's hand. While this tactic does not work on Portia, Shakespeare returns to this narrative in *Othello* with a female protagonist, Desdemona, on whom it does work. Othello is also related to the Prince of Morocco in their belief that their births, although foreign, are nonetheless worthy of the women they desire. During the famous casket test for Portia's hand, the Prince of Morocco does not hesitate to declare that he matches Portia in birth: 'I do in birth deserve her, and in fortunes, / In graces and in qualities of breeding' (*MV* 2.7.32–3). Thus, we see Shakespeare borrowing from and imitating the characterizations of villainous 'negro Moors' in his earlier work only to abandon those characterizations to create figures who are still rhetorically gifted but also high born and self-assured.

2. Places The geographic landscape of *Othello* also helps to reveal the early modern context into which Shakespeare was imagining this world. Like many of Shakespeare's plays, *Othello* has a split geography with the first act of the play taking place in Venice and the remaining acts taking place in Cyprus. In a comedic structure, this type of geographic split usually emphasizes the licensing freedom that is enabled outside of the city walls. Think, for example, of the geographic split in *A Midsummer Night's Dream* in which Athens represents the world of the law and patriarchal order (Egeus appeals to Theseus, the Duke of Athens, to force his daughter to marry Demetrius instead of Lysander), and the woods represent the world of holiday and licentiousness (in which the lovers end up paired according to the women's initial wishes: Hermia with Lysander and Helena with Demetrius). Of course, tragic tales can contain a geographic split as well in order to mark a break from order into chaos. Most famously, *King Lear*'s movement from the court to the heath marks the political, familial and emotional breaks that the titular hero experiences. In *Othello*, the geographic split seems to signify the movement from Christian civilization to an unstable outpost.

Venice, however, was not viewed as the same kind of city as London in early modern England. In fact, Venice was both lauded and reviled in the early modern English imagination. It was lauded for being a cosmopolitan and diverse city; for establishing a formidable maritime power; and for enabling most of Europe's trade with Africa and the East. Venice was a cosmopolitan city in which people from different races, ethnicities and religions lived and worked together, and had a 'reputation as a multicultural republic' (Drakakis, 3). Clearly, this was one of the factors that drew Shakespeare to making Venice the setting for *The Merchant of Venice* and *Othello*, two plays that investigate what it means to live in a cosmopolitan city during times of increasing international trade (one play explores this through a comedic lens and one through a tragic one). As already noted, Venice was also admired for its complex political and social structures. To the early modern English, then, Venice seemed wealthier, more sophisticated and more outward-facing than London. Although it could not have been fully clear at the time, Venice's international power was waning by 1600, prompted in part by the loss of Cyprus to the Turks in the Fourth Ottoman–Venetian War (1570–1573). Thus, the Duke's fears that Cyprus must be protected at all costs against the Turkish invasion reflect the growing awareness of the fragility of this 'multicultural republic'.

Yet Venice also became a symbol of hedonistic excess in the early modern English imagination. John Drakakis has claimed that 'By the 1590s Venice had clearly become a byword for the exoticism of travel' (Drakakis, 4). Associated with the goddess of love, Venus, Venice fascinated the early modern English because of the city's more liberal treatment of sexual relations where prostitution was actually regulated by the state and involved thousands of women. Writing a few years after the creation of *Othello*, Thomas Coryate included his impressions of the courtesans in Venice in a travel book he published in 1611:

> As for the number of these Venetian Courtesans it is very great. For it is thought there are of them in the whole city and other adjacent places, as Muraon, Malomocco, &c. at the least twenty thousand, whereof many are esteemed so loose, that they are said to pen their quivers to every arrow. A most ungodly thing without doubt that there should be a toleration of such licentious wantons in so glorious, so potent, so renowned a City.
>
> (Coryate, 264)

Thus, Iago gives voice to many early modern English stereotypes about Venice when he describes Othello and Desdemona as 'an erring Barbarian and a super-subtle Venetian' (1.3.356–7), tagging the former as the foreigner and the latter as the whore who are both granted too much liberty in Venice. Likewise, Iago activates the stereotype of the 'loose' Venetian woman when he tells Othello, 'I know our country disposition well – / In Venice they do let God see the pranks / They dare not show their husbands; their best conscience / Is not to leave't undone, but keep't unknown' (3.3.204–7). In this statement, Iago manages both to vilify Desdemona and denigrate Othello as an unschooled outsider in Venice.

In *Othello*, Cyprus looks as if it will represent the opposite of Venice: the margin instead of the centre. Cyprus is after all an island at the far east of the Mediterranean, marking it as closer to the religions and cultures of the East than to those of the West. Cyprus is the territory over which empires clash; it is the colony and not the empire itself. But as is true of so many of Shakespeare's plays with split geographies, the centre and margins end up bleeding together in significant ways. In *Othello* there is the uncanny sense that Venice and Cyprus are related in their mythological associations with Venus: Cyprus is thought to be Venus's birthplace (and another of Venus's names is Cypris). Cyprus is the contested ground over which empires battle, but it also serves to highlight the problems inherent in those empires. After all, the Turkish threat is destroyed by the natural forces of a storm, but the island releases the violence lurking beneath the surface of the Venetian defenders of the Christian faith. The play seems to be asking if the violence was inherent to them in the first place, or if there was something about Cyrpus that made them change.

Two other locations play roles in *Othello* even though they are not depicted and are only referenced: Aleppo and Barbary. Aleppo (currently in part of modern day Syria) was captured by the Turks in 1517, and the Turks 'integrated it into the commercial system of their empire as a major center for their silk trade' (Molà, 57). Othello commits suicide mentioning that he has 'done the state some service' (5.2.337) in Aleppo in the past, and that brief mention serves to conjure a past in which the Venetian empire might have won more of the East. It is a fantasy, of course, but one to which Othello clings especially at the moment of his death (Kastan, 108). Barbary, on the other hand, appears at first glance to represent a geographical region and a people who are wholly other and distant from the Venetians. In early modern English, Barbary was slang for the region of North Africa associated with Berbers or Moors, the so-called Barbary Coast of Africa. For instance, Iago, riling Brabantio with images of his daughter's sexual relations with Othello, states, 'you'll have your daughter covered with a Barbary horse' (1.1.109–10). In Iago's logic, Desdemona has not only disobeyed her father but also flung herself into a relationship with someone so different as to be bestial. And yet even the certainty of the cultural, religious and racial divides between the Venetians and those from Barbary begins to collapse when Desdemona sings the 'Willow Song' and explains that she learned it from her mother's maid, Barbary (4.3.24). Although Barbary is never mentioned again, the audience is left wondering who this maid was, how she came to be associated with Desdemona's family, and what exactly she meant to Desdemona in terms of Desdemona's understandings of race and class.

3. Peoples So what exactly was a Moor in Shakespeare's world? It is clear from the theatrical references already noted that Moor was an elastic term in the early modern period that could encompass Muslims (i.e., a religious group), Africans (i.e., a geographical group), blacks (i.e., a racial group), atheists (i.e., a non-religious group) and others. The *Oxford English Dictionary* provides the following definition for Moor:

> a native or inhabitant of ancient Mauretania [see 4.2.226], a region of North Africa corresponding to parts of present-day Morocco and Algeria. Later usually: a member of a Muslim people of mixed Berber and Arab descent inhabiting north-western Africa (now mainly present-day Mauritania), who in the 8th cent. conquered Spain. In the Middle Ages, and as late as the 17th cent., the Moors were widely supposed to be mostly black or very dark-skinned, although the existence of 'white Moors' was recognized. Thus the term was often used, even into the 20th cent., with the sense 'black person.'
>
> (*OED* n.2)

I include this long and wide-ranging definition to demonstrate that the term Moor was unstable when Shakespeare was writing *Othello*. As Anthony Barthelemy has cleverly written about the *OED*'s definition, 'Moor can mean, then, non-black Muslim, black Christian, or black Muslim. The only certainty a reader has when he sees the word is that the person referred to is not a [white] Christian' (Barthelemy, 7). Thus, the title of Shakespeare's play, *Othello: The Moor of Venice*, juxtaposes an unstable personal descriptor with a stable geographical location.

Hearing the title of his play, Shakespeare's audience members probably had various and potentially contradictory definitions and corresponding images in their minds. While not exactly analogous, I think something similar could be said for many in the US and the UK today for the word *Arab*: for some it will signify an ethnicity, for others it will signify a religious affiliation, for others it will signify a linguist grouping, and for still others it will signify a race. One can argue vociferously that the term *Arab* actually refers to an extremely heterogeneous panethnic grouping of peoples from western Asia, North Africa, the Horn of Africa and parts of the Arabian peninsula, but the terms *Arab* and *Muslim* often get conflated.[1] So it should not surprise us that there was confusion about Moors in the early modern period. It is not that the early modern English were quaint and unworldly, but rather that designations of identity often become fungible when race, nationality and/or religion are evoked.

How did the early modern confusion over the term Moor affect staging practices for *Othello*? What did Othello look like on Shakespeare's stage? While I will describe the performance history of *Othello* in more detail (see p. 67ff), it is important to address the history of performing Othello's Moorishness with

1 In 2004, *Slate Magazine* ran a scathing critique of *The New York Times* for publishing an article that purportedly examined 'Arab' donations to George W. Bush's campaign when in fact the article conflated Arabs, Muslims and others (Shafer).

5 *Members of the Theban Legion*, by Georgius Jehner von Orlamünde (courtesy of the W. E. B. Du Bois Institute for African and African American Research, Harvard University)

regards to race and colour here. We believe the title role was performed by Richard Burbage, the actor who also played the leading roles in *Hamlet* and *King Lear*, because elegies written at his death in 1619 include praise for his portrayal of Othello:

> But let me not forget one chiefest part
> Wherein, beyond the rest, he mov'd the heart,
> The grievèd Moor, made jealous by a slave,
> Who sent his wife to fill a timeless grave,
> Then slew himself upon the bloody bed.
> All these and many more with him are dead.
>
> (*Var*, 396)

From these remarks we know that *Othello* was a popular role with which Burbage's identity as an actor was attached: he was the 'grievèd Moor'.

Although few documents reveal much about early modern staging practices,[1] there is one unusual document that depicts Aaron, the Moor from *Titus Andronicus*: a drawing done by Henry Peacham around 1595 (now called the Longleat manuscript). The manuscript contains a drawing of several characters from *Titus Andronicus*, and Aaron, the Moor, who is figured in the drawing on the far right, is clearly portrayed as having black skin and a curly black Afro. Because the detailing of the drawing is imprecise, it is impossible to discern if Aaron's skin colour is a factor of dyeing or cloth covering. Nonetheless, Aaron's hair appears to be a wig affixed with a headband tied round his temples. It is now widely assumed that diverse prosthetics were used to convey racial differences in early modern performances: herb-based dyes (usually woad), soot, coal, jet, oil-based ointments, dyed black cloth (masks, gloves and stockings), exotic costuming and wigs.[2]

1 For more on early modern stage practices see Stern.

2 For more on the techniques used to make characters black on the early modern stage see, Karim-Cooper; Smith 'Othello'; and Smith, 'White'.

The text of *Othello* seems to suggest that Othello was portrayed as black on the early modern stage. While most of the racialized rhetoric comes from Roderigo, Iago and Brabantio before the audience ever sees Othello, scholars have debated whether the rhetoric is metadramatic, that is, indicating how Othello should be performed, or is in opposition to the man we eventually encounter with our own eyes (Vaughan, *Performing*, 93–110). For instance, Roderigo calls Othello 'thicklips' (1.1.65); Iago refers to him as 'an old black ram' (1.1.87) and later as 'black Othello' (2.3.29); Brabantio claims that Othello has a 'sooty bosom' (1.2.70); and the Duke, when praising Othello to Brabantio, states 'Your son-in-law is far more fair than black' (1.3.291). Even Othello himself refers to his blackness, wondering if Desdemona has been unfaithful because he is black: 'Haply for I am black / And have not those soft parts of conversation / That chamberers have' (3.3.267–9). And then he pronounces that Desdemona's virtue is now as black as his face: 'Her name, that was as fresh / As Dian's visage, is now begrimed and black / As mine own face' (3.3.389–91). When one places the Longleat manuscript drawing of Aaron, the Moor in blackface alongside these lines from *Othello* it appears that Othello's blackness could have been portrayed in a literal fashion on the early modern stage.

In fact, it was not until the early nineteenth century that Othello's blackness was questioned by scholars and actors. None other than Samuel Taylor Coleridge appears to be the first to question the validity of portraying Othello as a black man. In 1818 he wrote:

> Can we imagine him [Shakespeare] so utterly ignorant as to make a barbarous negro plead royal birth, – at a time, too, when negroes were not known except as slaves? . . . Besides, if we could in good earnest believe Shakespeare ignorant of the distinction [between a Moor and a 'negro'], still why should we adopt one disagreeable possibility instead of a ten times greater and more

H. Singleton del.
C. Taylor direx.t sculp.
RODERIGO,
Sir, Your daughter hath made a gross revolt.
London Publish'd July 1;1793 by C.Taylor No 10 near Castle Street,Holborn.

6 *Roderigo: Sir your daughter hath made a gross revolt, [Othello, act I, scene 1] [graphic] / H. Singleton del.; C. Taylor direxr., sculp* (1793), Charles Taylor, printmaker (used by permission of the Folger Shakespeare Library under a Creative Commons Attribution-ShareAlike 4.0 International Licence)

> pleasing probability? It is a common error to mistake epithets applied by the *dramatis personae* to each other as truly descriptive of what the audience ought to see or know. No doubt Desdemona saw Othello's visage in his mind; yet, as we are constituted, and most surely as an English audience was disposed in the beginning of the seventeenth century, it would be something monstrous to conceive this beautiful Venetian girl falling in love with a veritable negro. It would argue a disproportionateness, a want of balance, in Desdemona, which Shakespeare does not appear to have in the least contemplated.
>
> (Coleridge, 385–6)

Coleridge's logic is very strained in this argument, for he implicitly acknowledges that Othello was performed as black in the past, the 'disagreeable possibility', but he also wants to argue that performances should now move to the more 'pleasing probability' that Othello is not black but light-skinned. And finally he bluntly states that a good 'Venetian girl' could never love a 'veritable negro'. Despite the fact that Coleridge attempts to cloak his argument in historicist terms, his arguments against Othello's blackness are a clear reflection of his own time, the early nineteenth century when the transatlantic slave trade was fully established and anti-miscegenation laws were enacted.

While Coleridge's argument must seem flimsy, racist and sexist by today's standards, it proved extremely influential in the nineteenth century and helped to initiate what has come to be called the great 'Bronze Age of *Othello*',[1] the period in which Othello was portrayed as tanned, tawny, and off-white (i.e., definitively non-black). Edmund Kean, one of the most

1 I cannot determine who coined the term the 'Bronze Age of *Othello*' because it is often cited and never fully attributed. The earliest reference I have been able to find is from 1969, but even there scare quotes were employed for the term, indicating that the phrase was already in circulation (Carlisle, 194).

famous Shakespearean actors of the era, was the first to stage the new, lighter-skinned Othello. Writing in 1869, Kean's biographer discussed his race/colour decision:

> Kean regarded it as a gross error to make Othello either a negro or a black, and accordingly altered the conventional black to the light brown which distinguishes the Moors by virtue of their descent from the Caucasian race. . . . Betterton, Quin, Mossop, Barry, Garrick, and John Kemble all played the part with black faces, but it was reserved for Kean to innovate, and Coleridge to justify, the attempt to substitute a light brown for the traditional black. The alteration has been sanctioned by subsequent usage.
>
> (Hawkins, 221)

Thus, from the 1820s until the 1870s, it was standard practice to have Othello portrayed as light-skinned or bronzed. But as is clear from Coleridge's and Kean's biographer's comments, nineteenth-century artists were well aware that they were breaking from Shakespeare's tradition: they explicitly acknowledge that Othello was portrayed as black on the early modern stage. This point is frequently glossed over when scholars and performers today claim that the early modern understanding of Moor was vague, fungible and elastic. While the meaning of the term itself can be unclear, in the nineteenth century there was a tacit agreement that theatrical performances of Moors in early modern England were not: Othello was a black man (or, rather, a white man in black makeup).

While *Othello* explicitly portrays a Moor, the play implicitly asks its audience to imagine another distinct group, the Turks. After all, it is the Turks who pose the threat to Cyprus that makes the Venetians require their mercenary soldier, the Moor of Venice. So how were Turks conceived in the early modern period? Although the term Turk seems somewhat more precise than Moor, it too was elastic in early modern English usage, encompassing the Turkish people, Muslims in general and the Ottoman Empire. Early modern English texts catalogue the long litany of stereotypes associated with Turks: barbarous, cruel, despotic, tyrannical and sexually voracious (seraglios, the private living quarters for the Sultan's wives and concubines, were a favourite topic in early modern literature and drama).[1] Furthermore, there were widespread stories about the abduction and enforced slavery of Christians by Turkish pirates.[2] The underlying early modern English narrative was that the Turks threatened to engulf all Western civilization militarily, economically and even sexually.

Many early modern English fears were well founded. After all, the Ottoman Empire was large, powerful and rapidly expanding. In the 1580s, for instance, the Ottoman Empire controlled part or all of modern day Turkey, Syria, Iraq, Egypt, Libya, Tunisia, Algeria and much of Eastern Europe. Writing in 1603, Richard Knolles gives voice to early modern English anxieties about the strength of the Ottoman Empire:

> So that by this we haue alreadie said is easily to be gathered how much the Turke is too strong for any one the neighbor princes, either Mahometanes or Christians, bordering vpon him, and therefore to be of them the more feared. . . . As for the Turk, the most dangerous and professed enemie of the Christian commonweale, be his strength so great, yea and happily greater too than is before declared (the greatness of his dominions and empire considered) yet is he not to be thought therefore inuincible, or his power indeed so great as it in shew seemeth for to be.
>
> (Knolles, 5G2^{i})

Knolles suggests that the Ottoman Empire is too strong to be defeated by Muslims and Christians alone; divine intervention

1 For more on early modern English views of the Turks see Burton; and Vitkus, *Turning*.
2 For more on early modern captivity narratives see Vitkus, *Piracy*.

is required to defeat a 'strength so great'. In fact, the Ottoman Empire maintained a strong presence in Europe through the end of the seventeenth-century.

The anxiety about not only the power, but also the lure of the Turk was expressed in the early modern English colloquial phrase 'to turn Turk'. When the alarm bell is rung on the island of Cyprus during Cassio's drunken brawl, Othello enters asking:

> Why, how now, ho? From whence ariseth this?
> **Are we turned Turks?** and to ourselves do that
> Which heaven hath forbid the Ottomites?
> (2.3.165–7)

In early modern English, 'to turn Turk' was always used in a derogatory sense because, on the most basic level, this phrase signifies the threat of becoming barbaric or losing control. Yet the subtexts of the phrase reveal anxieties about (1) how to distinguish between groups, religions and racial identities; and (2) the nature of identity itself. If the emphasis is placed on the noun, 'to turn TURK', there is an implicit understanding that Englishness and Christianity are the opposites of Turkishness. 'To turn Turk' would then imply becoming something wholly separate, foreign and anathema to English Christianity. Yet if the emphasis is place on the verb, 'to TURN Turk', the implication is at odds with the previous sentiment. When the possibility of turning is emphasized, one gets the sense that identities are subject to change, self-constructions may be transient and impermanent, and one's identity may be altered by both internal desires (conversions) and external threats (forced conversions). In fact, a society would not need a phrase like 'to turn Turk' if (1) there were no anxieties about the differences between groups or the abilities to distinguish between groups; or (2) identity was conceived as fixed and stable. Yet it is clear that neither was the case in early modern England.

This is precisely the murky terrain that Shakespeare explores in *Othello*. After all, Brabantio is furious not only that his daughter has married without his permission, but also that the Venetian state fails to recognize the essential ways in which Othello is ill-suited for his daughter. He cannot fathom that the Duke will support the marriage: 'For if such actions may have passage free / Bond-slaves and pagans shall our statesmen be' (1.2.98–9). Brabantio believes in a world in which there are real, tangible and fixed differences between Venetian statesmen on the one hand, and pagan slaves on the other. Yet the world of *Othello*, in which there already exists a Moor of Venice, a mercenary soldier who has fought for the Christians against the Turks and Muslims, shows how out of touch Brabantio's beliefs are. Even though Brabantio's beliefs reveal him to be detached from his contemporary Venetian state, the play does not render those beliefs as foolish or incoherent. On the contrary, the play ends with Othello committing suicide, narrating a story about his divided sense of self as both Christian and Turk.

> Set you down this,
> And say besides that in Aleppo once,
> Where a malignant and a turbanned Turk
> Beat a Venetian and traduced the state,
> I took by th' throat the circumcised dog
> And smote him – thus!
>
> (5.2.349–54)

Othello commits suicide enacting the roles of both the Christian defender in the outposts of contested territory (Aleppo was controlled by the Ottoman Empire in the 1580s) and the 'turbanned Turk' who must be excised. It seems almost impossible to experience the end of *Othello* without hearing the pang of nostalgia for a world in which Christians and Turks are clearly and easily distinguished. In other words, there is an implicit longing for some certainty about the differences between barbarians and the civilized, Turk and Venetian, Muslim and Christian. The reader/audience member is left asking how near or far this nostalgic position is from Brabantio's?

The early modern investment in conversion is also implicated in *Othello*'s investigation of the colloquial phrase 'to turn Turk'. Thomas Kyd's *Soliman and Perseda* (1599) explicitly investigates the nature of religious conversions by staging an unwilling conversion to Islam. Shakespeare's *The Merchant of Venice* takes up the topic by presenting both a willing conversion to Christianity through Shylock's daughter Jessica and a forced conversion to Christianity through Shylock. In *Othello*, however, the eponymous hero's religion is left vague, once again inviting the audience to ponder precisely what it means for a character to be the Moor of Venice. When Othello relates the story of his life, he describes in equivocal terms how he was 'sold to slavery' and his 'redemption thence' (1.3.139). Does his use of 'redemption' in that sentence mean his salvation from slavery or his salvation through Christ? Things are further muddled in the famous temptation scene (3.3) when Othello kneels vowing 'black vengeance' (3.3.450). As Iago kneels beside him, stating 'Do not rise yet' (3.3.465), theatrically the scene can look like two men kneeling together in prayer. And several productions have interpreted this scene as Othello's reversion to Islam, in which men pray together without women present, by kneeling and touching their heads to the ground in supplication to Allah (see, for example, Stuart Burge's 1965 film version of *Othello* starring Laurence Olivier). If this interpretation was explicit in early modern stagings, then the colloquial phrase 'to turn Turk' would resonate in a horrifically literal sense: the 'turbanned Turk' who maligns the Venetian state in one of the farthest outposts of the Ottoman Empire should be smitten by the long arm of the Lord in a Christian narrative.

The scene in which Othello and Iago kneel together, however, also looks like a bizarre inversion of a marriage rite. After all, Iago pledges:

> Witness that here Iago doth give up
> The execution of his wit, **hands**, **heart**,
> To wronged Othello's service. Let him **command**
> And to **obey** shall be in me remorse
> What bloody business ever.
>
> (3.3.468–72)

By giving up his 'hands' and 'heart' and pledging that he will 'obey' Othello's command, Iago places himself in the role of a subordinate and perhaps also in the role of a wife, displacing Desdemona in Othello's heart. The scene ends with Iago punctuating this pledge by making himself Othello's property for eternity: 'I am your own for ever' (3.3.482). While many modern directors have interpreted this scene as revealing Iago's hidden motive – his homoerotic love for Othello – it may be slightly more complex than that. The scene implicitly links religious conversions with the conversions that women make when they become wives. Once again, we can see that Shakespeare was experimenting with this connection in his other Venetian play, *The Merchant of Venice*, in which Jessica's conversion to Christianity is linked with her conversion from being Shylock's daughter to being Lorenzo's wife. In *Othello*, Desdemona makes it clear that she has been made wholly new through her marriage to Othello. When Brabantio asks her to whom she owes her 'obedience' (1.3.180), she makes it clear that marriage converts a woman's duties from father to husband: 'But here's my husband: / And so much duty as my mother showed / To you, preferring you before her father, / So much I challenge that I may profess / Due to the Moor my lord' (1.3.185–9).

Just as there were early modern anxieties about the potential to revert to one's older religious beliefs (Jewish converts to Christianity, after all, were not labelled as 'Christians' but as 'Marranos' (swine) in Spain and Portugal) there were also anxieties about conversions and female sexuality. Linking the colloquial phrase 'to turn Turk' with female sexuality, Othello complains that Desdemona is all too ready to convert and turn whenever her desires are peaked:

> Sir, she can **turn**, and **turn**, and yet go on
> And **turn** again. And she can weep, sir, weep.
> And she's **obedient**: as you say, **obedient,**
> Very **obedient**.
>
> (4.1.253–6)

The problem with women, Othello seems to suggest, is that the qualities that men most value and praise – their willingness to turn from father to husband, and their obedience – can be the most dangerous ones. For if women are willing to stray from the duty they owe to their fathers, are they not already primed to stray from the duty they then owe their husbands? This sexist logic, of course, comes directly from Iago in the temptation scene, revealing that it is Othello and not Desdemona who is all too prompt to revert from his duties to a spouse (3.3.209–11). Yet Othello never acknowledges this fact even after he realizes that he has unjustly killed Desdemona ('speak / Of one that loved not wisely, but too well' 5.2.341–2). It is up to the audience to ponder the nature of conversions, faith and duty.

Othello presents a society in which there is so much global economic and political traffic that the distinctions between Venetian and Turk, Christian and Muslim, and father/daughter and husband/wife are increasingly challenged. The play is constantly setting up binaries, which are then destabilized. On the most fundamental level, the play asks what it is to be human and how humanity is differentiated from being an animal. As many readers and audience members quickly realize, *Othello* is riddled with references to animals and birds. Daws, rams, ewes, horses, guinea-hens, baboons, cats, puppies, asses, dogs, lions, parrots, goats, toads, monkeys, wolves, minxes, ravens, bears, crocodiles, dear, gulls, swans, vipers and other creatures litter the dialogue of *Othello* (my count puts the references around 40). Iago introduces most of the animal imagery at the beginning of the play, and then in the temptation scene pointedly asks Othello, 'Are you a man?' (3.3.377). It should not be surprising that Othello introduces most of the animal imagery from that point forward, including his infamous outburst to Lodovico, 'You are welcome, sir, to Cyprus. Goats and monkeys!' (4.1.263).

As scholars working in animal studies have noted, societies that draw sharp distinctions between, and hierarchies among, human and non-human animals often create sharp distinctions

7 Frontispiece of *Shakespeare's Othello* (mid to late nineteenth century) published by Pantographe-Gavard (used by permission of the Folger Shakespeare Library under a Creative Commons Attribution-ShareAlike 4.0 International Licence). Notice the abundance of animal imagery in this frontispiece.

between, and hierarchies among, different human races.[1] Thus, Iago's rhetoric at the beginning of the play reads as a classic example of an attempt to create and maintain social hierarchies based on race by linking Othello's race with non-human animals. Talking to Desdemona's father, Iago rails: 'you'll have your daughter covered with a Barbary horse; you'll have your nephews neigh to you' (1.1.109–11). The difference between Desdemona's Venetian identity and Othello's Moorish identity is as clear as the distinctions between humans and horses, Iago declares, emphasizing that their coupling is as unnatural as bestiality. Likewise, when Iago attempts to convince Othello that Desdemona is having an affair with Cassio, he paints their sexual behaviour in bestial terms, stating that it would be impossible to get the 'ocular proof' (3.3.363) of their affair even if they were 'as prime as goats; as hot as monkeys, / As salt as wolves in pride' (3.3.406–7).

Othello's adoption of Iago's terms, his unselfconscious echoing of the animals Iago uses to represent an overactive sexual drive, serves to signal his internalization of the social hierarchies Iago has established as well. For while Othello begins the play declaring that he is worthy of Desdemona both in terms of birth and value, he quickly begins to accept that his blackness renders him unworthy and that Desdemona's desire for him renders her untrustworthy. Furthermore, Desdemona, whom Othello once referred to in the most human terms as his 'fair warrior' (2.1.180) before he thought she had cuckolded him, is now linked almost exclusively with animals in his rhetoric: 'lewd minx' (3.3.478), 'chuck' (3.4.49) and 'crocodile' (4.1.245). Equally disturbing, however, is Othello's absorption of Iago's rhetoric that he himself is an animal. Tacitly accepting Iago's racist hierarchies in which Moors are non-human animals, Othello kills himself claiming that he is the 'turbanned Turk' who is a 'circumcised dog' (5.2.351, 353).

1 For an overview of animal studies see Haraway. For a specific reading of animal studies in early modern studies see Raber.

To Iago's earlier question, 'Are you a man?' (3.3.377) Othello ends by implicitly denying his humanity and proclaiming his animality.

Othello and the Audience

Iago's question about what distinguishes men from animals resonates particularly loudly throughout *Othello* because of the play's unique positioning of the audience. Unlike most other Shakespearean tragedies but similar to many comedies, the audience knows more than the titular tragic hero. Othello, after all, is tricked into committing murder, and the audience is made complicit in the trick by being Iago's confidant throughout the play: he speaks directly to us as he plots Othello's destruction. So the audience is positioned as distinctly different from Othello.

As many scholars and theatre artists have noted, the affordance of knowledge can make the audience extremely uncomfortable. More than with any other play, there are stories about audience members interrupting performances of *Othello*. The earliest extant account of an audience reaction actually records the fact that the audience is moved beyond measure by Desdemona's death. In 1610, Henry Jackson recorded the audience's reaction to a performance of *Othello* in Oxford:

> But truly the celebrated Desdemona, slain in our presence by her husband, although she pleaded her case very effectively throughout, yet moved [us] more after she was dead, when lying on her bed, entreated the pity of the spectators by her very countenance.[1]

The audience at the Oxford performance willingly suspend their disbelief, shelving their knowledge that the boy-actor who played Desdemona would live to perform again. Moreover,

1 First quoted in Latin in Tillotson. The original Latin text, as well as the English translation used here, is quoted in *Riv*, 1852.

there were numerous reports throughout history of audience members reacting as if the events are real. Patrons at a French performance of *Othello* in 1792, for example, were moved to 'a universal tumult. Tears, groans, and menaces resounded from all parts of the theatre; and what was still more demonstrative, and more alarming, several of the prettiest women in Paris fainted in the most conspicuous boxes and were publicly carried out of the house' (quoted in Rosenberg, 32).

More striking, however, are the accounts of audience members being so moved that they feel the need to interrupt the course of events. There is an anecdote about a woman at a nineteenth-century production of *Othello* in Charleston, South Carolina, who felt compelled to yell to Othello, who was delivering his speech over the sleeping Desdemona, that 'She did not do it' (quoted in Kolin, 4). Likewise, the French writer Stendhal records the following anecdote: 'Last year [August 1822] a soldier who was standing guard in the theatre in Baltimore, upon seeing Othello, in the fifth act of the tragedy of that name, about to kill Desdemona, cried out: "It will never be said that in my presence a damned nigger killed a white woman". At the same moment the soldier shot at the actor who was playing Othello and broke his arm' (Stendhal, 22). Stendhal comments, 'Now that soldier was entertaining an *illusion*: he believed in the reality of what was happening on the stage' (Stendhal, 22). And there are many other stories of audience members who entertain the illusion that *Othello* is reality. For instance, the director Margaret Webster writes about one girl's reaction to the 1943 Broadway production, 'Once, as Emilia, I was waiting in the extreme downstage corner for my last entrance while Othello and Desdemona played out their scene. I heard a young girl's voice from the front row whispering over and over again, "Oh God, don't let him kill her . . . don't let him kill her . . . don't let him kill her" ' (Webster, 114–15).

These anecdotes may not all be true, but they reveal a desire for agency on the audience's part: a desire to protect

Desdemona from an unjust death. While the events in *Hamlet, King Lear* and *Macbeth* are just as tragic, audience members do not feel compelled to intervene in Hamlet's duel with Laertes, or in Lear's banishment of Cordelia or even in Macbeth's employment of the murderers. Despite the tragic nature, these plots do not move the audience to engage directly because the audience is on equal footing with the tragic hero: the audience knows as much as the hero. In *Othello*, however, the audience knows much more than Othello and is therefore placed in the position of either being complicit with the tragic action (i.e., by watching silently and doing nothing) or attempting to thwart that tragedy (i.e., by protesting, shouting or disrupting the action).

While the latter behaviour may strike one as inappropriate in the theatre, many actors and directors wonder why more audience members do not intervene in *Othello*. Writing about Gregory Doran's 2004 RSC production in which he played Iago, Antony Sher explains, 'Throughout the run, I waited for the performance when someone would stand up and shout, "Stop it!" ' (Sher, 64). Sher continues explaining that by the end of the play, 'The dangerous wordsmith may be silent, but in my head this question always rang out: *You saw what was happening – why didn't you stop it*?' (Sher, 69). Likewise, the director Peter Sellars describes *Othello* as a play that is a 'permanent provocation' (Sellars, 7). Critiquing the play's structure, Sellars argues that the audience's complicity through silence not only renders the audience culpable but also vulnerable: 'Shakespeare creates a portrait of silence that is complicit with mass murder, that hopes by not uttering the truth to save its own skin, but that will in fact become the next victim when the lie follows the inexorable course' (Sellars, 10). The play, therefore, seems to be built on an uneven plain, one which forces the audience to take a side.

Making Objects Pornographic in *Othello*

Lynda Boose astutely writes, 'As most academics who teach Shakespeare know, the question the observant student wants to ask is the prurient one that is built into the text of this play: whether Othello and Desdemona did or did not consummate their marriage. The question is unavoidable. It is layered into the dynamics of the drama in a way that it is not, for instance, in *Romeo and Juliet*. Because we know what happened in Juliet's bedroom, the consummation never becomes an issue of obsessive curiosity to the audience. The dramatic construction of *Othello*, however, seduces its readers and watchers into mimicking Iago's first question to Othello: "Are you fast married?" ' (Boose, 'Let', 24). Did Othello and Desdemona do it before the action of the play? Or, did they do it immediately after Othello is given his assignment to go to Cyprus? Or, perhaps they did it that first night in Cyprus? Or, more frustratingly for them, perhaps they never consummated the marriage at all? Of course, there are no definitive answers in the text, and thus the audience member/reader is invited to ponder and imagine exactly what goes on in their bed and exactly when.

Sex is central to the plot of *Othello*: it is the action that Iago accuses Desdemona of performing outside of her marriage; and is never usually witnessed by anyone beyond the participants. Iago makes this clear when Othello demands 'ocular proof' (3.3.363), stating: 'Would you, the supervisor, grossly gape on? / Behold her topped?' (3.3.398–9). As Iago knows from first-hand experience, not seeing and only imagining others having sex can be as titillating as, and perhaps even more upsetting than, actually witnessing the act. Although Iago's motives for hating the Moor are notoriously muddled, he does state twice that he fears Othello has had an affair with his wife Emilia:

> I hate the Moor
> And it is thought abroad that 'twixt my sheets

He's done my office. I know not if't be true,
But I for mere suspicion in that kind
Will do as if for surety.

(1.3.385–9)

For that I do suspect the lusty Moor
Hath leaped into my seat, the thought whereof
Doth like a poisonous mineral gnaw my inwards . . .
And nothing can or shall content my soul
Till I am evened with him, wife for wife . . .

(2.1.293–7)

And Emilia makes it clear that she is aware that there are rumours of her infidelity with Othello, stating that 'The Moor's abused by some most villainous knave, / Some base notorious knave, some scurvy fellow' (4.2.141–2) because 'some such squire he was / That turned your [Iago's] wit the seamy side without / And made you to suspect me with the Moor' (4.2.147–9).

Many scholars, actors and directors have been inspired by Samuel Taylor Coleridge's argument that Iago's soliloquies reveal 'the motive-hunting of a motiveless malignity' (Coleridge, 388). That is to say, that Iago does not appear to have one fixed motive for his actions; rather, he hunts for ones that will appeal to others (like Roderigo and the audience in general). Following Coleridge's general argument, these scholars see Iago as embodying the improvisational qualities that the early modern English audience would have ascribed to the devil and Vice figures from morality plays.

Yet some directors have staged productions in which Iago's motive is clearly and simply to revenge a prior affair between Emilia and Othello (most famously Peter Sellars's 2009 production, starring Philip Seymour Hoffman as Iago). Emilia, after all, appears much more knowledgeable than Desdemona when it comes to sex, sexual desires and pragmatic justifications for extra-marital affairs. Responding to Desdemona's query if 'there be such women do abuse their husbands / In such gross

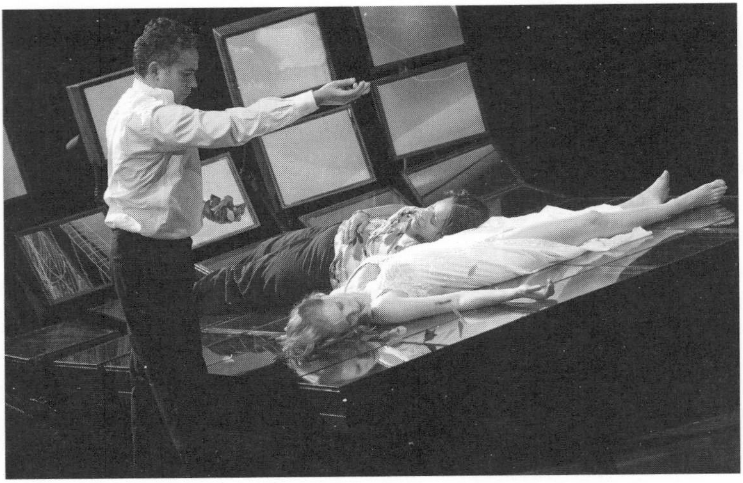

8 John Ortiz as Othello, Liza Colón-Zayas as Emilia, and Jessica Chastain as Desdemona in Peter Sellars' 2009 production at the Skirball Center, New York, © Birgit Hupfield

kind' (4.3.61–2), Emilia provides a lengthy justification for the 'abuse'. First, she jokes that she would only have an affair in the dark and not 'by this heavenly light' (4.3.65); then she rationalizes that 'The world's a huge thing: it is a great price / For a small vice' (4.3.68–9); and then she argues that men and women are the same and therefore have the same 'affections', 'Desires for sport', and 'frailty' (4.3.99, 100). In other words, Emilia appears to be well suited to Iago: they are both skilled and pragmatic rhetoricians, who pay attention to the intricacies of argumentation.[1] This point is further emphasized when certain lines are reassigned to Emilia. Honigmann reassigned

1 It should be noted that Emilia's speech about marital fidelity (4.3.85–102) is absent from the 1622 Quarto and present in the 1623 Folio. Ernst Honigmann argues that the Quarto text was based on a scribal copy of Shakespeare's foul papers, while the Folio text was based on the scribal copy of Shakespeare's fair copy. For a full account of the differences in the texts see Honigmann, *Texts*.

9 Emilia steals the handkerchief as Desdemona walks away in *Shakespeare's Othello* (mid to late nineteenth century) published by Pantographe-Gavard (used by permission of the Folger Shakespeare Library under a Creative Commons Attribution-ShareAlike 4.0 International Licence)

the line, 'This Lodovico is a proper man' (4.3.34–5) to be spoken by Emilia instead of Desdemona. In Emilia's mouth, the line echoes Iago's line, 'Cassio's a proper man' (1.3.391). There is no textual evidence to support this change (Honigmann states in the footnote that he agrees with a 'conjecture' that the line 'seems out of character' for Desdemona); rather, it is an interpretive decision that can and should be questioned. In Desdemona's mouth, however, the line might signal a momentary recognition that she could have made an easier marriage choice for herself.

Like the prurient questions that *Othello* inspires about the sexual relationship between Othello and Desdemona, it also inspires questions about the nature of the relationship between Iago and Emilia. After all, Emilia appears to be on very friendly terms with Desdemona, yet she steals the handkerchief and stands by without saying a thing when Desdemona searches frantically for it (3.4). Why would Emilia betray her friend in such a fashion? The only clue we get from Emilia is that Iago has 'a hundred times / Wooed [her] to steal it' (3.3.296–7). And then she has the enigmatic line about not knowing what Iago will do with it: 'Heaven knows, not I, / I nothing, but to please his fantasy' (3.3.302–3). Perhaps this signifies that Emilia does not know what Iago will do with the handkerchief, but she thinks she is nothing if she does not serve his desires. Or, it could mean that Emilia thinks that Iago only imagines her as serving his longings. Or, if one hears 'I' as 'Ay' (meaning 'yes'), then perhaps Emilia is saying that she knows nothing but how to please Iago's wants. Each interpretation implicates a different type of relationship between Emilia and Iago.[1]

Recently many productions of *Othello* figure the relationship as one defined by Iago's abuse of Emilia and/or Iago's closeted homosexuality. That is, it has become common to see productions of *Othello* in which Emilia is figured as a battered wife, who does her husband's bidding, even when it goes against her own wishes and/or moral compass, in order to keep him appeased and to maintain a type of peace (see, for example, Trevor Nunn's 1989 televised version of *Othello*, with Ian McKellen as Iago and Zoe Wanamaker as Emilia). Sometimes the battered wife interpretation is linked with an interpretation of Iago as a frustrated and repressed homosexual (see, for example, Oliver Parker's 1995 film version of *Othello* starring Kenneth Branagh as Iago). While in performance directors and actors must have

1 For more about what Shakespeare withholds from the audience see Honigmann, *Shakespeare*, 77–100.

clear motives for the characters, *Othello* as a text on the page is enigmatic and imprecise as to the nature of the relationship (sexual and emotional) between Iago and Emilia.

What is not enigmatic in *Othello*, however, is the way that specific objects become tied with courtship, love, marriage, sexual intercourse and cultural/racial differences. In particular, the play forces the reader and the audience member to focus on the handkerchief, the bedsheets and the bed itself. These objects get charged with meanings that transform when they are moved from the private realm to a public one. Although we see Desdemona with the handkerchief, it is Othello who alone claims for it especial value and significance. At first, Othello tells Desdemona that it was given to his mother by an Egyptian who claimed it would keep Othello's father 'subdue[d]' 'to her love' as long as she kept it (3.4.61, 62). Othello then claims it was made by a 200-year-old sibyl who used the silk of 'hallowed' worms and dyed it in the blood from the hearts of virgins (3.4.75, 76).

While presenting a handkerchief dyed in 'mummy' may seem like a horrific gift, dyeing handkerchiefs in mummy was not uncommon in early modern England. In fact, the practice was one that was both familiar (coming from contemporary medicinal practices) and foreign (coming from Egyptian burial practices). Richard Sugg details the four sources, types and methods for extracting mummy used in early modern medicine: 'One is mineral pitch [bitumen]; the second the matter derived from embalmed Egyptian corpses; the third, the relatively recent bodies of travellers, drowned by sandstorms in the Arabian deserts; and the fourth, flesh taken from fresh corpses (usually those of executed felons, and ideally within about three days) and then treated and dried by Paracelsian practitioners' (Sugg, 15). Far from being a practice that was viewed as wholly foreign, extracting mummy and dyeing a cloth in it was a practice that united Africa and Europe: it was both an ancient African practice and a contemporary English one. As Ian Smith reminds us when providing glosses for the uses of mummy in *Othello*, *Macbeth* and *The Merry Wives of Windsor*, 'Strange though this idea of eating desiccated human flesh might appear, its familiarity in England is registered by its frequent mention among authors, including Shakespeare' (Smith, 'Othello', 17).

The fact that the mummy-dyed handkerchief is the object that metonymically stands in for the missing 'ocular proof' that Othello desires to determine whether Desdemona has been unfaithful to him allows the reader or audience member to question how agentive the cloth actually is.[1] The handkerchief knits together Othello and Desdemona with his African past and her European present; it weaves their love together while it is in Desdemona's possession; and it unravels their lives when the Cypriot courtesan Bianca is ordered to 'take out the work' by Cassio (4.1.153). So are we as readers/audience members supposed to believe that there is 'magic in the web' of the handkerchief and that the tragic demise of Othello and Desdemona's relationship stems from the fact that Emilia steals it to give to Iago?

Is the handkerchief supposed to have agency, actually causing events to occur? Of course, this is another enigmatic moment in *Othello*, especially when one realizes that Othello tells a completely different story about the handkerchief's provenance at the end of the play. Othello justifies killing Desdemona to Emilia and Gratiano by explaining that he saw the handkerchief in Cassio's hand, 'It was a handkerchief, an antique token / My father gave my mother' (5.2.214–15). Is this contradiction an authorial oversight? Or perhaps it signals Othello's gift as a storyteller once again? After all, Othello won Desdemona's heart by telling her fantastical tales about his childhood; perhaps his story about her need to 'Make it a darling' (3.4.68) was simply

1 Ian Smith provides a fascinating reading of the handkerchief as black instead of white, arguing that the black colour would reflect early modern performance tropes in which blackness was frequently portrayed by cloth masks and gloves. A black handkerchief, Smith argues, 'constitutes a fitting, virtually self-explanatory symbol of the play's central but controversial interracial marriage' (Smith, 'Othello', 24).

just that – another good tale to make her do what he wants. This interpretation would render the handkerchief a lot less agentive and place power back in the mouth of the human storyteller.

As many scholars have noted, however, the handkerchief also serves as a symbol for the visual verification of consummating a marriage. Lynda Boose argues, 'What Shakespeare was representing was a visually recognizable reduction of Othello and Desdemona's wedding-bed sheets, the visual proof of their consummated marriage' (Boose, 'Othello', 363). Arguing along similar lines, Edward Snow writes that the handkerchief 'is potent as visible proof of Desdemona's adultery largely because it subconsciously evokes for Othello the blood-stained sheets of the wedding-bed and his wife's loss of virginity there' (Snow, 390). Boose and Snow, of course, are referring to another custom that seems to unite Africa with Europe – the act of displaying bloodied bedsheets after a wedding night to prove the newly betrothed woman was in fact a virgin. The handkerchief, which Iago describes as being 'Spotted with strawberries' (3.3.438), symbolizes in miniature the bedsheets which should be displayed with hymenial blood.

Othello and Desdemona's wedding sheets are discussed several times throughout the play. On their first night in Cyprus Iago proclaims to Cassio that Othello 'hath not yet made wanton the night' with Desdemona (2.3.16), and thus invites Cassio to drink with him and to toast 'happiness to their sheets' (2.3.26). Aurally the audience can hear an echo of Iago's earlier claim that he suspects that Othello has done his 'office' ''twixt [his] sheets' (1.3.387, 386).

Desdemona, of course, seems to cling to the idea that her 'wedding sheets' (4.2.107) are a private symbol of her love for Othello. That is precisely why she asks Emilia to 'lay' them on her bed after Othello calls her 'the cunning whore of Venice' (4.2.91). In her innocence, Desdemona believes that the sheets reveal her steadfastness, love and purity. She even asks to be buried in them if she should die suddenly ('If I do die before

B.
N°9
H.Singleton pinx.t
C.Taylor direxit et sculpsit
CASSIO.
—this is my ancient—this is my right hand
this is my left hand:—I am not drunk.
London,Published March 1.1793 by C.Taylor N°10 near Castle Street,Holborn.

10 *Cassio: This is my ancient . . . [Othello, act* II, *sc. 3] [graphic] / H. Singleton pinxt.; C. Taylor direxit et sculpsit* (1793), Charles Taylor, printmaker (used by permission of the Folger Shakespeare Library under a Creative Commons Attribution-ShareAlike 4.0 International Licence)

thee, prithee shroud me / In one of these same sheets' 4.3.22–3) because she continues to believe the sheets reveal, express and project her love. But the play reveals how easily private and personal objects can be endowed with pornographic meaning when trafficked in public discourse.

Thus, the play moves from small private objects, like the handkerchief, to larger ones, like the wedding sheets, and culminates with the whole bed. Tracing the way Desdemona's death on her bed was censored in performance, Michael Neill argues that the play tips towards pornography because it 'capitulate[s] to Iago's poisoned vision at the very moment when it has seemed poised to reaffirm the transcendent claims of their love' (Neill, 412). The final scene of *Othello*, after all, is dominated

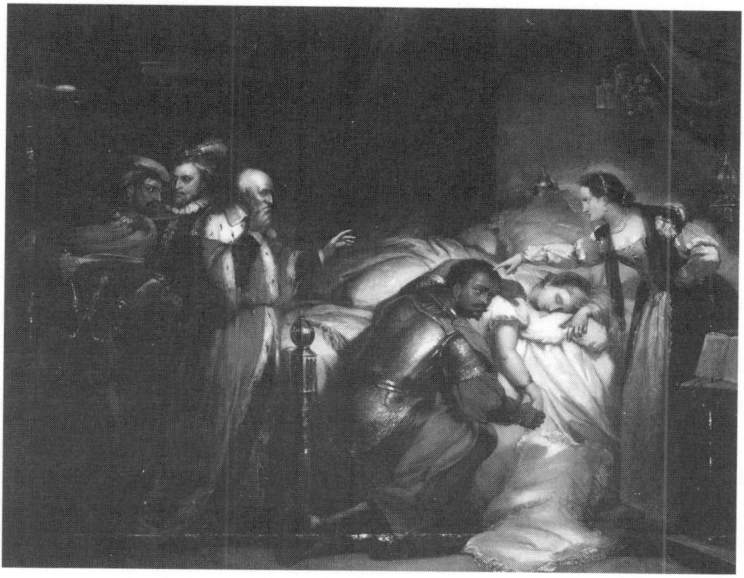

11 *Othello's Lamentation* (1857) by William Salter (used by permission of the Folger Shakespeare Library under a Creative Commons Attribution-ShareAlike 4.0 International Licence)

by the bed on which Desdemona sleeps and is killed, the corpse of Emilia is placed and Othello commits suicide. While the scene starts as a private encounter between Desdemona and Othello, it quickly turns into a public affair with Emilia, Montano, Gratiano, Iago, Lodovico and Cassio entering in at various points. Mirroring the audience whose gaze is never allowed to exist in an uninvolved way, these public figures (many of whom are representatives of the Venetian and Cypriot governments) come into Desdemona's bedroom as if clarity could be achieved through witnessing. But *Othello* throws cold water on one's desire to see. Certainty is never achieved through public viewing.

Othello and Scholarly Debates

Critical responses to *Othello* have ranged widely over the 400+ years since the play's debut. While at the beginning of the twenty-first century the play is firmly ensconced in the canon both in terms of its position in literature and drama curricula and its frequent revival on the stage (in 2015 there were at least 15 professional performances of *Othello* in the US and the UK alone), critical assessments of the play have not always been favourable. In fact, the first criticism published about *Othello* was entirely negative. Thomas Rymer, writing in 1693, included a scathing critique of *Othello* based on the improbability of the plot, the characters, and the play's structure overall.

> The Character of that State is to employ strangers in their Wars; But shall a Poet thence fancy that they will set a Negro to be their General; or trust a *Moor* to defend them against the *Turk*? With us a Black-amoor might rise to be a Trumpeter; but *Shakespear* would not have him less than a Lieutenant-General. With us a *Moor* might marry some little drab, or Small-coal Wench: *Shake-spear*, would provide him the Daughter and Heir of some great Lord, or Privy-Councellor: And

> all the Town should reckon it a very suitable match . . . Nothing is more odious in Nature than an improbable lye; And, certainly, never was any Play fraught, like this of *Othello*, with improbabilities.
>
> (Rymer, 134)

For Rymer it is completely improbable to think that a 'Negro' could rise to the level of a general and marry a woman of high birth and social standing. Rymer's critique is especially fascinating when he reveals that 'a *Moor*' might marry with a white woman from the working classes, like a 'drab' (i.e., prostitute) or a 'coal wench'. The problem in *Othello*, according to Rymer, is the combination of mixing races and classes.

Furthermore, a firm belief in clear class hierarchies permeates Rymer's objections to *Othello*. He argues of Othello's verbal abuse of Desdemona in 4.1: 'Some Drayman or drunken Tinker might possibly treat his drab at this sort of rate, and mean no harm by it: but for his excellency, a My lord General, to Serenade a Senator's Daughter with such a volley of scroundrel filthy Language, is sure the most absurd Maggot that ever bred from any Poets addle Brain' (Rymer, 158). The improbability of the race and class of Othello, then, lead Rymer to speculate that the play is more risible than tragic. In fact, he begins by joking that there is nothing the audience can really take away from the play except: 'First, This may be a caution to all Maidens of Quality how, without their Parents consent, they run away with Blackamoors. . . . Secondly, This may be a warning to all good Wives, that they look well to their Linnen. Thirdly, This may be a lesson to Husbands, that before their Jealousie be Tragical, the proofs may be Mathematical' (Rymer, 132).

Rymer ends his reflections on *Othello* by emphasizing that the play does not impart a moral lesson and is therefore closer to a comedy than a tragedy. 'What can remain with the Audience to carry home with them from this sort of Poetry, for their use and edification? . . . There is in this Play, some burlesk, some humour, and ramble of Comical Wit, some shew, and some *Mimickry* to divert the spectators: but the tragical part is, plainly none other, than a Bloody Farce, without salt or savour' (Rymer, 164). Rymer even suggests that the improbability that the handkerchief becomes the 'ocular proof' (3.3.363) Othello requires sets the audience up for comedy: 'So much ado, so much stress, so much passion and repetition about an Handkerchief! Why was not this call'd the *Tragedy of the Handkerchief*? . . . Had it been *Desdemona's* Garter, the Sagacious Moor might have smelt a Rat: but the Handkerchief is so remote a trifle, no Booby, on this side *Mauritania*, cou'd make any consequence from it' (Rymer, 160).

Interestingly, Charlotte Lennox, writing about 60 years after Rymer, takes a stance against Rymer's racism, arguing that it is not unusual for black men to marry white women. She writes, 'such Affections are not common indeed; but a very few Instances of them prove that they are not impossible; and even in *England* we see some very handsome Women married to Blacks, where their Colour is less familiar than at *Venice*; besides the *Italian* Ladies are remarkable for such Sallies of irregular Passions' (Lennox, vol 1, 131). As Ann Thompson notes, 'Lennox does not find a white-versus-black racist stereotyping in the play (she is full of praise for "the amiable Othello" and his many virtues), but she substitutes for it an equally stereotypical English-versus-Italian racism' (Thompson, An, 147). Lennox even critiques Rymer's account of the inconsistencies in the play, noting 'That of *Emilia* though more inconsistent than any, he has taken no Notice of' (Lennox, vol 1, 129). Unfortunately, Lennox's sanguine analysis of *Othello* and critique of Rymer went largely neglected for various complicated reasons that Ann Thompson explores in her recent essay on her life and work (Thompson, An).

While Rymer's argument about the improbabilities of *Othello* has not had a large scholarly influence (after all, there are lots of improbable situations in Shakespeare's plays, like people getting captured by pirates in *Hamlet* and *Pericles*, a father not recognizing his own son in *King Lear* and cross-dressed women who are never recognized as women in several plays such as *Twelfth Night* and *As You Like It*), his argument that *Othello* veers closer to comedy than tragedy has been picked up by others including Susan Snyder, Michael Bristol and Sheila Rose Bland. Snyder and Bristol both note the comedic underpinnings to the following plot structures: the daughter who thwarts her father's wishes; the January–May marriage; the improvisational clown-trickster who serves as the scourge of marriage (Synder; Bristol). Bland, however, argues that *Othello* should be staged as a comedy with an all-male white cast as it would have been staged in Shakespeare's time so that 'When my blackfaced white male Othello steals his last kiss from my white male Desdemona and falls on the bed alongside my white male Emilia . . ., the full impact of the homoeroticism will be felt . . . There will be joy. There will be humor. There will be titillation' (Bland, 40).

Writing in the early nineteenth century, Samuel Taylor Coleridge mounted a different kind of critique of *Othello*. Unlike Rymer, Coleridge had nothing but praise for Shakespeare as a writer, often extolling Shakespeare's talents in what would come to be termed a form of 'Bardolatry', that is, reverential worship of the playwright.[1] Coleridge writes of Shakespeare, 'But combine all, – wit, subtlety, and fancy, with profundity, imagination, and moral and physical susceptibility of the pleasurable, – and let the object of action be man universal; and we have – O, rash prophecy! say, rather, we have – a Shakespere!' (Coleridge, 394). For Coleridge, then, the fault is never in Shakespeare, the

1 George Bernard Shaw coined the term 'Bardolatry' in 1901 when he critiqued the Victorian custom of deeply editing the plays for performance: 'It is a significant fact that the mutilators of Shakespear, who never could be persuaded that Shakespear knew his business better than they, have ever been the most fanatical worshippers. . . . It was an age of gross ignorance of Shakespear and incapacity for his works that produced the indiscriminate eulogies with which we are familiar. It was the revival of genuine criticism of those works that coincided with the movement for giving genuine instead of spurious and silly representations of his plays. So much for Bardolatry!' (Shaw, xxxi).

playwright; instead, Coleridge critiques the tradition of staging Othello as a 'blackamoor or negro' (Coleridge, 385). Like Rymer, Coleridge argues that there are improbabilities that mar *Othello*: 'Besides, if we could in good earnest believe Shakespeare ignorant of the distinction [between a Moor and a "negro"], still why should we adopt one disagreeable possibility instead of a ten times greater and more pleasing probability?' (Coleridge, 385). Coleridge effectively starts the line of argument that Othello could not be black; a line of argument which changed performance practices for roughly 100 years.

Coleridge's other influential argument was that Iago had 'the coolness of a preconceiving experimenter', and that his rhetorical skills allowed him to coin 'Iagoism[s]' (Coleridge, 384 and 388). The notion that Iago is somehow more adaptive, socially spontaneous and improvisational has gripped scholars and performers alike as a unique quality that differentiates him not only from everyone else in the play, but also from the standard early modern constructions of identity. Stephen Greenblatt argued that Iago represents the way concepts of identity modified from medieval notions of fixed identities to early modern notions of fluid ones (Greenblatt, 222–57). As already noted (see p. 45), however, Coleridge's argument was also tied to a belief that Iago did not have a clear motive for his actions: 'The remainder – Iago's soliloquy – the motive-hunting of a motiveless malignity – how awful it is!' (Coleridge, 388). As Antony Sher writes about playing Iago in 2004, though, 'I'm angry with Samuel Coleridge. His analysis of Iago as a villain possessed by "motiveless malignity" has somehow lodged in the public consciousness, even though it's complete nonsense' (Sher, 57). Coleridge's criticism of *Othello*, then, has cast a long shadow.

In the twentieth century, *Othello* scholarship took a different turn with critics debating the play's place among Shakespeare's great tragedies. A.C. Bradley, for instance, argued that *Othello* was one of Shakespeare's greatest tragedies, often assessing it more favourably than *Hamlet, Macbeth* and *King Lear*. Bradley declared, 'What is the peculiarity of *Othello*? What is the distinctive impression it leaves? Of all Shakespeare's tragedies, I would answer, not even excepting *King Lear, Othello* is the most painfully exciting and the most terrible' (Bradley, 168). Bradley attributed the intensity of the drama to its structure (a play without a subplot), the 'sense of shame and humiliation' (Bradley, 169) audience members feel about the topic of sexual jealousy and the modern feeling the play evokes: '*Othello* is a drama of modern life; when it first appeared it was a drama almost of contemporary life, for the date of the Turkish attack on Cyprus is 1570. . . . Besides this, their [the characters'] fortunes affect us as those of private individuals more than is possible in any of the later tragedies with the exception of *Timon*' (Bradley, 171). For Bradley, then, *Othello* rises above *Hamlet* and *Macbeth* because it has the power to 'affect' audience members more precisely because it is a play about private matters instead of state ones (Bradley, 173).

Bradley challenged Coleridge's reading of *Othello* on two important fronts. First, he forcefully declared that Shakespeare 'imagined Othello as a black man, and not as a light-brown one', noting, 'we must remember that the brown or bronze to which we are now accustomed in the Othellos of our theatres is a recent innovation. Down to Edmund Kean's time, so far as is known, Othello was always quite black' (Bradley, 187–8). But Bradley hedged his argument in a lengthy footnote in which he essentially took up Charles Lamb's argument that certain Shakespearean plays are better experienced as read pieces than in performance. This may seem like a strange argument for twenty-first century readers who are used to experiencing Shakespeare as both texts studied in school and performance pieces seen onstage (although there is a strong pedagogical movement currently that Shakespeare should be studied as a performance piece because kinesthetic learning enables deeper and more sustained understanding[1]), but that has not always been the case. While in Shakespeare's time

1 For more about current trends in Shakespearean pedagogy see Thompson and Turchi.

his plays would have been experienced primarily as performance pieces, by the early nineteenth century Shakespeare was considered a great author whose plays needed to be studied and experienced through reading.

Bradley seems to straddle the fence between these worlds, but he lands down firmly on the reading side when it comes to *Othello* precisely because of his discomfort with seeing Othello's race. He writes:

> I will not discuss the further question whether, granted that to Shakespeare Othello was a black, he should be represented as a black in our theatres now. I dare say not. We do not like the real Shakespeare. We like to have his language pruned and his conceptions flattened into something that suits our mouths and minds. And even if we were prepared to make an effort, still, as Lamb observes, to imagine one thing and to see is another. Perhaps if we saw Othello coal-black with the bodily eye, the aversion of our blood, an aversion which comes as near to being merely physical as anything human can, would overpower our imagination and sink us below not Shakespeare only but the audiences of the seventeenth and eighteenth centuries.
>
> (Bradley, fn.1, 190–1)

Bradley's argument is amazingly forthcoming about the presumed differences between an early twentieth-century audience and a Shakespearean one. He is the first critic to implicitly acknowledge that the intervening years between 1604 (one of the earliest recorded stagings of *Othello*) and 1904 (when Bradley published his lectures) render the signification of a black man's body differently. While the history of the transatlantic slave trade does not enter into Bradley's argument explicitly, it lurks in the shadows haunting Bradley's footnote.

Bradley also disagrees with Coleridge's assessment that Iago lacks a clear motive for his actions, and he mounts one of the first sustained analyses of Iago as a metadramatic figure: that is, as a character who operates as if he understands the conventions of theatre. Bradley declares that Iago finds satisfaction in the knowledge that 'he is the master of the General who has undervalued him and of the rival who has been preferred to him; that these worthy people, who are so successful and popular and stupid, are mere puppets in his hands, but living puppets, who at the motion of his finger must contort themselves in agony' (Bradley, 213–14). Arguing that Iago's motives are not only intelligible but also essentially creative, Bradley aligns Iago with Shakespeare: 'But Iago, finally, is not simply a man of action; he is an artist. His action is a plot, the intricate plot of a drama, and in the conception and execution of it he experiences the tension and the joy of artistic creation. . . . Here at any rate Shakespeare put a good deal of himself into Iago' (Bradley, 215). While other scholars and artists had linked Shakespeare with Hamlet and Prospero, Bradley was the first to analyse Iago's desire to 'bring this monstrous birth to the world's light' (1.3.403) as an artistic impulse that would have been familiar to Shakespeare.

Bradley's view of *Othello*, however, was challenged. T.S. Eliot, whom G.K. Hunter claimed 'virtually invented the twentieth-century Shakespeare in a collection of asides' (Hunter, 299), implicitly responded to Bradley's claims that the titular character was the first of a new type of hero for Shakespeare. Bradley proclaimed, 'There is in most of the later heroes something colossal, something which reminds us of Michael Angelo's figures. They are not merely exceptional men, they are huge men; as it were, survivors of the heroic age living in a later and smaller world. . . . Othello is the first of these men' (Bradley, 168). Disagreeing, Eliot responds that 'there is, in some of the great tragedies of Shakespeare, a new attitude. . . . [I]t is modern, and it culminates, if there is ever any culmination, in the attitude of Nietzsche' (Eliot, 110). Eliot continued, 'It is the attitude of self-dramatization assumed by some of Shakespeare's heroes at the moments of tragic intensity'

(Eliot, 110). To prove this claim, Eliot focuses on Othello's death speech, arguing that it was not an expression of heroic greatness but rather a speech in which Othello seems to be '*cheering himself up*' (Eliot, 111). Eliot proclaims, 'nothing dies harder than the desire to think well of oneself', which he labels as '*bovarysme*, the human will to see things as they are not' (Eliot, 111). As Jason Harding has argued about Eliot's reading of *Othello*, 'what is modern about Eliot's Shakespeare is his capacity to see self-dramatisation and self-deception as everyday, rather than tragic, flaws' (Harding, 166).

In many ways, Eliot's argument that Othello suffers from everyday flaws instead of grand tragic ones sets the terms for critical debates in the mid- to late-twentieth century criticism: debates about whether Othello is a noble hero and whether the play should be considered one of Shakespeare's greatest tragedies. In a typical essay, F.R. Leavis argued stringently against Bradley's assessment of the play by aligning himself with Eliot's. Writing in stark terms, Leavis claimed, 'And yet it is of *Othello* that one can say bluntly, as of no other of the great tragedies, that it suffers in current appreciation an essential and denaturing falsification' (Leavis, 259). For Leavis only the 'denaturing falsification' of a rose-tinted reading sees Othello as a 'noble hero' (Leavis, 283) because he argues that Othello is 'egotistic', one who is prone to 'self-dramatization' (Leavis, 265). Interestingly, Leavis's view of Othello shows a high level of similarity with Iago's. While Leavis's line of argumentation was not often followed, a strange obsession around *Othello*'s place in the Shakespearean canon has persevered.

This critical trend came to an end, however, around the turn of the twenty-first century when scholars and artists began to ask different questions about race, gender and representation. Although it is difficult to pinpoint the exact start of this new scholarly trend, one could make the case that a collection of essays published in 1996 by 'black writers' responding to *Othello* helped initiate new approaches to the play. Edited by

Mythili Kaul and published by a historically black university in Washington DC, Howard University Press, *Othello: New Essays by Black Writers* made it clear that black readers, audience members, scholars and artists may be experiencing a different play from white ones. Debates about whether the play was among Shakespeare's greatest were immediately made irrelevant as these scholars and artists grappled with the ways the play not only illuminated the racial thinking of Shakespeare's time, but also affected contemporary constructions of race. As Kaul wrote in the preface, 'The one thing that all the contributors do share in common, however, is the recognition that the issues raised by the play are, indeed, of utmost relevance today in terms of politics, colonial exploitation, cultural relativism, and, above all, race. From the other side, the essays collectively also make clear the extent to which an engagement with *Othello* can enable black writers to discuss these pressing contemporary issues in ways that are both pointed and complex' (Kaul, xii). Suddenly, then, *Othello* became a text through which our contemporary world could and should be explored.

This was clearly the case when Ben Okri, the Nigerian poet and novelist, included an essay on *Othello* in his 1997 collection, *A Way of Being Free*. In five short 'meditations' on *Othello*, Okri traces the way the play symbolizes how blacks and whites share a long and contentious history. Okri argues that Othello must be viewed as 'the white man's myth of the black man' because 'It is possible that Othello actually is a blackened white man' (Okri, 76 and 78). Othello, then, should not be viewed as a fully formed character with a clear psychology because he really represents a white myth or a stereotype about black masculinity. Even with this knowledge, though, Okri writes, 'The black person's response to Othello is more secret, and much more anguished, than can be imagined. It makes you unbearably lonely to know that you can empathise with them [white people], but they will rarely empathise with you. It hurts to watch Othello' (Okri, 80). And Okri ends his meditations by suggesting that productions of *Othello* may add to racial tensions instead of relieving them: 'What matters is that because of Shakespeare's genius Othello haunts the English stage. He won't go away. He is always there on the stage, a reminder of his unexplained presence in the white consciousness, and a symbol of the fact that black people and white are bound on the terrible bed of history. Doomed to his relentless cycle, he will not vanish from our dreams. And yet I dream of ways of liberating him from that bondage' (Okri, 86). Like the writers included in *Othello: New Essays by Black Writers*, Okri reads *Othello* not only as representing the cultural historical moment in which it was created, but also as a text and performance piece that continues to inform and even potentially create modern cultural historical moments – for both good and ill.

Although writing from a scholarly perspective, Dympna Callaghan, in her essay ' "Othello was a white man": Properties of race on Shakespeare's stage', argues along similar lines that the *Othello* experienced on the contemporary stage is strained precisely because of the performance modes established in the early modern period. Through a historicist lens, Callaghan examines records from the early modern period that document the use of Africans in court entertainments and the impersonation of blackness on the stage by white actors. She argues that there were 'two distinct, though connected, systems of representation crucially at work in the culture's preoccupation with racial others and singularly constitutive of its articulation of racial difference: the display of black people themselves (exhibition) and the simulation of negritude (mimesis)' (Callaghan, *Shakespeare*, 77). Traditionally, she argues, in exhibition modes the audience is given all the power because the bodies displayed are represented as passive objects. And in mimetic modes actors are given the lion's share of power because of their control over the 'embodied performance' (Callaghan, *Shakespeare*, 77). And then Callaghan goes on to note that for African American and female actors 'mimesis and exhibition tend to overlap because the actor is always already construed as an exhibition in a representational context that severely curtails the actor's creative control' (Callaghan, *Shakespeare*, 78). This framework not only helps to position early modern performances of *Othello*, but also to situate the difficulties performances of *Othello* can pose in later historical moments.

While I elaborate on the history of the changes in performance practices for *Othello* in the next section (see p. 67ff), many theatre critics and scholars point to Paul Robeson's performances as Othello in the 1930s, 1940s and 1950s as watershed moments in the history of *Othello*. Many proclaimed that seeing an actual black man play the role of the Othello made it feel as if they were 'seeing the tragedy for the first time . . . because the fact that he was a true Negro seemed to floodlight the whole drama' (Wilson *Othello*, x). Writing the introduction to the Cambridge edition of *Othello* in 1957, John Dover Wilson revealed, 'Everything was slightly different from what I had previously imagined; new points, fresh nuances, were constantly emerging; and all had, I felt, been clearly intended by the author. The performance convinced me in short that a Negro Othello is essential to the full understanding of the play' (Wilson *Othello*, x).

By the 1980s, Othello had become a role that only black male actors performed: no more white actors in makeup. Writing against this tradition, however, the black British actor Hugh Quarshie wondered if Othello is actually a role to which black actors should aspire. Addressing the University of Alabama Hudson Strode Theatre in 1998, Quarshie pointedly asked:

> if a black actor plays Othello does he not risk making racial stereotypes seem legitimate and even true? When a black actor plays a role written for a white actor in black make-up and for a predominantly white audience, does he not encourage the white way, or rather the wrong way, of looking at black men, namely that black men, or 'Moors', are over-emotional, excitable and unstable. . . . Of all parts in the canon, perhaps Othello

> is the one which should most definitely not be played by a black actor.
>
> (Quarshie, 5)

Implicitly supporting Callaghan's claims that when black actors play parts written for white actors in blackface it 'curtails the actor's creative control', Quarshie attempts to imagine a production of *Othello* that would enable more creative, cultural and political control for the black actor. Yet in the end, he admits, 'But, you may say, that's another *Othello*, not Shakespeare's. That's rather the point, isn't it?' (Quarshie, 23).

Quarshie's frank comments about his reluctance to play Othello helped to open the door for more critical assessments of casting in general, and this area of scholarship brings us up to the most current trends in *Othello* criticism. Celia Daileader's essay 'Casting Black Actors: Beyond Othellophilia' (published in 2000) was one of the first to think through the way *Othello* actually casts a long shadow on the way black actors are cast in other classical roles. Analysing the way 'Othello's racialist rhetoric hinges upon the pairing of a black man and a white woman in such a way as to render the former a vehicle for misogynist figurations of a woman's sexual besmirching or "blackening", with all the voyeuristic (and potentially racist) titillation such a spectacle provides' (Daileader, 178), Daileader traces the way black actors in the 1980s and 1990s were cast in supposedly non-traditional or colour-blind productions but which replicated the racialist rhetoric of *Othello* nonetheless. Daileader dubs this phenomenon 'Othellophilia' and argues that the 'modern Anglo-American myth of the sexually potent black male and his morally dubious white female target can be traced to . . . *Othello*' (Daileader, 178). My own scholarship has likewise tracked the way casting practices are particularly fraught for modern productions of *Othello*, arguing that the continued cultural force of Bardolatry renders it difficult to create appropriative productions that enable an oppositional gaze for race in performance (Thompson, Ay, *Passing*, 96–117). In order to understand this line of argument, though, one first needs to know the fascinating performance history of Shakespeare's *Othello*.

Othello Onstage, Part 1: Stage Histories

From the title page of the first quarto published in 1622, we know that *Othello* was 'diuerse times acted at the Globe, and at the Black-Friers, by his Maiesties seruants'. We also know that *Othello* was played at Court by the King's Men on 1 November 1604, in Oxford in 1610 and again at Court in 1612–13 during the courtly celebrations for Princess Elizabeth's marriage to Prince Frederick of Heidelberg. These multiple performances in different locations and venues not only speak to the play's popularity, but also to its versatility. Performances at The Globe, for instance, could accommodate up to 3,000 audience members, and therefore the performances had to be larger in their performance modes (volume, gesture, scale, etc.). Blackfriars, the private indoor theatre that the King's Men began to lease in 1608, only seated up to 700 people with admission prices sufficiently higher to attract a wealthier audience base. Plays as performed in this indoor theatre, then, were more intimate in their size, scale and content. And while any play could be called upon to be reprised at court, the nature of the performance had to change to suit the new environment in a smaller space with a much smaller audience. Like several other Jacobean plays of the King's Men, *Othello* was performed in these diverse environments, which reveals the play's chameleon-like nature: it can be staged as a large military tragedy or as a small domestic one.

As already noted (see p. 28), Richard Burbage (1567–1619) is thought to have originated the role of Othello. The prime tragedian in the Lord Chamberlain's Men and then the King's Men, Burbage played the leading roles in *Richard III*, *Hamlet*, *Othello* and *King Lear*. We know next to nothing about his performances as Othello except that in his eulogy he is praised for playing the 'grievèd Moor' as his 'chiefest part' (*Var*, 396).

The performance history of *Othello* is slightly more detailed during the Restoration when the newly re-opened theatres allowed women onstage for the first time in English history. In fact, *Othello* is thought to be the first of Shakespeare's tragedies staged during the Restoration, but performance historians are not sure which actress played Desdemona first. Writing in 1800 about 1660, Edmund Malone noted, 'The first woman that appeared in any regular drama on a publick stage, performed the part of Desdemona; but who that lady was, I am unable to ascertain. . . . Mrs. [Margaret] Hugh[e]s performed the part of Desdemona when the company removed to Drury-Lane, and obtained the title of the Kings Servants' (Malone, 138). Malone continues by providing an epilogue which he claims was recited at the conclusion of the play in the Restoration:

> And how do you like her? Come, what is't ye drive at?
> She's the same thing in publick as in private;
> As far from being what you call a whore;
> As Desdemona, injur'd by the Moor:
> Then he that censures her is such a case,
> Hath a soul blacker than Othello's face.
>
> (qtd Malone, 140)

The epilogue's attention to the differences between honest women and whores employs themes from *Othello* to emphasize that women should be allowed public lives. It is interesting to think that a play about taboo relationships was revived precisely so that it could usher in a new era in performance modes.

The change in acting customs to allow women onstage did not obscure the praise for the great actors who played Othello. While it seems as though Nicholas Burt was the first Othello on the Restoration stage, when the King's Company merged with the Duke's Company in 1682 the famous Restoration actor Thomas Betterton (1635–1710) made Othello his own. Betterton's heroic acting style was reflected in the fact that 'his aspect was serious, venerable, and majestic . . . His Voice was low and grumbling, though he could time it by an artful Climax, which enforc'd universal attention, even from the *Fops* and *Orange-girls*' (qtd Rosenberg, 20). Likewise, Sir John Perceval, writing a humorous and hyperbolic letter to his cousin Elizabeth Southwell on 20 September 1709, comments: 'I declare that they [the audience members] who cannot be moved at Othello's story so artfully worked up by Shakespeare, and justly played by Betterton, are capable of marrying again before their husbands are cold, of trampling on a lover when dying at their feet, and are fit to converse with tigers only' (qtd Spencer, 26).

Nevertheless, as the Restoration moved into the eighteenth century a 'clamor in criticism for Decorum' (Rosenberg, 20) began to alter the *Othello* audience members experienced. While many acting scripts were edited to cleanse *Othello* of indecorous language, 'the deepest and cruelest cuts were made to reduce the atmosphere of sexuality into which Othello was betrayed' (Rosenberg, 35). Thus, many lines and scenes were edited or cut altogether (most famously 4.1 in which Bianca confronts Cassio, and Othello and Iago debate what exactly is signified by sexual language: 'Lie with her? lie on her?' 4.1.35). With these excisions, it is believed the eighteenth-century actors who played Othello emphasized the character's noble and heroic qualities. Marvin Rosenberg argues, 'the actor was supposed to bear the air of Decorum's hero' (Rosenberg, 36). Furthermore, Lois Potter notes that the eighteenth-century actors who played Othello also played two other 'famous black roles: . . . the title character in Thomas Southerne's *Oroonoko* (1695), based on a novella of 1688 by Aphra Behn, and Zanga, the villain of Edward Young's *The Revenge* (1721)' (Potter, 13). Because both of these plays explicitly addressed the enslavement of Africans (and *Oroonoko* was perceived to be and employed as an anti-slavery play), and because the movement of actors between the three plays made connections between them resonate, Othello's reluctance to speak at length about his being 'sold to slavery' (1.3.139) 'came to signify [the] depths of [his] stoic endurance' (Potter, 14).

12 *Othello, act II, scene I, a platform – Desdemona, Othello, Iago, Cassio, Roderigo, Emilia, &c. [graphic] / painted by Thos. Stothard; engraved by Thos. Ryder* (1799), Thomas Ryder printmaker (used by permission of the Folger Shakespeare Library under a Creative Commons Attribution-ShareAlike 4.0 International Licence)

The nineteenth century, however, saw another large set of changes to performances of *Othello*. First, the acting text for *Othello* was actually 'fixed' during this period. As Charles Shattuck notes:

> a production of *Othello* in those days might have been handsome or might have been shabby, but in the essentials of 'the book' – the text and basic stage business – it would not stray far from the forms established by the histrionic tradition and community. The book of *Othello* was quite rigidly fixed, precisely because it was played so often and because every

> aspiring tragedian had to be ready on call to perform either of its leading roles.
>
> (Shattuck, 3)

Virginia Vaughan has compared the surviving promptbooks from the time (including ones from provincial theatres in the UK and the US) and argues that the 'blockings and stagings were similar in most performances' (Vaughan, *Othello*, 148). She continues, 'One promptbook (Folger promptbook 26 . . .) was the property of the Edinburgh theatre and includes blocking for all the eminent Othellos who played there – Edmund Kean, Edwin Forrest, [Charles] Macready, J.W. Wallack, and Edwin Booth' (Vaughan, *Othello*, 148). In other words, the *Othello* that audience members saw onstage during the nineteenth century was a stable textual and visual entity on both sides of the Atlantic, permitting easy transfer of the actors who played both Othello and Iago to move between the various venues that sprang up in the heyday of popular theatre.

As already noted (see p. 31ff), Edmund Kean (1789–1833), one of the great actors of the nineteenth century, helped to usher in the great 'Bronze Age of *Othello*' in which white actors performed in light, bronze or tawny makeup as opposed to in dark or blackfaced makeup. While Kean's colour alteration impacted performances for the rest of the nineteenth and early twentieth centuries, his interpretation of Othello as an intensely emotional character also cast a long shadow on future performances. Small in stature, Kean decided that his Othello had to be explosive in his passions: a character who controlled the attention of senators with his calm demeanour but who also could ignite into fury easily. Writing in the *London Magazine* in 1820, William Hazlitt was overwhelmed by 'the fitful fever in the blood, the jealous madness of the brain: his heart seemed to bleed with anguish, while his tongue dropped broken, imperfect accents of woe' (Hazlitt, 444). There are many accounts of audience members being swept away by the emotion of Kean's performance: 'his imitation of the hysterical sob under powerful agitation caused fine ladies to faint, and [Lord] Byron to weep, from nervous sympathy' (Young, 57). The politician Lord Granville Leveson Gower wrote of Kean's Othello, 'Should tragedy be quite so natural? . . . I was frightened, alarmed; I cannot account for what I felt. I wished to be away, and saw those eyes all night, and hear "D – n her! D – n her!" still – it was too horrible' (Granville, 457).

When Kean was tried for adultery in 1825, his acting career was almost over: audience members frequently booed him and pelted him with rotten vegetables. Yet when he returned as Othello opposite Charles Macready as Iago, audience members were surprised by the power of his performance despite his 'drunken hoarseness' (Lewes, 5). George Lewes wrote, 'I remember the last time I saw him play Othello, how puny he appeared beside Macready, until the third act, when roused by Iago's taunts and insinuations, he moved towards him with a gouty hobble, seized him by the throat, and, in a well-known explosion, "Villain! be sure you prove", &c., seemed to swell into a stature that made Macready appear small. . . . old men leaned their heads upon their arms and fairly sobbed' (Lewes, 4–5). Kean cemented his reputation as giving it all onstage when he collapsed playing Othello opposite his son Charles Kean as Iago in 1833. His biographer writes, 'He was able to groan out a few words, in Charles' ear – "I'm dying – speak to them for me"; after which . . . he was borne from the stage' (Cornwall, 241). Kean died a few days later.

Despite the fact that the nineteenth century was the era of the superstar theatre actor and there are many well-noted Othellos from the period, Othello acting modes fell into two distinct camps over which actors, critics and audience members fought. There was an acting style that emphasized the 'thunder and lightning of sorely grieved Moors' as represented by the Italian actor Tommaso Salvini, and the acting style that emphasized the 'cooler troubled' Moor in a 'refined guise' as represented by Edwin Booth (Rosenberg, 80). Salvini (1829–1915) was born in Milan to acting parents. While Salvini played in many non-Shakespearean plays, he became famous for his presentation of Othello, which he performed for the first time in 1856 in Venice. Shortly thereafter, he began making frequent trips to the UK and the US to perform in *Othello*. Despite the fact that he only ever performed in Italian (the rest of the cast would speak in English in the UK and the US), audience members and critics frequently debated the 'southern voluptuousness' of his performance (*Ath*, 498). In fact, a review in April 1875 in the *Athenaeum Magazine* notes, 'Othello has not been a favourite character with English exponents, happier always in presenting the sombre rage of Northern blood than the fierce and burning passion of the South' (*Ath*, 498). Salvini's performance was interpreted as being 'terribly natural' in that his Moor has only a 'veneer of civilization' which Iago effectively peels off thereby exposing the 'barbarian' within (*Ath*, 498).

Part of this interpretation stemmed from the fact that Salvini's performance was remarkably physical. Fanny Kemble noted that English actresses would not willingly participate in 'the full fury of his assault' on Desdemona (Kemble, 'Salvini', 376). The physicality apparently started in the temptation scene when Salvini rushed upon his Iago:

> Seizing fiercely Iago by the throat, he crushes the cowering miscreant to the ground, and in the whirlwind of his passion lifts his foot to stamp the heel upon his head, it might even be to kick out his brains. Recalled however to reason, he turns away, and with averted head he stretches out his hand, and penitently, yet with a species of loathing, raises the prostrate wretch from the ground. In this scene, the one profoundly electrical effect of the interpretation is reached.
>
> (*Ath*, 498)

But Salvini's Othello was primarily remembered for the way he stalked and then thrashed Desdemona to death in the final scene of the play. Reminiscing about seeing Salvini, John Ranken Towes, the long-time theatre critic for the *New York Evening Post*, wrote in 1910:

> Salvini, convulsed, with fixed and flaming eyes, half-crouched, slowly circled the stage toward her, muttering savagely and inarticulately as she cowered before him. Rising at last to his full height with extended arms, he pounced upon her, lifted her into the air, dashed with her across the stage and through the curtains [of her bed, which was upstage], which fell behind him. You heard a crash as he flung her on the bed, and growls as of a wild beast over his prey. It was awful . . . such a picture of a man, bereft by maniacal jealousy of mercy and reason, reduced to primeval savagery.
>
> (Towes, 163)

Salvini's decision to portray Othello as reverting to a 'primeval savagery' was, of course, precisely what made his performances so controversial.

Yet the actors, audience members and critics who praised Salvini's style did so on the grounds that it was a presentation of the natural African. The novelist Henry James wrote about Salvini's Othello, 'It is the rage of an African, but of a nature that remains generous to the end; and in spite of the tiger-paces and tiger-springs, there is through it all, to my sense at least, the tremor of a moral element' (James, 175). Salvini fed into the racist views that his violent performance was a reflection of natural African character traits by claiming that he studied the mannerisms and emotive expressions of Moors when he travelled to Gibraltar. Interestingly, the Russian actor and director Konstantin Stanislavsky, the founder of the Stanislavsky System of acting which stressed realism, was influenced by seeing an early performance of Othello by Salvini.

Edwin Booth (1833–1893), whose acting style represents the opposite side of the interpretive debates in the nineteenth century, actually played Iago to Salvini's Othello in a few productions. Like Salvini, Booth was born into a theatrical family. The English actor Junius Brutus Booth had three illegitimate sons in the United States who would go on to have acting careers: Junius Brutus Booth, Jr. (who never achieved great success as an actor), Edwin Booth (who became a celebrated Shakespearean actor) and John Wilkes Booth (whose acting successes were eventually overshadowed by his assassination of President Abraham Lincoln in 1865). Slight of figure, Edwin Booth was best-known for his portrayal of Hamlet, but his Othello became famous for the way it represented Victorian restraint. An 1881 appraisal in the *Saturday Review of Politics* noted that Booth 'takes a poetical view of Othello, the view which has always seemed to us the true one. Unless the romantic nobleness of the character is insisted upon, it surely becomes difficult to find any acceptable explanation either of Desdemona's love for the Moor or the complete confidence placed in him by the Seigneury' (*SRP*, 177).

Reflecting back, Booth recounted his performance choices to the late nineteenth-century literary scholar Horace Howard Furness, emphasizing what Marvin Rosenberg named 'a Byronic Moor, quick to sadness, melancholy, [and] foreboding' (Rosenberg, 82). For instance, Booth is quoted as saying, 'The keynote of [Othello's] nature, a modest, simple-hearted *gentleman*, not a braggart as Iago would make him out' (*Var*, 32). And even at the height of the temptation scene, Booth attempted to emphasize Othello's humanity: 'Although the savage blood is up, let a wave of humanity sweep over his heart at these words. Breathe out " 'Tis gone" with a sigh of agony which seems to exhale love to heaven' (*Var*, 209). The restraint that Booth demonstrated as his Othello apparently helped his most famous Desdemona, Ellen Terry (1847–1928). In her autobiography she writes, 'Booth's Othello was very helpful to my Desdemona. It is difficult to preserve the simple, heroic blindness of Desdemona to the fact

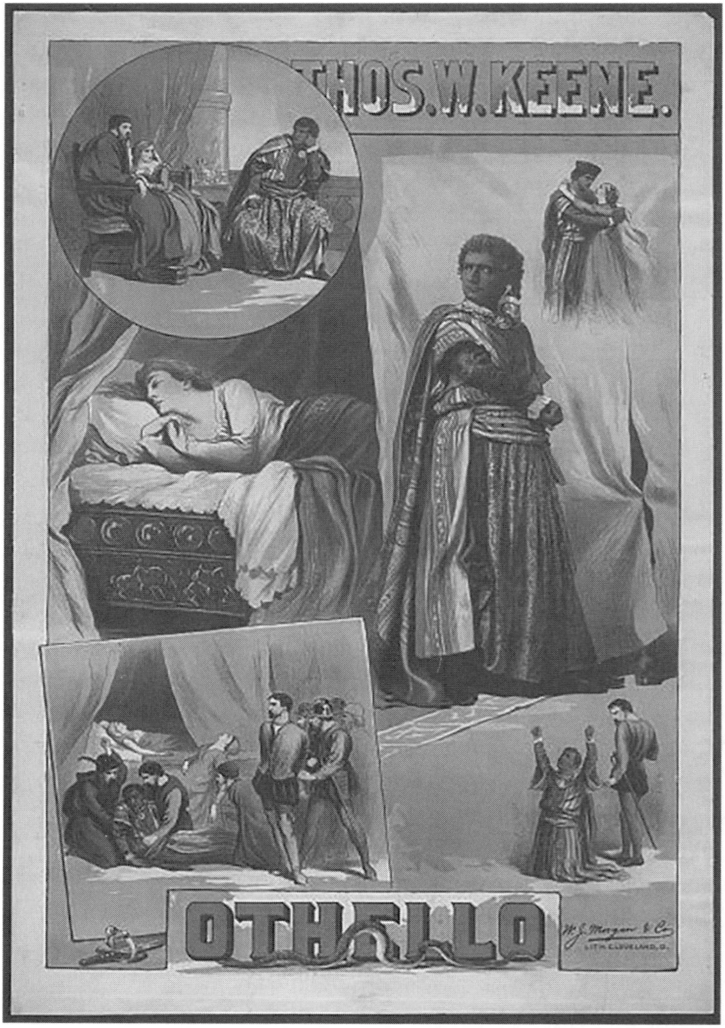

13 Poster for 1884 production of *Othello*, starring Thomas W. Keene as Othello (1884) (W. J. Morgan & Co. Lith., courtesy of the Library of Congress)

that her lord mistrusts her, if her lord is raving and stamping under her nose. Booth was gentle with Desdemona' (Terry, *Story*, 223). Booth's emphasis on Othello's gentleness and humanity, though, necessitated significant cuts to the text, including all references to 'sheets', 'bed' and 'body'; substituting words for 'whore', 'bawdy' and 'strumpet'; and 'obscuring the details of sexual relationships' (Rosenberg, 87).

Another *Othello* innovation came when Booth was in a six-week run at the Lyceum Theatre in London in which he and the British actor Henry Irving (1838–1905) exchanged the roles Othello and Iago weekly. Ellen Terry praised Booth's restraint as Othello but criticized his 'deadly commonplace' Iago; and praised Irving's Iago ('Could one ever forget those grapes which he plucked in the first act, and slowly ate, spitting out the seeds, as if each one represented a worthy virtue to be put out of his mouth . . .?'), but criticized his Othello because he 'screamed and ranted and raved . . . [and] lost his voice' (Terry, *Story*, 224, 224, 225). While the critics tended to agree with Terry's assessment of her leading men, the experiment proved a fruitful one in terms of thinking through which character should dominate the action. Iago has more lines than Othello, but the play remains in the end Othello's. By alternating the roles, these actors were able to show the versatility required to master both parts. While this was possible when both actors were white, the opportunity to perform this type of theatrical experiment has been inadvertently thwarted by the contemporary practice of casting actors of colour almost exclusively as Othello. And yet there is the opportunity to appropriate and revise this experiment if Iago and Othello are both performed by actors of colour. While the swapping of roles by actors of colour has not been done on any professional stage yet, I am hopeful it will occur soon. Such an experiment could help spur new conversations about *Othello* as a text, performance piece, cultural artefact and cultural producer of constructions of race.

Another seismic innovation for *Othello* performances occurred in the nineteenth century, but was not recognized as such until the late twentieth century: the first actors of colour began to play Othello. James Hewlett was probably the first black actor to play Othello, and the first productions were held in New York City at the African Grove Theatre in 1822 (n.b.: this was five years before the complete abolition of slavery in New York State) (White, 113–14). Furthermore, the African Company actually toured the eastern seaboard starting in 1823, with write-ups in several regional papers including one in the *Providence Gazette* noting that the company was refused a licence despite the fact that Hewlett 'was a very good Othello without paint' (*PG*, 3).

While we do not know that much about Hewlett's life except for the fact that he was a ship's steward, a profession that afforded him the opportunity to travel to several foreign countries, we know a lot about his protégé Ira Aldridge (1807–1867). Aldridge attended the African Free School where he received a classical education, and as a young teen, he worked in African Grove Theatre. By 1824 (at the age of seventeen) Aldridge travelled to England in the hopes of performing Shakespeare in non-segregated theatres. By May 1825, he performed *Othello* at the Royalty Theatre in London's East End. Travelling throughout England, Scotland, Ireland and much of Eastern Europe for forty years, Aldridge hoped to return to the United States after the emancipation of slaves and the conclusion of the Civil War but he died while on tour in Lodz, Poland in 1867 at the age of sixty. Aldridge reached a level of fame and financial security that was virtually unknown to free blacks at the time, but he could not achieve this fame in New York or London; instead, he was a star in Warsaw, Kiev and Moscow. While he was celebrated by European artists like Richard Wagner, Théophile Gautier and Taras Shevchenko, he was also reviled and mocked by theatre critics in New York and London.[1]

1 For more about Aldridge's reception in Eastern Europe see Hill, 17–27; and Courtney, 103–22.

Aldridge's performances of Othello implicitly challenged Edmund Kean's establishment of Othello as a tawny Moor (see, p. 31ff). Aldridge was not a light-skinned black man, and he could not perform Othello as a tawny Moor. In fact, he frequently fabricated an African heritage and adopted the monikers the 'African Tragedian', 'African Prince' and 'African Roscius' to explain his blackness and sell his performances (Courtney, 106–7). Despite the fact that Aldridge's style went against the grain, many European critics marvelled that he became a 'true Othello'. As Krystyna Courtney discovered in the archives in Eastern Europe, 'An 1854 review in *Czas* [Kracow, Poland] (9 November 1854) stated that "it is the first time we have seen a true Othello", while the reviewer in *Pamietnik muzyczny i teatralny* [Warsaw, Poland] assured his readers that "Othello is a perfect fit for Mr. Aldridge" because "he himself is a Negro" ' (Courtney, 112).

Yet this nineteenth-century history was largely forgotten by the time that Paul Robeson (1898–1976) played *Othello* in 1930 in London, 1943 in New York and 1959 in Stratford-upon-Avon. In fact, Robeson was often heralded as the first black Othello, and many reputable scholars discuss the performance history of *Othello* as falling into two time periods: pre- and post-Paul Robeson. While this may be a slight overstatement, Robeson's impact was huge, especially in the US where the theatres were still segregated in the 1940s. Robeson, who was extremely large in stature (6′3″) and who had a famously rich, deep voice, loomed large onstage opposite his Desdemonas who were played by Peggy Ashcroft, Uta Hagen and Mary Ure respectively. While it was assumed that English audience members would object less than American ones to the sight of a black male actor playing opposite a white female actor, Robeson nonetheless was extremely nervous and reflected later that, 'For the first two weeks in every scene I played with Desdemona that girl couldn't get near to me, I was backin' away from her all the time. I was like a plantation hand in the parlor, that clumsy. But the notices were good. I got over it' (qtd van Gelder).

Robeson's unease was not simply an expression of the humility topos or actorly nerves; rather, he was keenly aware of the tightrope he had to walk as the first black Othello in the twentieth century. He had to make his Othello less threatening sexually and emphasize his naïveté in matters of the heart. This was complicated by the fact that Robeson actually had affairs with two of his Desdemonas: Peggy Ashcroft and Uta Hagen. In many ways, though, *Othello* helped awaken Robeson politically. Although he was playing at the Savoy Theatre, he was not allowed to stay in the adjoining Savoy Hotel because the hotel would not permit black guests. Robeson became much more involved in social and political movements, famously becoming a member of the Communist Party. By the time Robeson was headlining on Broadway in 1943, he was much more confident in both his acting abilities and his political views. He used the popularity of his run in *Othello* on Broadway and then on tour to raise social and political issues in the popular media, including promoting the desegregation of major league baseball and opposing the exploitation of Africa by colonial powers. The reviews were glowing, and the critics wrote openly about the change they were experiencing seeing a black man play Othello. For instance, writing in *Variety* in 1943, Rudolph Elie, Jr. enthused, 'Robeson playing opposite a white girl' was 'electric' and that 'no white man should dare presume to play [Othello] again' (Elie).

Despite the sense that Robeson's performances in *Othello* were viewed as a sea change in acceptable performance modes, white actors continued to dominate the role until the 1980s. Most famously, Laurence Olivier (1907–1989) played the role from 1964 to 1965 at the National Theatre production directed by John Dexter. Olivier indicated that he styled his performance on recent West Indian immigrants to the UK so he made himself up in heavy black makeup which covered his entire body, adopted a different gait and even lowered the timbre of his

14 Paul Robeson in the Savoy Theatre London stage production *Othello* (courtesy of Billy Rose Theatre Division, The New York Public Library for the Performing Arts, Astor, Lenox and Tilden Foundations)

voice significantly. In his book *On Acting*, Olivier describes how he developed the walk, voice and mannerisms first. But he ends by describing the colour: 'Black all over my body, Max Factor 2880, then a lighter brown, then Negro Number 2, a stronger brown. Brown on black to give a rich mahogany. Then the great trick: that glorious half yard of chiffon with which I polished myself all over until I shone. . . . The lips blueberry, the tight curled wig, the white of the eyes, whiter than ever, and the black, black sheen that covered my flesh and bones, glistening in the dressing-room lights' (Olivier, 109). In other words, Olivier's Othello was no tawny Moor, and was, in fact, a full-on racial impersonation.

Occurring precisely at the birth of the Black Arts Movement in the United States, the artistic incarnation of the Civil Rights Movement and the Black Power Movement, the National's production looked immediately dated. Despite the fact that the production was lucrative enough to occasion a film version for which all the principals received Academy Award nominations (directed by Stuart Burge and released in 1965), the reviews of the production were mixed precisely because of Olivier's blackface performance.

In the UK the reviews were primarily positive. For instance, Philip Hope-Wallace writing in *The Guardian* praised 'the inventiveness of it above all, the sheer variety and range of the actor's art which made it an experience in the theatre altogether unforgettable by anyone who saw it' (qtd Tynan, 101). But in the US there was a sense that Olivier's performance mode crossed several uncomfortable lines. Writing in the *New York Times* in February 1966, Bosley Crowther was incredulous: 'He plays Othello in blackface! That's right, blackface – not the dark-brown stain that even the most daring white actors do not nowadays wish to go beyond. . . . The consequence is that he hits one – the sensitive American, anyhow – with the by-now outrageous impression of a theatrical Negro stereotype. He does not look like a Negro (if that's what he's aiming to make the Moor) – not even a West Indian chieftain, which some of the London critics likened him to. He looks like a Rastus or an end man in an American minstrel show. You almost wait for him to whip a banjo out from his flowing, white garments or start banging a tambourine' (Crowther). Another American critic noted, 'I was certainly in tune with the gentleman sitting next to me who kept asking, "When does he sing *Mammy*?" ' (qtd in Higgins). For American critics, then, Olivier's performance mode was too close to the blackface minstrel show tradition in which white actors impersonated black characters through performance stereotypes (for more on this topic, see p. 102ff).

Despite the critical outrage, white actors continued to play Othello until about the 1980s. Soon, however, a consensus formed that the part should be played by actors of colour, and performance modes began to shift once again. One major trend in the early twenty-first century is the emphasis on the military themes in the play. Thus, Nicholas Hytner's 2013 production at the National Theatre starring Adrian Lester employed the retired army veteran Jonathan Shaw to advise the actors on military ranks, comportment and off-duty behaviours, as well as the effects of post-traumatic stress disorder on veterans. As Lester communicated, these issues were much more in the forefront of his character preparation than Othello's race (Lester). In many ways, at the dawn of the twenty-first century the UK and the US are preoccupied with the effects of war on our collective social consciousness and on our personal psychology. After all, the seemingly never-ending wars waged against Iraq and Afghanistan make the effects of militarism on societies and individuals immediately pressing topics. Yet it is interesting to note that at precisely the historical moment when black actors dominate the role of Othello many productions choose to de-emphasize themes of racial difference in order to emphasize themes involving the personal strains on *all* military personnel. In fact, this is precisely the justification the

Norwegian director Stein Winge employed when he cast the white American actor Bill Pullman (1953–) to star in *Othello* in Norway in 2015. As Rob Weinert-Kendt notes, 'Winge wondered: What if Othello were the story of an American Navy man adrift in Norway? And what if his confusion and isolation grew not from racial alienation but from that disconnect? At the very least, they agreed, the concept . . . could give Pullman a chance to dig into a role few white, English-speaking actors would even dare to approach' (Weinert-Kendt). In the end, it might be that black actors' desires to de-emphasize the significance of Othello's race may re-open the door for white actors to play the part – with all the complications of that performance mode still unresolved.

Othello Onstage, Part 2: Black Actors, White Actresses

Of course, actors of all colours have had various reactions to playing Othello. Even Laurence Olivier wrote, 'I felt that Othello was a loser from the word go', because 'It's Iago's piece' (Olivier, 101, 104). Olivier's response is a fairly representative one: actors are always attempting to figure out how to manage the 'many climaxes' and to avoid the temptation to 'bellow away like a dying moose' (Olivier, 104). These are some of the issues that all actors, regardless of race, have to face when playing Othello. Yet it must be acknowledged that black actors have other, more complicated responses to the role and the play precisely because their performance modes are not considered as impersonations but rather as embodiments. Responses to the role by black actors, then, tend to fall into three types: (1) the role is viewed positively as a vehicle for racial uplift; (2) the role is viewed negatively as a tool for racial oppression; and (3) the role is viewed as a neutral one because it is race neutral.

Although one can find examples of all three responses in different time periods, for the most part they are split into the pre-Civil Rights era, the post-Civil Rights era and the millennial moment. For instance, James Hewlett, the first black actor to play Othello professionally albeit without a white Desdemona, employed quotes from *Othello* to combat Charles Mathews's lampooning of the actors in the African Grove theatre:

> Why these reflections on our color, my dear Matthews [sic], so unworthy your genius and humanity, your justice and generosity? Our immortal bard says, (and he is *our* bard as well as yours, for we are all descendants of the Plantagenets, the white and red rose;) our bard Shakespeare makes sweet Desdemona say,
>
> 'I saw Othello's *visage* in his mind'.
>
> Now when you were ridiculing the 'chief black tragedian', and burlesquing the 'real negro melody', was it my 'mind', or my 'visage', which should have made an impression on you? Again, my dear Matthews [sic], our favorite bard makes Othello, certainly an interesting character, speak thus:
>
> '*Haply*, for I am black'.
>
> That is as much to say 'tis happy that I am black. Here then we see a General proud of his complexion.
>
> (Hewlett)

For Hewlett, lines from *Othello* are self-consciously employed to bolster his arguments against racism. Despite the fact that he mistakes the meaning of 'haply' [perhaps], Hewlett attempts to demonstrate his mastery of *Othello* and to make a claim for his own Shakespearean descent ('he is *our* bard'). Likewise, Othello's character and words, and Desdemona's thoughts about him, are interpreted in the most positive light: to be Othello is to be a powerful, proud and strong black man.

This view was held by Ira Aldridge as well, who went a step further than Hewlett by attempting to re-fashion his identity to resemble more directly Othello's. Despite the fact that Aldridge was born in New York City, he frequently claimed that 'his forefathers were princes of the Fulah tribe, whose dominions were Senegal, on the banks of the river of that name, on the west coast of Africa' (*Memoir*, 8). A typical insert in a playbill, this one from the Surrey Theatre in 1833, claimed:

> Mr. Aldridge, a native of Senegal, and known by the appellation 'The African Roscius!' is engaged at this theatre for two nights; and will have the honour of making his first appearance on Monday next, April 22 in Shakespeare's play of 'Othello'. N.B. – The circumstance of a man of colour performing Othello, on the British Stage, is, indeed, an epoch in the history of theatricals; and . . . is as highly creditable to the native talent of the sunny climes of Africa, as to the universal liberality of a British Public.
>
> (qtd *Memoir*, 18)

To put it plainly, Aldridge assumed that a fake African heritage which clearly connected him personally to his performance of *Othello* would be an effective marketing strategy to sell seats in the theatre. It should not be surprising, then, that many audience members and critics reacted to the performance as natural: 'From his first step on the stage the African artist captivated the entire audience by his harmonious and sonorous voice, by his simple, natural, and dignified declamation' (qtd Hill, 25). By all accounts there was never any reluctance on Aldridge's part to play Othello; on the contrary, he appears to have intentionally appropriated *Othello*. The custom was for white actors to perform scenes featuring comedic and stereotypical black characters alongside scenes from *Othello*. Aldridge orchestrated performing the *Othello* scenes first in the evening, thereby implicitly challenging the more stereotypical portrayals of black characters in the scenes that followed. Bernth Lindfors argues, 'Only now, having already witnessed his polished performance in a serious role [Othello], they [the audience] knew that he was playing the *fool* – in short, that he was acting a part, not manifesting his own innate racial peculiarities' (Lindfors, 7). Thus, for Aldridge Othello was always a heroic and noble character.

While Paul Robeson never had to play scenes from *Othello* alongside scenes from minstrel shows, he too consistently interpreted the role and the play as symbols of racial uplift. Robeson was anxious to prove he could perform Shakespeare effectively, and he capitalized on the success of his performances to help promote civil rights. James Earl Jones (1943–), who played Othello seven times professionally between 1956 and 1982, most notably in Central Park in 1964 (the same year Olivier blacked up in London), was the heir apparent to Robeson's efforts. And like Robeson, Jones viewed Othello as noble with 'no sense of inferiority' (Jones and Niven, 165). In fact, Jones's father introduced him to *Othello* and told him, 'you have to come to him strong and clean' and that Othello 'has greater dignity than any other of Shakespeare's men' (Jones and Niven, 145). Despite the fact that the producer of the 1964 Central Park show, Joseph Papp, urged Jones to use his performance to express 'black rage' because it was the onset of the Civil Rights Movement in the United States, Jones could not interpret the role in that vein (Jones and Niven, 158). Papp's urgings, however, signalled a change that was coming to interpretations of *Othello* because even the celebrated film star, Sidney Poitier, told Jones that he refused to play the part: 'I cannot go on stage and give audiences a black man who is a dupe' (qtd Jones and Niven, 298).

Sentiments like the one expressed by Poitier were frequently expressed by black actors to each other quietly, but it was not until the British actor Hugh Quarshie (1954–) gave a talk at the University of Alabama in 1998 that a black actor publicly articulated the sense that *Othello* was a racist play. Quarshie summarized his argument thus:

> My contention is, firstly, that, in adapting and elaborating Cinthio's story about a jealous, uxoricidal Moor,

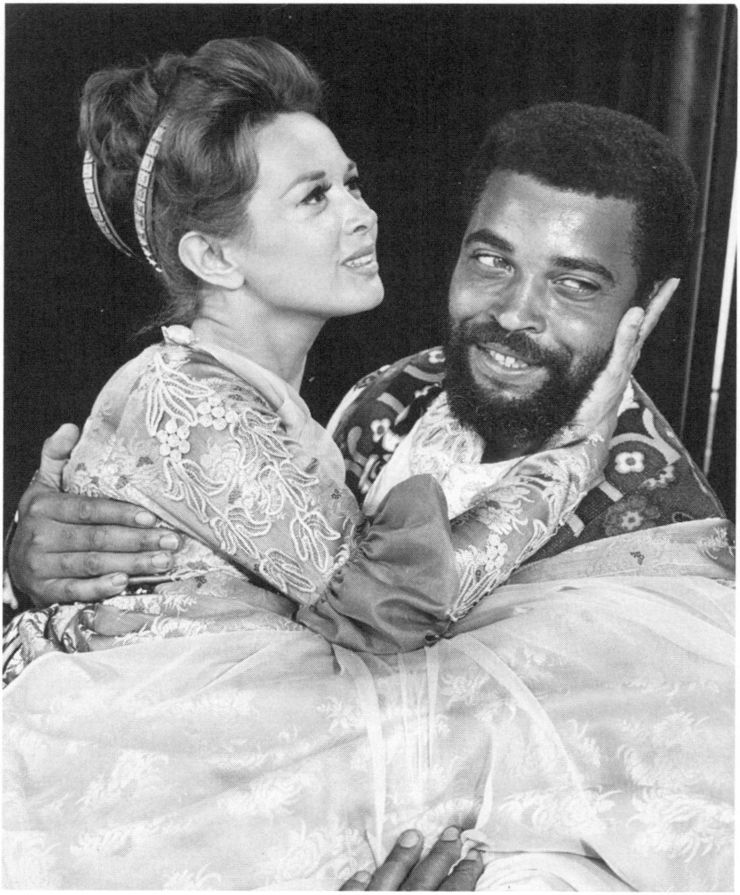

15 Julienne Marie as Desdemona and James Earl Jones as Othello in Gladys Vaughan's 1964 production at the Delacorte Theater, New York (photograph by Friedman-Abeles © The New York Library for the Performing Arts)

Shakespeare was endorsing a racist convention; secondly, that performance conventions and conventional interpretations have further reinforced racist views; and, thirdly, that, while it may never be possible to avoid the

> conclusion that Othello behaves as he does because he is black, a non-racist interpretation may nevertheless be possible, but only with careful editing of text and a radical re-reading of key passages.
>
> (Quarshie, 3)

A celebrated classically trained actor, who was educated at Christ Church, Oxford, and who was a member of the Royal Shakespeare Company, Quarshie noted that he had 'seen more productions of this one play [*Othello*] than any other' (Quarshie, 4). While this included many productions featuring white actors as Othello, Quarshie's 'interest in watching white men imitate black men waned' and he became more interested in seeing productions featuring black actors in the title role. Nonetheless, Quarshie writes, 'I am left with a nagging doubt: if a black actor plays Othello does he not risk making racial stereotypes seem legitimate and even true?' (Quarshie, 5). Othello, then, is no longer interpreted as a noble and heroic character and is instead seen as a stereotypical one: one that was created by a white author, to be played by a white actor in blackface, for a white audience. This is a far cry from the public views espoused by actors like Robeson and Jones, and Quarshie's challenge enabled other black actors to open up about their refusals to play the part.

For instance, Harry J. Lennix (1964–), most well-known for his portrayal of Aaron, the Moor in Julie Taymor's 1999 film *Titus*, played *Othello* at the Cort Theatre in Chicago in 1992, a few years after he graduated from Northwestern. While he received good reviews, and while he has gone on to have an impressive Shakespearean résumé both on stage and on film, he states flatly, 'I guess many people continue to do it [*Othello*]. I never want to do it again' (Thompson, Ay, 'Two', 51). In a published conversation with Laurence Fishburne (1961–), who played Othello in Oliver Parker's 1995 film, Lennix declares, 'it's impossible to play Othello properly if you're a black man. . . . If you're a *black man* . . . If you're a man and have any pride. It's an extraordinarily problematical character to play' (Thompson, Ay, 'Two', 46). Again, this sentiment is the polar opposite of the view that Othello is an uplifting character to perform; for Lennix and Fishburne, the assumption is that Shakespeare was 'racist' because 'the world was racist at that time' (Thompson, Ay, 'Two', 49). While Fishburne states that he is more than willing to play Othello again, he agrees that 'it is extremely challenging [to play Othello] and it's challenging to that aspect of having pride in one's own race and one's people. Very, very difficult' (Thompson, Ay, 'Two', 46).

More recently, black actors have expressed a belief that *Othello* is not actually about race, thereby avoiding the debates about whether the part is uplifting or oppressive. As already noted (see p. 83), the 2013 production at the National Theatre in London focused much more heavily on the military aspects of Othello's character. Adrian Lester (1968–), who starred in that production, was very aware of the debates and was dismayed 'how often critics talk about colour and then not character' (Lester). So he 'wanted to strip that away' so that the audience could see the character before the colour (Lester). This was partially achieved by having several other actors of colour in the production so that Lester was not the only black actor on the stage. This is a trend that has become very popular in millennial productions of *Othello* with many actors of colour filling in other roles, most notably Iago, Emilia and Cassio.[1]

It is not just actors of colour who have struggled with *Othello*, though; many actresses have struggled with how to play Desdemona. While scholarly debates about Desdemona's character have ranged from misogynistic to recuperative and everything in between, the Desdemonas that have graced the stage have fallen primarily into two camps: performances that stress Desdemona's passivity and performances that stress her

1 For more about these casting trends see Pao.

strength. Edward Pechter argues that Desdemona provides a type of litmus test for *Othello*: 'Desdemona provides the major confirmation – or, more precisely, disconfirmation of the beliefs originally impressed on us by the play' (Pechter, 42). Yet as Carol Carlisle argues, 'We must go all the way to the twentieth century to reach the only actor-criticisms that present Desdemona as a seriously flawed character' (Carlisle, 242). Like performance modes for Othello, the split in Desdemona performance trends divides historically between pre- and post-late nineteenth-century productions.

While we know that the first actors to play Desdemona were boys in Shakespeare's era, we do not know which actor precisely. We also do not know who the first female Desdemona was on the Restoration stage, although there are conjectures (see p. 68). We only begin to have reliable historical information about the women who played Desdemona and the acting styles they employed beginning in the eighteenth century, when the trend appears to have been to edit the text radically so as to eliminate many of Desdemona's scenes, including most notably the Willow Scene (4.3). This was the era in which the propriety of the play was questioned, and Desdemona's function in making the play acceptable meant that performances could not contain any scenes in which she discusses sexual desires (or bedsheets for that matter!). Francis Gentleman, writing in his *Dramatic Censor, or Critical Companion* in 1770, summarizes the eighteenth-century view of the necessity of editing that scene: 'if Desdemona was to chaunt the lamentable ditty, and speak all that Shakespeare has allotted for her in this scene, an audience, as Foigard says, would not know whether to laugh or cry, and Aemilia's quibbling dissertation on cuckold-making, is contemptible to the last degree' (Gentleman, 146). By the mid-nineteenth century, then, it became typical to have actresses emphasize Desdemona's meekness. Charlotte Vandenhoff's (1790–1861) performances were praised thus: 'It is an unalloyed delight, mingled with sorrowful sympathy, when the woman is forgotten in the actress, to follow her gentle madness, as Ophelia . . .; or to see her sad, fearful, yet gentle as a bruised dove, bend meekly to the implacable jealousy of the swart Othello, and receive her death, while kissing the hand which gives it' (E.F.R., 168). For two decades it appears as if actresses were made to play Desdemona as not only meek, but also willing to die at her husband's hands.[1]

As Carol Carlisle argues, though, Desdemona's supposed meekness made the role less and less appealing by the late nineteenth century when the actor 'star system was in its heyday' (Carlisle, 245). Carlisle writes, 'There were numerous occasions when the Desdemona of the evening was an actress who normally rose no higher in the Shakespearean scale than Celia, Hero, Virgilia, or Lady Macduff' (Carlisle, 240). And she goes on to note, 'No ambitious actress would attempt to build her reputation on the drooping, wavering creature the critics described – especially when she is flanked in the same play by the passionate Othello and the devilishly fascinating Iago' (Carlisle, 245). Helen Faucit (1817–1898) and Fanny Kemble (1809–1893) were two of the first stars to accept the role and to begin to transform it. For example, Faucit writes that she always loved Desdemona's character and was surprised to learn that 'Desdemona is usually considered a merely amiable, simple, yielding creature, and that she is generally so represented on the stage' (Faucit, 48). Faucit always felt that:

> [Desdemona] was in all things worthy to be a hero's bride, and deserving the highest love, reverence, and gratitude from the noble Moor. . . . I cannot think [Wordsworth] would have singled her out in his famous sonnet, had he not thought her as brave as she was generous, as high of heart as she was sweet of nature, or had he regarded her as a soft, insipid, plastic creature,

1 For a similar argument about performances of Lavinia's death in *Titus Andronicus* see Aebischer, 56–63.

> ready to do anyone's bidding, and submit placidly to any ill-usage from mere weakness and general characterless docility. Oh, no!
>
> (Faucit, 48)

Remarkably, Faucit goes on to boast, 'It was well for me that I never saw Desdemona, or indeed any of Shakespeare's heroines, on the stage, before I had to impersonate them myself. I was thus hampered by no traditions' (Faucit, 49).

Likewise, Fanny Kemble changed the performance tradition by having her Desdemona fight during the murder scene when she was playing opposite Charles Macready in 1848. Writing to a friend, Kemble mused:

> I think I shall make a desperate fight for it, for I feel horribly at the idea of being murdered in my bed. The Desdemonas that I have seen, on the English stage, have always appeared to me to acquiesce with wonderful equanimity in their assassination. . . . but I did think I should like not to be murdered, and therefore, at the last, got on my knees on my bed, and threw my arms tight round Othello's neck (having previously warned Mr. Macready, and begged his pardon for the liberty).
>
> (Kemble, *Records*, 551)

While it appears that Kemble was not able to repeat her 'desperate fight' for Desdemona's life, the moment signalled a sea change for performances of Desdemona. She no longer had to acquiesce to be performed and interpreted as worthy, good and chaste. It should not be surprising that Kemble initiated this sea change in performance modes when one remembers that she was a staunch abolitionist who often wrote about the horrors of slavery from a feminist perspective. As Catherine Clinton writes, 'Kemble was not only a writer concerned with the inhumanity of slaveowners toward slaves, but also a woman struggling against the patriarchal prerogatives within her society' (Clinton, 74).

Ellen Terry also helped to change performances of Desdemona by performing her as an unconventional woman. Terry proclaimed that 'Shakespeare has suffered from so much misconception. The general idea seems to be that Desdemona is a ninny, a pathetic figure chiefly because she is half-baked' (Terry, *Four*, 129). Yet Terry argued that 'a great tragic actress with a strong personality and a strong method, is far better suited to it, for Desdemona is strong, not weak' (Terry, *Four*, 129). Faucit, Kemble and Terry, then, helped to make Desdemona a character that stars wanted to play, and they also made her a character who was presented as both good and strong, even potentially fighting for her life at the end of the play. With the restoration of the Willow Scene in twentieth-century productions, actresses have been fighting to stem the 200-year history of productions that were 'consistently replacing Desdemona's voice with silence and transforming her presence into absence' (Pechter, 130).[1]

By the mid-twentieth century, many actresses were following Terry's lead, arguing that Desdemona is a strong figure. Peggy Ashcroft (1907–1991), who played opposite Robeson in the 1930 production, was adamant that Desdemona is not only a strong character but also a proto-feminist: 'It seems to me amazing that women can think of Shakespeare as anti-feminist. Take Desdemona: some people see her as a sort of softy, a milk-and-watery character. I think she has enormous strength – and the courage of the step she took. She is of course the victim of the play, and perhaps victims are written off when they are not the main protagonist. But she is a wonderfully drawn character' (Ashcroft, 19). Yet the courage that Ashcroft had in playing the

1 The Willow Song (4.3.39–56), however, provides another instance of textual variation between the 1622 Quarto and the 1623 Folio versions of *Othello*. The reasons for this variation are explored by Honigmann, *Texts*, 10–11.

role as a strong woman opposite Robeson was not easily replicated. In her autobiography, Margaret Webster notes how difficult it was to get a white actress to play the role opposite Paul Robeson on Broadway in 1943: 'It had been all right, they said, for Peggy Ashcroft to do it in London, but she was English and that was London. In America – a white girl play love scenes with a *black* man . . . they were appalled' (Webster, 107). Yet, Uta Hagen (1919–2004), who was eventually cast for the role, made it clear from the beginning of rehearsals that her Desdemona would be strong. Webster continues, 'She was comparatively inexperienced, but she had the strength and enough classical training to meet the demands of the part – no dewy-eyed lamb-to-the-slaughter for Uta' (Webster, 108).

By the time Maggie Smith (1934–) played opposite Laurence Olivier in the 1964 production at the National Theatre, the

16 Desdemona (Olivia Vinall) and Othello (Adrian Lester) embrace in Cyprus, surrounded by soldiers in Nicholas Hytner's 2013 production at the National Theatre (Johan Persson / ArenaPAL)

death of the ninny Desdemona had fully occurred. Alan Seymour writes about Smith's performance, 'The milksop Desdemona has been banished from this stage and a girl of real personality and substance comes into her own. Fighting back, not soppily "hurt", but damned angry, she makes the conjugal battle less one-sided and so more interesting and certainly more exciting' (qtd Tynan, 16). Yet even with Desdemona's strength taken as a given, millennial productions have reverted to presenting Desdemona as extremely young, naïve and in love for the first time. Thus, Olivia Vinall, who played opposite Adrian Lester in the 2013 production at the National Theatre, resolutely declares, 'Desdemona is a young girl, who has at the start of the play just fallen completely in love. She's married Othello, who is more than twice her age in our production, and her father had no idea she was going to do this' (National Theatre). It is interesting to note that Vinall no longer feels it necessary to promote Desdemona's strength; yet she does feel it necessary to explain the importance of her youth and inexperience. While there have always been young Desdemonas onstage, the shift away from discussions of her strength to discussions of her inexperience is remarkable. Similarly, the RSC's 2015 production of *Othello*, directed by Iqbal Khan, featured Hugh Quarshie as Othello (age 60) and Joanna Vanderham as Desdemona (age 23). With close to a 40-year age difference between them, Desdemona's youth, inexperience and naïveté were prominently featured. The primary relationship in productions like the National's and the RSC's, then, becomes the one between Othello and Iago because there is such a disparity between Othello and Desdemona. What would it mean if directors and actors moved away from assumptions about Desdemona's youth, and presented the newlyweds as having a less visible age gap? This might fruitfully challenge assumptions about the cultural significance of Desdemona's sexual knowledge and could present a more feminist-leaning interpretation of the play.

Othello Onstage, Part 3: *Othello* in the World

The performance histories that I have provided thus far have skewed heavily towards UK and US productions, falsely giving the impression that *Othello* lives only in Western, English-speaking countries. This, of course, is far from the truth, and Shakespeare's presence globally cannot be underestimated. While there is only space to discuss three specific non-UK/US *Othello* productions, it is important to realize that Shakespeare's life as an early modern writer who was interested in the globe and Shakespeare's afterlife as a dramatist whose works get produced globally have become huge areas of scholarly research.[1] What is fascinating about productions of *Othello* outside the UK and the US is the fact that the cultural weight of the significance of Othello's racial, ethnic and religious differences translate in unique ways.

In 1987 the white South African actress Janet Suzman (1939–) made her directorial debut staging *Othello* at the Market Theatre in Johannesburg, South Africa. While *Othello* had been performed before in South Africa, this was the first production in which a black actor, John Kani (1943–), would play Othello, and it was seven years *before* the end of apartheid in South Africa. While the Market Theatre had allowed desegregated audience members since its opening in 1976, and while the Immorality Act which barred sexual relations across racial and ethnic lines had been repealed in 1985, the production was viewed as inherently political. As Adele Seeff writes, 'John Kani was himself a living example of the consequences of the Population Act. As a black South African, Kani's place of residence was prescribed (forcibly reassigned according to apartheid's terms) and he lived in Soweto, the largest township in South Africa. . . . The first

1 For a great resource that includes many videos of global productions see MIT's Global Shakespeares open access website (MIT).

run-through of the play, for example, was postponed because police cordoned off Soweto in preparation for the funeral of a murdered activist. Police roadblocks were a constant challenge for Kani as he made his way from Soweto to the Market Theatre in downtown Johannesburg' (Seeff, 378–9). In interviews Kani regularly voiced his view that 'he regarded his entire acting career as an extension of the black struggle against apartheid in South Africa' (Battersby). The *New York Times* quotes Kani saying, 'When I am offered work, I am very selective . . . I want my work to contribute toward creating a better society, toward bringing people together. That is always the first consideration, not the money' (Battersby).

Nonetheless, the production provoked a lot of negative responses with audience members walking out when Othello and Desdemona, played by Joanna Weinberg, touched for the first time onstage. 'Ms. Suzman said that by the time the production closed, "hate mail" from theatregoers and some who had not seen the play had piled up' (Battersby). Kani felt the dialogues that the production inspired and enabled were worth the trouble and he voiced his appreciation that Shakespeare was conscripted into their political activist theatre: 'There goes the native causing more trouble, and this time he has Shakespeare to do it for him' (Battersby). So while this global production of *Othello* presented and worked through familiar Western racialized discourses, the explicit politicization of both Shakespeare and the production's performance mode render it noteworthy in the global context. The production employed a fairly conservative mise en scène with vaguely early modern costumes and sets, but the impact of the production was anything but conservative: it was charged with progressive politics.

Ong Keng Sen's *Desdemona* (2000) demonstrates the wide variety of global Shakespeares. In fact, it is probably more effective to think about global productions in terms of the specific cultural legacies they bring to Shakespeare; instead of thinking about the ways Shakespeare ties them together. Ong

Keng Sen (1963–), a Singaporean director who attended NYU on a Fulbright Fellowship, is interested in creating intercultural theatre through rich juxtaposition. Thus, his productions often feature several art and cultural forms from different countries and regions in Asia which remain independent of each other but which enable dialogues about the politics of interculturalism. *Desdemona*, which premiered at the Adelaide Festival in Australia, was also staged in Munich, Hamburg and Singapore. The production was a collaboration between actors, musicians, designers and video installation artists from India, Korea, Myanmar, Indonesia and Singapore, and they all performed in traditional styles, some of which are dying out. Helena Grehan explains, 'For example, Madhu Margi, who, along with another actor, performs Othello in *Desdemona*, is only one of a small number of people who still practices *kudiyattum* [the only surviving example of ancient Sanskrit theatre] in Kerala, India. As a collaborator in this project he uses his extensive skills in *kudiyattum* to inform his portrayal of Othello. . . . *Desdemona* allows him to experience other art forms and to collaborate with both traditional and contemporary practitioners' (Grehan, 115).

As his second Shakespearean production (he directed the much-heralded *Lear* in 1997), Ong Keng Sen was interested in the ways that Shakespeare's *Othello* could serve as a vehicle to explore 'archetypal killing of an intercultural couple. One kills the other and that was just our point from which we projected out' (qtd Grehan, 119). In the programme notes, Ong Keng Sen also states that *Desdemona* was 'a journey through difference in Asia, traditional performing arts, gender, ritual and contemporary art; a process of reinvention' (Sen, '*Desdemona*', 5). As must be clear from these statements, though, there is a vast difference between Ong Keng Sen's relationship with Shakespeare and John Kani's or Janet Suzman's. Ong Keng Sen does not approach Shakespeare as a political ally but instead as a vehicle for asking questions about interculturalism. He writes, 'For me, interculturalism in performance is increasingly less about finding a better way of telling a story and more about asking, Why engage in interculturalism at all? Hence the work naturally shifts from one character to actor and I must say that these are issues that we cannot answer directly at this point in time. Questions with no answers' (Sen, 'On', 118). Shakespeare's play, then, is not the final product, and is instead 'a seed, a provocation' (Grehan, 117). In the end, Ong Keng Sen's *Desdemona* was similar to Suzman's 1987 South African production in its desire to politicize Shakespeare but radically different in its instrumentalization of *Othello*.

One final example of a global production of *Othello* comes from the 2009 Deutsches Theater Berlin German-language production directed by Jette Steckel (1982–), starring Susanne Wolff (1973–) as Othello. In a radically pared-down script translated into German by Frank-Patrick Steckel (the director's father), the text was nonetheless remarkably close to Shakespeare's text with a near verbatim translation. Therefore the few textual alterations were that much more remarkable because of the closeness of the textual translation. The largest textual change was the excision of the term 'Moor' to describe Othello. While the archaic German word 'Mohr' is the closest translation for the English word 'Moor' (in fact, Steckel's published translation is called *Die Tragödie von Othello, Dem Mohren von Venedig*), the text consistently uses variations of the German word 'Schwarze', or 'black man' in lieu of 'Moor'.

This textual alteration is further emphasized by the fact that Othello is played by the white, German actress Susanne Wolff who never appears physically disguised or made up to look like a black man. Instead, she appears in the first act in a white dress shirt and black slacks (as is the entire cast) with her long straight hair down; in the second and third acts she appears in a three-piece brown suit with a short wig complete with side burns; towards the end of the temptation scene (3.3) she applies and then proceeds to wipe off white clown makeup, complete with a Joker-like red smile; in act four she dons a realistic looking gorilla costume, takes it off and then reappears in a strapless red dress, blonde wig and black high heels; and in the final act, she appears in the bedroom scene wearing only an oversized Public Enemy t-shirt. Likewise, Othello has slight black marks across his middle knuckles from the second act until the end of the production. There is nothing mimetic about this performance mode; everything is conveyed through representational metaphors which render Othello's race less of a stable physical marker and more of a fractured and performative one.

Steckel's production rendered racialization as only ever barely about the body itself and more about the ways we code certain objects, the cultural narratives we construct about those objects and the performance modes that are enabled by those narratives as racialized. Thus, the gorilla suit is not discussed in the production in any explicit way, but it is allowed to drip silently with the various uncomfortable racialized narratives that do not necessarily stem from the early modern period (for more on the animal imagery in the play, see p. 38ff). In a performance mode that renders the distinction between mimesis and exhibition completely indeterminate, the gorilla costume renders racialized discourses, narratives and performance modes as constructed entities that often have nothing whatsoever to do with real bodies. In this production, race has nothing to do with either exhibition or mimesis because anybody can be rendered racialized in a social system that is determined to racialize: race becomes, then, inescapable.

These three examples of global productions of *Othello* differ widely in their approaches to Shakespeare, *Othello* and the frames that are useful and necessary to make compelling theatre. Again, it is important to realize that global *Othello*s are only ever united in the fact that Shakespeare's text is their jumping off point. Why *Othello* provides the jumping off point, what cultural work they want Shakespeare's reputation to play and what themes, performance modes and dialogues they hope to inspire are all unique to the cultural moment and place on the globe in which the production occurs.

Othello: Restaged / Rewritten

While it is fruitful to think about theatrical productions of *Othello* as types of adaptations or afterlives for Shakespeare's text, there are also many examples of new plays that seek to rewrite *Othello*. Although this may strike twenty-first century readers as a very modern approach, adaptations and appropriations of *Othello* date back to at least the nineteenth century. Again, there is not enough space in this introduction to provide a thorough overview of these appropriations, so I will limit my remarks to a handful of examples that fall into three categories: minstrel show rewritings, appropriations by black playwrights and feminist appropriations. I began the introduction discussing the ways *Othello* is a play about storytellers, their tall-tales and their effects on gullible listeners. As I argued, storytelling matters in very explicit and tangible ways in the play, and the playwrights who have appropriated *Othello* seem to have been attracted to the power of controlling the frame, the story, of *Othello*. So it is fitting that I end this introduction with a section on the theatrical afterlives of *Othello*.

Minstrel show versions of *Othello* were very popular in the nineteenth century, and they were the most popular blackface adaptations of Shakespeare. We have playtexts for the following *Othello* burlesques: Maurice Dowling, *Othello Travestie: An Operatic Burletta* (1834); T.D. Rice, *Otello: A Burlesque Opera* (1853); Griffin and Christy's Minstrels, *Othello: A Burlesque* (1870); and Anonymous, *Desdemonum: An Ethiopian Burlesque, in Three Scenes* (1874). I begin with them as the first set of theatrical appropriations because it is clear now that these burlesques were an attempt to employ *Othello* to frame narratives about black masculinity as

Plate 2
OTHELLO.
Moved to jealousy by the disclosure of wicked Mr Iago.
Oth. What hath he said ?
Iago. 'Faith, that he did, ———

17 *Othello: an interesting drama, rather! / by Alexander Do Mar; with illustrations after Rembrandt* (c. 1850), Alexander Do Mar (used by permission of the Folger Shakespeare Library under a Creative Commons Attribution-ShareAlike 4.0 International Licence)

18 Front cover of *Desdemonum: An Ethiopian Burlesque, in Three Scenes* (c. 1874) (used by permission of the Folger Shakespeare Library under a Creative Commons Attribution-ShareAlike 4.0 International Licence)

monstrous, laughable and yet potentially threatening if not properly controlled. While the history of blackface minstrelsy is complicated, we know that it began around 1830 when Thomas Dartmouth 'T.D.' Rice 'jumped Jim Crow' after a New York performance of *Othello*. The practice was for white actors to apply burnt cork to their skin to appear as poor, Southern, buffoon-like black slaves, who would dance, sing and talk in an exaggerated black dialect. Minstrelsy began as a humorous interlude between scripted performances (an entr'acte), but Rice formalized the tradition and even published lyrics for his specific 'Jim Crow' songs so that minstrel performances were then staged on their own as stand-alone productions.

As Joyce Green MacDonald notes, the cultural moment in which these burlesques were born was loaded: Edmund Kean began performing the Moor as tawny instead of black for the first time in 1820; the black American actor Ira Aldridge made his first appearance onstage in London in 1825; the Slavery Abolition Act was passed in the UK in 1833; and *Othello* burlesques began appearing around 1834 (MacDonald, 232–3). The minstrel show appropriations of *Othello* were all comical in nature; several associated Othello with the nineteenth-century slave trade making him explicitly Haitian or Jamaican; and several included a scene never shown in Shakespeare's original – the elopement of Desdemona and Othello. MacDonald argues, 'The Othello burlesques work hard to divest Shakespeare's climactic scene of the marriage-bed murder of a white girl by her black husband of its power to assault the sensibilities of whiteness' (MacDonald, 243). Dowling's *Othello Travestie: An Operatic Burletta* (1834), for instance, ends with an explicit call to 'let the past be all forgot' (Dowling, 43). Even though Othello has killed Desdemona, her ghost rises up to sing a song that scares him and actually revives her. Desdemona sings: 'You see I am not dead – not I', which helps to resolve everything:

RODERIGO	Then let the past be all forgot –
OTHELLO	Agreed!
DESDEMONA	Agreed!
IAGO	Agreed!
GHOST	Why not?

(Dowling, 43)

Of this ending MacDonald argues, 'Silencing Othello and having all the assembled characters agree simply to forget what has happened to them doubly revises *Othello*, both revisions suggesting the kinds of tensions which Shakespearean blackface may be designed to address' (MacDonald, 248). In other words, it squashes fears of racial pretension and renders black rage as both laughable and controllable. Most of the minstrel show versions of *Othello* perform this type of cultural work: they denigrate black masculinity but also neutralize the effects of its potential threats to white sexuality.

In an entirely different appropriative move, the Black Arts Movement, the artistic arm of the Civil Rights Movement and the Black Power Movement, saw the first black authors responding to *Othello* in their own rewritings of the play. Publishing at the time under the name LeRoi Jones, Amiri Baraka (1934–2014) wrote the twinned plays *Dutchman* and *Slave* in 1964, and they are said to 'represent the ultimate African American revision of *Othello*' (Andreas, 50). While *Slave* has an explicit reference to *Othello*, *Dutchman*'s plot is clearly an active appropriation of Shakespeare's interracial narrative. Clay, a young black man, meets Lulu, a young white woman, on the New York metro. They talk and flirt, but their encounter grows charged and aggressive, ending with Lulu stabbing Clay and ordering the other white Metro riders to throw his corpse off the train. As James Andreas writes, 'The myth of the ritual murder of innocent white virgins is, in *Dutchman*, fully deconstructed or inverted to reflect more accurately the relationship between the races that has existed throughout Western history. . . . Baraka is suggesting that the true victim in the biracial sexual struggle is the black *male*, and he is the partner who is ritually sacrificed in *Dutchman*' (Andreas, 50). Jason Demeter contextualizes the play effectively, explaining that *Dutchman* played at roughly the same moment when Gladys Vaughan's *Othello* appeared in New York's Central Park (starring James Earl Jones) and John Dexter's *Othello* appeared in London (starring Laurence Olivier) (Demeter). In his manifesto on theatre, 'The Revolutionary Theatre', Baraka explains that 'Clay, in *Dutchman*, Ray, in *The Toilet*, Walker in *The Slave*, are all victims. In the Western sense they could be heroes. But the Revolutionary Theatre, even if it is Western, must be anti-Western. It must show horrible coming attractions of *The Crumbling of the West*. Even as Artaud designed *The Conquest of the Mexico*, so we must design *The Conquest of the White Eye*, and show the missionaries and wiggly Liberals dying under blasts of concrete' (L. Jones, 4–5). Shakespeare's *Othello*, then, was one of the pillars that had to be rewritten in order for 'The Crumbling of the White Eye' to occur in Baraka's artistic-political imagination.

Iago (1979) by C. Bernard Jackson (1927–1996) took a different approach to appropriating *Othello*, making Iago a Moor who is less the aggressor and more a victim of racism as well. Cassio, in Jackson's play, becomes the scheming force, with Emilia attempting to set the story straight to the 'Author'. Unlike Baraka, however, Jackson weaves in many of Shakespeare's lines, but it becomes clear how unsatisfying Cinthio's and Shakespeare's versions have become when Emilia proclaims at the end, 'They came and asked me what had happened and Cinthio wrote it all down. And though I told him exactly what I'm telling you, he changed the facts as he saw fit, so I vowed to squat and wait here in this house which I have built over my husband's grave and will not leave nor let my spirit rest until what truly happened here is known and the story is set straight' (Jackson, 91). Jackson's play, then, makes explicit how unsatisfying the older narratives are because they ignore the viewpoints of women and people of colour. For those silenced voices to be heard, playwrights like Jackson decided they needed to return to Shakespeare's text to script those voices literally.

One final example of a black playwright appropriating *Othello* comes from Caleen Sinnette Jennings (1950–), whose one-act play *Casting Othello* (1999) looks closely at the politics of performance for actors of colour in a Shakespearean production. A metadramatic play, *Casting Othello* has a black character named Georgia who openly struggles with the racial politics in Shakespeare's *Othello*: 'Desdemona loves Othello because he's the exotic black buck. Othello loves Desdemona because she's Miss Anne. Now I've got to play the maid to the alabaster goddess who Mandingo over here, played by my *husband*, is drooling all over. . . . I'm gonna tell you straight up, people, this is a struggle' (Jennings, 88). Employing racial stereotypes and caricatures that post-date Shakespeare's *Othello* (the black buck, Miss Anne and Mandingo), Georgia nonetheless draws a clear line from *Othello* to nineteenth- and twentieth-century racial narratives. Not resolving the crisis, Jennings' play allows the audience to see the challenges actors of colour face when they are cast in Shakespeare's *Othello*. *Casting Othello* makes it apparent that it is not merely Shakespeare's politics that need to be addressed in contemporary performances of *Othello*, but also the ensuing history of racial portrayals.

This provides a natural segue into the final group of *Othello* appropriations – those by feminist playwrights. As both Jackson's *Iago* and Jennings' *Casting Othello* make clear, racialized appropriations of *Othello* often include explicit investigations of modern gender constructions. In many ways, the appropriations by black and feminist playwrights demonstrate the ways *Othello* can enable discussions about intersectionality; that is, that systems of oppression operate on multiple axes of identity simultaneously, like race, gender and class. In fact, the feminist appropriations of *Othello* often make intersectionality a central issue. Take, for example, *Desdemona, a play about a handkerchief* (1994) by Paula Vogel (1951–). In Vogel's play, the historical setting of Shakespeare's *Othello* remains the same, but the entire play takes place in the kitchen, in which only Desdemona, Emilia and Bianca traverse: the men do not enter this domestic space and therefore do not appear in the play. While there are moments of female solidarity in Vogel's play, the class distinctions between the three women are portrayed in stark terms as defined by the dramatis personae:

> DESDEMONA – Upper-class. Very.
> EMILIA – Broad Irish Brogue.
> BIANCA – Stage Cockney.
> (Vogel, 4)

As such, Desdemona behaves in an entitled fashion that is not explicitly revealed in Shakespeare's play; she is sexually adventurous, even pretending to be a prostitute with Bianca, and she relies on Emilia to keep her secrets in return for small favours that she promises to her and Iago. The power differentials between the women are revealed to be entirely based on their class differences.

And yet the women are united in the fact that they are dependent on the men who are entirely absent from *Desdemona*. In fact, Emilia is constantly asking for Desdemona to ask Othello to give Iago a promotion. When Desdemona asks why, especially considering the fact that Emilia hates Iago, Emilia reveals that her entire way of being is defined by her need for financial independence:

> You see, miss, for us in the bottom ranks, when man and wife hate each other, what is left in a lifetime of marriage but to save and scrimp, plot and plan? The more I'd like to put some nasty rat-ridder in his stew, the more I think of money – and he thinks the same. . . . I'd like to rise a bit in the world, and women can only do that through their mates – no matter what class

> buggers they all are. I says to him each night – I long for the day you make me a lieutenant's widow!
>
> (Vogel, 14)

Thus, Vogel works within Shakespeare's plot structure of *Othello* to expose the way the play is as much about gender and class as it is about race. The absent superstructure, which the play implies is created by white upper-class men, oppresses all others, while presenting the guise that power sharing may occur for some. As Desdemona prepares for bed, scared that Othello will kill her, Vogel lets the audience know that no one can survive in this system of oppression: black, female and the lower classes will be all smothered together.

Harlem Duet (1997) by Djanet Sears (1959–) does not maintain Shakespeare's socio-historical framework for *Othello* and instead transposes the play to three different time periods in Harlem: 1860, 1928 and the 'present day'. Circling around three different relationships between black men and black women, Sears wants to excavate and recover the voices of the black women who are absent from Shakespeare's *Othello*. In her introductory notes to the play, Sears explains, 'As a veteran theatre practitioner of African Descent, Shakespeare's *Othello* had haunted me since I first was introduced to him. . . . In an effort to exorcise this ghost, I have written *Harlem Duet. Harlem Duet*, a rhapsodic blues tragedy, explores the effects of race and sex on the lives of people of African descent. It is a tale of love. . . . [T]his is Billie's [the black woman's] story' (Sears, 'Notes', 14–15). Through the multiple time frames, the play implicitly asks why black women are denigrated by black men in favour of white women. The love between black men and black women is presented as true and passionate, and yet their relationships crumble under the social constructions that render white femininity as the standard for all beauty and desirability. In the end, the female protagonist from present day Harlem, Billie, who is clearly named after the black blues

19 Rokia Traoré as Barbary and Tina Benko as Desdemona in *Desdemona*, scripted by Toni Morrison and directed by Peter Sellars, at the Amandier Theater in Nanterre, 2011 © P Vitor / ArtComArt

singer Billie Holiday whose own life was racked by tragedy, sits in a psychiatric ward attempting to find forgiveness for Othello who left her for the white Mona. Part of her problem, though, is that she dreams that her white doctor has 'flashing blue eyes'. While her doctor does not know what this dream means, Billie says, 'Her eyes were flashing blue. She could only see my questions through her blue eyes' (Sears, *Harlem*, 115). In other words, the hope for mutual understanding is strained because it is too hard to see through other people's eyes when race is concerned. For Sears, then, Shakespeare's *Othello* comes to emblematize the problems posed to cross-/inter-racial communication, empathy and even love.

Desdemona (2012) by Toni Morrison (1931–) with lyrics by Rokia Traoré likewise interrogates the possibilities of cross-/inter-racial communication and love. Speaking at a symposium about *Desdemona* at the University of California, Berkeley in 2011, Morrison indicated her dissatisfaction with Shakespeare's *Othello* and its performance history: 'the place of spectacle and exoticism that *Othello* presents – not just in the play, but as I have long noticed in the performances, none of which I have ever really liked – is not as a complicated human being but as a kind of male, Africanist, black warrior/symbol of something' (Morrison). Morrison's re-vision, then, provided a vehicle to explore what could happen if the characters were all fuller, more complicated and freed from the bounds of time. In fact, the play takes place after death, which Morrison presents as timeless. Thus, Desdemona and Othello have the luxury of time to discuss all the facets of their relationship. By their final scene together, it is clear that Desdemona has fully grasped what timelessness means in terms of relationships and love. She tells Othello that he misunderstood her love for him when they were alive:

> DESDEMONA You believed I loved
> Othello the warrior. I did not.
> I was the empire you had already conquered.
> Alone together we could have been
> invincible.
> OTHELLO And now? Together? Alone? Is it too late?
> DESDEMONA 'Late' has no meaning here. Here there is
> Only the possibility of wisdom.
> (Morrison and Traoré, 54–5)

Desdemona's final words are, 'We will be judged by how well we love' (Morrison and Traoré, 56), and as Peter Sellars writes in the foreword to the published play, 'The apologies that we have waited four hundred years to hear are finally spoken. We are not simply left with tragedy' (Sellars, 11).

What makes *Desdemona* a particularly interesting feminist appropriation of *Othello*, though, is the relationship that Morrison depicts between Desdemona and her mother's servant, Barbary, who in Shakespeare's play taught her the

'Willow Song' and in Morrison's play is named Sa'ran. Sounding like many contemporary white liberals, Desdemona assumes that she and Barbary 'shared so much' (Morrison and Traoré, 45). But Sa'ran flatly declares,

> We shared nothing.
> . . .
> I mean you don't even know my name.
> Barbary? Barbary is what you call Africa.
> Barbary is the geography of the foreigner,
> the savage.
> . . .
> I was your slave.
> (Morrison and Traoré, 45)

While Barbary finally tells Desdemona that her real name is Sa'ran and also admits that Desdemona 'never hurt or abused' her, she does not express an interest in engaging Desdemona further. Instead, she ends declaring:

> I have thought
> long and hard about my sorrow. No more
> 'willow'. Afterlife is time and with time there
> is change. My song is new.
> (Morrison and Traoré, 48)

Sa'ran's new song celebrates the fact that she is comforted by a mysterious breath that 'caresses' the tears from her eyes:

> And I hear a call – clear, so clear:
> 'You will never die again'.
> What bliss to know
> I will never die again.
> (Morrison and Traoré, 49)

Desdemona responds, 'We will never die again', rendering her understanding of Sa'ran and Sa'ran's song unclear. Are we to interpret Desdemona's inclusion of her own suffering with Sa'ran's as an epiphany about their conjoined future in the afterworld, or is it merely a return to the unthinking collapse of all female suffering, one that implicitly whitewashes the unequal treatment of black and white bodies? While the play presents a very hopeful outcome for Desdemona's afterlife relationship with Othello, it presents a much more complicated portrait of her relationship with Sa'ran. Like Sears's play, *Desdemona* posits that cross-/inter-racial relationships can only be successful through hard work and long, sustained, and at times uncomfortable, dialogues.

It is important to note as well that there are myriad film, novelistic and artistic appropriations of *Othello*. There are simply too many to do justice to them in this introduction, but there is excellent scholarship on *Othello*'s afterlives in these various media.[1]

Concluding Thoughts

I feel compelled to return to storytelling as I conclude this introduction to William Shakespeare's *Othello* because the play provides a story that will not remain stable; it will not sit still. Even if it were possible to divine Shakespeare's true thoughts about and intentions for *Othello*, that platonic ideal of an Ur-text *Othello* could not erase the histories and stories that proliferate out of it. The play invites revisions, retellings, appropriations and adaptations because it shows just how powerful it is to control the master narrative. As I said before, he who controls the storytelling controls the world in *Othello*. It should be noted, though, that proliferation is not necessarily a positive force (e.g., cancer cells proliferate through

1 For more on *Othello*'s afterlives in poetry, novels and the visual arts see Erickson. For more on *Othello*'s afterlives on film see Hatchuel and Vienne-Guerrin. And for a comprehensive bibliography of *Othello* on film see Fernández.

metastasis). In the end, then, *Othello*'s most constructive energy may be geared toward the listeners of tall-tales.

The beginning of 1.3 is often cut in productions because it is a self-contained scene of about 50 lines in which the Duke and Senators receive conflicting news about the Turkish fleet. The reports provide different numbers for the Turkish galleys (107, 140 and 200), and other reports indicate that the fleet is heading to Rhodes instead of Cyprus. When the Duke questions the meaning of 'this change' in news (1.3.18), the first Senator provides a model for engaged listening. He says:

> This cannot be,
> By no assay of reason: 'tis a pageant
> To keep us in false gaze. When we consider
> Th'importancy of Cyprus to the Turk,
> And let ourselves again but understand
> That as it more concerns the Turk than Rhodes
> So may he with more facile question bear it,
> For that it stands not in such warlike brace
> But altogether lacks th'abilities
> That Rhodes is dressed in. If we make thought of this
> We must not think the Turk is so unskilful
> To leave that latest which concerns him first,
> Neglecting an attempt of ease and gain
> To wake and wage a danger profitless.
>
> (1.3.18–31)

The Senator, in fact, provides the perfect model for a reader or audience member who is not only engaged and thoughtful, but also sceptical and wary. He does not accept at face value the claim that the Turks will forsake the importance of gaining Cyprus for the ease of gaining Rhodes because to do so would mean that the Turks are 'unskilful' in their quest to increase their empire. In effect, the Senator forestalls the proliferation of this story by being an attentive audience member who questions the evidence and provides well-reasoned counter-arguments for the validity of that evidence. In fact, the Senator convinces the Duke who determinedly declares, ‘Nay, in all confidence, he’s not for Rhodes’ (1.3.32). Both the Senator and the Duke are proven correct when the next messenger enters and reveals that the Turkish fleet went to Rhodes simply to meet up with thirty additional ships to take with them to Cyprus.

I end with this short scene because it encapsulates what so many characters in the play fail to do: listen with a sceptical ear. While *Othello* continues to inspire artists, audience members and scholars to re-tell the story as a way to control the play’s stories, frames and contexts, it really should inspire a new breed of listener, one who can discern the significance and validity of those stories, frames and contexts.

THE TRAGEDY OF OTHELLO, THE MOOR OF VENICE

LIST OF ROLES

OTHELLO	the Moor [a general in the service of Venice]
BRABANTIO	*father to Desdemona* [*a Venetian senator*]
CASSIO	*an honourable lieutenant* [*who serves under Othello*]
IAGO	*a villain* [*Othello's ancient or ensign*]
RODERIGO	*a gulled gentleman* [*of Venice*]
DUKE	*of Venice*
SENATORS	[*of Venice*]
MONTANO	*governor of Cyprus* [*replaced by Othello*]
GENTLEMEN	*of Cyprus*
LODOVICO *and* GRATIANO	*two noble Venetians [Desdemona's cousin and uncle*]
SAILOR	
CLOWN	
DESDEMONA	*wife to Othello* [*and Brabantio's daughter*]
EMILIA	*wife to Iago*
BIANCA	*a courtesan* [*and Cassio's mistress*]

[Messenger, Herald, Officers, Gentlemen,
Musicians and Attendants
Scene: Act 1, Venice; Acts 2–5, Cyprus]

THE TRAGEDY OF OTHELLO, THE MOOR OF VENICE

[1.1] *Enter* RODERIGO *and* IAGO.

RODERIGO
Tush, never tell me, I take it much unkindly
That thou, Iago, who hast had my purse
As if the strings were thine, shouldst know of this.

IAGO
'Sblood, but you'll not hear me. If ever I did dream
Of such a matter, abhor me.

RODERIGO
Thou told'st me
Thou didst hold him in thy hate.

IAGO
Despise me
If I do not. Three great ones of the city,

LIST OF ROLES. See LN.

1.1 For the act and scene divisions, see p. 359, and *Texts*, 31. Location: a street outside Brabantio's house in Venice. Shakespeare is vague about many details (*this*, 3, *him*, 6, *her*, 73): we have to piece them together. Iago and Roderigo, it seems, have been arguing for some time. It is night (*Awake*, 78).

1 **Tush** a mild oath, removed from some play-texts as 'profanity' (Marlowe, 2, 247). Such exclamations (cf. *'Sblood*, 4) could be treated as extra-metrical.
much unkindly with much dissatisfaction

2 **thou** might be misread as *you* (cf. Q; *Texts*, 83)
Iago three syllables

3 **strings** 'threaded strings by drawing which the mouth of a purse is closed' (*OED*); hence, to hold the purse strings

4 **'Sblood** God's blood, an oath expurgated in F (see pp. 358–9)

4–5 **If . . . matter** semi-proverbial (Dent, D592, 'He never dreamed of it')

4–6 For the scansion, see *Texts*, 122–3.

5 **abhor** '*Abhor* retains the literal sense of the Latin *abhorreo*, "shrink from me in horror" ' (Kittredge).

6 **him** Othello: not identified until 32, and persistently misrepresented by Iago in 1.1

7 **great ones** Did Shakespeare know of Venice's *Savii Grandi* (elected by the Senate to superintend boards beneath it, in effect ministers of state)? See Wotton, 1.413n.

1.1] *Actus Primus. Scoena Prima. F; not in Q* 0.1 RODERIGO *and* IAGO] *as F (Rodergo) throughout; Iago* and *Roderigo Q (Rodorigo) throughout* 1 Tush] *Q; not in F* 2 thou] *F;* you *Q* hast] *F;* has *Q* 3 the] yͤ *F* 4–7] *as F; Q lines* heare me, / abhorre me. / hate. / Citty 4 'Sblood] *Q; not in F* you'll] you'l *F;* you will *Q*

In personal suit to make me his lieutenant,
Off-capped to him, and by the faith of man
I know my price, I am worth no worse a place.
But he, as loving his own pride and purposes,
Evades them, with a bombast circumstance
Horribly stuffed with epithets of war,
And in conclusion
Nonsuits my mediators. For 'Certes,' says he,
'I have already chose my officer.'
And what was he?
Forsooth, a great arithmetician,
One Michael Cassio, a Florentine,
A fellow almost damned in a fair wife
That never set a squadron in the field

8 **lieutenant** In *H5* Ancient Pistol is also 'lieutenant' (2.1.26, 39): Cassio is a different kind of lieutenant, hence the sharp distinction in 31, 32. See LN.

9 **Off-capped** took off their caps (any headdress for men, not a modern cap), as a sign of respect

10 **price** worth; suggesting 'the price by which my support may be purchased' (*OED* 4), i.e. the lieutenancy

12 **Evades** avoids giving a direct answer, puts off (a questioner) (*OED* 3b, first here)
bombast (cotton or cotton wool, used as stuffing for clothes): bombastic (language)
circumstance circumlocution; formality (*OED* 6, 7)

13 **stuffed** padded; crammed (of speech: *OED* 9)
epithets terms, expressions. Cf. *MA* 5.2.66, 'Suffer love! a good epithite!' (Q)

15 **Nonsuits** stops the suit of, refuses (legal: causes the voluntary withdrawal of the petition) (unique in Shakespeare)
mediators suitors, go-betweens
Certes truly (an 'upper-class' word; could be monosyllabic). As QF use no quotation marks, we could read ' "For, certes," says he'.

16 **my officer** The captain appoints and dismisses his own officers (see LN, 1.1.8), hence is their *master* (41ff.).

17 **And . . . he?** seems to complete 14 as one pentameter (cf. 5.2.81ff.). Perhaps Iago raises his voice at *And* (14, 17), suggesting an interrupted line.

18 **Forsooth** sneering at 'genteel' oaths: cf. Iago's *'Sblood*, 4, Othello's *Certes*, 15.
arithmetician sneering at Cassio's lack of experience of battle (cf. *bookish theoric*, 23). Yet others think differently, appointing Cassio to succeed Othello (4.1.236).

19 **Florentine** Machiavelli was seen as the quintessential Florentine, hence 'a crafty devil'. Cf. 3.1.41n., 2.1.235–46.

20 **A . . . wife** unexplained. Perhaps a line deleted by Shakespeare: an unmarried Cassio suits his plot better (*Texts*, 36). See LN.

21 **squadron** a body of soldiers drawn up in square formation

9 Off-capped] *F;* Oft capt *Q* 11 purposes] *QF;* purpose *Theobald* 14] *Q; not in F* 16–17| *one line QF* 16 chose] *F;* chosen *Q* 20 damned] dambd *Q;* damn'd *F*

Nor the division of a battle knows
More than a spinster – unless the bookish theoric,
Wherein the toged consuls can propose
As masterly as he. Mere prattle without practice
Is all his soldiership – but he, sir, had th'election
And I, of whom his eyes had seen the proof
At Rhodes, at Cyprus and on other grounds,
Christian and heathen, must be be-leed and calmed
By debitor and creditor. This counter-caster
He, in good time, must his lieutenant be
And I, God bless the mark, his Moorship's ancient!

RODERIGO

By heaven, I rather would have been his hangman.

IAGO

Why, there's no remedy, 'tis the curse of service:

22 **division** methodical arrangement
battle a body of troops or the main body of an army (*OED* 8, 9)

23 **unless** but for

24 **toged** togèd. Both Q and F are possible, *toged* from Lat. *togatus*, wearing the toga (the garb of peace), *tongued* as in *Cym* 3.2.5, 'as poisonous tongued as handed'. Tongue could be spelled *tong* (*R2* 5.5.97, Q), so this may be misreading (*Texts*, 83), as in Q *MV* 1.1.112 (togue) and F *Cor* 2.3.115 (*tongue* for *toge*).
consuls councillors
propose hold forth

25 **prattle . . . practice** Cf. Dent, P550.1, 'more prattle than practice' (first recorded 1611; echoing *Oth*?).

26 **election** formal choosing of a person for an office, usually by a vote (*OED* 1a, c). Whether or not others voted, Iago believes that it was Othello's decision.

27 **his** i.e. Othello's

28 **on . . . grounds** in . . . lands

29 **be-leed** left without wind (of ships), left high and dry
calmed becalmed

30 **By . . . creditor** by a mere bookkeeper. Or is it hinted that Cassio was promoted to pay back a favour? Cf. *Cym* 5.4.168.
counter-caster a coinage; 'one who counts with the assistance of counters or an abacus, but here much the same as the *arithmetician* [18]' (Ridley)

31 **in good time** indeed (ironical, expressing amazement, incredulity: *OED* time 42c). Cf. *Forsooth*, 18.

32 **God . . . mark** Dent, G179.1, 'God bless (save) the mark': cf. *RJ* 3.2.53. 'An apologetic or impatient exclamation when something horrible or disgusting has been said' (*OED* mark 18).
Moorship's Shakespeare's coinage, on the analogy of kingship, generalship, worship (sarcastic)
ancient a standard-bearer, ensign. 'Our "colour-sergeant" or perhaps "regimental sergeant-major" would be an approximation' (Ridley).

34 **no remedy** no help for it, no alternative. Cf. *TN* 3.4.296, 305, 333.
service public or military service; serving a master

24 toged] *Q;* Tongued *F* 26 th'] *F;* the *Q* 28 Cyprus] *F* (Ciprus*); Q (Cipres) throughout* other] *Q;* others *F* 29 Christian] *Q;* Christen'd *F* be be-leed] *F;* be led *Q* 32 God] *Q; not in F;* Sir *Q2 (*Sir (blesse the marke) . . .*)* Moorship's] *as F;* Worships *Q* 34] *QF lines* remedy, / seruice, / Why] *F;* But *Q*

Preferment goes by letter and affection
And not by old gradation, where each second
Stood heir to th' first. Now sir, be judge yourself
Whether I in any just term am affined
To love the Moor.

RODERIGO I would not follow him then.

IAGO

O sir, content you!
I follow him to serve my turn upon him.
We cannot all be masters, nor all masters
Cannot be truly followed. You shall mark
Many a duteous and knee-crooking knave
That, doting on his own obsequious bondage,
Wears out his time much like his master's ass
For nought but provender, and, when he's old,
cashiered.
Whip me such honest knaves! Others there are

35 i.e. promotion comes if you have supporting letters and the goodwill of friends, viz. by favouritism. Cf. 7: did *three great ones* really plead for Iago?

36 **old gradation** advancing step by step, according to seniority, as of old

38 **Whether** could be monosyllabic ('whe'er')
term respect; footing. Usually plural, 'in . . . terms'.
affined bound

39 **follow** serve

40 **content you** don't worry about that!

41 **serve my turn** common (= to serve my purpose), less usual with *upon*. Hinting at 'to turn the tables upon him'?

42 **We . . .[1] masters** Dent, M107: 'Every man cannot be a master' (from 1592).

43 **truly** faithfully
shall mark i.e. may observe

44 **duteous** subservient
knee-crooking bowing, making a leg, as in *Ham* 3.2.61, 'crook the pregnant hinges of the knee' (Ridley) (unique in Shakespeare)
knave servant; anyone of low status

45 **obsequious** obedient, dutiful; cringing (*OED* 1, 2)
bondage slavery; subjection (*OED* 2, 3)

46 **Wears out** passes, spends
time life-time (*OED* 7). Cf. *AYL* 2.7.142, 'one man in his time plays many parts'.

47 **provender** food; fodder (for animals). Apprentices and servants often received board and lodging in their master's house.
cashiered i.e. he's cashiered. But this word, hanging loose in the sentence, could be an exclamation: 'and when he's old – cashiered! –'

48 **me** as far as I'm concerned (ethic dative, 'for me'). Almost 'for my sake'. Petty offenders (usually *dishonest knaves*) were whipped.

36 And . . . by] *F;* Not by the *Q* 37] *as F; two lines Q* first: / to th'] to' th' *F;* to the *Q* 38 affined] *F;* assign'd *Q* 42 all be] *F;* be all *Q* 47 nought] noughe *Q;* naught *F* 48–51] *as F; Q lines* knaues: / formes, / hearts, / throwing / Lords, /

Who, trimmed in forms and visages of duty,
Keep yet their hearts attending on themselves
And, throwing but shows of service on their lords,
Do well thrive by them, and, when they have lined
their coats,
Do themselves homage: these fellows have some soul
And such a one do I profess myself. For, sir,
It is as sure as you are Roderigo,
Were I the Moor, I would not be Iago.
In following him I follow but myself:
Heaven is my judge, not I for love and duty
But seeming so, for my peculiar end,
For when my outward action doth demonstrate
The native act and figure of my heart
In complement extern, 'tis not long after

49 **trimmed** dressed up
forms images; customary ways; set methods of behaviour (*OED* 2, 11, 14)
visages assumed appearances (*OED* 8); i.e. faces like masks, concealing their feelings

50 Cf. the 'clever slave' of classical comedy who boasts 'My dependence is wholly on myself (e.g. Terence, *Phormio*, 139).

51 **throwing** directing (*OED* 15, 16)

52 elide: *by 'm, they've* (see *Texts*, 121)
lined their coats Dent compares 'to line one's purse' (P664; from 1521).

53 **Do . . . homage** i.e. pay themselves their due, serve their own interests. Here we begin to see two Iagos.
soul i.e. spirit. Cf. Othello's use of the word!

54 **For, sir** extra-metrical

56–7 ***Were . . . myself**: F follows Q's colon and full stop, but this punctuation is probably without authority (*Texts*, 127ff.). Reversing the colon and stop we make the lines slightly less baffling. 'Were I the Moor, I would not wish to be Iago. [But, being Iago,] I only follow him to follow my own interests.'

58 **Heaven . . . judge** Dent, G198.1, 'God (Heaven) is my judge.'
not . . . love I do not follow him out of love.

59 **peculiar end** private purpose

60 **demonstrate** (probably stressed on second syllable) manifest, exhibit

61 **native** innate, i.e. secret
act activity or active principle (*OED* 3; Hulme, 288)
figure appearance; design

62 **complement extern** outward show or completeness. Complement and compliment were not distinguished: Iago implies outward 'civility' or 'complement' to the inner. 'When his actions exhibit the real intention and motives of his heart *in outward completeness*' (Knight, in Furness).

52–3] *QF lines* 'em, / coates, / homage, / soule, / 52 them] *F;* 'em *Q* 53 these] *F;* Those *Q* 54 For, sir] *as QF; om. Pope* 56–7 Iago. . . . myself:] *this edn;* Iago: . . . my selfe. *QF* 60 doth] *F;* does *Q*

SECRET *

But I will wear my heart upon my sleeve → *once I show*
my innerself,
then I'm dead.

For daws to peck at. I am not what I am.

↳ *I am the Anti-God,*
⟨audience aware⟩

RODERIGO

What a full fortune does the thicklips owe ———— 65
If he can carry't thus!

bluntly racist thing.

IAGO Call up her father,

Rouse him, make after him, poison his delight, *Desdemona's*
father
Proclaim him in the streets, incense her kinsmen,
And, though he in a fertile climate dwell,
Plague him with flies! Though that his joy be joy 70
Yet throw such changes of vexation on't
As it may lose some colour.

RODERIGO

Here is her father's house, I'll call aloud.

IAGO

Do, with like timorous accent and dire yell
As when by night and negligence the fire 75

63 **wear . . . sleeve** 'I will expose my feelings to everyone' (*OED* heart 54f). Cf. Greene's *Planetomachia* (1585), Elb, 'they weare their hearts in their handes . . . their thoughts in their tongues end'; Dent, F32, 'He pins his faith (etc.) on another man's sleeve.' Servants wore their master's badge on their sleeve.

64 **daws** jackdaws, proverbially foolish
I . . . am appears to mean 'I am not what I seem' (cf. *TN* 3.1.141). Profanely alluding to God's 'I am that I am' (Exodus 3.14: cf. 1 Corinthians 15.10).

65 **full fortune** perfect good fortune
thicklips unique in Shakespeare (but cf. *Tit* 4.2.175, the Moor to his child, 'you thick-lipp'd slave')
owe own, possess

66 **carry't** carry it off, win the day (*OED* 15). Cf. *MW* 3.2.69–70.

67 **him . . . him . . . his** i.e. Brabantio. Some editors think 'the "him" throughout is Othello' (Walker), because of F's punctuation: yet F's punctuation has little authority (*Texts*, 127ff.).
make after pursue

69 **though** even though (he already dwells in a fertile climate, plague him with more flies)

70–2 **Plague . . . colour** plague him with further irritations; though his delight be (unalloyed) delight, yet direct such various harassments against it that it may lose some reason for its existence (*OED* colour 12b). Some editors prefer F *chances* (*OED* 2: mischances, accidents).

70 **Though that** i.e. though

74 **timorous** fear-inspiring, terrible
accent tone, voice

75 elliptical: as when a fire which gained hold by negligence at night

64 daws] *F;* Doues *Q* 65 full] *Q;* fall *F* thicklips] *Q;* Thicks-lips *F* Thicks-lips *F* 66 't] *F;* 'et *Q* 68 streets, incense] streete, incense *Q;* Streets. Incense *F* 71 changes] *Q;* chances *F* on't] *F;* out *Q* 74 timorous] timerous *QF*

Is spied in populous cities.

RODERIGO

What ho! Brabantio, Signior Brabantio ho!

IAGO

Awake, what ho, Brabantio! thieves, thieves, thieves!
Look to your house, your daughter and your bags!
Thieves, thieves!

plays on fear

BRABANTIO [*appears above*] *at a window.*

BRABANTIO

What is the reason of this terrible summons?
What is the matter there?

RODERIGO

Signior, is all your family within?

manipulation

Fear

IAGO

Are your doors locked?

BRABANTIO Why? Wherefore ask you this?

IAGO

Zounds, sir, you're robbed, for shame put on your gown!
Your heart is burst, you have lost half your soul,
Even now, now, very now, an old black ram

78, 80 **thieves** Iago's repetitions generate hysteria: cf. 87.
79 **bags** money bags
80.1 ****window*** Some Elizabethan play-houses had an upper stage or balcony and/or upper windows.
81 **What is** scan *what's*
terrible stronger than today: terrifying
85 **Zounds** = by God's (or Christ's) wounds
for shame fie. How characteristic of Iago to accuse Brabantio of shamelessness just when he himself speaks so shamelessly!
gown coat; or, senator's gown
86 **burst** broken
87 **very** (intensive) i.e. at this very moment
old the first hint as to Othello's age
ram Cf. *OED* rammish: lustful, lascivious. An old husband with a young wife was a traditional butt of comedy (Plautus, *Miles Gloriosus*, 965; see pp. 38–41).

77 Signior] Seignior *Q (throughout);* Siginor *F* 78 ³thieves] *Q; not in F* 79 ²your] *F;* you *Q* 80.1] *this edn;* Brabantio *at a window. Q; Bra. Aboue. F(SP)* 81 terrible summons?] *Q; F lines* terrible / there? / 84 your . . . locked] *F;* all doore lockts *Q* Why?] *F;* Why, *Q* 85 Zounds] *Q; not in F* you're] y'are *F;* you are *Q* 87 ²now] *F; not in Q*

Is tupping your white ewe! Arise, arise,
Awake the snorting citizens with the bell
Or else the devil will make a grandsire of you,
Arise I say!

BRABANTIO What, have you lost your wits?

RODERIGO
Most reverend signior, do you know my voice?

BRABANTIO
Not I, what are you?

RODERIGO My name is Roderigo.

BRABANTIO
The worser welcome!
I have charged thee not to haunt about my doors:
In honest plainness thou hast heard me say
My daughter is not for thee; and now in madness,
Being full of supper and distempering draughts,
Upon malicious bravery dost thou come
To start my quiet?

RODERIGO
Sir, sir, sir –

BRABANTIO But thou must needs be sure
My spirit and my place have in them power
To make this bitter to thee.

88 **tupping** (of rams) copulating with. Cf. 3.3.399, *topped.*
white white (as opposed to black); pure, unstained; precious, beloved (*OED* 7, 9)

89 **snorting** snoring, sleeping heavily; or, snorting like animals
bell alarm bell

90 **devil** monosyllabic. Othello, because devils were thought to be black. Cf. 1.2.63, 'Damned as thou art', 5.2.129.

92 **reverend** respected
know my voice It is too dark to see him.

94 **worser** double comparative, not unusual (Abbott, 11)

98 **distempering draughts** intoxicating liquor

99 **Upon . . . bravery** in bravado, in defiance (*OED* 1). F *knauerie* 'is slightly redundant after *malicious*' (Ridley).

100 **start** startle

101 **Sir . . . sir** extra-metrical. Brabantio's two half-lines really make a pentameter: Roderigo attempts to interrupt, perhaps several times, as Brabantio speaks on (cf. Hankey, 143).
But . . . sure You had better be clear about this.

102 **spirit . . . place** character . . . social position

103 **bitter** painful

90–1 Or . . . say!] *F; one line Q* 94 worser] *F (*worsser*);* worse *Q* 99 bravery] *Q;* knauerie *F* 100 quiet?] *Q;* quiet. *F* 102 spirit] *Q;* spirits *F* them] *Q;* their *F*

RODERIGO Patience, g

BRABANTIO

What tell'st thou me of robbing? This i
My house is not a grange.

RODERIGO Most grave Bra

In simple and pure soul I come to you –

IAGO Zounds, sir, you are one of those that will not serve God, if the devil bid you. Because we come to do you service, and you think we are ruffians, you'll have your daughter covered with a Barbary horse; you'll have your nephews neigh to you, you'll have coursers for cousins and jennets for germans!

BRABANTIO What profane wretch art thou?

IAGO I am one, sir, that comes to tell you your daughter and the Moor are now making the beast with two backs.

BRABANTIO

Thou art a villain!

103 **Patience, good sir!** could be 'Patience! good sir –'

105 **grange** country house or outlying farmhouse, i.e. more vulnerable than a house in a city

grave respected

106 **simple** free from duplicity, honest (*OED* 1)

pure unblemished, sincere

110 **covered** Cf. *OED* cover 6: of a stallion, to copulate with a mare.

Barbary Barbary, the home of Berbers or Moors (see pp. 24–5, 40, 112–14), could refer to all Saracen countries along the north coast of Africa (*OED* 4). Barbary horse = barb, Arab horse, i.e. Othello.

111 **nephews** grandsons, descendants

neigh Notice the alliteration in 111, 112: and *neigh* would echo *neph*[ews] if *-gh-* was sounded as in enough, laugh, etc. Cf. Jeremiah 5.8, 'In the desire of uncleanly lust they are become like the stoned horse, every man neigheth at his neighbour's wife'; 13.27, 'Thy adulteries, thy neighings . . . thy abominations have I seen.'

112 **coursers** could be a powerful horse, ridden in battle, or a racehorse

jennets small Spanish horses. (He chooses this word because the Moors had settled in Spain?)

germans close relatives

113 **profane wretch** foul-mouthed despicable person

115 **making . . . backs** copulating. Cf. Dent, B151, 'the beast with two backs' (Fr. and It. proverb); Rabelais, 1.3, '*faisoient . . . la beste a deux doz*', and 5.30. Shakespeare seems to have known the works of Rabelais. Cf. *AYL* 3.2.225, 'Gargantua's mouth'.

116 **Thou . . . You** *Thou* is contemptuous or familiar, *You* is (usually but not here) respectful.

104–5] *as Q; F lines* Robbing? / Grange. / 104 What] *F;* What, *Q* 107 Zounds] *Q; not in F* 109 and] *F; not in Q* 112 jennets for germans] Iennits for *Iermans Q;* Gennets for Germaines *F* 114 comes] *F;* come *Q* 115 now] *Q; not in F*

You are a <u>senator!</u> *political*

we hate politicians.
(universal)

ΛNTIO

This thou shalt answer. I know thee, Roderigo!

RODERIGO

Sir, I will answer anything. But I beseech you,
If't be your pleasure and most wise consent,
As partly I find it is, that your fair daughter 120
At this odd-even and dull watch o'th' night,
Transported with no worse nor better guard
But with a knave of common hire, a gondolier,
To the gross clasps of a lascivious Moor –
If this be known to you, and your allowance, 125
We then have done <u>you bold and saucy wrongs.</u>
But if you know not this, my manners tell me
We have your wrong rebuke. Do not believe
That from the sense of all civility
I thus would play and trifle with your reverence. 130
Your daughter, if you have not given her leave,
I say again, hath made a gross revolt,
Tying her duty, beauty, wit and fortunes

116 **a senator** contemptuous (perhaps he spits as he speaks). Pause after *You* or *are* or *a*? Notice the class feeling. Between equals, the epithet *villain* would lead to a duel.

117 **answer** answer for. Brabantio knows Roderigo, not Iago.

119 **pleasure** delight; will (sarcastic)
wise fully aware, as in modern 'he's wise to that one' (Ridley)

120 **As . . . is** 'as, by your refusal to listen to us, I am half inclined to believe it *is*' (Kittredge)

121 ***odd-even** a coinage = (?)neither one thing nor the other, neither night nor day. Cf. 'What is the night? / Almost at odds with morning, which is which' (*Mac* 3.4.125–6).
dull drowsy, lifeless
o'th' so F. Perhaps a scribal contraction of

o'the (see *Texts*, 140).

122–3 elliptical (Roderigo stumbles, speaking hastily): he means 'your daughter *has been* transported . . . *than* with a knave'.

123 **But** One expects 'Than'.
knave male servant
gondolier F *Gundelier* suggests two syllables, accent on first.

124 **clasps** embraces

125 **and your allowance** and has your approval

126 **saucy** insolent

127 **manners** good breeding

129 **from** away from, without
civility civilized behaviour

130 **your reverence** a respectful form of address, in general use

132 **gross** great (Folger); or, disgusting

119–35] *F; not in Q* 121 odd-even] *Malone;* odde Euen *F*

In an extravagant and wheeling stranger
Of here and everywhere. Straight satisfy yourself:
If she be in her chamber or your house
Let loose on me the justice of the state
For thus deluding you.

BRABANTIO Strike on the tinder, ho!
Give me a taper, call up all my people.
This accident is not unlike my dream, ← daughter running away
Belief of it oppresses me already.
Light, I say, light! *Exit above.*

IAGO Farewell, for I must leave you.
It seems not meet, nor wholesome to my place,
To be produced, as, if I stay, I shall, Go back & say he's
Against the Moor. For I do know the state, loyal to Othello.
However this may gall him with some check,
Cannot with safety cast him, for he's embarked
With such loud reason to the Cyprus wars,
Which even now stands in act, that for their souls
Another of his fathom they have none

134 **In** i.e. to. Could be corrupt.
extravagant roaming, vagrant, as in *Ham* 1.1.154, the 'extravagant and erring spirit hies / To his confine': cf. 'erring Barbarian' (1.3.356)
wheeling (?)reeling, hence giddy, unstable. Though first recorded 1661, *wheedling* (= using soft flattering words) is not impossible (cf. *Per* 5, chor. 5, *neele* for *needle*).
135 **Of . . . everywhere** of uncertain background
138 **Strike . . . tinder** strike a light with the tinderbox
139 **taper** candle; light
140 **accident** occurrence, (unforeseen) event
143 **meet** fitting, proper
place i.e. as Othello's ensign (lightly ironic)
144 ***produced** F may be correct but would be meaningless today.
146 **gall** vex
check reprimand
147 **cast** discharge
for the third *for* in six lines. A copyist's error? Omit?
embarked involved (*OED* 2); or, loosely speaking, his belongings are embarked
148 **loud** urgent
148–9 **wars . . . stands** Shakespeare sometimes has the plural verbal *-s* (Abbott, 338), but these could be misprints (*Texts*, 85).
149 **act** action, i.e. have started
for their souls to save their souls
150 **fathom** ability (*OED* 2b)

134 wheeling] *F;* wheedling *Collier*[2] 138 thus . . . you] *F;* this delusion *Q* 142 SD] *F; not in Q* 143 place] *F;* pate *Q* 144 produced] *Q;* producted *F* 146 However] How euer *Qu, F;* Now euer *Qc* 147 cast him] *Q;* cast-him *F* 150 fathom] *Q;* Fadome *F* none] *F;* not *Q*

To lead their business – in which regard,
Though I do hate him as I do hell-pains,
Yet for necessity of present life
I must show out a flag and sign of love,
Which is indeed but sign. That you shall surely find him,
Lead to the Sagittary the raised search,
And there will I be with him. So farewell. *Exit.*

fake, another secret

Enter BRABANTIO *in his night-gown and Servants with torches.*

BRABANTIO
It is too true an evil, gone she is,
And what's to come of my despised time
Is nought but bitterness. Now Roderigo,
Where didst thou see her? – O unhappy girl! –
With the Moor, say'st thou? – Who would be a father? –
How didst thou know 'twas she? – O, she deceives me

151 **business** three syllables
in which regard for which reason. Notice how loosely this speech hangs together.
152 ***hell-pains** the torments of hell (cf. hell-fire, hell-hound, etc.)
153 i.e. because it is necessary for my livelihood
154 **sign** Lat. *signum* = (1) token, sign; (2) military standard, banner. Iago is Othello's ancient or standard (sign)-bearer.
155 **sign** show, pretence
156 **Sagittary** an inn or house with the sign of Sagittarius (= the Centaur: a mythological figure, with head, trunk, arms of a man and lower body and legs of a horse. Alluding to Othello's 'divided nature'?). Cf. *CE* 1.2.9. Either Q or F may be correct (*Texts*, 85), but cf. *TC* 5.5.14, 'the dreadful Sagittary' (Q and F).
search search party
157.1 ***night-gown*** dressing-gown
159 and what lies ahead in my despised life: despised because a father whose daughter has eloped suffers from loss of face (like a cuckolded husband)
160–5 Cf. Shylock's reported distraction after Jessica's elopement (*MV* 2.8.15ff.), a comedy routine. 'O treason of the blood' = Shylock's 'My own flesh and blood to rebel!' (3.1.34).
161 **unhappy** miserable, wretched cf. p. 395

152 hell-pains] hells paines *Q;* hell apines *F* 155–6] *as F; Q lines* surely / search, / 156 Sagittary] Sagittar *Q;* Sagitary *F* 157.1] *as Q (*Barbantio*); Enter Brabantio, with Seruants and Torches. F* 160 nought] *Q;* naught *F* bitterness. Now] *F;* bitternesse now *Q* 161–4] *F uses brackets:* (Oh vnhappie Girle) . . . (Who . . . Father?) . . . (Oh she . . . thought:) 163 she deceives] *F (*deccaues*);* thou deceiuest *Q;* she deceaued *(Furness)*

Past thought! – What said she to you? – Get more tapers,
Raise all my kindred. Are they married, think you?

RODERIGO

Truly I think they are.

BRABANTIO

O heaven, how got she out? O treason of the blood!
– Fathers, from hence trust not your daughters' minds
By what you see them act. – Is there not charms
By which the property of youth and maidhood
May be abused? Have you not read, Roderigo,
Of some such thing?

RODERIGO Yes sir, I have indeed.

BRABANTIO

Call up my brother. – O, would you had had her!
Some one way, some another. – Do you know
Where we may apprehend her and the Moor?

RODERIGO

I think I can discover him, if you please
To get good guard and go along with me.

BRABANTIO

Pray you lead on. At every house I'll call,
I may command at most: get weapons, ho!
And raise some special officers of night.
On, good Roderigo, I'll deserve your pains. *Exeunt.*

164 **Past thought!** beyond comprehension
more F *moe* = more
167 **O heaven** extra-metrical
treason . . . blood (1) betrayal of her father and family; (2) rebellion of the passions (Folger)
169 **Is . . . charms** are there not magical powers
170 **property** nature
171 **abused** perverted; deceived; violated
173 **brother** Cf. 5.2.199n.
176 **discover** expose to view, find
180 **officers of night** Discussed by Lewkenor, who prints 'Officers of night' in the margin.
181 **deserve your pains** requite the trouble you take

164 more] *Q;* moe *F* 167] *as Q; F lines* out? / blood. / 170 maidhood] *F;* manhood *Q* 172 thing] *QF;* things *Q3* Yes . . . indeed] *F;* I haue sir *Q* 173 would] *F;* that *Q* 178 you lead] *F;* leade me *Q* 180 night] *Q;* might *F* 181 I'll] *Q;* I will *F*

[1.2] *Enter* OTHELLO, IAGO *and Attendants with torches.*

IAGO

Though in the trade of war I have slain men
Yet do I hold it very stuff o'th' conscience
To do no contrived murder: I lack iniquity
Sometimes to do me service. Nine or ten times
I had thought t'have yerked him here, under the ribs.

OTHELLO

'Tis better as it is.

IAGO Nay, but he prated

And spoke such scurvy and provoking terms
Against your honour,
That with the little godliness I have
I did full hard forbear him. But I pray, sir,
Are you fast married? Be assured of this,
That the magnifico is much beloved
And hath in his effect a voice potential

1.2 Location: a street outside the Sagittary (cf. 1.1.156n.)

1 **trade** business (cf. Othello's *occupation*, 3.3.360)

2 **stuff** (?)stock-in-trade (*OED* 1j); (?) alluding to 'the stuffs of war', the munitions of an army (*OED* 1c)

3 **contrived** còntrived. Cf. *H5* 4.1.162, 'premeditated and contriv'd murther'.

4 **Nine . . . times** With Iago's pretended indecisiveness, cf. 2.3.149ff.

5 **yerked** to yerk or yark = strike, esp. with rod or whip; Iago means with a dagger. Q *ierk'd* (jerked) is possible (facetious understatement).

him Roderigo (hence 58)? But could refer to Brabantio.

6 **prated** chattered foolishly

7 **scurvy** contemptible

10 **I . . . him** I put up with (or spared) him with great difficulty.

11 **fast** firmly (*OED* 4: firmly tied). So *MM* 1.2.147, 'she is fast my wife'. Sometimes a couple could be divorced (cf. 14) if the marriage was not consummated: that may be Iago's point.

12 **magnifico** 'The chief men of Venice are by a peculiar name called *Magnifici*, i.e. Magnificoes' (Tollet, quoted Ridley). So *MV* 3.2.280.

is . . . beloved has many good friends

13 **effect** i.e. power

potential potent; possible as opposed to actual, latent (*OED* 1, 2)

13–14 **a . . . duke's** Shakespeare 'supposed (erroneously) that the "duke" had a casting vote, and so, on an equal division, two votes'; Iago says Brabantio is so popular that he can 'get his own way as effectively as if he also had two votes' (Ridley).

1.2] *Scena Secunda. F; not in Q* 0.1 *and*] *Q; not in F* 2 stuff o'th'] *F;* stuft of *Q* 4 Sometimes] *Q;* Sometime *F* 5 t'] *F;* to *Q* yerked] *F;* ierk'd *Q* 10 pray] *Q;* pray you *F* 11 Be assured] *F;* For be sure *Q*

As double as the duke's: he will divorce you
Or put upon you what restraint or grievance
The law, with all his might to enforce it on,
Will give him cable.

OTHELLO Let him do his spite;
My services, which I have done the signiory,
Shall out-tongue his complaints. 'Tis yet to know –
Which, when I know that boasting is an honour,
I shall promulgate – I fetch my life and being
From men of royal siege, and my demerits
May speak unbonneted to as proud a fortune
As this that I have reached. For know, Iago,
But that I love the gentle Desdemona
I would not my unhoused free condition
Put into circumscription and confine
For the sea's worth. But look, what lights come yond?

Enter CASSIO, *with Officers and torches.*

15 **grievance** infliction, oppression
16 **his** could refer to Brabantio or to the law (*his* = modern *its*)
enforce it on press it home
17 **cable** i.e. scope. For Iago's nautical metaphors, cf. 1.1.29, 150, 2.3.59, etc.
do his spite do his spiteful worst
18 **signiory** the governing body (Signoria) of Venice
19 **out-tongue** outspeak, i.e. get the better of (unique in Shakespeare)
'Tis . . . know i.e. it is not yet known (Folger)
21 **promulgate** make publicly known. Q *provulgate* means the same but was a rarer word, and could well be Shakespeare's (Lat. *promulgare, provulgare*).
22 **siege** rank (lit. seat); Q *height* (= high rank, *OED* 7) is possible
demerits merits; deficiencies
23 **speak . . . to** appeal to (*OED* 13c); or (loosely), claim
unbonneted Fr. *bonneter* = to put off one's bonnet (headdress), out of respect; *unbonneted* seems to mean 'without removing my bonnet', but some editors prefer 'having removed my bonnet'. Cf. 1.1.9.
proud high, grand
26 **unhoused** unhousèd. Othello had lived in tents (1.3.86).
free unmarried
27 i.e. restrict and confine (*confine* = confinement)
28 **For . . . worth** for all the treasures buried in the sea

14 duke's] *QF;* Duke *Q3* 15 or] *F;* and *Q* 16 The] *F;* That *Q* 17 Will] *F;* Weele *Q* 18 services] *QF;* service *Q3* 20 Which . . . know] *F; not in Q* 21 promulgate] *F;* provulgate *Q* 22 siege] *F (*Seige*);* height *Q* 28 sea's] *Theobald;* seas *QF;* seas' *Cam (anon.)* yond] *F;* yonder *Q* 28.1] *Enter* Cassio *with lights, Officers, and torches. Q opp.* 28; *Enter Cassio, with Torches. F*

IAGO

Those are the raised father and his friends,
You were best go in.

OTHELLO Not I, I must be found.
My parts, my title and my perfect soul
Shall manifest me rightly. Is it they?

IAGO

By Janus, I think no.

OTHELLO

The servants of the Duke? and my lieutenant?
The goodness of the night upon you, friends.
What is the news?

CASSIO The duke does greet you, general,
And he requires your haste-post-haste appearance,
Even on the instant.

OTHELLO What's the matter, think you?

CASSIO

Something from Cyprus, as I may divine;
It is a business of some heat. The galleys
Have sent a dozen sequent messengers
This very night, at one another's heels,
And many of the consuls, raised and met,

29 **raised** raisèd = roused, for attack or defence; roused from sleep
30 **I . . . found** it is fitting that I be found
31 **parts** (good) qualities; actions
title legal right or claim
perfect flawless, blameless; 'fully prepared for what may occur' (Hart)
32 **manifest me rightly** reveal me correctly as I am
33 **Janus** Roman god with two faces, at front and back of the head. Iago, himself 'two-faced', may mean 'by the god who sees what others cannot see', because it is dark.
34 This line could be *either* one or two questions, *or* one or two exclamations ('!' was often printed '?'). For F's punctuation, see *Texts*, 127ff.
35 May the goodness of the night (peace? rest?) light upon you.
36 **general** Cf. 53, *captain*; see LN, 1.1.8.
37 **haste-post-haste** urgent. Often written as a command on letters, here used as an adjective. Cf. 1.3.47.
40 **heat** i.e. urgency
galleys still used in Venice in the seventeenth century, not in England
41 **sequent** successive
43 **consuls** Cf. 1.1.24n.
raised roused (from sleep), or gathered (*OED* 4, 26)

29 Those] *F;* These *Q* 32 Is . . . they?] *F;* it is they. *Q* 34 Duke *Q;* Dukes *F* Duke? . . . lieutenant?] *as Q; F lines* Dukes? / Lieutenant? / 35 you, friends.] you (Friends) *F;* your friends, *Q* 38 What's] *Q;* What is *F* 41 sequent] *F;* frequent *Q*

Are at the duke's already. You have been hotly called
for,
When, being not at your lodging to be found,
The Senate hath sent about three several quests
To search you out.

OTHELLO 'Tis well I am found by you:
I will but spend a word here in the house
And go with you. [*Exit*.]

CASSIO Ancient, what makes he here?

IAGO
Faith, he tonight hath boarded a land carrack:
If it prove lawful prize, he's made for ever.

CASSIO
I do not understand.

IAGO He's married.

CASSIO To whom?

IAGO
Marry, to –

Enter OTHELLO.

Come, captain, will you go?

OTHELLO Ha' with you.

44 **hotly** urgently
45 **When** whereupon; inasmuch as, since
46 **about** around, in the city
quests searches
48 **spend** utter (cf. *R2* 2.1.7, *Ham* 5.2.131). It may be that Othello does not exit and re-enter but speaks to someone in the doorway.
49 **makes he** is he doing
50 **boarded** gone on board of, entered (a ship), often with sexual implications: Paris 'would fain lay knife aboard' (*RJ* 2.4.202), 'board her, woo her, assail her' (*TN* 1.3.57)
carrack treasure ship (usually Spanish)
51 **lawful prize** i.e. if he's legally married (*prize* = capture, booty). Cf. 11n.
52 ***To whom?** Cf. 3.3.94ff., where Cassio seems to know all that has happened. Some think he feigns ignorance here. The 'inflection of *who* is frequently neglected' (Abbott, 274, citing also 2.3.15, 4.2.101); yet *whom* might be misread as *who* (*Texts*, 89).
53 **Marry** (originally) by the Virgin Mary, a mild exclamation
captain Cf. 36n., 2.1.74.
***Ha' with you** = I'm ready (cf. *AYL* 1.2.256). Q mistook *Ha* as an exclamation, so *Ha* must have stood in the Q manuscript; F modernized to *Haue*.

46 hath . . . about] *F;* sent aboue *Q* 48 I will but] *F;* Ile *Q* 49 Ancient] *F (*Anciant*)* SD] *Rowe; not in QF* 50 carrack] Carrick *Q;* Carract *F* 51 he's made] *Q;* he' made *F* 52 whom] *Q2;* who *QF* 53 SD] *Rowe (after* go?*); not in QF* Ha' with you] Ha, with who? *Q;* Haue with you. *F*

CASSIO

Here comes another troop to seek for you.

Enter BRABANTIO, RODERIGO, *with Officers and torches and weapons.*

IAGO

It is Brabantio: general, be advised,
He comes to bad intent.

OTHELLO

Holla, stand there!

RODERIGO

Signior, it is the Moor.

BRABANTIO

Down with him, thief!

[*They draw on both sides.*]

Rodergo can't hurt him.

IAGO

You, Roderigo! come sir, I am for you. ← Intentional.

OTHELLO

Keep up your bright swords, for the dew will rust them.
Good signior, you shall more command with years
Than with your weapons.

BRABANTIO

O thou foul thief, where hast thou stowed my daughter?

54.1–2 Cf. John 18.1–11. Like Jesus, Othello is challenged by enemies in the dark (*officers*, with *torches* and *weapons*), and is led off to a higher authority. Compare 59 and John 18.11, 'Jesus said unto Peter, Put up thy sword into the sheath' (Mrs Rosamond K. Sprague, private communication). Note that the SD differs in Q and F. Just a coincidence?

55 **advised** careful

56 **to bad intent** with bad intention

Holla stop! or, a shout to excite attention (*OED* 1, 2)

58 **You . . . you** Iago picks on Roderigo as if to confirm that Roderigo *prated* (6) and was the cause of Othello's trouble. Perhaps 'I'm for you!'

59 Cf. 54 SD n., *KJ* 4.3.79, 'Your sword is bright, sir, put it up again.' When Kean spoke this famous line, it was as if his voice 'had commanded where swords were as thick as reeds', according to John Keats; Salvini's voice was 'touched with gallant laughter' (Rosenberg, 62–3, 105).

60 **you** Cf. 62, *thou*!

62 **foul** loathesome; wicked; ugly (*OED* 1, 7, 11)

stowed placed, i.e. hidden

54.1–2] *Enters* Brabantio, Roderigo, *and others with lights and weapons. Q (after* To who *52); Enter Brabantio, Rodorigo, with Officers, and Torches. F* 55 Brabantio: general,] *subst. F* 57 SP BRABANTIO] *F; Cra. Q* SD] *Rowe; not in QF* 58 You . . . come] *as Q;* You, *Rodorigoc?* Cme *F* 59–61] *as Q; prose F* 59 them] *F;* em *Q;* 62] *as Q; F lines* Theefe, / Daughter? /

Damned as thou art, thou hast enchanted her,
For I'll refer me to all things of sense,
If she in chains of magic were not bound,
Whether a maid so tender, fair and happy,
So opposite to marriage that she shunned
The wealthy, curled darlings of our nation, men.
Would ever have, t'incur a general mock,
Run from her guardage to the sooty bosom
Of such a thing as thou? to fear, not to delight.
Judge me the world if 'tis not gross in sense
That thou hast practised on her with foul charms,
Abused her delicate youth with drugs or minerals
That weakens motion: I'll have't disputed on,
'Tis probable and palpable to thinking.
I therefore apprehend and do attach thee
For an abuser of the world, a practiser
Of arts inhibited and out of warrant. → witchcraft
Lay hold upon him; if he do resist
Subdue him at his peril!

Non-Christian thing.

63 **Damned . . . art** Devils were thought to be black, so black implied damnation ('his soul may be as damn'd and black / As hell', *Ham* 3.3.94; 'the complexion of a devil', said of Morocco, *MV* 1.2.130).
enchanted cast a spell on
64 **refer me** submit my case
things of sense persons (*OED* 10)
66 **tender** delicate; gentle; sensitive
fair unblemished (of character or reputation)
happy contented; perhaps = successful (?conventional) in doing what the circumstances require (*OED* 5)
67 **opposite** opposed
68 **curled** curlèd. May imply artificial curls, worn by men.
69 **mock** mockery
70 **guardage** guardianship (first recorded here)
71 **thing** (contemptuous)
to . . . delight *either* 'run . . . to fear, not to delight' (two nouns), *or* 'a thing . . . to fear (frighten) not to delight' (two infinitives)
72 **gross in sense** obvious in meaning
73 **practised on** plotted against
74 **minerals** mineral medicines or poisons (*OED* 4c)
75 **weakens** Hanmer's *waken* is attractive (*Texts*, 88).
motion desire, inclination (so 1.3.331); or, inward impulse or prompting (i.e. against Othello)
disputed on looked into (lit. debated)
77 **attach** arrest
78 **abuser** deceiver
79 **inhibited** prohibited
out of warrant illegal
81 **Subdue** overpower

64 things] *F;* thing *Q* 65] *F; not in Q* 68 darlings] *Q;* Deareling *F* 69 t'] *F;* to *Q* 72–7] *F; not in Q* 75 weakens] *F;* waken *Hanmer* 78 For] *F;* Such *Q*

HELLO Hold your hands,
Both you of my inclining and the rest:
Were it my cue to fight, I should have known it
Without a prompter. Where will you that I go
To answer this your charge?

BRABANTIO To prison, till fit time
Of law, and course of direct session
Call thee to answer.

OTHELLO What if I do obey?
How may the duke be therewith satisfied,
Whose messengers are here about my side
Upon some present business of the state,
To bring me to him?

OFFICER 'Tis true, most worthy signior,
The duke's in council, and your noble self
I am sure is sent for.

BRABANTIO How? the duke in council?
In this time of the night? Bring him away:
Mine's not an idle cause, the duke himself,
Or any of my brothers of the state,
Cannot but feel this wrong as 'twere their own.
For if such actions may have passage free
Bond-slaves and pagans shall our statesmen be. *Exeunt.*

81 **Hold** i.e. don't move
82 **my inclining** my side ('you who incline towards me')
83 **cue** Q's *Qu.* is Shakespeare's spelling elsewhere (*Texts*, 160).
84 **Where** F *Whether* is a variant spelling of whither, where.
86 **direct session** 'normal process of law' (Ridley)
90 **present** immediate, urgent
93 **I am** read 'I'm'
94 **In** at (Abbott, 161)
95 **idle** groundless; frivolous
cause (legal) case
96 **brothers . . . state** fellow Senators (Sanders)
97 **as** as if
98 **passage** the fact of 'passing current' or being generally accepted (*OED* 6)
99 **Bond-slaves** Cf. 1.3.139: Othello was once a slave. Brabantio's *pagans* implies (rightly or wrongly) that he was or is a heathen (see pp. 35–6). For slaves as their masters' masters in a topsy-turvy world, the same sarcasm, see Cicero, *Letters to Atticus*, 2.1: 'Are we to be slaves of freedmen and slaves?'

83 cue] *F* (Cue); Qu. *Q* 84 Where] *Q;* Whether *F* 85 To] *F;* And *Q* 87 I] *Q; not in F* 91 bring] *F;* beare *Q*

[1.3] *Enter* DUKE *and* Senators, *set at a table, with lights and Attendants.*

DUKE
There is no composition in these news
That gives them credit.

1 SENATOR Indeed, they are disproportioned.
My letters say a hundred and seven galleys.

DUKE
And mine a hundred forty.

2 SENATOR And mine two hundred.
But though they jump not on a just account –
As in these cases, where the aim reports,
'Tis oft with difference – yet do they all confirm
A Turkish fleet, and bearing up to Cyprus.

world flipped upside down

DUKE
Nay, it is possible enough to judgement:
I do not so secure me in the error
But the main article I do approve
In fearful sense.

Othello = most important.

turks invaded, duke & senators,

SAILOR (*within*) What ho, what ho, what ho!

1.3 Location: a council chamber. For the importance of this scene, see pp. 114–16.

1.3.0.1 DUKE i.e. the Doge (a word not used in *Oth* or *MV*)

1 **composition** consistency
news reports

2 **credit** credibility
disproportioned out of proportion

3–4 Cf. *JC* 4.3.175ff.

5 **jump** agree
just account exact estimate. For the same QF variants, cf. 2.1.288.

6 **aim** guess, conjecture. Before modern methods of communication were invented the movements of foreign armies and navies were reported to the Privy Council (or guessed at) exactly as here: cf. HMC, Hatfield House, Part 12 (1602), 386.

8 **bearing up** proceeding

9 **to judgement** i.e. when you think about it

10 **secure** feel overconfident (because of the discrepancy of the numbers)

11–12 But I believe the chief point (that a Turkish fleet is making for Cyprus) to be true, with frightening implications (for us).

12–17 In F the 'sailor shouts "within" and is then introduced by the officer. In Q "one within" [the sailor?] shouts and the sailor then introduces himself (Ridley). This passage, and others in this scene, may have been rewritten by Shakespeare (*Texts*, 16–18).

1.3] *Scoena Tertia. F; not in Q* 0.1–2] *Q; Enter Duke, Senators, and Officers. F* 1 There is] *Q;* There's *F* these] *Q;* this *F* 4 forty] *F;* and forty *Q* 5 account] *Q;* accompt *F* 6 the aim] *F;* they aym'd *Q* 10 in] *F;* to *Q* 11 article] *F;* Articles *Q* 12] *as F;* In fearefull sense. *Enter a Messenger. / One within.* What ho, . . . *Q*

Enter Sailor.

OFFICER
A messenger from the galleys.

DUKE
Now? what's the business?

SAILOR
The Turkish preparation makes for Rhodes,
So was I bid report here to the state
By Signior Angelo.

DUKE
How say you by this change?

1 SENATOR
This cannot be,
By no assay of reason: 'tis a pageant
To keep us in false gaze. When we consider
Th'importancy of Cyprus to the Turk,
And let ourselves again but understand
That as it more concerns the Turk than Rhodes
So may he with more facile question bear it,
For that it stands not in such warlike brace
But altogether lacks th'abilities
That Rhodes is dressed in. If we make thought of this

15 **preparation** force, or fleet (prepared for action)

17 **By . . . Angelo** The 'governor of Cyprus' (cf. 2.1.0.1n.) would be the appropriate person to report 'to the state': Shakespeare could have confused Angelo and Montano. A deleted half-line, printed in error by F?

18 **by** about

19 **assay** trial, judgement
pageant show; trick (*OED* 1c)

20 **in false gaze** 'looking in the wrong direction, with our attention diverted' (Sanders); 'a specific metaphor from hunting' (Ridley)

21 **importancy** importance; import, significance

22 **again** moreover

24 'carry it (in the military sense of "win it") with less arduous fighting' (Ridley, adding 'but question is not elsewhere used in Shakespeare in that sense'). Perhaps *question* = a subject of debate or strife (*OED* 4), viz. physical 'argument', fighting.

25 **For that** because
brace state of defence (*OED* lc, the only entry); or a coinage from the verb (*OED* brace 4: to brace oneself), i.e. 'bracedness', resoluteness

26 **abilities** power, means

27 **dressed in** prepared with

13 galleys] *F;* Galley *Q* 14] *as F;* Now, the businesse? *Q* 17 By . . . Angelo] *F; not in Q* 18–19 This . . . pageant] *F; Q lines* reason – / Pageant, / 21 Th'] *F;* The *Q* 25–31 For . . . profitless.] *F; not in Q*

We must not think the Turk is so unskilful
To leave that latest which concerns him first,
Neglecting an attempt of ease and gain
To wake and wage a danger profitless.

DUKE

Nay, in all confidence, he's not for Rhodes.

OFFICER

Here is more news.

Enter a Messenger.

MESSENGER

The Ottomites, reverend and gracious,
Steering with due course toward the isle of Rhodes,
Have there injointed with an after fleet –

1 SENATOR

Ay, so I thought; how many, as you guess?

MESSENGER

Of thirty sail; and now they do re-stem
Their backward course, bearing with frank appearance
Their purposes toward Cyprus. Signior Montano,
Your trusty and most valiant servitor,
With his free duty recommends you thus

28 a more respectful view of non-Europeans than Iago's (346, 356, 399ff.)

31 **wage** risk, hazard (*OED* 5)

34 **Ottomites** Turks, Ottomans
reverend and gracious respected and gracious (senators)

35 **due** appropriate

36 **injointed** joined. Why did F insert *them?* Perhaps intending *enjoined them*. 'Injoint' is first recorded by *OED* in *Oth.* Cf. *AC* 1.2.92, 'jointing their force 'gainst Caesar'.
after fleet unexplained. Perhaps 'a following fleet'. In 1570 a Turkish fleet sailed towards Rhodes, then joined another fleet to attack Cyprus, as here: Shakespeare must have known this (see Honigmann, 'Date of *Othello*', 218–19).

38–9 **they . . . course** they navigate back again (*stem* = to keep on a fixed course, of a ship)

39 **frank** unchecked; open

41 **servitor** servant. He is the governor of Cyprus (*Texts*, 37), hence *relieve him* (43).

42 **free duty** willing service (Walker); 'unstinted devotion' (Kittredge)
recommends you reports to you

32 Nay] *F;* And *Q* 33.1 *a* Messenger *F; a* 2. *Messenger Q* 34 Ottomites] *Ottamites QF* 36 injointed] *as Q;* inioynted them *F;* injoin'd *Rowe* 37] *F; not in Q* 38 re-stem] *F;* resterine *Q* 40 toward] *F;* towards *Q*

And prays you to relieve him.

DUKE

'Tis certain then for Cyprus.
Marcus Luccicos, is not he in town?

1 SENATOR

He's now in Florence.

DUKE

Write from us to him; post-post-haste, dispatch.

1 SENATOR

Here comes Brabantio and the valiant Moor.

Enter BRABANTIO, OTHELLO, CASSIO, IAGO, RODERIGO *and Officers.*

DUKE

Valiant Othello, we must straight employ you
Against the general enemy Ottoman.
[*to Brabantio*] I did not see you: welcome, gentle signior,
We lacked your counsel and your help tonight.

BRABANTIO

So did I yours. Good your grace, pardon me,
Neither my place nor aught I heard of business

43 ***relieve** QF *beleeue* is feeble, in such a situation, and *relief* is sent immediately.

45 **Marcus Luccicos** a strange name, probably a misreading (but with the same spelling in Q and F). Some think it alludes to Paulo Marchi Luchese, master of an Italian inn in London: unlikely.
in town *OED* town 4b: in the town (pre-Shakespearian)

47 **post-post-haste** a variant of *haste-post-haste* (1.2.37)
dispatch send (*OED*: 'the word regularly used for the sending of official messengers')

48–9 **Moor . . . Othello** Others mostly speak *of* him as the Moor, *to* him as Othello.

50 Against the general enemy (of all Christians), the Turk. *Ottoman* is oddly placed, if an adjective: perhaps we should read *Ottoman enemy*, or *enemy, Ottoman* (transpose, or insert comma).

51 **gentle** a polite form of address to a gentleman

54 **place** (official) position or rank
aught anything

43 relieve] *Johnson (T. Clark);* beleeue *QF*   45 Luccicos] *QF; Lucchese / Capell* he] *F;* here *Q*   47] *as Q; F lines* vs, / dispatch. / to] *F;* wish *Q*   48.1–2] *as F; Enter* Brabantio, Othello, Roderigo, Iago, Cassio, Desdemona, *and Officers. Q (after 47)*   51 SD] *Theobald; not in QF*   52 lacked] *F;* lacke *Q*

Hath raised me from my bed, nor doth
care
Take hold on me, for my particular grief
Is of so flood-gate and o'erbearing nature
That it engluts and swallows other sorrows
And it is still itself.

DUKE
Why? What's the matter?

BRABANTIO
My daughter, O my daughter!

1 SENATOR
Dead?

BRABANTIO
Ay, to me:
She is abused, stolen from me and corrupted
By spells and medicines bought of mountebanks,
For nature so preposterously to err
Being not deficient, blind, or lame of sense,
Sans witchcraft could not.

DUKE
Whoe'er he be, that in this foul proceeding
Hath thus beguiled your daughter of herself,
And you of her, the bloody book of law
You shall yourself read, in the bitter letter,
After your own sense, yea, though our proper son

55 **from my bed** an afterthought, hence extra-metrical?
care anxiety, concern
56 **particular** private
57 **flood-gate** (sluice-gate; hence, of the water held back) torrential
58 Dent, G446, 'The greater grief drives out the less.'
engluts devours
59 **And . . . itself** i.e. it is unaffected by other sorrows
61 **abused** wronged; cheated, deceived. Notice how Brabantio surrenders to a fixed idea, as Othello does later.
62 **mountebanks** quacks, charlatans. Sidney referred scornfully to 'the mountebanks at Venice' (*Apology*, ed. G. Shepherd [1965], 131); cf. Jonson, *Volpone*, 2.2.4ff.
63–5 Confusing, because of a change of construction: 64 and 65 need *err*, not *to err*, in 63. 'For, without witchcraft, nature – as long as it is not deficient, blind or defective in sense – could not err so preposterously.'
67 i.e. made her act so unlike herself
68–70 **the . . . sense** 'you shall yourself pronounce the sentence (from) the death-decreeing book of law, (taking it) in its (most) severe interpretation, according to your own judgement'. Witchcraft (65) was a capital crime (Sanders).
70 **our proper** i.e. my own

56 hold on] *F;* any hold of *Q* grief] *F;* griefes *Q* 59 Why?] *F;* Why, *Q* 60 SP 1 SENATOR] *Sen. F; All. Q* 64] *F; not in Q* 65 Sans] *F;* Since *Qu* (Saunce *Qc)* 70 your] *F;* its *Q* yea] *F; not in Q*

ood in your action.

ABANTIO Humbly I thank your grace.

Here is the man, this Moor, whom now it seems
Your special mandate for the state affairs
Hath hither brought.

ALL We are very sorry for't.

DUKE [*to Othello*]

What in your own part can you say to this?

BRABANTIO

Nothing, but this is so.

OTHELLO

Most potent, grave, and reverend signiors,
My very noble and approved good masters:
That I have ta'en away this old man's daughter
It is most true; true, I have married her.
The very head and front of my offending
Hath this extent, no more. Rude am I in my speech
And little blest with the soft phrase of peace,
For since these arms of mine had seven years' pith
Till now some nine moons wasted, they have used
Their dearest action in the tented field,
And little of this great world can I speak
More than pertains to feats of broil and battle,

71 **Stood . . . action** were (the other) party in your legal action (*OED* stand 95)

74 SP ALL Probably one senator speaks, others indicate agreement (see Honigmann, 'Stage direction').

75 **in** i.e. on

76 **but** except

78 **approved** proved (by experience); esteemed

79 **this old man's** A tactless way of speaking of his new father-in-law, perhaps triggered by 72, 'Here is the man'.

81 **head and front** (*OED* head 41, first here) height, highest extent

82 **Rude** Lat. *rudis*, rough, unskilled

83 **soft** pleasing; gentle; quiet
phrase style of expression, language

84 **pith** strength. He has helped in battles from the age of 7 (cf. 133, 'from my boyish days'), like the Boy in *H5*.

85 **wasted** gone; with a hint of squandered, as he devotes his life to war (Adamson, 62)

86 **dearest** worthiest
tented Cf. 1.2.26n.

87 **this great world** Perhaps he bows to the senators. Venice was an independent state and cultural centre in 1600.

88 **broil** confused disturbance, tumult, turmoil

75 SD] *Theobald; not in QF* 82 extent, no more.] extent no more. *Q;* extent; no more. *F* 83 soft] *F;* set *Q* 88 feats of broil] feate of broyle *Q;* Feats of Broiles *F*

And therefore little shall I grace my cause
In speaking for myself. Yet, by your gracious patience,
I will a round unvarnished tale deliver
Of my whole course of love, what drugs, what
  charms,
What conjuration and what mighty magic –
For such proceeding I am charged withal –
I won his daughter.

BRABANTIO A maiden never bold,
Of spirit so still and quiet that her motion
Blushed at herself; and she, in spite of nature,
Of years, of country, credit, everything,
To fall in love with what she feared to look on?
It is a judgement maimed and most imperfect
That will confess perfection so could err
Against all rules of nature, and must be driven
To find out practices of cunning hell
Why this should be. I therefore vouch again
That with some mixtures powerful o'er the blood
Or with some dram conjured to this effect
He wrought upon her.

DUKE To vouch this is no proof,

91 **round** honest, plain
unvarnished unpolished (unique in Shakespeare)

92–5 Note the change of construction: *either* 'with what drugs . . . I won', *or* 'what drugs . . . won'. Perhaps *with* was dropped because of *withal* (= with), 94.

95 **never bold** How well does he know his daughter?

96 **motion** (any) inward impulse or desire (*OED* 9)

97 **in . . . nature** i.e. in spite of *differences of* nature

98 **credit** reputation

100 **maimed** F *main'd* is a variant spelling.

101 **err** go astray

102 **and . . . driven** i.e. and *sound judgement* must be driven

103 **practices** intrigues, treacheries

104 **vouch** affirm

105 **blood** (the supposed seat of) passion; sexual appetite (*OED* 5, 6)

106 **dram** a small draught of medicine
conjured (accent on second syllable) made by magic

107 **wrought upon** worked on, influenced (*OED* work 30)
To . . . proof Dent, S1019, 'Suspicion (Accusation) is no proof.'

91 unvarnished] *as Q;* vn-varnish'd u *F* 92] *as Q; F lines* Loue. / Charmes, / 94 proceeding] *F;* proceedings *Q* I am] *F;* am I *Q* 95–6 bold . . . so] *F subst.;* bold of spirit, / So *Q* 99 on?] *Q;* on; *F* 100 maimed] *Q;* main'd *F* 101 could] *F;* would *Q* 107 SP] *Q; not in F* vouch] *F;* youth *Q*

Without more certain and more overt test
Than these thin habits and poor likelihoods
Of modern seeming do prefer against him.

1 SENATOR

But, Othello, speak:
Did you by indirect and forced courses
Subdue and poison this young maid's affections?
Or came it by request and such fair question
As soul to soul affordeth?

OTHELLO

I do beseech you,
Send for the lady to the Sagittary,
And let her speak of me before her father.
If you do find me foul in her report
The trust, the office I do hold of you
Not only take away, but let your sentence
Even fall upon my life.

DUKE

Fetch Desdemona hither.

OTHELLO

Ancient, conduct them, you best know the place.
And till she come, as truly as to heaven

Exeunt [Iago and] two or three.

108 **overt** manifest. An overt act (in law) was 'an outward act, such as can be clearly proved to have been done, from which criminal intent is inferred' (*OED* 2b).
test proof; trial; witness; evidence (*OED sb.* 1, 3)
109 **thin** implausible
habits (clothes; appearances, hence) suggestions
poor likelihoods weak probabilities
110 **modern seeming** commonplace appearance. Is this an appeal against racial prejudice?
prefer bring
112 **indirect** devious
forced forcèd: constraining
113 **poison** pervert morally (*OED* 3)
114 **question** talk; questioning. 'Or did it come about by (your or her) request and such blameless talk as one soul can grant another?' Hinting that (1) Desdemona took the initiative, (2) it was a 'soul to soul' relationship.
116 **Sagittary** Cf. 1.1.156n.
117 **before** in the presence of
118 **foul** wicked; guilty
119 **office** position (as general)
122 **Desdemona** He knows her name without being told. The leading Venetians are a closed circle; Othello is very much an outsider.

108 certain . . . overt] *Q* (ouert); wider . . . ouer *F* 109 Than these] *F;* These are *Q* 110 seeming do] *F;* seemings, you *Q* 111 SP] *Q; Sen. F* 116 Sagittary] Sagittar *Q;* Sagitary *F* 119] *F; not in Q* 123] *as Q; F lines* them: / place. / Ancient] *Q;* Auncient *F* 124 till] *Q;* tell *F* truly] *F;* faithfull *Q* SD] *Exit two or three. Q; not in F*

I do confess the vices of my blood
So justly to your grave ears I'll present
How I did thrive in this fair lady's love
And she in mine.

DUKE
Say it, Othello.

OTHELLO
Her father loved me, oft invited me,
Still questioned me the story of my life
From year to year – the battles, sieges, fortunes
That I have passed.
I ran it through, even from my boyish days
To th' very moment that he bade me tell it,
Wherein I spake of most disastrous chances,
Of moving accidents by flood and field,
Of hair-breadth scapes i'th' imminent deadly
breach,
Of being taken by the insolent foe
And sold to slavery; of my redemption thence

125 **vices** depravities; or, faults ('without implication of serious wrong-doing': *OED* 4)
blood Cf. 105n.
126 **justly** faithfully
present (legal) lay before a court
128 **And . . . mine** perhaps read 'And she *did thrive* in mine' (Proudfoot, private note)
Say it an unusual turn of phrase, not quite the same as 'Speak'. Also, a short line: something missing (see previous note)?
129 **Her . . . [1]me** Did Othello or Brabantio deceive himself? How does Brabantio react to this line?
oft i.e. the lovers took their time (cf. 85, *nine moons*)
130 **Still** constantly
131 **From . . . year** This half-line adds nothing essential; perhaps cancelled, and printed in error (*Texts*, 36–7)?
132 **passed** gone through; escaped
135 **spake** for *o:a* misreading, see *Texts*, 83.
disastrous ill-starred, unlucky (*OED* 1)
chances 'Chance' seems to have been against Othello from an early age, so he thinks: cf. 5.2.339, 'these unlucky deeds'.
136 **moving** changeful; affecting (the feelings)
accidents occurrences
flood and field by water and by land; or, by sea (fight) and on the (battle) field
137 **scapes** escapes
imminent hanging over one's head, ready to fall
breach a gap in a fortification made by battery
138 **insolent** overbearing; insulting; exulting

125] *F; not in Q* 131 battles] *Q;* Battaile *F* fortunes] *Q;* Fortune *F* 134 To th'] Toth' *QF* 135 spake] *Q;* spoke *F* 136 accidents by] *F;* accident of *Q* 139 of] *F;* and *Q*

And portance in my travailous history; 140
Wherein of antres vast and deserts idle,
Rough quarries, rocks and hills whose heads touch
 heaven
It was my hint to speak – such was my process –
And of the cannibals that each other eat,
The Anthropophagi, and men whose heads 145
Do grow beneath their shoulders. This to hear
Would Desdemona seriously incline,
But still the house affairs would draw her thence,
Which ever as she could with haste dispatch
She'd come again, and with a greedy ear 150

[marginal annotation: fantastical]

140 **portance** bearing, behaviour. Cf. *Cor*
2.3.224.
 ***travailous** toilsome, wearisome. Q
trauells perhaps resulted from the phonetic
spelling of *-ous* as *-es* or *-s*, as in *Ham*
2.1.3, 'meruiles [F 'maruels'] wisely' (Q2);
TC 1.2.136, 'a maruel's white hand' (QF).
141 **antres** caves (Lat. *antrum*); *OED* first
records here.
 vast . . . idle Both words could mean empty
(Lat. *vastus*).
 deserts As Venice did not possess (or wage
war in) deserts he refers to a time before he
entered the service of Venice.
142 **quarries** perhaps = large masses of stone
or rock (*OED* 2); or in the modern
sense, places where men (?slaves) hew
rocks
143 **hint** occasion, opportunity. Could be *hent*
in the seventeenth century (so Q).
 process proceeding (cf. 94); drift; story
145 **Anthropophagi** 'man-eaters', cannibals.
With Q's *-ie* ending, cf. '*Andronicie*' (*Tit*
2.3.189).
145–6 **men . . . shoulders** See p. 17; cf. *Tem*
3.3.44ff., 'Who would believe . . .

that there were such men / Whose heads
stood in their breasts?', *Patient Grissill*,
5.1.25 (Dekker, 1.278). The F reading is
possible if there is a heavy pause after
'Grew—' (Shakespeare's revision?).
146 **This to hear** *Either* hearing this would
make Desdemona incline earnestly, *or* in
order to hear this Desdemona would
incline (towards me) earnestly. Incline =
physical or mental inclination (bend
towards, or bend mind or heart towards).
For the QF variants, see *Texts*, 35–6.
148 Desdemona seems to be a mother-less girl,
in charge of household affairs, partly
because her mother is not mentioned
(except as a memory, 4.3.24).
149 **Which** A Latin construction: '(And) ever
as she could dispatch them (which), she'd
come again'.
150 **greedy ear** Cf. *Faerie Queene*, 6.9.26,
'Whylest thus he talkt, the knight with
greedy eare / Hong still upon his melting
mouth attent' (Malone). But *greedy . . .
Devour* has stronger implications (cf. *MA*
3.1.28, 'greedily devour the treacherous
bait').

140 portance in] *F;* with it all *Q* travailous] *(R. Proudfoot (N&Q, NS 21 [1974], 130–1));* trauells *Q;*
Trauellours *F* 141 antres] Antrees *Q;* Antars *F* 142 and hills] *Q;* Hills *F* heads] *Q;* head *F* 143 hint]
F; hent *Q* ²my] *F;* the *Q* 144 other] *Q;* others *F* 145 Anthropophagi] *Anthropophagie Q;*
Antropophague F 146 Do grow] *Q;* Grew *F* This] *Q;* These things *F* 148 thence] *Q;* hence *F* 149
Which] *F;* And *Q* 150 She'd] *as Q;* She'l'd *F*

Devour up my discourse; which I, observing,
Took once a pliant hour and found good means
To draw from her a prayer of earnest heart
That I would all my pilgrimage dilate,
Whereof by parcels she had something heard
But not intentively. I did consent,
And often did beguile her of her tears
When I did speak of some distressful stroke
That my youth suffered. My story being done
She gave me for my pains a world of sighs,
She swore in faith 'twas strange, 'twas passing strange,
'Twas pitiful, 'twas wondrous pitiful;
She wished she had not heard it, yet she wished
That heaven had made her such a man. She thanked me
And bade me, if I had a friend that loved her,
I should but teach him how to tell my story
And that would woo her. Upon this hint I spake:
She loved me for the dangers I had passed
And I loved her that she did pity them.

151–4 **which . . . dilate** i.e. Othello took the very first step

152 **pliant** suitable (*OED* 2c); or, an hour when she was easily influenced (transferred epithet)

153 **earnest** intense, ardent

154 **pilgrimage** i.e. life's journey, implying that his was a dedicated life
dilate relate

155 **by parcels** in bits and pieces (parcel = part). Cf. *2H4* 4.2.36, 'the parcels and particulars of our grief.

156 **intentively** attentively, with steady application

157 **often** implying that the story was told more than once or over a period of time
beguile A smiling allusion to 'practices of cunning hell' (103)?

158 **distressful** 'A literary and chiefly poetical word' (*OED*). Of how many other words in Othello's longer speeches could the same be said?
stroke blow; calamitous event (*OED* 3b, first entry 1700)

161 **swore** affirmed emphatically
passing very, surpassingly

164 **made her** Romance heroines sometimes wish they were men (*MA* 4.1.317), but this could also mean 'made such a man *for her*'.

166 **but** only

167 **hint** occasion, opportunity; a suggestion conveyed indirectly (first here)

168–9 How well does he understand her love, or his own?

169 **that** because

155 parcels] *F;* parcell *Q* 156 intentively] *Q;* instinctiuely *F* 158 distressful] *F;* distressed *Q* 160 sighs] *Q;* kisses *F* 161 in faith] *F;* Ifaith *Q* 167 hint] *F;* heate *Q*

This only is the witchcraft I have used:

Enter DESDEMONA, IAGO, *Attendants.*

Here comes the lady, let her witness it.

DUKE
I think this tale would win my daughter too.
Good Brabantio, take up this mangled matter at the
best:
Men do their broken weapons rather use
Than their bare hands.

BRABANTIO I pray you, hear her speak.
If she confess that she was half the wooer,
Destruction on my head if my bad blame
Light on the man. Come hither, gentle mistress:
Do you perceive, in all this noble company,
Where most you owe obedience?

DESDEMONA My noble father,
I do perceive here a divided duty.
To you I am bound for life and education:
My life and education both do learn me
How to respect you; you are the lord of duty,

170 Shakespeare probably recalled Pliny's account of a former bondslave, C. Furius Cresinus, who, accused of acquiring wealth by 'indirect means, as if he had used sorcery', pointed to his plough and farm implements and said 'Behold, these are the sorceries . . . and all the enchantments that I use' (E. H. W. Meyerstein, quoted Bullough, 211).
only alone

171 **lady** For her age, see p. 96.
witness furnish evidence concerning, bear witness to

173 **Good Brabantio** extra-metrical
mangled mutilated; i.e. 'accept this less than perfect business in the best possible way'. Cf. Dent, B326, 'Make the best of a bad bargain'.

177 **bad** incorrect, mistaken (*OED* 2, first entry 1688)

178 **Light on** fall or descend on
gentle mistress This is not how a father normally addressed his daughter.

179 **noble** perhaps an error, anticipating *noble*, 180 (Walker)

182 **bound** tied, united; obliged; subjected
education upbringing

183 **learn** teach

184 **lord** master. She distinguishes two kinds of *lord* (cf. 189) and duty: 'you are the master of my duty hitherto, but now I owe a wife's duty to the Moor, my new lord'. Cf. *KL* 1.1.91ff.

170.1 *Attendants*] *F; and the rest. Q; SD follows 171 QF* 177 on my head] *F;* lite on me *Q* 184 the lord of] *F;* Lord of all my *Q*

I am hitherto your daughter. But here's my husband:
And so much duty as my mother showed
To you, preferring you before her father,
So much I challenge that I may profess
Due to the Moor my lord.

BRABANTIO

God be with you, I have done.
Please it your grace, on to the state affairs;
I had rather to adopt a child than get it.
Come hither, Moor:
I here do give thee that with all my heart
Which, but thou hast already, with all my heart
I would keep from thee. For your sake, jewel,
I am glad at soul I have no other child,
For thy escape would teach me tyranny
To hang clogs on them. I have done, my lord.

DUKE

Let me speak like yourself, and lay a sentence
Which as a grise or step may help these lovers
Into your favour.

185 **hitherto** implying that her new identity as wife now supersedes the previous one as daughter
187 **preferring** placing; loving (you more than)
188 **challenge** claim (as a right). In effect she also challenges her father (and later Othello: 3.3.60ff.).
189 **the Moor** Cf. 48–9n., 249, 253. **my lord** the male head of a household, as in the Bible (e.g. Matthew 24.45)
190 probably four syllables originally, 'God bye (= God be with you), I've done', making a complete verse line with 189
191 **Please it** may it please
192 **get** beget
194 i.e. in the circumstances he is glad to be rid of her
195 **but thou hast** except that thou hast it
196 **For your sake** because of you
198 **escape** elopement; outrageous transgression (*OED* 7)
199 **clogs** blocks of wood, etc., attached to the neck or legs of man or beast to prevent escape
200–2 Could be prose.
200 **like yourself** i.e. by giving advice; or, as ideally you would speak
lay expound
sentence opinion; decision (of a court); pithy saying or maxim. He adopts the conventional wisdom that 'What cannot be eschew'd must be embrac'd' (*MW* 5.5.237).
201 **grise** stairway; step

190] *F;* God bu'y, I ha done *Q* 195] *F; not in Q* 199 them] *F;* em *Q* 200] *as Q; F lines* selfe: / Sentence, / 202 Into your favour] *Q; not in F*

When remedies are past the griefs are ended
By seeing the worst which late on hopes depended.
To mourn a mischief that is past and gone
Is the next way to draw new mischief on.
What cannot be preserved when fortune takes,
Patience her injury a mockery makes.
The robbed that smiles steals something from the
 thief,
He robs himself that spends a bootless grief.

BRABANTIO

So let the Turk of Cyprus us beguile,
We lose it not so long as we can smile;
He bears the sentence well that nothing bears
But the free comfort which from thence he hears.
But he bears both the sentence and the sorrow
That, to pay grief, must of poor patience borrow.
These sentences to sugar or to gall,
Being strong on both sides, are equivocal.
But words are words: I never yet did hear
That the bruised heart was pierced through the ear.

203 Cf. Dent, R71.1, 'Where there is no remedy it is folly to chide'; i.e. 'when it is too late for remedies'.
griefs suffering; sorrows

204 i.e. because we have seen the worst happen, which formerly was subject to hopes (that it would not happen); or, *hope* = expectation 'of ill as well as of good, and so is sometimes practically equivalent to "fear" ' (Kittredge)

205 **mischief** evil; misfortune; injury

206 **next** nearest

207–8 When fortune takes away what cannot be saved, (your) patience makes a mockery of (= mocks, defeats) fortune's wrongful action.

210 **spends** expends; wastes
bootless pointless

213–14 He bears your *sentence* (200) well who suffers only the free (?cheap) consolation which he hears (and not the grief that occasioned it). *Bears the sentence* 'plays on the meaning, "receives judicial sentence" ' (Bevington).

216 **pay** pacify

217 **gall** (bile, hence) bitterness

218 **equivocal** equally appropriate

219 **words are words** Dent, W832, 'Words are but words'.

220 **bruised** crushed, battered (a stronger word than today)
pierced piercèd: 'That the crushed heart was relieved by mere words that reach it through the ear.' *Through* could be disyllabic (*thorough*) but probably isn't here. F has two errors, *eares* (the rhyme supports Q *eare*), and *pierc'd*. Kittredge preferred 'piecèd' (= mended, cured).

206 new] *F;* more *Q* 211 So let] *QF;* So, let *Theobald* 220 pierced] *Q;* pierc'd *F;* pieced *Warburton* ear] *Q;* eares *F*

I humbly beseech you, proceed to th'affairs of state.

DUKE The Turk with a most mighty preparation makes for Cyprus. Othello, the fortitude of the place is best known to you, and, though we have there a substitute of most allowed sufficiency, yet opinion, a sovereign mistress of effects, throws a more safer voice on you. You must therefore be content to slubber the gloss of your new fortunes with this more stubborn and boisterous expedition.

OTHELLO

The tyrant custom, most grave senators,
Hath made the flinty and steel couch of war
My thrice-driven bed of down. I do agnize
A natural and prompt alacrity
I find in hardness, and do undertake

222–9 The switch to prose is all the more jolting after two speeches of rhymed couplets. We move from private to public business, and this makes Othello's verse rhythms (230ff.) sound self-indulgent.

222 **preparation** Cf. 15n.

223 **fortitude** physical or structural strength; ?fortification

224 **substitute** deputy. This seems to refer to Montano, the 'governor of Cyprus': see *Texts*, 37.

225 **allowed** praised. The sense 'acknowledged' is not recorded before 1749 (*OED* 3).
sufficiency ability; qualification
opinion Lat. *opinio* (feminine, hence *mistress*, 226). 'General opinion, which finally determines what ought to be done, will feel safer with you in command' (Ridley).

226 **effects** purposes; results
voice preference; vote

227 **slubber** obscure; smear, sully
gloss lustre; fair semblance

228 **stubborn** difficult; rough ('more' so than the 'gloss of . . . new fortunes')

229 **boisterous** (painfully) rough, violent
expedition military enterprise; haste (cf. 277)

230 **custom** Dent, C933, 'Custom makes all things easy'. Cf. Henry Howard in *A Defensative* (1583), 'That irregular and wilfull tyraunt Custome' (Kittredge); *Ham* 3.4.161, 'that monster custom'.

231 **flinty and steel** He refers to sleeping on the ground in armour (Sanders).

232 **thrice-driven** 'softest possible; a current of air drifted the finer and lighter feathers away from the coarser and heavier' (Ridley)
agnize acknowledge. 'I acknowledge (that) I find a natural and ready eagerness (in myself) in (situations of) hardship.'

233 **natural** inherent, innate
alacrity cheerful readiness

234 **hardness** difficulty; (sleeping on) the hard ground
undertake take in charge

221] *as F;* Beseech you now, to the affaires of the state. *Q* 222 a most] *F;* most *Q* 225 a] *Q;* a more *F* 230 grave] *F;* great *Q* 231 couch] *Pope;* Cooch *Q;* Coach *F* 233 alacrity] *Q;* Alacartie *F* 234 do] *F;* would *Q*

This present war against the Ottomites.
Most humbly therefore, bending to your state,
I crave fit disposition for my wife,
Due reverence of place, and exhibition,
With such accommodation and besort
As levels with her breeding.

DUKE
Why, at her father's.

BRABANTIO I'll not have it so.

OTHELLO
Nor I.

DESDEMONA Nor would I there reside
To put my father in impatient thoughts
By being in his eye. Most gracious duke,
To my unfolding lend your prosperous ear
And let me find a charter in your voice
T'assist my simpleness.

DUKE
What would you, Desdemona?

DESDEMONA
That I did love the Moor to live with him

235 ***war** For the QF plural, 'common errors' and final *-s* errors, see *Texts*, 85, 89, 90.
236 **bending . . . state** submitting to your high office. He may bow respectfully as he speaks.
237 **crave** request
disposition arrangements
238 proper respect for her place (as my wife) and maintenance
239 **accommodation** room and suitable provision (*OED* 7, first here); supply of necessities
besort suitable company (*OED*, first here). A coinage: cf. the verb, *KL* 1.4.251, 'Such men as may besort your age' (first here).
240 **levels with** equals, is on a par with
breeding upbringing
242 Removing Q's first *I*, F softens Desdemona's refusal (*Texts*, 16–18).
244 **eye** sight. So *Ham* 4.4.6, 'We shall express our duty in his eye.'
245 **unfolding** what I shall unfold (say)
prosperous favourable
246 **charter** privilege; pardon
voice expressed judgement (*OED* 3)

235 war] *Q2;* warres *QF* Ottomites] *Ottamites QF* 238 reverence] *Q;* reference *F* 239 With] *F;* Which *Q* accommodation] *Q (*accomodation?*)* 241 Why, . . . father's.] Why at her Fathers? *F;* If you please, bee't at her fathers. *Q* I'll] *as Q;* I will *F* 242 Nor would I] *F;* Nor I, I would not *Q* 245 your prosperous] *F;* a gracious *Q* 247 T'assist] *F;* And if *Q* simpleness.] *F;* simplenesse. – *Q* 248 you, Desdemona?] *F;* you – speake. *Q* 249 did] *Q; not in F*

My downright violence and scorn of fortunes
May trumpet to the world. My heart's subdued
Even to the very quality of my lord:
I saw Othello's visage in his mind,
And to his honours and his valiant parts
Did I my soul and fortunes consecrate,
So that, dear lords, if I be left behind,
A moth of peace, and he go to the war,
The rites for which I love him are bereft me,
And I a heavy interim shall support
By his dear absence. Let me go with him.

250 **downright** positive, absolute
violence i.e. violent rupture with conventional behaviour
scorn Both *scorn* and *storm* of fortune were commonplaces (cf. Q and F): thus Heywood, *Edward the Fourth* (1600), 'stormes of fortune' (Part 1, B3b), 'ouerthrowne, / By fortunes scorne' (Part 2, 16a). Also *TC* 1.3.47, 'storms of fortune' (classical in origin: Seneca, *Agamemnon*, 594: *procella Fortunae*). Both are possible here; each could be misread as the other.

250 **fortunes** So QF: a misreading of *fortune?*

251 **trumpet** proclaim (*OED*, here first with this sense)

252 **quality** profession (Malone); nature, moral and mental identity (Cowden-Clarke, quoted Furness). The thought is as in *Son* 111, 'My nature is subdued / To what it works in, like the dyer's hand': her inmost being (*OED* heart 6) has been assimilated to Othello's nature (and military profession). Q *vtmost pleasure* looks like a first thought, changed because it might suggest sexual pleasure.

253 'I saw (the colour of) Othello's face in (the quality of) his mind', i.e. his face was transformed, in her eyes, by his mind. She does not refer to his colour directly but seems to be half apologizing for it.

254 **parts** personal qualities or attributes (*OED* 12), as in *MA* 5.2.60–1, 'For which of my bad parts didst thou first fal in loue with me?' (Q).

256 **dear** worthy, honoured

257 **moth** *either* drone, idler; *or* alluding to the moth's attraction to light: if he goes away to war, she, deprived of his *honours* and *valiant parts*, will be like a moth in the dark. Cf. *Cor* 1.3.82ff., 'You would be another Penelope: yet they say, all the yarn she spun in Ulysses' absence did but fill [Ithaca] full of moths.'

258 **rites** *Right* and *rite* were interchangeable spellings. Probably both are intended here: *right* = enjoyment of privileges, 'sharing his life and dangers' (Walker); *rite* as in *rites of love*, a cliché (cf. *R3* 5.3.101, *AW* 2.4.41).
bereft ('with double object: to bereave *any one a possession*', *OED* 1c), i.e. the rights-rites are taken from me. So *2H6* 3.1.84–5, 'all your interest in those territories / Is utterly bereft you'.

259 **heavy** distressful
support endure (with quibble on propping up something heavy)

260 **dear** grievous (cf. *Son* 37, 'Fortune's dearest spite')

250 scorn] *Q;* storme *F, Q2* 252 very quality] *F;* vtmost pleasure *Q* 258 which] *Q;* why *F*

OTHELLO

Let her have your voice.
Vouch with me, heaven, I therefore beg it not
To please the palate of my appetite,
Nor to comply with heat, the young affects
In me defunct, and proper satisfaction,
But to be free and bounteous to her mind.
And heaven defend your good souls that you think
I will your serious and great business scant
When she is with me. No, when light-winged toys
Of feathered Cupid seel with wanton dullness
My speculative and officed instrument,
That my disports corrupt and taint my business,

261 **voice** support, approval
262 **Vouch** bear witness (*OED* 5b, first here)
263 **palate** taste; liking
appetite (sexual) desire
264 **comply with** act in accordance with; satisfy
heat passion; sexual excitement in animals, esp. females
affects appetites, lusts
265 **defunct** extinct, dead (Hulme, 153–4)
***proper** in conformity with rule (*OED* 4, 10), permissible; correct. 'Nor to satisfy sexual passion – the youthful appetites that are extinct in me – and permissible gratification of desire.' Many editors feel that the passage is corrupt. For the misreading of final *-e*/*-y* (as apparently in *me*/*my* here), see *Texts*, 85.
266 **free** generous, liberal
her mind Cf. *his mind*, 253. They both almost repudiate the body: how well do they know themselves?
267 **defend** forbid
268 **scant** stint, neglect
269 **light-winged** (?)insubstantial, trifling (a coinage)
toys amorous sport, dallying; light caresses; trumpery, rubbish (*OED* 1, 2, 5)
270 **feathered** referring to Cupid's wings or arrows
seel close (the eyes), alluding to blind Cupid. In falconry, young hawks were trained by having their eyes seeled (hooded).
wanton dullness drowsiness, resulting from amorous dalliance
271 'my organ of sight, which has this particular function (i.e. to see clearly)'. *Speculative* (of faculties), exercised in vision; *officed*, having a particular office or function; *instrument*, a part of the body with a special function, an organ. Q's *foyles* = overthrows; *active instruments* = hands and feet (Malone).
272 **disports** (sexual) sports
taint injure
business diligence; care; official duties (*OED* 1, 6, 12)

261–2 Let . . . heaven] *F;* Your voyces Lords: beseech you let her will, / Haue a free way *Q* 265 me] *Capell (Upton);* my *QF* defunct] *QF;* distinct *Theobald* 266 [2]to] *F;* of *Q* 268 great] *F;* good *Q* 269 When] *F;* For *Q* 270 Of] *F;* And *Q* seel] *F;* foyles *Q* 271 officed instrument] *F;* actiue instruments *Q*

Let housewives make a skillet of my helm
And all indign and base adversities
Make head against my estimation.

DUKE
Be it as you shall privately determine,
Either for her stay or going: th'affair cries haste
And speed must answer it.

1 SENATOR You must away tonight.

DESDEMONA
Tonight, my lord?

DUKE This night.

OTHELLO With all my heart.

DUKE
At nine i'th' morning here we'll meet again.
Othello, leave some officer behind
And he shall our commission bring to you,
And such things else of quality and respect
As doth import you.

OTHELLO So please your grace, my ancient:
A man he is of honesty and trust.

273 **housewives** Perhaps 'hussies'?
skillet cooking pot, a metal container similar in shape to a helmet but lacking its dignity (Elliott, 15)
helm helmet
274 **indign** shameful (unique in Shakespeare)
275 **Make head** advance, rise up
estimation the way I am valued; reputation. Five syllables.
277 **cries** calls for (*OED* 7: first here)
278 **answer it** i.e. be answerable (corresponding) to it; with quibble on *cries* and *answer*
tonight viz. their wedding night
279 **With . . . heart** 'Othello gazes longingly, even despairingly, at his new wife . . . then says with a sigh . . . "With all my heart" ' (Mack, 141). Or he pretends, covering up his disappointment, or to persuade Desdemona.
280 **we'll meet** The Duke and senators will meet; Othello will have sailed. Note that Iago leaves later but arrives in Cyprus before Othello: hence 2.1.67ff.
283–4 'and such other things as concern your rank and the respect due to you'; import = relate to
285 **honesty** could = honour; integrity; good reputation

273 housewives] *F;* huswiues *Q* skillet] *F;* skellet *Q* 275 estimation] *F;* reputation *Q* 277 her] *F; not in Q* th'affair cries] *F;* the affaires cry *Q* 278–9] And speede must answer, you must hence to night, / *Desd.* To night my Lord? / *Du.* This night. / *Q;* And speed must answer it. / *Sen.* You must away to night. / *F* 280 nine] *F;* ten *Q* i'th'] *F;* i'the *Q* 283 And] *F;* With *Q* and] *F;* or *Q* 284 import] *F;* concerne *Q* So please] *F;* Please *Q*

To his conveyance I assign my wife,
With what else needful your good grace shall think
To be sent after me.

DUKE Let it be so.
Good-night to everyone. And, noble signior,
If virtue no delighted beauty lack 290
Your son-in-law is far more fair than black.

1 SENATOR
Adieu, brave Moor, use Desdemona well.

foreshadowing

BRABANTIO
Look to her, Moor, if thou hast eyes to see:
She has deceived her father, and may thee.
 Exeunt [Duke, Brabantio, Senators, Officers].

Time

OTHELLO

Double time.

we see

3 days

But

it's rlly

1 week.

My life upon her faith. Honest Iago, 295
My Desdemona must I leave to thee:
I prithee, let thy wife attend on her
And bring them after in the best advantage.
Come, Desdemona, I have but an hour
Of love, of worldly matter and direction 300
To spend with thee. We must obey the time.
 Exeunt Othello and Desdemona.

286 **conveyance** escort(ing)
287 'with whatever else your good grace shall
 think needful'
290 **delighted** delightful
291 **fair** fair-skinned; free from moral stain
 (*OED* 9), after *virtue*, 290
294 Cf. Dent, D180, 'He that once deceives is
 ever suspected.'
 SD As Brabantio turns to leave,
 Desdemona 'is often directed to kneel to
 him for a blessing, and his rejection is
 another shock to her' (Rosenberg, 213).
295 **My . . . faith** '(I would wager) my life on
 her good faith.'
 Honest 'a vague epithet of appreciation or
 praise, esp. as used in a patronizing way to

an inferior' (*OED* 1c); cf. 'good Iago'
(2.1.97).
297 He does not ask Desdemona whether this
 arrangement suits her. As she has just
 eloped, this will be the first time Emilia
 attends on her.
298 **in . . . advantage** as opportunity best
 serves (Ridley)
300 **love** (?)loving talk; not 'love-making' (cf.
 2.3.9)
 direction instruction. He is in charge.
301 **obey the time** i.e. 'we must comply with
 the needs of this emergency'. In effect
 she must obey. Cf. Dent, T340.2, 'To obey
 the time' (probably Shakespeare's
 coinage).

293 if . . . see] *F*; haue a quicke eye to see *Q* 294 and may] *F*; may doe *Q* SD *Exeunt*] *Q*; *Exit F* 298
them] *F*; her *Q* 300 worldly] *Q*; wordly *F* matter] *F*; matters *Q* 301 the] *Q*; the the *F* SD] *Exit
Moore and* Desdemona. *Q*; *Exit. F*

RODERIGO Iago!

IAGO What sayst thou, noble heart?

RODERIGO What will I do, think'st thou?

IAGO Why, go to bed and sleep.

RODERIGO I will incontinently drown myself.

IAGO If thou dost, I shall never love thee after. Why, thou silly gentleman?

RODERIGO It is silliness to live when to live is torment; and then have we a prescription to die, when death is our physician.

IAGO O villainous! I have looked upon the world for four times seven years, and since I could distinguish betwixt a benefit and an injury I never found a man that knew how to love himself. Ere I would say I would drown myself for the love of a guinea-hen I would change my humanity with a baboon.

303 **thou** Iago's ascendancy has grown since 1.1, where he addressed Roderigo as *you* and *sir*; *noble heart* (drawled?) is close to insolence.

304 **What . . . do** Cf. Terence, *Phormio*, 540, '*Geta.* Quid faciam? *Antiph.* Invenias argentum' (*G.* What am I to do? *A.* You must raise the money), and 'Put money in thy purse', 340.

306 **incontinently** immediately; with unconscious quibble on sexual incontinence, since he cannot control his 'love'

drown myself clearly not a heroic death. Cf. the Clown in *Mucedorus* (1598), B2a, 'I wil go home and put on a cleane shirt, and then goe drowne my selfe.'

307–8 **Why . . . gentleman**? could be a question or an exclamation

310 **prescription** doctor's prescription; ancient custom (*OED* 4c)

310–11 **death . . . physician** Cf. Dent, D142.3, 'Death is a physician' (could be post-Shakespearian).

312 **villainous** shameful

313 **four . . . years** Why does Shakespeare make such a point of Iago's precise age? Cf. *Ham* 5.1.143–62; *Oth* 3.4.173ff. (a similar round-about calculation). Iago is younger than Othello and older than young Roderigo (5.1.11).

316 **guinea-hen** a showy bird with fine feathers (Johnson); (?)prostitute (*OED* 2b, 'slang': but not recorded in this sense before *Oth*). Since *hen* could = female, and *ginny* = cunning, ensnaring, seductive (*OED*, first recorded 1615), perhaps 'cunning female'. Pliny mentions 'Ginnie or Turkey Hens . . . in great request' in Numidia (p. 296).

317 **change** exchange

baboon sometimes glossed as simpleton, i.e. a fitting victim for a 'ginny hen'. Baboons were, thought to be particularly lecherous (*TNK* 3.5.132, 'the bavian [baboon] with long tail and eke long tool').

304 think'st] *F;* thinkest *Q* 307 If] *F;* Well, if *Q* after] *F;* after it *Q* 307–8 Why, thou . . . gentleman?] Why, thou . . . Gentleman. *Q;* Why thou . . . Gentleman? *F* 309 torment] *F;* a torment *Q* 310 have we] *F;* we haue *Q* 312 O villainous! I have] *as F;* I ha *Q* 314 betwixt] *F;* betweene *Q* a man] *Q;* man *F*

RODERIGO What should I do? I confess it is my shame to be so fond, but it is not in my virtue to amend it.

IAGO Virtue? a fig! 'tis in ourselves that we are thus, or thus. Our bodies are gardens, to the which our wills are gardeners. So that if we will plant nettles or sow lettuce, set hyssop and weed up thyme, supply it with one gender of herbs or distract it with many, either to have it sterile with idleness or manured with industry – why, the power and corrigible authority of this lies in our wills. If the balance of our lives had not one scale of reason to poise another of sensuality, the blood and baseness of our natures would conduct us to most preposterous conclusions. But we have reason to cool our raging motions, our carnal stings, our unbitted lusts; whereof I take this, that you call love, to be a sect or scion.

319 **fond** infatuated; foolish
virtue power; moral excellence
320 **a fig!** contemptuous exclamation (cf. *2H4* 5.3.118); an obscene gesture 'which consisted in thrusting the thumb between two of the closed fingers or into the mouth' (*OED* fig 2)
in ourselves i.e. in our own power
320–1 **thus, or thus** Cf. *STM*, 'It is in heaven that I am thus and thus' (Addition III.1, sometimes ascribed to Shakespeare).
321 **gardens** alluding to Galatians 6.7, 'whatsoever a man soweth, that shall he also reap'. Iago's speech is a mock sermon, using theological commonplaces: cf. St Teresa on the good Christian as a gardener (*The Life*, ch. 18), or Robert Mason, *Reasons Monarchie* (1602), 71–3, on the 'motions of lust . . . against Reason'.
322 See LN.
323 **set** plant
324 **gender** kind
distract it with divide it among
325 **sterile with idleness** unproductive because of our inactivity
manured managed; cultivated; enriched with manure; worked upon by hand (*OED* 1–4)
326 **power** control (of oneself)
corrigible authority corrective power to influence others (*OED* authority 4)
327 **balance** scales; equilibrium. F *braine* could be a misreading of *beame* (= the bar from the ends of which the scales of a balance are suspended; or, 'the balance itself' [*OED* 6]).
328 **poise** hold in equilibrium, counterpoise
329 **blood** (the supposed seat of) animal appetite, fleshly nature
330 **preposterous** perverse, irrational (placing last what should be first)
conclusions results
331 **motions** impulses
332 **unbitted** i.e. unrestrained
lusts pleasures; appetites; sexual desires
333 **sect** cutting
scion graft; sucker

321 gardens] *Q;* our Gardens *F* 323 hyssop] *F (*Hisope*);* Isop *Q* 327 balance] *Q;* braine *F;* beam *Theobald* 332 our] *Q;* or *F* 333 sect] *QF;* Set *Johnson* scion] syen *Q;* Seyen *F*

RODERIGO It cannot be.

IAGO It is merely a lust of the blood and a permission of the will. Come, be a man! drown thyself? drown cats and blind puppies. I have professed me thy friend, and I confess me knit to thy deserving with cables of perdurable toughness. I could never better stead thee than now. Put money in thy purse, follow thou the wars, defeat thy favour with an usurped beard; I say, put money in thy purse. It cannot be that Desdemona should long continue her love to the Moor – put money in thy purse – nor he his to her. It was a violent commencement in her, and thou shalt see an answerable sequestration – put but money in thy purse. These Moors are changeable in their wills – fill thy purse with money. The food that to him now is as luscious as locusts shall be to him shortly as

335 **permission** perhaps alluding to God's 'permissive will', which tolerates the existence of evil (see *Paradise Lost*, 3.685)

336 **be a man** Cf. 4.1.66.

337 **blind** i.e. new-born, therefore helpless

338 **deserving** desert, worthiness

cables strong ropes. Cf. Polonius, 'Those friends thou hast, and their adoption tried, / Grapple them unto thy soul with hoops of steel' (*Ham* 1.3.62–3).

339 **perdurable** imperishable

stead help, serve the needs of

340 **Put . . . purse** Cf. 304n. He means 'sell your assets to raise money' and Roderigo understands (380).

follow i.e. as a hanger-on, not as a soldier

341 **defeat** destroy the beauty of, disfigure

favour appearance; face

usurped false, counterfeit; i.e. make yourself less pretty by wearing a false beard (Roderigo is too young to have a beard of his own: see 313n., 5.1.11n.). Cf. *TN* 5.1.250, 'my masculine usurp'd attire' (Ridley). Kittredge thinks 'spoil thy pretty face by growing a beard to which it has no right'.

344–8 The dashes come from Q. I suspect that Iago is 'otherwise engaged' as he speaks – tying a lace? fencing with his shadow? – and throws out 'Put money . . .' as if it's no concern of his. Cf. Rosenberg, 126.

346 **answerable** corresponding

sequestration (lit. an act of sequestering or cutting off); here probably = cessation, or sequel (Lat. *sequor*, I follow). Cf. Dent, B262, 'Such beginning such end'; N321, 'Nothing violent can be permanent.'

347 **wills** desires; whims; wilfulness

349 **locusts** 'The carob groweth in Apulia . . . so full of sweet juice that it is used to preserve ginger . . . [This is] thought to be that which is translated *locusts*' (Gerard's *Herball*, 1597, quoted Ridley).

337 have professed] *F;* professe *Q* 340 thou the] *F;* these *Q* 342 be] *Q;* be long *F* 343 should long] *Q;* should *F* to] *F;* vnto *Q* 344 his] *F; not in Q* 345 in her] *F; not in Q*

acerb as coloquintida. She must change for youth; when she is sated with his body she will find the error of her choice: she must have change, she must. Therefore, put money in thy purse. If thou wilt needs damn thyself, do it a more delicate way than drowning – make all the money thou canst. If sanctimony, and a frail vow betwixt an erring Barbarian and a super-subtle Venetian, be not too hard for my wits and all the tribe of hell, thou shalt enjoy her – therefore make money. A pox of drowning thyself, it is clean out of the way: seek thou rather to be hanged in compassing thy joy than to be drowned and go without her.

RODERIGO Wilt thou be fast to my hopes, if I depend on the issue?

IAGO Thou art sure of me – go, make money. I have told thee often, and I re-tell thee again and again, I

350 **acerb** bitter (from Cinthio's *acerbissimo*: see p. 382)
coloquintida colocynth, a bitter apple. Its bitterness and use as a purgative were noted in herbals.
for youth for a younger man than Othello
351 **sated** satiated
353–4 **wilt needs** must
354 **delicate** (ironical) delightful; finely sensitive
355 **make** raise
355–6 **sanctimony** lit. holiness; pretended holiness (*OED* 3, from 1618): cf. 262, 'Vouch with me, heaven'. Or perhaps more general, pretended goodness.
356 **erring** wandering; straying; sinning. Cf. *extravagant*, 1.1.134n.
Barbarian native of Barbary, the Berber country; foreigner; a savage. Cf. *Barbary horse*, 1.1.110.
357 **super-subtle** super-crafty, referring to Desdemona as a typically depraved Venetian (see pp. 22–3) (unique in Shakespeare)
358 **tribe** i.e. population; 'and all the tribe of hell' may be an aside
360 **clean . . . way** vaguely facetious (because a drowned body is clean and out of the way?) and colloquial. We would say 'that's barking up the wrong tree'. *Clean* = completely.
hanged (as a rapist?)
361 **compassing** obtaining; embracing
363–4 **fast . . . issue** firmly fixed (to support) my hopes, if I await the outcome. Both *fast* and *depend* (*OED* 1: hang down, be suspended) imply tying.
365 **Thou . . . me** Cf. 3.3.482, 'I am your own for ever.'
art sure can be sure

350 acerb as] acerbe as the *Q;* bitter as *F* She . . . youth] *F; not in Q* 352 error] *Q;* errors *F* she must . . . must] *Q; not in F* 357 a] *Q; not in F* 359 of] *F;* a *Q* thyself] *F; not in Q* 359–60 it is] *F;* tis *Q* 363–4 if . . . issue] *F; not in Q* 366 re-tell] *F;* tell *Q*

hate the Moor. My cause is hearted, thine ha
less reason: let us be conjunctive in our revenge
against him. If thou canst cuckold him, thou dost
thyself a pleasure, me a sport. There are many events
in the womb of time, which will be delivered.
Traverse, go, provide thy money: we will have more
of this tomorrow. Adieu!

RODERIGO Where shall we meet i'th' morning?

IAGO At my lodging.

RODERIGO I'll be with thee betimes.

IAGO Go to, farewell. – Do you hear, Roderigo?

RODERIGO What say you?

IAGO No more of drowning, do you hear?

RODERIGO I am changed. I'll sell all my land. *Exit.*

IAGO Go to, farewell, put money enough in your purse.
Thus do I ever make my fool my purse:
For I mine own gained knowledge should profane
If I would time expend with such a snipe

367 **hearted** fixed in the heart, determined

368 **conjunctive** united. Occurs twice in Shakespeare ('She is so conjunctive to my life and soul', *Ham* 4.7.14); Q *communicatiue* (= in touch, in communication) occurs nowhere else in Shakespeare.

369 **cuckold** make (him) a cuckold (by seducing his wife)

370 **sport** amusement
events (from Lat. *evenire*, to come out or forth) consequences, outcomes

371 **delivered** i.e. brought forth (like a new-born child); declared, made known (in due time)

372 **Traverse** a military command (cf. *2H4* 3.2.272) of uncertain meaning; perhaps 'quick march!'

376 **betimes** early, in good time

377, 381 **Go to** a favourite phrase of his, used to jolly others along, sometimes almost meaningless (= come on; well then). Also biblical (Genesis 11.4, James 4.13, 5.1). 'The Folio compositor, one guesses, jumped from *Go too, farewell*, opening 377, to the later line which also opens with *Go to, farewell*, and omitted the intervening words. A conflation of Folio and Quarto is necessary to restore the original text' (Sisson, *Readings*, 2.249).

378–81 **What . . . purse** For the different readings of Q and F, see *Texts*, 47.

382 **ever** Iago is already a hardened cheater.

383 **profane** treat (the sacred) irreverently. He cynically misuses the word, since his *knowledge* is evil, not sacred as usually understood.

384 **expend** spend
snipe fool (*OED*: a term of abuse, first recorded here); woodcock (a long-billed bird like a snipe) meant 'gull' or 'dupe' before Shakespeare

367 hath] *F;* has *Q* 368 conjunctive] *F;* communicatiue *Q* 370 me] *F;* and me *Q* 378–80 What . . . changed.] *Q; not in F* 380 I'll . . . land.] *F; not in Q;* Ile goe sell . . . land. *Q2* 381 Go . . . purse.] *Q; not in F*

profit. I hate the Moor
oroad that 'twixt my sheets
ıce. I know not if't be true,
suspicion in that kind
for surety. He holds me well,
shall my purpose work on him.
a proper man: let me see now,
To get his place, and to plume up my will
In double knavery. How? How? let's see:
After some time to abuse Othello's ear
That he is too familiar with his wife.
He hath a person and a smooth dispose
To be suspected, framed to make women false.
The Moor is of a free and open nature
That thinks men honest that but seem to be so,

385 **sport** Cf. 370, 2.3.374.

386 **And** 'Rarely is a conjunction used so effectively: the hate is prior, and a motive is then discovered' (Heilman, 31).

abroad i.e. generally, widely

387 **He's** *Has* (or, *h'as*, *ha's*) could = he has: cf. 2.1.67.

office service, duty, function. A curious word for marital intercourse. Cf. 4.3.86, 'Say that they slack their duties'.

388 **in that kind** of that nature

389 **do** proceed; perhaps picking up '*done* my office' (387), i.e. 'do *his* office' (cf. 2.1.293–7). Cf. *2H4* 2.1.41–2, 'do me your offices'.

for surety for certain (*OED* 4c), i.e. as if it's a certain fact

holds . . . well He is well-disposed towards me.

391 **proper** handsome; also admirable, perfect; appropriate (*OED* 6–9)

let me see . . . Cf. the free-wheeling improvisations of the 'clever slave' of classical comedy, and 402n.

392 **his place** Cf. 1.1.7ff.

plume up uncertain. Perhaps = ruffle the feathers, like a bird that 'displays', hence make a show of, exhibit. Cf. *Lust's Dominion* (printed 1657, dated *c.* 1600), 'Ambition plumes the *Moor* . . . to act deeds beyond astonishment' (Dekker, 4. 182).

will inclination; pleasure; determination

395 **he** Cassio

his Othello's

396 **person** bodily presence

smooth dispose insinuating disposition

397 **framed** made, formed

398 **free** spontaneous, frank, unreserved

open not given to concealing thoughts or feelings; without defence or protection (*OED* 16, 15). Curiously, Ben Jonson echoed these words in describing Shakespeare.

399 Cf. Dent, T221, 'They that think none ill are soonest beguiled.'

387 He's] Ha's *Q;* She ha's *F* 388 But] *F;* Yet *Q* 392 his] *F;* this *Q* plume] *F;* make *Q* 393 In] *F;* A *Q* knavery. How? How?] *F;* knauery – how, how, – *Q* let's] *F;* let me *Q* 394 ear] *Q;* eares *F* 396 hath] *F;* has *Q* 398] *F;* The Moore a free and open nature too, *Q* 399 seem] *F;* seemes *Q*

And will as tenderly be led by th' nose
As asses are.
I have't, it is engendered! Hell and night
Must bring this monstrous birth to the world's light. *Exit.*

[2.1] *Enter* MONTANO *and two* Gentlemen.

MONTANO
What from the cape can you discern at sea?

1 GENTLEMAN
Nothing at all, it is a high-wrought flood:
I cannot 'twixt the haven and the main
Descry a sail.

MONTANO
Methinks the wind hath spoke aloud at land,
A fuller blast ne'er shook our battlements:
If it hath ruffianed so upon the sea
What ribs of oak, when mountains melt on them,

400 **tenderly** easily, gently (sarcastic)
led . . . nose Cf. Dent, N233, 'To lead one by the nose (like a bear, ass)'.

402 **I have't** Cf. the clever slave's *habeo!* (= I've got it, I've solved the problem!) in Latin comedy: e.g. Terence, *Andria*, 344, 498, etc. Echoed by Elizabethan dramatists: cf. *TS* 1.1.189, *Ham* 4.7.154ff., 'Soft, let me see . . . I ha't!'
engendered begotten, conceived

403 **birth** (*OED* 3b:) that which is borne in the womb. Cf. 371.

2.1.0.1 MONTANO probably the governor of Cyprus replaced by Othello: see t.n. and Honigmann, *Stability*, 44–6

1 **cape** projecting headland, land jutting into the sea. Presumably the Gentleman speaks from the side or back of the stage. In classical plays those on stage sometimes observe a ship at sea (Plautus, *Rudens*, 162ff.; cf. *WT* 3.3.88ff.).

2 **high-wrought** agitated to a high degree (*OED*); or, flinging itself high into the air (cf. 12ff.) (unique in Shakespeare)
flood (body of) water

3 **main** main sea, open ocean

4 **Descry** 'To catch sight of, esp. from a distance, as the scout or watchman who is ready to announce the enemy's approach' (*OED* 6)

5 **at land** on the land

6 **fuller** more complete (as in 'full flood', 'full tide': *OED* 8d)

7 **ruffianed** acted the ruffian (unique in Shakespeare as verb)

8 **ribs** curved frame-timbers of a ship
mountains i.e. huge masses of water. Cf. 'hills of seas', 184. Adapted from Judges 5.5, 'The mountains melted from before the Lord' (Steevens).

400 led . . . nose] led bit'h nose *Q;* lead by' th' Nose *F* 402 have't] *F;* ha't *Q* 403 SD] *Q; not in F* **2.1**] *Actus* 2. / *Scoena* I. *Q; Actus Secundus. Scena Prima. F* 0.1] *F; Enter* Montanio, *Gouernor of* Cypres, *with two other Gentlemen. Q* 3 haven] *Q;* Heauen *F* 5 hath spoke] *F;* does speake *Q* 7 hath] *F;* ha *Q* 8 when . . . them] *F;* when the huge mountaine meslt *Q*

Can hold the mortise? What shall we hear of this?

2 GENTLEMAN

A segregation of the Turkish fleet:
For do but stand upon the foaming shore,
The chidden billow seems to pelt the clouds,
The wind-shaked surge, with high and monstrous mane,
Seems to cast water on the burning bear
And quench the guards of th'ever-fired pole.
I never did like molestation view
On the enchafed flood.

MONTANO If that the Turkish fleet
Be not ensheltered and embayed, they are drowned.
It is impossible to bear it out.

Enter a Third Gentleman.

9 ***hold the mortise** keep their joints intact (Sanders)

10 **segregation** dispersion, separation (unique in Shakespeare)

11 **foaming** Q *banning*, the 'harder reading', could mean cursing, chiding; an easy misreading, improbable here

12 **chidden** i.e. repelled by the shore
pelt strike, beat (stronger than today: cf. *KL* 3.4.29, 'the pelting of this pitiless storm')
clouds See LN.

13 **wind-shaked** unique in Shakespeare (but cf. *wind-shaken, Cor* 5.2.111)
surge a high rolling swell of water
mane with high-flying mane like a monstrous beast. Knight's spelling brings out the mane–main quibble. Furness compared *2H4* 3.1.20ff., where *surge* and *winds* 'take the ruffian billows by the top, / Curling their monstrous heads'. According to Sisson, *Readings*, the 'sense of main is as in "with might and main" ' (= power), and *monstrous* = portentous (2.250). But *monstrous* could = huge, gigantic (*OED* 4), and the line's imprecision may be deliberate.

14 **bear** the constellation Ursa Minor (i.e. the Little Bear), 'since the *guards* are the two stars in that constellation next in brightness to the Pole Star' (Ridley)

15 See LN.

16 **molestation** unique in Shakespeare; from Cinthio (cf. p. 375). Lat. *molestia* = trouble, vexation; Shakespeare seems to mean turmoil.

17 **enchafed** (probably enchafèd, eliding *the* to *th'*): excited, furious
If that if

18 **ensheltered** unique in Shakespeare
embayed unique in Shakespeare (= sheltered in a bay)

19 **bear it out** hold out, survive it

9 mortise] morties *QF* 10 SP] 2 *Gent. Q; 2 F* 11 foaming] *F;* banning *Q* 12 chidden] *F;* chiding *Q* 13 mane] *Knight;* mayne *Q;* Maine *F* 15 ever-fired] euer fired *Q;* euer-fixed *F* 19 to] *F;* they *Q* 19.1 Third] *Q; not in F*

3 GENTLEMAN
News, lads: our wars are done!
The desperate tempest hath so banged the Turks
That their designment halts. A noble ship of Venice
Hath seen a grievous wrack and sufferance
On most part of their fleet.

MONTANO How? Is this true?

3 GENTLEMAN
The ship is here put in,
A Veronessa; Michael Cassio,
Lieutenant to the warlike Moor, Othello,
Is come on shore; the Moor himself at sea,
And is in full commission here for Cyprus.

MONTANO
I am glad on't, 'tis a worthy governor.

3 GENTLEMAN
But this same Cassio, though he speak of comfort

Enter CASSIO.

Touching the Turkish loss, yet he looks sadly
And prays the Moor be safe, for they were parted

20 **lads** With the QF variants, cf. *TC* 3.1.108, lad (Q), Lord (F); and *Texts*, 83, on *a:o* misreading.
21 **desperate** terrible
22 **designment** enterprise
halts (lit. 'is lame') is in doubt; stops
noble great, stately
23 **wrack** disaster, destruction (cf. 'wrack and ruin'); shipwreck
sufferance damage (inflicted on)
26 See LN.
29 and is (heading) for Cyprus with full delegated authority here (*OED* commission 5)
30 **governor** ungrudging praise from the man replaced as governor: see 2.1.0.1n.
31 **comfort** support, relief; a cause of satisfaction (*OED* 5)
*31.1 Cassio must enter earlier than QF direct, as he overhears Montano's speech. SDs were often placed in the margins of a text, not precisely where required (see Honigmann, 'Stage direction').
32 **sadly** gravely

20 SP] 3 *Gent. Q;* 3 *F (throughout)* lads] *F;* Lords *Q* our] *F;* your *Q* 21 Turks] *F; Turke Q* 22 A noble] *F;* Another *Q* 24 their] *F;* the *Q* 25–6] *as Q; one line F* 25 in,] in: *QF* *26* Veronessa] *Q; Verennessa F* 28 on shore] *F;* ashore *Q* himself] *QF;* himself's *Rowe* 30] *as Q; F lines* on't: / Gouernour. / 31.1] *this edn; after 42 QF* 33 prays] *Q;* praye *F*

With foul and violent tempest.
MONTANO Pray heavens he be,
For I have served him, and the man commands
Like a full soldier. Let's to the seaside, ho!
As well to see the vessel that's come in
As to throw out our eyes for brave Othello,
Even till we make the main and th'aerial blue
An indistinct regard.
3 GENTLEMAN Come, let's do so,
For every minute is expectancy
Of more arrivance.
CASSIO
Thanks, you the valiant of this warlike isle
That so approve the Moor. O, let the heavens
Give him defence against the elements,
For I have lost him on a dangerous sea.
MONTANO
Is he well shipped?
CASSIO
His bark is stoutly timbered, and his pilot
Of very expert and approved allowance,
Therefore my hopes, not surfeited to death,

34 **With** by
35 **served** served under
36 **full** perfect
39 **aerial** atmospheric: 'even till our eyes make the sea and atmospheric blue a single indistinguishable sight'
41 **expectancy** expectance (a new word *c.* 1600)
42 **arrivance** (a coinage, unique in Shakespeare) i.e. more arrivals
44 **approve** commend
48 **bark** a sailing vessel; 'in 17th century sometimes applied to the *barca-longa* of the Mediterranean' (*OED* 3)
49 **approved** proved
allowance acknowledgement (*OED* 3), i.e. is acknowledged to be skilled and proved good by experience
50–1 **not . . . cure** not indulged in excessively, persist in their optimism (*OED* stand 72; *bold* = confident, *cure* = care). 'A verbal bubble that disappears if one examines it too closely' (Ridley).

34 heavens] *F;* Heauen *Q* 38 throw out] *Q;* throw-out *F* 39–40 Even . . . regard] *F; not in Q* 39 aerial] *Pope;* Eriall *F;* Ayre all *Q2* 40 SP] *as Q; Gent. F* 42 arrivance] *Q;* Arriuancie *F* 43 Thanks, you] Thankes you, *F;* Thankes to *Q* this] *Q;* the *F* warlike] *F;* worthy *Q* 44 O] *F;* and *Q* 45 the] *F;* their *Q* 48 pilot] *F* (Pylot)*;* Pilate *Q* 50 hopes, not . . . death] hope's not . . . death *Q;* hope's (not . . . death) *F*

Stand in bold cure.

A VOICE (*within*) A sail! a sail! a sail!

CASSIO

What noise?

2 GENTLEMAN

The town is empty: on the brow o'th' sea
Stand ranks of people, and they cry 'A sail!'

CASSIO

My hopes do shape him for the governor. *A shot.*

2 GENTLEMAN

They do discharge their shot of courtesy,
Our friends at least.

CASSIO I pray you sir, go forth
And give us truth who 'tis that is arrived.

2 GENTLEMAN

I shall. *Exit.*

MONTANO

But, good lieutenant, is your general wived?

CASSIO

Most fortunately: he hath achieved a maid
That paragons description and wild fame;
One that excels the quirks of blazoning pens
And in th'essential vesture of creation

51 SD ***within*** i.e. off stage
53 **brow** projecting edge of a cliff (overlooking the sea)
54 **ranks** rows
55 **shape** shape him (in imagination) to be the governor; portray
56 **shot of courtesy** a cannon shot, in friendly salute (off stage)
60 **wived** not quite the same as 'married'. Cf. 3.4.195, 'womaned'.
61 **achieved** acquired
62 **paragons** surpasses (*OED* 3, first here)
wild fame report at its wildest
63 **quirks** verbal subtleties
blazoning describing; boasting; proclaiming
64 **And . . . creation** = (?)in the essential clothing in which she was created. I suggest 'in her innermost nature' (*essential vesture* = soul, not body). Or, in the 'vesture that is her essence' (Capell).

51 *opp.* cure] *Enter a Messenger. Q* SP] *Mess. Q; Within. F* 53 SP] *Mess. Q; Gent. F* 55 governor] *F;* guernement *Q* SD] *Q (after* least *57); not in F* 56 SP] *Q; Gent. F* their] *F;* the *Q* 57 friends] *F;* friend *Q* 59 SP] *Q; Gent. F* SD] *Q; not in F* 63 quirks of] *F; not in Q* 64 th'] *F;* the *Q*

Does tire the inginer.

Enter Second Gentleman.

How now? Who has put in?

2 GENTLEMAN

'Tis one Iago, ancient to the general.

CASSIO

He's had most favourable and happy speed.
Tempests themselves, high seas, and howling winds,
The guttered rocks and congregated sands,
Traitors ensteeped to clog the guiltless keel,
As having sense of beauty, do omit
Their mortal natures, letting go safely by
The divine Desdemona.

MONTANO What is she?

CASSIO

She that I spake of, our great captain's captain,

65 **tire the inginer** = (?)exhaust the (powers of the) divine inventor (God); i.e. she is God's masterpiece. Inginer (= author, inventor) is modern 'engineer', but stressed on first syllable; could = a human artist (a painter, or one who describes verbally), i.e. exhausts the one who tries to do her justice. Muir notes that ' "tyre" can mean "attire", as well as "weary". Possibly "tire" was suggested by "vesture" through an unconscious quibble.' Not too clear, hence Q's weak substitution.
put in landed

66 **ancient . . . general** i.e. Iago was attached to the general rather than to the army: see p. 339.

67 **happy** fortunate; successful
speed 'includes the idea of "fortune", as well as that of celerity' (Ridley)

68–73 The idea may come from the Orpheus legend: Orpheus' music made wild animals *omit* their deadly natures.

69 **guttered** furrowed, grooved (by wind and water). Ovid mentioned the rocks that surround Cyprus (*Metamorphoses*, 10.6).
congregated sands sandbanks

70 **ensteeped** under water (a coinage). Q *enscerped* could = enscarped (= sloping, from *escarp*: Hulme, 282).
clog obstruct
guiltless having no familiarity with or experience of (these 'traitors') (*OED* 3, from 1667)

71 **omit** forbear to use

72 **mortal** deadly

73 **divine Desdemona** Cf. 'divine Zenocrate' in *1 Tamburlaine*, 5.1.135.

74 **captain's captain** So *AC* 3.1.22; cf. *Oth* 2.3.305, 'Our general's wife is now the general', *R3* 4.4.336, 'Caesar's Caesar', *TN* 3.1.102, 'Your servant's servant'.

65 tire the inginer] *F (*tyre the Ingeniuer*);* beare all excellency *Q* SD] *Q (after 65); Enter Gentleman. F (after* Ingeniuer*)* How] *F; not in Q* 66 SP] *as Q; Gent. F* 67 SP] *as F; not in Q* He's] He has *Q;* Ha's *F* 68 high] *F;* by *Q* 69 guttered rocks] *Q;* gutter'd-Rockes *F* 70 ensteeped] *F;* enscerped *Q* clog] *Q;* enclogge *F* 72 mortal] *F;* common *Q* 74] *F lines* of: / Captaine, / spake] *F;* spoke *Q*

Left in the conduct of the bold Iago,
Whose footing here anticipates our thoughts
A se'nnight's speed. Great Jove, Othello guard,
And swell his sail with thine own powerful breath
That he may bless this bay with his tall ship,
Make love's quick pants in Desdemona's arms,
Give renewed fire to our extincted spirits
And bring all Cyprus comfort! –

Enter DESDEMONA, IAGO, RODERIGO *and* EMILIA.

O, behold,
The riches of the ship is come on shore:
You men of Cyprus, let her have your knees!
Hail to thee, lady, and the grace of heaven,
Before, behind thee, and on every hand
Enwheel thee round!

DESDEMONA I thank you, valiant Cassio.
What tidings can you tell me of my lord?

CASSIO
He is not yet arrived, nor know I aught
But that he's well, and will be shortly here.

75 **conduct** charge, conducting
76 **footing** setting foot upon land (*OED* 1b, first here)
76–7 **Whose . . . speed** occurs earlier than we expected by a week. She left after Cassio and Othello, who sailed together (91; 1.3.278).
77–8 In Renaissance maps and pictures supernatural beings blow ships, etc., across the seas.
79 **tall** tall-masted
80 **love's quick pants** 'The quick breathing that accompanies and ensues upon the orgasm' (Partridge, 162). Perhaps, but note that Cassio later resists sexual imagery applied to Desdemona (2.3.14ff.). The 'panting of loving hearts' was a commonplace (Lyly, 2.373, and Lyly, *Sapho*, 1.1.22), 'quick pants' less so.
81 **extincted** extinguished (unique in Shakespeare)
84 **let . . . knees** kneel to her (out of courtesy)
85–7 Cassio uses (familiar) *thee* here, but *you* later (165). An echo of 'Hail Mary', reinforced by kneeling and 'the grace of heaven'?
86 Could Shakespeare have known Donne's (unpublished) Elegy 19, 'Going to Bed'? 'License my roving *hands*, and let them, go / *Before, behind*, between, above, below'. **on every hand** on all sides
87 **Enwheel** encircle: a coinage

80 Make . . . in] *F;* And swiftly come to *Q* 82 And . . . comfort!] *Q; not in F* SD] *as F; Enter* Desdemona, Iago, Emillia, *and* Roderigo. *Q (after 80)* 83 on shore] *F;* ashore *Q* 84 You] *F;* Ye *Q* 88 me] *Q; not in F*

DESDEMONA

O, but I fear . . . how lost you company?

CASSIO

The great contention of the sea and skies
Parted our fellowship. (A VOICE *within:* 'A sail! a sail!')
But hark! a sail!

[*A shot is heard.*]

2 GENTLEMAN

They give their greeting to the citadel:
This likewise is a friend.

CASSIO

See for the news.

[*Exit Gentleman.*]

Good ancient, you are welcome. [*to Emilia*] Welcome, mistress.
Let it not gall your patience, good Iago,
That I extend my manners; 'tis my breeding
That gives me this bold show of courtesy.

[*He kisses Emilia.*]

IAGO

Sir, would she give you so much of her lips
As of her tongue she oft bestows on me
You'd have enough.

DESDEMONA

Alas! she has no speech.

93 **Parted our fellowship** separated our ships

96, 97 **Good . . . good** Note the touch of condescension in *good.*

97 **gall** vex. For Iago's delayed response, cf. 167ff.

98–9 **That . . . courtesy** i.e. that I offer a polite greeting to your wife; it is my good manners (or upbringing) that prompt me to this bold display of elegant behaviour (kissing the ladies). Such kissing was 'an English habit rather than an Italian one' (Bullough, 219).

99.1 *Perhaps Emilia accepts the kiss too willingly, irritating Iago. Does she have to *give . . . her lips?*

101 **her tongue** Iago coarsely hints at kissing, as well as scolding, with the tongue. **bestows** confers as a gift (sarcastic)

102 **Alas . . . speech** Poor thing! you have put her out; or, alas, she's not a talker.

91] *as Q; F lines* feare: / company? / 92 the sea] *Q;* Sea *F* 93 [1]SD] *[within.] A saile, a saile. Q (after 91); Within.* A Saile, a Saile. *F (after 93)* [2]SD] *Guns / Capell; not in QF* 94 their] *Q;* this *F* 95 See . . . news] *F;* So speakes this voyce: *Q* SD] *Capell; not in QF* 96 SD] *Rowe; not in QF* 99 SD] *as Johnson; not in QF* 100 Sir] *F;* For *Q* 101 oft bestows] *F;* has bestowed *Q* 102 You'd] *Q;* You would *F*

IAGO

In faith, too much!
I find it still when I have list to sleep.
Marry, before your ladyship, I grant,
She puts her tongue a little in her heart
And chides with thinking.

EMILIA

You have little cause to say so.

FEMININITY

IAGO

Come on, come on, you are pictures out of doors,
Bells in your parlours, wild-cats in your kitchens,
Saints in your injuries, devils being offended,
Players in your housewifery, and housewives in . . .
Your beds!

women different inside & out.

DESDEMONA O, fie upon thee, slanderer!

IAGO

Nay, it is true, or else I am a Turk:

104 **still** always
list inclination. F *leaue* is possible: when I have her permission to sleep (because she still goes on talking).
105 **before** in the presence of
106–7 'holds her tongue and thinks the more' (Ridley)
109–13 prose in F, verse in Q: could be either. Cf. Dent, W702, 'Women are in church saints, abroad angels, at home devils.' There were many variations before Shakespeare, e.g. 'a shrew in the kitchen . . . an ape in the bed'.
109 **you** He cheekily includes Desdemona!
pictures 'silent appearances (of virtue)' (Sanders). Or, pretty as pictures, when you put on your best clothes to go out, 'with a suggestion that they owe their beauty to painting' (Kittredge).
110 **Bells** i.e. jangling bells
parlours A parlour was originally a room for conversation (Fr. *parler*).
wild-cats Cf. *TS* 1.2.196, 'Will you woo this wild-cat?'
kitchens i.e. in defending your territories
111 **Saints . . . injuries** 'When you have a mind to do injuries, you put on an air of sanctity' (Johnson); or, (you pretend to be) innocent when others have injured you.
112 **Players** i.e. you play at housekeeping; it is not what you give serious attention to
***housewives** After the antitheses of 111, one expects 'workers in your beds'. Housewife = a woman who manages her household with skill, or a 'light' woman, now *hussy* (*OED* 1, 2). Hence 'you are skilful managers in your beds' (notice the plural: he includes Desdemona).'
114 **or . . . Turk** a variant of 'I am a Jew (rogue, villain) else' (Dent, J49.1)

103 In faith] *F;* I know *Q* 104 it . . . have] *F;* it, I; for when I ha *Q* list] *Q;* leaue *F* 108 have] *F;* ha *Q* 109–13 Come . . . beds] *prose F; Q lines as verse* adores: / Kitchins: / offended: / beds. / 109 of doors] adores *Q;* of doore *F* 112–13 in . . . / Your beds] *this edn* 113 SP] *F; not in Q*

You rise to play, and go to bed to work.

EMILIA

You shall not write my praise.

IAGO

No, let me not.

DESDEMONA

What wouldst thou write of me, if thou shouldst praise
me?

IAGO

O, gentle lady, do not put me to't,
For I am nothing if not critical.

DESDEMONA

Come on, assay. There's one gone to the harbour?

IAGO

Ay, madam.

DESDEMONA

I am not merry, but I do beguile
The thing I am by seeming otherwise.
Come, how wouldst thou praise me?

IAGO

I am about it, but indeed my invention
Comes from my pate as birdlime does from frieze,

115 **You** He speaks even more directly to Desdemona than at 109, attacking her sense of sexual privacy. Cf. the voyeurism of 1.1.109ff., 3.3.413ff., 4.1.1ff.

117–64 'One of the most unsatisfactory passages in Shakespeare' (Ridley). Yet it shows how Iago wins an ascendancy over others, his improvising skills (note how Cassio is overshadowed), and that Desdemona understands sexual innuendo.

117 **of me** She is not asking for compliments, but wants to stop the marital bickering and places herself in the firing line (as later with Othello-Cassio).
shouldst were to; had to

118 **put me to't** challenge me to (do) it (*OED* put 28)

119 **critical** censorious

120 **assay** try, put me to the test
one someone

122–3 **I . . . otherwise** perhaps an aside. Cf. *AW* 2.2.60–1, 'I play the noble housewife with the time, / To entertain it so merrily with a fool.'

122 **beguile** disguise; divert attention from. An ominous echo of Iago's 'I am not what I am' (1.1.64)?

123 **The . . . am** i.e. the fact that I am an anxious wife

125 **invention** inventiveness; the thing invented. Slur as 'my 'nvention'. But 125–8 may be meant as prose.

126 **birdlime** a viscous preparation spread on bushes to snare birds (Ridley)
frieze coarse woollen cloth; i.e. comes from my thick head just as sticky birdlime comes (with difficulty) from frieze

117 wouldst thou] *Q;* would'st *F* 120] *as Q; F lines* assay. / Harbour? / 125–8] *as Q (verse); prose F*

It plucks out brains and all; but my muse labours
And thus she is delivered:
If she be fair and wise, fairness and wit,
The one's for use, the other useth it.

DESDEMONA

Well praised. How if she be black and witty?

IAGO

If she be black, and thereto have a wit,
She'll find a white that shall her blackness fit.

DESDEMONA

Worse and worse.

EMILIA

How if fair and foolish?

IAGO

She never yet was foolish that was fair,
For even her folly helped her to an heir.

127–8 **but . . . delivered** quibbles on being in labour and giving birth; *my muse* = my inspiring goddess (jocular: he compares himself with Homer and classical poets who invoke their Muse). Iago affects a gentlemanly facility as versifier: cf. Jonson's Stephano, who will 'write you your halfe score or your dozen of sonnets at a sitting' (*Jonson*, 3.228), and *LLL* 4.2.50ff.

129–30 **If . . . it** semi-proverbial. Cf. Dent, F28, 'Fair and foolish, black and proud, long and lazy, little and loud'; *fair* = beautiful, or fair-haired; *wit* = intellect, wisdom.

130 **The . . . it** Perhaps = each one is for use, and the other (beauty or brains) makes use of it, i.e. they both need each other.

131 **black** dark-haired.

witty endowed with good judgement

133 **find** Cf. 245–6, 'the woman hath found him already'.

white a quibble on *wight* (cf. 158) = person; man. Here *black* and *white* hint at a mixed union like Othello's and Desdemona's. Q *hit* is possible: cf. *The Wit of a Woman* (1604), B1b, 'when you haue your mistresse, hange your selfe, if you can not teach her a right hit it', and *LLL* 4.1.125–8.

blackness could = pudendum. 'To hit the white' = to hit the centre of the target (cf. *TS* 5.2.186), and 'shall her blackness hit' may quibble accordingly.

134 said admiringly in wit combats (Lyly, *Endimion*, 4.2.52; *Midas*, 1.2.101); i.e. 'progressively worse' (*OED* 1c)

137 **folly** foolishness; unchastity (cf. 5.2.130: 'She turned to folly, and she was a whore') (Sanders)

an heir to marry an heir; to have a bastard child

127 brains] *F;* braine *Q* 129–30, 132–3, 136–7, 141–2, 148–58, 160] *as Q; italics F* 130 useth] *F;* vsing *Q* 131] *as Q; F lines* prais'd: / Witty? / 133 fit] *F;* hit *Q* 137 an heir] *F;* a haire *Q*

DESDEMONA These are old fond paradoxes to make fools laugh i'th' alehouse. What miserable praise hast thou for her that's foul and foolish?

IAGO

There's none so foul, and foolish thereunto,
But does foul pranks which fair and wise ones do.

DESDEMONA O heavy ignorance, thou praisest the worst best. But what praise couldst thou bestow on a deserving woman indeed? One that in the authority of her merit did justly put on the vouch of very malice itself?

IAGO

She that was ever fair and never proud,
Had tongue at will, and yet was never loud,
Never lacked gold, and yet went never gay,
Fled from her wish, and yet said 'now I may',
She that, being angered, her revenge being nigh,
Bade her wrong stay, and her displeasure fly,

138 **fond** foolish
paradoxes contradictory or absurd sayings

139 **miserable** miserly, stingy; wretched; despicable

140 **foul** ugly; dirty

142 **pranks** i.e. sexual pranks or acts (cf. 3.3.205). Iago's rhymes have become more and more overtly sexual.
do Cf. 3.3.435n.

143 **heavy** grievous; distressing

143–4 **thou . . . best** (because he has said less in dispraise of the worst?)

145 **indeed** 'freq. placed after a word in order to emphasize it' (*OED* 1b), i.e. 'a truly deserving woman'. Thinking of herself? Or pointing to Emilia?

146 **put on** encourage, urge on (*OED* 46h), as in *KL* 1.4.208, 'That you protect this course and put it on / By your allowance.' Hence, 'one who, authorised by her merit, did reasonably encourage (others to give) the testimony of malice itself': i.e. one who, sure of her own merit, did not fear the worst that could be said against her.

148–60 **She . . . beer** Cf. the nonsense verses in *KL* 3.2.81 ff., spoken by the Fool. Here Iago plays the fool to mask his true character, as in 2.3.64ff., and to show off his cleverness.

149 **Had . . . will** was never lost for words. Hart compared Plutarch's *Lives* (Cato), 'he became a perfect pleader, and had tongue at will'.

150 **gay** finely dressed

151 i.e. modestly refrained from what she wanted, and yet knew when she might have it

153 i.e. did not seek to right her wrong and commanded her anger to cease. Cf. Plautus, *Stichus*, 119 ff., 'The best proof of a woman's excellence of character. Her . . . having the chance to do wrong and the self-restraint not to.' Cf. *Son* 94.1, 'They that have power to hurt and will do none'.

138 fond] *F; not in Q* 139 i'th'] *F;* i' the *Q* 142 wise ones] *Q; wise-ones F* 143 thou praisest] *F;* that praises *Q* 146 merit] *F;* merrits *Q*

She that in wisdom never was so frail
To change the cod's head for the salmon's tail,
She that could think, and ne'er disclose her mind,
See suitors following, and not look behind,
She was a wight, if ever such wights were –

DESDEMONA
To do what?

IAGO
To suckle fools, and chronicle small beer.

DESDEMONA O, most lame and impotent conclusion! Do not learn of him, Emilia, though he be thy husband. How say you, Cassio, is he not a most profane and liberal counsellor?

CASSIO He speaks home, madam, you may relish him more in the soldier than in the scholar.

IAGO [*aside*] He takes her by the palm; ay, well said, whisper. With as little a web as this will I ensnare as great a fly as Cassio. Ay, smile upon her, do: I will gyve thee in thine own courtesies. You say true, 'tis

154 **frail** weak; morally weak, unable to resist temptation (cf. Mrs Frail in Congreve's *Love for Love*)
155 See LN.
156 Cf. *AYL* 3.2.249, 'Do you not know I am a woman? when I think, I must speak.'
158 **wight** creature, person. Iago now pretends to be stuck. Cf. 4.1.32n.
160 **chronicle** register, record; 'be concerned with trivialities' (Sanders)
small beer trivialities (*OED*, first here, but likely to be earlier)
161 **lame** (crippled, hence) weak
impotent ineffective, weak
164 **profane** brutal in expression (Johnson); irreverent
liberal unrestrained, licentious; could = gentlemanly (as in 'liberal education'). Cassio picks up the second sense.
165 **home** directly, to the point
relish appreciate
166 **in** in the role of
scholar an unfortunate remark, as Cassio's bookishness particularly irritates Iago (1.1.23ff.)
167 **palm** could = hand (*OED* 1); but cf. 252
well said Cf. 4.1.116n.
168 **web** could = a subtly woven snare, something flimsy and unsubstantial (*OED* 4c). Iago stands aside, like a spider watching a fly. If Cassio still holds Desdemona's hand when Othello enters, this could be a poisonous image in Othello's mind later.
169 **fly** i.e. simpleton
170 ***gyve** fetter, shackle
courtesies courtly or elegant gestures
say true ironic: he does not hear what Cassio says, ridiculing his body language

157] *F; not in Q* 158 wights] *F;* wight *Q* 167 SD] *Rowe; not in QF* 168 With] *F; not in Q* 1] *F; not in Q* 169 fly] *F;* Flee *Q* 170 gyve . . . courtesies] giue thee in thine owne Courtship *F;* catch you in your owne courtesies *Q*

ed. If such tricks as these strip you out of ieutenantry, it had been better you had not d your three fingers so oft, which now again you most apt to play the sir in. Very good, well kissed, and excellent courtesy: 'tis so indeed! Yet again, your fingers to your lips? would they were clyster-pipes for your sake! (*Trumpets within*) The Moor! I know his trumpet!

CASSIO 'Tis truly so.

DESDEMONA

Let's meet him and receive him.

Enter OTHELLO *and Attendants.*

CASSIO Lo, where he comes!

OTHELLO

O my fair warrior!

DESDEMONA My dear Othello!

OTHELLO

It gives me wonder great as my content
To see you here before me! O my soul's joy,

171 **tricks** capricious or foolish acts; feats of dexterity (*OED* 2, 5). Could also refer to Iago's own tricks.
172 **lieutenantry** lieutenancy (*OED*, first here)
173 See LN.
174 **apt** ready, disposed
sir gentleman. For Iago's 'class hatred', see pp. 17–18.
176 **clyster-pipes** 'a tube or pipe for administering clysters' (*OED*, first here). A clyster was a medicine injected into the rectum. Ridley glossed as 'syringe for a (vaginal) douche'. The imagery (fingers, lips, pipes) is partly sexual.
178 **trumpet** could = trumpeter; trumpet call; or, the instrument. 'Distinguished people had their own recognizable calls . . . [cf.] *KL* 2.1.80 . . . [and] "Your husband is at hand; I hear his trumpet" (*MV* 5.1.121)' (Ridley).
179 **receive** i.e. welcome
SD Notice the build-up for this entry.
180 **warrior** Cf. 1.3.249ff., 3.4.152. In love poetry the woman is sometimes addressed as a warrior (in love): cf. Spenser's *Amoretti*, 57.1, 'Sweet warriour! when shall I have peace with you?' Is it significant that Othello turns first to Desdemona, though he arrives on official duty as governor?
181 **content** pleasure, contentment; repeated (189, 194) the word acquires overtones of self-indulgent 'satisfaction'
182 **soul's joy** Notice how often he refers to his soul.

173 kissed] *F;* rist *Q* 174 Very] *F; not in Q* 175 and] *F;* an *Q* 176 to] *F;* at *Q* clyster-pipes] *as Q;* Cluster-pipes *F* 177 SD] *Q (opp. 178); not in F* 178 The . . . trumpet!] *speech cont. Q; new line F* 179 SD] *after* trumpet *178 Q; after* comes *179 F* 182] *Q; F lines* me. / Ioy: /

If after every tempest come such calms
May the winds blow till they have wakened death,
And let the labouring bark climb hills of seas,
Olympus-high, and duck again as low
As hell's from heaven. If it were now to die
'Twere now to be most happy, for I fear
My soul hath her content so absolute
That not another comfort like to this
Succeeds in unknown fate.

DESDEMONA The heavens forbid
But that our loves and comforts should increase
Even as our days do grow.

OTHELLO Amen to that, sweet powers!
I cannot speak enough of this content,
It stops me here, it is too much of joy.
And this, and this the greatest discords be *They kiss.*

183 Cf. Dent, S908, 'After a storm comes calm'; *calms* = calms at sea; inner tranquillity.

184 **wakened** aroused, summoned into existence, i.e. till they threaten our death

186 **Olympus-high** (a coinage) as high as Mount Olympus, the fabled abode of the gods in Greek mythology

187–91 **If . . . fate** a common sentiment in classical writers. Cf. Virgil, *Aeneid*, 4.660, Terence, *The Eunuch*, 551–2, 'O heavens! this is a moment when I could bear dissolution for fear life pollute this exultation with some distress.'

187 **If it were** elliptical: if it were (my fate) now . . .

189 **content** quibble on content = containing capacity (*OED* 5)

190 **comfort** delight, gladness; relief (after distress)

191 **Succeeds . . . fate** can follow in our unknown, predetermined futures. After *Olympus-high, unknown fate* has Greek overtones.

191–2 **forbid / But that** double negative, i.e. ensure that

193 **grow** increase

Amen . . . powers *Amen* is biblical, *sweet powers* suggests the pagan classical gods (esp. after 186, 191) (but cf. *Ham* 3.1.141, 'Heavenly powers, restore him!'). Cf. 5.2.217, 'O heauenly God' (Q), 'oh heauenly Powres' (F).

194 **speak enough of** perhaps 'speak highly enough of' or 'my words cannot express'. But Shakespeare may have intended 'I cannot speak. Enough of this content!' (referring back to 181, 189).

195 **stops** chokes (*OED* 9). Preparing for his later choking, esp. 4.1.36.

here pointing to his throat?

196 **discords** absence of harmony (music); disagreement, strife. From Lat. *cor* = heart (cf. 197). Iago takes it in the musical sense.

183 calms] *F;* calmenesse *Q* 192] *as Q; F lines* Loues / encrease / 193 powers] *F;* power *Q* 194 speak . . . content] *QF* 196 discords] *F;* discord *Q* SD] *Q; not in F*

That e'er our hearts shall make.
IAGO [*aside*]
O, you are well tuned now: but I'll set down
The pegs that make this music, as honest
As I am.
OTHELLO Come, let us to the castle.
News, friends, our wars are done, the Turks are
drowned.
How does my old acquaintance of this isle?
Honey, you shall be well desired in Cyprus,
I have found great love amongst them. O my sweet,
I prattle out of fashion, and I dote
In mine own comforts. I prithee, good Iago,
Go to the bay and disembark my coffers.
Bring thou the master to the citadel,
He is a good one, and his worthiness
Does challenge much respect. Come, Desdemona;
Once more, well met at Cyprus.
[*Exeunt all but Iago and Roderigo.*]

198 **set down** slacken (the strings or pegs of a musical instrument); perhaps also 'bring low, or take down the (human) pegs (= Othello, Desdemona) that make this joyful music' (*OED* set 143)

199–200 ***as . . . am** for all my supposed honesty (Ridley). Why does Iago suddenly bridle at the thought of his honesty? I suspect that we need to complete 197: 'That e'er our hearts shall make. Honest Iago!' (Othello greets Cassio warmly, and merely nods to Iago saying 'Honest Iago!', i.e. well met, then turns back to Desdemona).

202 **old acquaintance** old friend(s). Cf. *1H4* 5.4.102, 'What, old acquaintance! could not all this flesh / Keep in a little life?' (Hal to Falstaff); *Auld Lang Syne*, 'Should auld acquaintance be forgot'.

203 **desired** sought after; with dramatic irony, since Roderigo and Iago desire her more literally

205 **out of fashion** improperly, contrary to what is expected (*OED* 11). Cf. *Tem* 3.1.57, 'I prattle / Something too wildly'.

207 **coffers** trunks, baggage. In Latin comedy a slave or servant sometimes has to disembark his master's luggage (e.g. Plautus, *Amphitruo*, 629; cf. *CE* 5.1.410). Othello treats Iago almost as a personal servant.

208 **master** captain (of merchant vessel) or navigating officer (of ship of war) (*OED* 2)

210 **challenge** deserve

211 **at** As they are in Cyprus, *at* may be an error, anticipating *at*, 212.

198 SD] *Rowe; not in QF* 198–200 O . . . am] *this edn; prose F; Q lines* now, / musique, / am. / 201] *as Q; F lines* done: / drown'd. / 202 does my] *F;* doe our *Q* this] *F;* the *Q* 211 SD] *Exit. Q; Exit Othello and Desdemona. F*

IAGO Do thou meet me presently at the harbour. Come hither: if thou be'st valiant – as, they say, base men being in love have then a nobility in their natures, more than is native to them – list me. The lieutenant tonight watches on the court of guard. First I must tell thee this: Desdemona is directly in love with him.

RODERIGO With him? why, 'tis not possible.

IAGO Lay thy finger thus, and let thy soul be instructed. Mark me with what violence she first loved the Moor, but for bragging and telling her fantastical lies – and will she love him still for prating? let not thy discreet heart think it. Her eye must be fed, and what delight shall she have to look on the devil? When the blood is made dull with the act of sport, there should be, again to inflame it, and to give satiety a fresh appetite, loveliness in favour, sympathy in years, manners and

212 **Do . . . harbour** Perhaps addressed to a soldier, as Iago tells Roderigo to meet him at the citadel (281). *Exit* does not have to mean that Iago and Roderigo are left alone (211, QF).
presently in a little while
213–15 **as . . . them** This could be an aside. Cf. Dent, D216, 'Despair (love) makes cowards courageous.'
213 **base** worthless, ignoble
215 **native** natural
list listen to
216 **watches** is on duty or on guard
court of guard body of soldiers on guard (*OED*, corps de garde); or, the watchpost occupied by the soldiers on guard
217 **directly** plainly; completely
219 **thus** 'On thy mouth, to stop it while thou art listening to a wiser man' (Johnson). Cf. *TC* 1.3.240, 'Peace, Troyan, lay thy finger on thy lips!'; Judges 18.19, 'Hold thy peace: lay thine hand upon thy mouth, and come with us.'
let . . . instructed a mock catechism, with Iago as priest!
221 **but . . . lies** Iago dislikes Othello's high-flown speech (cf. 1.1.12–13); *but* = only; *fantastical* = existing only in imagination, fabulous.
222 **still** always, constantly
prating boasting; idle chatter
discreet discerning, judicious
223 **fed** *Feed* = gratify (the vanity or passion of); *feed one's eyes* is pre-Shakespearian (cf. *Faerie Queene*, 2.7.4).
224 **devil** Cf. 1.1.90n.
225 **dull** sluggish, listless
sport sexual intercourse: cf. 5.2.210, 'the act of shame'
226 **satiety** satiation
227 ***loveliness** loveableness; beauty. For the QF 'common error' in punctuation, see *Texts*, 100.
favour attractiveness; appearance (*OED* 8, 9)
sympathy affinity; likeness

213 hither] *Q;* thither *F* 215 list me] *Q;* list-me *F* 216 must] *F;* will *Q* 217 thee this:] *F;* thee, this *Q* 221–2 ²and . . . love] *Q;* To loue *F* 222 thy] *F;* the *Q* 223 it] *F;* so *Q* 225 again] *Q;* a game *F* ²to] *F; not in Q* 226–7 appetite, loveliness] *Theobald;* appetite. Loue lines *Q;* appetite. Louelinesse *F*

beauties, all which the Moor is defective in. Now for want of these required conveniences, her delicate tenderness will find itself abused, begin to heave the gorge, disrelish and abhor the Moor – very nature will instruct her in it and compel her to some second choice. Now sir, this granted – as it is a most pregnant and unforced position – who stands so eminent in the degree of this fortune as Cassio does? a knave very voluble, no farther conscionable than in putting on the mere form of civil and humane seeming, for the better compassing of his salt and most hidden loose affection. Why none, why none: a slipper and subtle knave, a finder out of occasions, that has an eye, can stamp and counterfeit advantages, though true advantage never present itself – a devilish knave;

229 **required** necessary
conveniences correspondences; aptitudes; advantages; comforts
230 **tenderness** youthfulness; sensitiveness to impression (*OED* 1, 3)
abused cheated; injured
230–1 **heave the gorge** vomit
231 **disrelish** *OED* dis- 6: *dis-* forms compound verbs which reverse the action of the simple verb. She relished what went down as food but does not relish what comes up as vomit.
very nature natural instincts themselves (Ridley)
233 **pregnant** obvious, cogent
234 **unforced position** natural proposition
eminent high
235 **degree** (lit. step, one of a flight of steps) stairway leading to
fortune good fortune
knave crafty rogue
236 **voluble** inconstant, variable; fluent or glib of tongue (more true of Iago than Cassio!)
conscionable governed by conscience
236–7 **putting on** feigning (*OED* put 46e); putting on the mask of
237 **form** prescribed behaviour
civil . . . seeming well-bred and courteous appearance
238 **compassing** attaining; embracing
salt lecherous (cf. 3.3.407)
239 **loose** wanton, immoral
affection emotion; lust
slipper slippery
240 **subtle** skilful; crafty, cunning
occasions opportunities
241 **eye** perhaps a roving eye. Cf. 2.3.21, 'What an eye she has!'
stamp make a coin; engender. Cf. *Cym* 2.5.4ff.: 'my father was I know not where / When I was stamped. Some coiner with his tools / Made me a counterfeit'.
advantages opportunities
***though** Q *the* must be a misreading of *tho* (*Texts*, 44).
242 **true** honest, virtuous

232 in it] *F;* to it *Q* 234 eminent] *F;* eminently *Q* 236 farther] farder *Q;* further *F* 237 humane seeming] *F;* hand-seeming *Q* 238 compassing] *Q;* compasse *F* 238–9 most . . . affection] *F;* hidden affections *Q* 239 Why . . . [2]none] *F; not in Q* 239–40 slipper and subtle] *F;* subtle slippery *Q* 240 out of occasions] *Q;* of occasion *F* has] *Q;* he's *F* 241–2 advantages . . . advantage] *F;* the true aduantages *Q* 242 itself . . . knave] *as F;* themselues *Q*

besides, the knave is handsome, young, and hath all those requisites in him that folly and green minds look after. A pestilent complete knave, and the woman hath found him already.

RODERIGO I cannot believe that in her, she's full of most blest condition.

IAGO Blest fig's-end! The wine she drinks is made of grapes. If she had been blest she would never have loved the Moor. Blest pudding! Didst thou not see her paddle with the palm of his hand? Didst not mark that?

RODERIGO Yes, that I did, but that was but courtesy.

IAGO Lechery, by this hand: an index and obscure prologue to the history of lust and foul thoughts. They met so near with their lips that their breaths embraced together. Villainous thoughts, Roderigo: when these mutualities so marshal the way, hard at hand comes the master and main exercise, th'in-

244 **folly** foolishness; wickedness; wantonness
green immature
245 **look after** search for
pestilent poisonous, confounded (*OED* 4, often used humorously)
246 **found** unclear (deliberately?); 'seen sympathetically what he is after' (Sanders); or perhaps = had. Cf. 133, *KL* 5.1.10–11, 'have you never found my brother's way / To the forfended place?'
247 **I . . . her** Like Sir Andrew (*TN* 1.3.67) he is comically overemphatic.
248 **condition** disposition; nature; quality
249 **fig's-end** Cf. 1.3.320n.
249–50 **The . . . grapes** one of Iago's vague general assertions, which we have to interpret for ourselves. Cf. Dent, W466, 'No wine made of grapes but hath lees, no woman created of flesh but hath faults' (1580).
251 **pudding** could = sausage (as in black pudding). I suspect euphemisms for 'blest vagina' (249), 'blest penis' (251).
252 **paddle** toy, fondle. So *Ham* 3.4.185, 'paddling in your neck with his damned fingers', *WT* 1.2.115.
255 **index** table of contents prefixed to a book; preface, prologue
obscure unclearly expressed, hidden
259 **mutualities** intimacies
hard close
260 **master** (adj.) principal
exercise action, exertion, (sexual) 'sport'
260–1 **incorporate** 'united in one body', i.e. the 'beast with two backs' (1.1.115). Cf. *VA* 539–40, 'Her arms do lend his neck a sweet embrace; / Incorporate then they seem, face grows to face.'

246 hath] *F;* has *Q* 251 Blest pudding] *F; not in Q* 252–3 Didst . . . that?] *F; not in Q* 254 that I did] *F; not in Q* 255 obscure] *F; not in Q* 258 Villainous . . . Roderigo] *F; not in Q* 259 mutualities] *Q;* mutabilities *F* hard] *F;* hand *Q* 260 master and] *F; not in Q* th'] *F;* the *Q*

corporate conclusion. Pish! But, sir, be you ruled by me. I have brought you from Venice: watch you tonight. For the command, I'll lay't upon you. Cassio knows you not, I'll not be far from you, do you find some occasion to anger Cassio, either by speaking too loud or tainting his discipline, or from what other cause you please which the time shall more favourably minister.

RODERIGO Well.

IAGO Sir, he's rash and very sudden in choler, and haply with his truncheon may strike at you: provoke him that he may, for even out of that will I cause these of Cyprus to mutiny, whose qualification shall come into no true trust again but by the displanting of Cassio. So shall you have a shorter journey to your desires, by the means I shall then have to prefer them, and the impediment most profitably removed, without the which there were no expectation of our prosperity.

RODERIGO I will do this, if you can bring it to any opportunity.

IAGO I warrant thee. Meet me by and by at the citadel:

261 **Pish!** Cf. 4.1.42: exclamation of disgust or vexation, it shows Iago reacting to his own voyeurism (or is he pretending?).
261–2 **But . . . me** Iago switches to *sir* and *you*: he is coming to the point.
261 **ruled** guided
263 **For . . . you** As for taking the lead (in our joint action), I'll leave it to you; 'I'll arrange for you to be appointed, given orders' (Bevington).
266 **tainting** disparaging
discipline military skill or professionalism
268 **minister** supply
270 **sudden** impetuous, abrupt, suddenly roused
choler (one of the four 'humours') in an irascible state
271 **haply** perhaps; by good luck
truncheon staff (carried by officers)
273 **mutiny** riot
qualification condition, nature; or, pacification: i.e. the Cypriots will not be trustworthy again except by the cashiering of Cassio
274 **displanting** removal
276 **prefer** advance
277 **profitably** advantageously
278 **prosperity** success. Note how Iago befogs with abstractions.
281 **warrant** assure, promise
thee Iago has won him over, and reverts to *thee*.

261 Pish] *F; not in Q* 263 the] *F;* your *Q* 267 cause] *Q;* course *F* 270 he's] *F;* he is *Q* 271 haply] *Q;* happely *F* with . . . truncheon] *Q (*Trunchen*); not in F* 274 trust] *Q;* taste *F* again] *F;* again't *Q* 278 the which] *F;* which *Q* 280 if you] *F;* if I *Q*

I must fetch his necessaries ashore. Farewell.
RODERIGO Adieu. *Exit.*
IAGO
That Cassio loves her, I do well believe it,
That she loves him, 'tis apt and of great credit.
The Moor, howbeit that I endure him not,
Is of a constant, loving, noble nature,
And I dare think he'll prove to Desdemona
A most dear husband. Now I do love her too,
Not out of absolute lust – though peradventure
I stand accountant for as great a sin – responsible
But partly led to diet my revenge, for revenge
For that I do suspect the lusty Moor
Hath leaped into my seat, the thought whereof
Doth like a poisonous mineral gnaw my inwards . . .
And nothing can or shall content my soul
Till I am evened with him, wife for wife . . .
Or, failing so, yet that I put the Moor
At least into a jealousy so strong

282 **necessaries** i.e. coffers, 207.
Farewell Iago dismisses him. *Adieu*, 283, is more 'upper-class'.
284 **loves** For Iago's curious reasoning, and the meaning of 'love', see Honigmann, *Seven Tragedies*, 87.
285 **apt** likely; fitting (in view of the theories he has expounded, 220ff.)
credit credibility
286 **howbeit** however it may be
endure him not cannot stand him
289 **dear** fond, loving
290 **absolute** mere, pure and simple
peradventure as it happens
291 **accountant** responsible
as . . . sin i.e. revenge
292 **diet** Why not 'feed'? Because revenge needs a special diet.
293 **For that** because
lusty lustful
294 **Hath . . . seat** Cf. *OED* leap 9: 'of certain beasts: to spring upon (the female) in copulation'; *1H4* 1.2.9, 'leaping-houses' (= brothels); *Son* 41.9, 'Ay me, but yet thou mightst *my seat* forbear'; *H5* 5.2.139, 'I should quickly leap into a wife'. *Seat* = sexual seat, his wife.
295 hinting at ulcers?
mineral Cf. 1.2.74n.
296 echoing 189, 'My soul hath her content so absolute'
297 **evened** Cf. *womaned* (3.4.195), *weaponed* (5.2.264): made even or quits.
wife for wife Cf. Exodus 21.1, 23–4, 'These are the laws . . . life for life, eye for eye, tooth for tooth'.

284 it] *Q;* 't *F* 286 howbeit] *F;* howbe't *Q* 287 loving, noble] *F;* noble, louing *Q* 291 accountant] *Q;* accomptant *F* 292 led] *F;* lead *Q* 293 lusty] *F;* lustfull *Q* 296 or] *F;* nor *Q* 297 evened] *F (*eeuen'd*);* euen *Q* ²wife] *Q;* wift *F* 299 jealousy] *as Q;* Ielouzie *F*

That judgement cannot cure; which thing to do,
If this poor trash of Venice, whom I trash
For his quick hunting, stand the putting on,
I'll have our Michael Cassio on the hip,
Abuse him to the Moor in the rank garb –
For I fear Cassio with my night-cap too –
Make the Moor thank me, love me, and reward me
For making him egregiously an ass,
And practising upon his peace and quiet
Even to madness. 'Tis here, but yet confused:
Knavery's plain face is never seen, till used. *Exit.*

[**2.2**] *Enter Othello's* Herald, *with a proclamation.*

HERALD [*Reads.*] *It is Othello's pleasure, our noble and valiant general, that, upon certain tidings now arrived,*

300 **That . . . cure** that no one's good sense can cure it

301 **poor trash** worthless person

***trash** See LN.

302 **For . . . hunting** 'to prevent him from hunting too fast. Iago has had to restrain and pacify Roderigo many times, no doubt' (Kittredge). Cf. *for* = 'to prevent' in *2H6* 4.1.73–4, 'dam up this thy yawning mouth / For swallowing the treasure of the realm'.

quick energetic (ironic)

stand . . . on goes along with my incitement (*OED* put 46h)

303 **our** vaguely contemptuous: cf. 2.3.57.

on the hip at a disadvantage (a wrestling term). Cf. *MV* 4.1.334, Dent, H474, 'To have one on the hip'.

304 **Abuse** slander

rank lustful

garb manner of doing anything, behaviour (*OED* 3); i.e. misrepresent him as lecherous

305 **night-cap** a head covering, worn in bed. Not likely to be worn by a lover: Iago's sense of humour runs away with him.

308 **practising upon** plotting against

309 **Even to** even till I bring him to

here here in my head. Cf. the clever slave in classical comedy (Plautus, *Pseudolus*, 576).

confused not yet clearly worked out

310 **plain** simple, honest (sarcastic). Cf. *Luc* 1532.

seen i.e. seen clearly, until the moment comes when it has to be used

2.2.0.1 *Herald The Herald probably addresses the audience, as if it consists of Cypriots. It is not clear how much is read, how much spoken. QF print in roman throughout, I print 1–7 in italics (assuming that this is proclaimed, the rest spoken).

2 ***upon*** on the occasion of (*OED* 7a)

301 ^{2}trash] *Steevens;* crush *Q;* trace *F* 304 rank] *Q;* right *F* 305 night-cap] *Q;* Night-Cape *F* 2.2] *Scena Secunda. F; not in Q* 0.1] *as F; Enter a Gentleman reading a Proclamation. Q* 1 SP] *F; not in Q* SD] *not in QF* 1–7] *italics this edn; roman QF*

importing the mere perdition of the Turkish fleet, every man put himself into triumph: some to dance, some to make bonfires, each man to what sport and revels his addiction leads him. For besides these beneficial news, it is the celebration of his nuptial. – So much was his pleasure should be proclaimed. All offices are open, and there is full liberty of feasting from this present hour of five till the bell have told eleven. Heaven bless the isle of Cyprus and our noble general Othello! *Exit.*

[**2.3**] *Enter* OTHELLO, CASSIO *and* DESDEMONA.

OTHELLO
Good Michael, look you to the guard tonight.
Let's teach ourselves that honourable stop
Not to outsport discretion.

CASSIO
Iago hath direction what to do,
But notwithstanding with my personal eye
Will I look to't.

OTHELLO Iago is most honest.
Michael, good night. Tomorrow with your earliest
Let me have speech with you. Come, my dear love,

3 ***importing*** communicating, stating
mere perdition total destruction
4 ***triumph*** public festivity, revelry (cf. the Venetian carnival)
6 ****addiction*** inclination; *addition* would = rank
beneficial beneficent, good
8 **offices** kitchens, butteries, etc. (Ridley)
9 **liberty** freedom of behaviour, beyond what is recognized as proper (*OED* 5), as in *MM* 1.3.29, 'liberty plucks justice by the nose'
10 **told** counted; proclaimed; tolled
2.3.2 **stop** restraint
3 not to carry our revelling beyond the bounds of discretion; *outsport*: unique in Shakespeare
7 **with your earliest** at your earliest convenience

3 *every*] *as F;* that euery *Q* 4 ²*to*] *F; not in Q* 6 *addiction*] *Q2*; minde *Q;* addition *F* 7 *nuptial*] *as F;* Nuptialls *Q* 9 of feasting] *F; not in Q* 10 have] *F;* hath *Q* 10–11 Heaven bless] *Q;* Blesse *F* 12 SD] *F; not in Q* 2.3] *new scene Theobald; scene cont. QF* 0.1] *as Q; Enter Othello, Desdemona, Cassio, and Attendants. F* 2 that] *F;* the *Q* 4 direction] *F;* directed *Q* 6 't] *F;* it *Q*

The purchase made, the fruits are to ensue:
That profit's yet to come 'tween me and you.
Good-night. *Exeunt Othello and Desdemona.*

Enter IAGO.

CASSIO Welcome, Iago, we must to the watch.

IAGO Not this hour, lieutenant, 'tis not yet ten o'th' clock. Our general cast us thus early for the love of his Desdemona – whom let us not therefore blame; he hath not yet made wanton the night with her, and she is sport for Jove.

CASSIO She's a most exquisite lady.

IAGO And I'll warrant her full of game.

CASSIO Indeed she's a most fresh and delicate creature.

IAGO What an eye she has! methinks it sounds a parley to provocation.

CASSIO An inviting eye; and yet methinks right modest.

IAGO And when she speaks is it not an alarum to love?

9 **purchase** (a richer word than now) acquisition; gain; bargain; prize; something bought
fruits anything resulting from an action (*OED* 7), implying that the marriage has still to be consummated (see p. 44). Cf. *Homilies*, 446 ('Of matrimony'): marriage was instituted by God 'to bring forth fruit', i.e. children.

10 **profit** benefit; but after *purchase* the commercial sense is also present

13–17 **Iago** switches to prose; Cassio (weakly?) follows suit.

13 **Not this hour** not for an hour yet
ten Cf. 2.2.10, *five*.

14 **cast** got rid of

15 ***whom** Cf. 1.2.52n.

16 **hath . . . her** i.e. has not yet slept with her

17 **sport** Cf. 2.1.225.
Jove Jupiter, a notorious womanizer in classical legends

18 **exquisite** accomplished; consummately perfect or beautiful

19 **game** sport, spirit; 'expert in love-play' (Ridley)

20 Cassio comes halfway to Iago's view. He might speak thus of a prostitute (cf. *Per* 4.2.6–10, 'We were never so much out of creatures . . . let's have fresh ones'); *fresh* could = in prime condition; *delicate* could = pleasing to the palate. Is he weak – or innocent?

21 **What . . . has** Cf. Marlowe, *The Jew of Malta*, 4.2.127, 'What an eye she casts on me?' (Ithamore of the courtesan).
parley makes a trumpet call to an opponent: the usual love–war metaphor

22 **provocation** challenge, defiance (military or sexual)

23 **right** properly; very

24 **alarum** call to arms; sudden attack

10 That] *F;* The *Q* 'tween] *F;* twixt *Q* 11 SD] *Q; Exit. F* 13–14 o'th' clock] *F;* aclock *Q* 15 whom] *F2;* who *QF* 18 She's] *F;* She is *Q* 20 she's] *F;* she is *Q* 21–2] *QF lines (as verse?)* has? / prouocation. / 22 to] *F;* of *Q* 23–4] *F lines* eye: / modest. / speakes, / Loue? / 24 alarum] *F;* alarme *Q*

CASSIO She is indeed perfection.

IAGO Well: happiness to their sheets! Come, lieutenant, I have a stoup of wine, and here without are a brace of Cyprus gallants that would fain have a measure to the health of black Othello.

CASSIO Not tonight, good Iago, I have very poor and unhappy brains for drinking. I could well wish courtesy would invent some other custom of entertainment.

IAGO O, they are our friends. But one cup, I'll drink for you.

CASSIO I have drunk but one cup tonight, and that was craftily qualified too, and behold what innovation it makes here! I am unfortunate in the infirmity, and dare not task my weakness with any more.

IAGO What, man, 'tis a night of revels, the gallants desire it.

CASSIO Where are they?

IAGO Here, at the door, I pray you call them in.

CASSIO I'll do't, but it dislikes me. *Exit.*

IAGO

If I can fasten but one cup upon him,

25 **perfection** Cf. 1.3.101.

26 **sheets** Cf. *Pigmalions Image* (1598), 'Sweet sheetes . . . Sweet happy sheetes' (lover to loved one's bedsheets) (John Marston, *Poems*, ed. A. Davenport [Liverpool, 1961], p. 58).

27 **stoup** flagon, tankard (of varying sizes)
without outside
brace couple (Iago may understate, to get Cassio to agree)

28 **fain** gladly
measure liquid measure, i.e. toast

31 **unhappy** troublesome; unfortunate (*OED* 1, 3)

33 **entertainment** social behaviour; receiving guests (*OED* 4, 11)

34 **cup** wine cup (which could have a foot and stem and lid); or, a cup with the wine it contains, a cupful

37 **craftily** skilfully
qualified diluted
innovation revolution, change. What is Iago to *behold*? Is Cassio unsteady on his legs (= *here*, 38)?

39 **task** test

40 **man** (less polite, putting pressure on Cassio)
gallants (military) followers; men of pleasure

44 **it dislikes me** I'm not happy about it

45 **fasten . . . upon** induce acceptance of: 'if I can get him to drink just one cupful'

25 She] *F;* It *Q* 29 black] *F;* the blacke *Q* 36 have] *F;* ha *Q* 38 unfortunate] *as Q;* infortunate *F*

With that which he hath drunk tonight already
He'll be as full of quarrel and offence
As my young mistress' dog. Now my sick fool,
  Roderigo,
Whom love hath turned almost the wrong side out,
To Desdemona hath tonight caroused
Potations pottle-deep, and he's to watch.
Three else of Cyprus, noble swelling spirits
That hold their honours in a wary distance,
The very elements of this warlike isle,
Have I tonight flustered with flowing cups,
And the watch too. Now 'mongst this flock of
  drunkards
Am I to put our Cassio in some action
That may offend the isle.

Enter CASSIO, MONTANO *and* Gentlemen.

But here they come.

47 **offence** aggressiveness, readiness to give or take offence
48 **As . . . dog** as any young lady's lapdog (some small dogs are especially aggressive)
sick love-sick
Roderigo extra-metrical
49 perhaps 'whom love has made almost the opposite of what he was'. Cf. 4.2.148, 'turned your wit the seamy side without'.
50 **caroused** drunk (a health); drunk repeatedly
51 **Potations** drinks, draughts
pottle-deep a coinage: to the bottom of a half-gallon tankard
watch i.e. for Cassio: 2.1.260ff.
52 **else** others
swelling proud, haughty
53 that keep their honours cautiously at a distance (from disgrace), i.e. that are quick to take offence
54 **elements** essential constituents, i.e. the life-blood. This word was sometimes spoken 'in inverted commas' (cf. *TN* 3.1.58, 3.4.124).
this warlike isle Cf. 2.1.43.
55 **flustered** befuddled
flowing poured out without stint. So *H5* 4.3.55.
56 **the** F *they* is possible. For final *-y* and final twirls misread in Q and F, see *Texts*, 85.
watch (military) watchmen or sentinels
flock One thinks of sheep or geese.
57 **Am I to** I have to, the plan is to
our Cf. 2.1.303n.
58 **offend** vex; injure

48] *as Q; F lines* dogge. / *Rodorigo*, / 49 hath] *F;* has *Q* out] *F;* outward *Q* 51 watch.] *F;* watch *Q* 52 else] *F;* lads *Q* 53 honours] *F;* honour *Q* 56] *as Q; F lines* too. / drunkards / the] *Q;* they *F* 57 Am I] *F;* I am *Q* to put] *Q;* put to *F* 58 SD] *F (after 58); Enter* Montanio, Cassio, *and others. Q (opp. 58)*

If consequence do but approve my dream
My boat sails freely, both with wind and stream.

CASSIO 'Fore God, they have given me a rouse already.

MONTANO Good faith, a little one, not past a pint, as I am a soldier.

IAGO Some wine, ho!

[*Sings.*]

And let me the cannikin clink, clink,
And let me the cannikin clink.
A soldier's a man,
O, man's life's but a span,
Why then let a soldier drink!

Some wine, boys!

CASSIO 'Fore God, an excellent song!

IAGO I learned it in England, where indeed they are most potent in potting. Your Dane, your German, and your swag-bellied Hollander – drink, ho! – are nothing to your English.

59 if that which follows only confirms my daydream, i.e. if the result bears out my hopes

60 Cf. Dent, W429, 'Sail with wind and tide'; *freely* = without hindrance, just as I want. For similar summing-up lines, cf. *TC* 2.3.266, 'Light boats sail swift, though greater hulks draw deep'; *JC* 5.1.67, 'Why now blow wind, swell billow, and swim bark!', *Cym* 4.3.46.

61 **rouse** carouse, a full bumper

65ff. For the song cf. p. 401.

65 **cannikin** small drinking can; *-kin* is diminutive (= German *-chen*), as probably in napkin (*OED* -kin, suffix)
clink i.e. against someone else's

68 Cf. Dent, L251, 'Life is a span', from Psalms 39.6, 'thou hast made my days as it were a span long'; *span* = a short distance or space of time.

72 **in England** This draws attention to the play as a play: cf. *Ham* 5.1.148ff.

73 **potent in potting** go in for drinking in a big way. Drinking songs before *Oth* praised the superior potting of the English (Lyly, *Sapho*, 3.2.76ff., 'O! thats a roring Englishman, / Who in deepe healths do's so excell, / From Dutch and French he beares the bel') or of the singers themselves (Lyly, *Mother Bombie*, 2.1.149ff.).

73–9 **Your** Note the force of Iago's repeated *your* (not quite the same as the indefinite article or 'a typical Dane', etc.): Iago wants to generate camaraderie.

74 **swag-bellied** with a belly that sags or wobbles

61 God] *Q;* heauen *F* 62–3] *prose F; verse Q* pint, / Good faith] *Q;* Good-faith *F* 64.1] *Rowe; not in QF* 65–9, 85–92] *italics QF (except 85 Q)* 65 cannikin] *Q; Cannakin F* 66 clink] *F; clinke, clinke Q* 67–8] *one line QF* 68 O, man's] *F; a Q* 71 God] *Q;* Heauen *F*

CASSIO Is your Englishman so exquisite in his drinking?

IAGO Why, he drinks you with facility your Dane dead drunk; he sweats not to overthrow your Almain; he gives your Hollander a vomit ere the next pottle can be filled.

CASSIO To the health of our general!

MONTANO I am for it, lieutenant, and I'll do you justice.

IAGO O sweet England!

[*Sings.*]

King Stephen was and-a worthy peer,
His breeches cost him but a crown,
He held them sixpence all too dear,
With that he called the tailor lown.
He was a wight of high renown
And thou art but of low degree,
'Tis pride that pulls the country down,
Then take thine auld cloak about thee.

Some wine, ho!

CASSIO 'Fore God, this is a more exquisite song than the other!

IAGO Will you hear't again?

CASSIO No, for I hold him to be unworthy of his place

76 **exquisite** accomplished. Cassio, drunk, gets 'stuck' on this word, which he had used before (2.3.18); slurred by some actors as 'ex-qust'.
78 **he . . . overthrow** he can easily outdrink
Almain German
79 **pottle** a half-gallon tankard
82–3 **do you justice** drink level with you (Ridley)
85ff. See LN.
85 **and-a** Cf. *TN* 5.1.389, 'When that I was and a little tine boy'; *KL* 3.2.74. A metrical 'fill in' used in ballads (Furness).
86 **a crown** five shillings
88 **lown** loon, rogue; a man of low birth
89–91 Does Iago sing these lines at Cassio, thus provoking 105ff.?
91 perhaps 'it is extravagance in dress that causes hard times in our country' (Kittredge)
92 **auld** old, as in 'auld lang syne' (dialectal)
97 **unworthy** Vaguely aware of professional misconduct, he is too befuddled to pin down or complete his thought.

76 Englishman] *Q;* Englishmen *F* exquisite] *F;* expert *Q* 82 I'll] *F;* I will *Q* 84 SD] *not in QF* 85 and-a] *F;* a *Q* 87 them] *F;* *'em Q* 92 Then] *Q; And F* thine] *Q; thy F* auld] *owd Q; awl'd F* 94 'Fore God] *Q;* Why *F* 97 to be] *F; not in Q*

that does . . . those things. Well, God's above all, and there be souls must be saved, and there be souls must not be saved.

IAGO It's true, good lieutenant.

CASSIO For mine own part, no offence to the general nor any man of quality, I hope to be saved.

IAGO And so do I too, lieutenant.

CASSIO Ay, but, by your leave, not before me. The lieutenant is to be saved before the ancient. Let's have no more of this, let's to our affairs. God forgive us our sins! Gentlemen, let's look to our business. Do not think, gentlemen, I am drunk: this is my ancient, this is my right hand, and this is my left. I am not drunk now: I can stand well enough, and I speak well enough.

GENTLEMAN Excellent well.

CASSIO Why, very well then; you must not think then that I am drunk. *Exit.*

MONTANO
To th' platform, masters, come, let's set the watch.

IAGO
You see this fellow that is gone before,

98 **God's above all** Cf. Dent, H348, 'Heaven (God) is above all.'
99 **be saved** find salvation, go to heaven. Cf. Matthew 10.22, 'he that endureth to the end shall be saved'.
102–3 Cf. Sir Andrew (*TN* 1.3.117–18) who thinks himself as good as 'any man in Illyria, whatsoever he be, under the degree of my betters'.
103 **quality** high birth, good social position (i.e. excluding Iago)
105 **not . . . me** Cf. *MA* 4.2.19–20, 'write God first, for God defend but God should go before such villains!'
107 **affairs** i.e. duties
107–8 **God . . . sins** Cf. the Lord's Prayer.
110 **right . . . left** Cf. Dent, H74, 'He knows not (knows) his right hand from his left.'
116 **platform** gun-platform
masters gentlemen
set the watch mount the guard
117 **fellow** man; but could = worthless person (*OED* 9, 10c), i.e. obliquely contemptuous

98 does . . . those] *this edn;* does those *QF* God's] *Q;* heau'ns *F* 99 ^{1}must] *F;* that must *Q* 99–100 and . . . saved] *F; not in Q* 101 It's] *F;* It is *Q* 104 too] *F; not in Q* 106 have] *F;* ha *Q* 107 God] *Q; not in F* 110 left] *F;* left hand *Q* 111 I speak] *F;* speake *Q* 113 SP] *Gent. F; All. Q* 114 Why] *F; not in Q* ^{2}then] *F; not in Q* 116 To th' platform] *F;* To the plotforme *Q*

He is a soldier fit to stand by Caesar
And give direction. And do but see his vice,
'Tis to his virtue a just equinox,
The one as long as th'other. 'Tis pity of him:
I fear the trust Othello puts him in
On some odd time of his infirmity
Will shake this island.

MONTANO But is he often thus?

IAGO
'Tis evermore the prologue to his sleep:
He'll watch the horologe a double set
If drink rock not his cradle.

MONTANO It were well
The general were put in mind of it.
Perhaps he sees it not, or his good nature
Prizes the virtue that appears in Cassio
And looks not on his evils: is not this true?

Drunk

Enter RODERIGO.

IAGO [*aside*]
How now, Roderigo?

Distract Montano. (pouring drink)

118 **stand by Caesar** i.e. as an equal; or, as his right-hand man

120 It counterbalances his virtue as exactly as day and night are equal at the equinox.

121 **pity of** a pity about

122 **trust** position of trust. But Capell's *in him* (for *him in*) may be right.

123 at some unusual (or, unexpected) time, when he suffers from his infirmity

124 **shake** (?)convulse (deliberately vague?)

125 **evermore** emphatic form of 'ever'

126 He'll stay awake twice round the clock or *horologe* ('while the clock strikes two rounds, or four-and-twenty hours' [Johnson]).

127 **cradle** unexplained; perhaps 'if drink doesn't rock him asleep, like a baby in a cradle'. But this is suspiciously abrupt: cf. *2H4* 3.1.19–20, 'Seal up the ship-boy's eyes, and rock his brains / In cradle of the rude imperious surge', which is immediately intelligible. Perhaps a misreading (*cradle* for *nodle*)? Viz. 'if drink doesn't unsteady his brain'. Cf. *TS* 1.1.64, 'your noddle' (= your head).

128 **put in mind** made aware

130 **Prizes** esteems
virtue unusual ability

131 **looks not on** disregards
evils i.e. faults

118 He is] *Q;* He's *F* 122 puts] *F;* put *Q* 125 the] *Q;* his *F* 127–8 It were . . . it] *as F; one line Q* 127 It were] *F;* Twere *Q* 130 Prizes] *F;* Praises *Q* virtue] *F;* vertues *Q* 131 looks] *F;* looke *Q* 132 SD] *Capell; not in QF*

I pray you, after the lieutenant, go! *Exit Roderigo.*

MONTANO

And 'tis great pity that the noble Moor

Should hazard such a place as his own second 135

With one of an ingraft infirmity.

It were an honest action to say so

To the Moor. Not I, for this fair island.

IAGO

I do love Cassio well, and would do much

 A cry within: 'Help! help!'

To cure him of this evil. But hark, what noise? 140

Enter CASSIO *pursuing* RODERIGO.

CASSIO Zounds, you rogue! you rascal! ← *angry*

MONTANO What's the matter, lieutenant?

CASSIO A knave teach me my duty? I'll beat the knave

 into a twiggen bottle!

RODERIGO Beat me? *Innocence → Cassio looks* 145

CASSIO Dost thou prate, rogue? *like a drunken idiot,*

MONTANO Nay, good lieutenant! I pray you, sir, hold

 your hand. *→ "Are you talking back to me, jerk?!" (2018 vers)*

CASSIO Let me go, sir, or I'll knock you o'er the

 mazzard. 150

135–6 should risk such a place as that of his own deputy by entrusting it to one with an ingrained weakness (*ingraft* = engraffed, grafted on)

137 **action** three syllables. Perhaps 'so' should begin 138.

140.1 Q '*driuing in*' = *Tem* 5.1.255, '*Enter Ariell, driuing in Caliban*', i.e. chasing on to the stage, whereas usually *in* = off stage, like *within* (cf. 5.2.84ff.). See *Texts*, 161.

143 **beat** Social inferiors were beaten, equals had to be challenged. In classical comedy and its derivatives beatings were a comic routine: cf. *TS* 4.1.165, etc., *CE* 2.2.23.

144 **twiggen** made of twigs or wicker-work (= Q *wicker*), 'like a Chianti flask' (Ridley); i.e. the criss-cross of weals on his body will look like wicker-work

146 **prate** chatter; could = speak boastfully or officiously

150 **mazzard** cup, bowl; (jocular) head. Cf. *Ham* 5.1.89. No doubt bottles and drinking cups were used in this scene.

133 SD] *Q; not in F* 137–8 It were . . . Moor] *as F; one line Q* 138 Not] *F;* Nor *Q* 139 SD] *Helpe, helpe, within Q; not in F* 140.1] *pursuing F; driuing in Q* 141 Zounds] *Q (*Zouns*); not in F* 143 duty? I'll] *as F;* duty: but I'le *Q* 144 twiggen bottle] Twiggen-Bottle *F;* wicker bottle *Q* 147–50] *as Q; F lines as verse* Lieutenant: / hand. / (Sir) / Mazard. / 147 Nay . . . I pray you] *F;* Good . . . pray *Q*

MONTANO Come, come, you're drunk.
CASSIO Drunk? *They fight.*
IAGO [*aside to Roderigo*]
Away, I say, go out and cry a mutiny. [*Exit Roderigo.*]
Nay, good lieutenant! God's will, gentlemen –
Help ho! Lieutenant! sir – Montano – sir –
Help, masters, here's a goodly watch indeed. *A bell rings.*
Who's that which rings the bell? Diablo, ho!
The town will rise, God's will, lieutenant, hold,
You will be shamed for ever!

Enter OTHELLO *and Attendants.*

OTHELLO
What is the matter here?
MONTANO Zounds, I bleed still;
I am hurt to th' death: he dies! [*Lunges at Cassio.*]
OTHELLO Hold, for your lives!
IAGO
Hold, ho! Lieutenant! sir – Montano – gentlemen –
Have you forgot all sense of place and duty?
Hold, the general speaks to you: hold, for shame!
OTHELLO
Why, how now, ho? From whence ariseth this?

153 **mutiny** riot
155 **ho!** could = *whoa*, a call to stop or cease what one is doing (*OED* int. 2)
156 **goodly** fine (ironical)
157 **the bell** the alarm bell
Diablo devil. Only once in Shakespeare in this Spanish form (Iago is a Spanish name: see p. 338).
158 **rise** take up arms; revolt
159 **shamed** disgraced (*Texts*, 118, 141)
161 **he dies** I'll kill him (cf. 5.1.10). Some, following Q2, treat *he dies* as a SD, but (1) Montano does not die, (2) the metre requires *he dies.*
for your lives if you value your lives
163 *Hanmer's transposition must be right.

151 you're] *F;* you are *Q* 152 SD] *Q; not in F* 153 [1]SD] Aside *Capell; not in QF* [2]SD] *not in QF; Exit* Rod. *Q2* 154 God's will] *Q;* Alas *F* 155 Montano – sir] *Montanio*, sir, *Q; Montano: F* 156 SD] *A bell rung: Q opp. 153; not in F* 157 which] *F;* that *Q* 158 God's will] *Q;* Fie, fie *F* hold] *Q; not in F* 159 You . . . shamed] *Q;* You'le be asham'd *F* 159.1] *F; Enter* Othello, *and Gentlemen with weapons. Q* 160 Zounds] *Q; not in F* 160–1 I bleed . . . dies] *one line F* 161 th'] *F;* the *Q* he dies!] He dies. *F; not in Q; he faints. Q2 (SD)* SD] *this edn; not in QF;* assailing Cassio again. *Capell* 162 ho] *F;* hold *Q* sir – Montano –] *sir Montanio, Q;* Sir *Montano, F* 163 sense of place] *Hanmer;* place of sence *QF* 164 hold] *F;* hold, hold *Q* 165 ariseth] *F;* arises *Q*

Are we turned Turks? and to ourselves do that
Which heaven hath forbid the Ottomites?
For Christian shame, put by this barbarous brawl;
He that stirs next, to carve for his own rage,
Holds his soul light: he dies upon his motion.
Silence that dreadful bell, it frights the isle
From her propriety. What is the matter, masters?
Honest Iago, that look'st dead with grieving,
Speak: who began this? on thy love I charge thee.

Othello = Christian.

IAGO

I do not know, friends all, but now, even now,
In quarter and in terms like bride and groom
Divesting them for bed; and then, but now,
As if some planet had unwitted men,
Swords out, and tilting one at other's breasts
In opposition bloody. I cannot speak
Any beginning to this peevish odds,
And would in action glorious I had lost
Those legs that brought me to a part of it.

Remind Othello of Dd.

166–7 See LN.
168 **put by** give up
barbarous Cf. 1.3.356n.
169 **carve** cut, cleave. Cf. Dent, C110, 'To be one's own carver'; *Faerie Queene*, 2.8.22, 'I can carve with this inchaunted brond [sword]'. Perhaps alluding to 'carving' meat at table.
170 **light** of small value
upon his motion the instant he moves (Ridley)
171 **dreadful** (stronger than now) terrifying
172 **propriety** proper character, own nature (i.e. peacefulness)
masters (He recognizes their social standing.)
174 **on . . . thee** By your love (affection) for me, I order you (to speak).
175 **all**, Some editors drop F's comma.
but only
176 **quarter** relations with, conduct towards, another (*OED* 17)
terms language
like . . . groom Is this meant to be cheeky (glancing at Othello and Desdemona)?
177 **Divesting them** undressing themselves
178 **unwitted** deprived of wits (*OED*, first here). It was thought that planets, if they came too near, could make men mad. Cf. Dent, P389, 'To be planet-struck', and 5.2.108–10.
179 **tilting** thrusting
180 **speak** reveal (*OED* 28)
181 **peevish** senseless; headstrong (*OED* 1, 4)
odds disagreement, quarrel (*OED*: in sixteenth century regularly construed as singular)
183 **a . . . it** i.e. take part in it

167 hath] *F;* has *Q* 169 for] *F;* forth *Q* 172 What is] *F;* what's *Q* 173 look'st] *Hanmer;* lookes *QF* 175 all,] *F;* all *Q* 177 for] *F;* to *Q* 179 breasts] *F;* breast *Q* 183 Those] *F;* These *Q*

OTHELLO

How comes it, Michael, you are thus forgot?

CASSIO

I pray you pardon me, I cannot speak.

OTHELLO

Worthy Montano, you were wont to be civil:
The gravity and stillness of your youth
The world hath noted, and your name is great
In mouths of wisest censure. What's the matter
That you unlace your reputation thus
And spend your rich opinion for the name
Of a night-brawler? Give me answer to it.

MONTANO

Worthy Othello, I am hurt to danger:
Your officer Iago can inform you,
While I spare speech, which something now offends
  me,
Of all that I do know; nor know I aught
By me that's said or done amiss this night
Unless self-charity be sometimes a vice,
And to defend ourselves it be a sin
When violence assails us.

OTHELLO Now, by heaven,

My blood begins my safer guides to rule
And passion, having my best judgement collied,

184 **are thus forgot** have thus forgotten yourself
186 **civil** civilized (as befits a citizen)
187 **stillness** quietness of temper
188 **great** i.e. greatly praised
189 **In . . . censure** in the mouths of men of wisest judgement
190 **unlace** undo (the laces of a purse); cut or carve (a boar or rabbit: a hunting term) (*OED* 1, 3)
191 **spend** waste, destroy
opinion reputation
192 **night-brawler** unique in Shakespeare
193 **to danger** to the point of danger
195 **something** somewhat
offends hurts (understatement)
198 **self-charity** regard for one's self (unique in Shakespeare). Many new compounds with 'self' appeared in the sixteenth and seventeenth centuries; Shakespeare coined several (cf. 3.3.203).
201 **blood** passion, anger
202 **collied** darkened: so *MND* 1.1.145, 'Brief as the lightning in the collied night'

184 comes . . . are] *F;* came . . . were *Q* 186 Montano . . . wont to] *F; Montanio* . . . wont *Q* 189 mouths] *F;* men *Q* 192 it] *F;* 't *Q* 198 sometimes] *F;* sometime *Q* 202 collied] *F;* coold *Q;* quell'd *Capell*

Assays to lead the way. Zounds, if I once stir,
Or do but lift this arm, the best of you
Shall sink in my rebuke. Give me to know
How this foul rout began, who set it on,
And he that is approved in this offence,
Though he had twinned with me, both at a birth,
Shall lose me. What, in a town of war
Yet wild, the people's hearts brimful of fear,
To manage private and domestic quarrel?
In night, and on the court and guard of safety?
'Tis monstrous. Iago, who began't?

MONTANO Othello trusts him.

If partially affined or leagued in office
Thou dost deliver more or less than truth
Thou art no soldier.

Misjudgement

IAGO Touch me not so near.

I had rather have this tongue cut from my mouth
Than it should do offence to Michael Cassio,
Yet I persuade myself to speak the truth

203 **Assays** tries
stir begin to act, bestir myself
205 **sink** fall; go down to hell (*OED* 2, obsolete)
my rebuke the shameful check (or, disgrace; reprimand) that I shall give him
206 **foul rout** disgraceful brawl
207 **approved** confirmed (guilty)
208 **twinned . . . birth** been my twin, both born at one birth. Twins can be born close together or with an interval between them.
209 **town of war** garrison town
210 **wild** unruly, uncontrolled
the . . . fear But cf. 2.1.201, 'our wars are done'.
211 **manage** conduct
domestic internal
212 **In night** usually 'in th(e) night': in Shakespeare's hand *th* sometimes looked like a meaningless squiggle (*Texts*, 84), so was dropped by a copyist
and on . . . safety and on the courtyard and (during) the guard duty meant to protect our general safety. But Theobald's transposition, 'of guard and', may be right (cf. 163).
213 **monstrous** a trisyllable (monsterous) (Malone)
214 ***If . . . office** if bound (to Cassio) by partiality, or because he's a colleague
215 **more . . . truth** Cf. Dent, T590, 'The truth, the whole truth, and nothing but the truth'.
216 **Touch** charge, take to task (*OED* 19)
near closely
218 **offence** harm

203 Zounds] *as Q; not in F* once] *F; not in Q* 210 brimful] *Q;* brim-full *F* 211 quarrel] *F;* quarrels *Q* 212 and guard of] *QF;* of Guard and *as Theobald* 213 began't] *F;* began *Q* 214 partially] *F;* partiality *Q* leagued] *Pope;* league *QF* 217 have] *F;* ha *Q* cut] *F;* out *Q*

Shall nothing wrong him. Thus it is, general:
Montano and myself being in speech,
There comes a fellow crying out for help
And Cassio following him with determined sword
To execute upon him. Sir, this gentleman
Steps in to Cassio and entreats his pause,
Myself the crying fellow did pursue
Lest by his clamour, as it so fell out,
The town might fall in fright. He, swift of foot,
Outran my purpose, and I returned the rather
For that I heard the clink and fall of swords
And Cassio high in oath, which till tonight
I ne'er might say before. When I came back,
For this was brief, I found them close together
At blow and thrust, even as again they were
When you yourself did part them.
More of this matter cannot I report.
But men are men, the best sometimes forget;
Though Cassio did some little wrong to him,
As men in rage strike those that wish them best,
Yet surely Cassio, I believe, received
From him that fled some strange indignity

220 **nothing** (adverb) not at all, in no way
Thus it is so *Cor* 1.3.96
223 **him** perhaps an error (anticipating *him*, 224) (Malone)
determined transferred epithet: Cassio was determined
sword At 2.1.269ff. Iago spoke of what might happen. At 2.3.143 Cassio said he would *beat* Roderigo, perhaps with the flat of his sword.
224 **execute upon** bring (a weapon) into operation against; but also implies 'put to death' (*OED* 1b, 6)
this gentleman Montano
225 **his pause** i.e. him to pause
229 **the rather** all the more quickly
230 **fall** downward stroke (of a sword): so *R3* 5.3.111
231 **high** loud (as in 'high words')
235 This short line may mark a pause (Iago wipes his brow?). It also marks a change of tactics: having described what happened, he 'defends' Cassio.
237 Cf. Dent, M541, 'Men are (but) men'; B316.1, 'The best go astray'; *forget* = forget themselves, or, forget their responsibilities.
238 **him** Montano
239 **those . . . best** even those who are most favourably disposed towards them
241 **indignity** insult

220 Thus] *Q;* This *F* 229 the] *Q*; then *F* 231 oath] *F;* oaths *Q* 232 say] *F*; see *Q* 236 cannot I] *F;* can I not *Q*

Which patience could not pass.

OTHELLO I know, Iago,
Thy honesty and love doth mince this matter,
Making it light to Cassio. Cassio, I love thee,

Enter DESDEMONA, *attended.*

But never more be officer of mine.
Look if my gentle love be not raised up!
I'll make thee an example.

DESDEMONA
What is the matter, dear?

OTHELLO All's well now, sweeting,
Come away to bed. – Sir, for your hurts
Myself will be your surgeon. Lead him off.

[*Montano is led off.*]

Iago, look with care about the town
And silence those whom this vile brawl distracted.
Come, Desdemona: 'tis the soldier's life
To have their balmy slumbers waked with strife.

Exeunt [*all but Iago and Cassio.*]

IAGO What, are you hurt, lieutenant?

242 **pass** let pass, agree to

243 **love** affection (for Cassio). The word is used three times in four lines, with different connotations.
mince this matter Cf. Dent, M755, 'To mince the matter'. Viz. make light of or extenuate this fault.

244 **Making . . . Cassio** making light of it for Cassio's benefit

245 Cf. LN, 1.1.8 and 1.1.16n. Othello personally appoints and dismisses his officers.

247 Cf. Dent, E212.1, 'To make one an example'.

248 **sweeting** sweetheart

250 I'll make it my business that your wounds are properly treated, presumably by the general's surgeon (5.1.100). Some think that Othello himself dresses Montano's wounds (Bradshaw, 151, 164).
Lead him off. 'I am persuaded, these words were originally a marginal direction' (Malone), i.e. were accidentally printed as dialogue. Cf. *Texts*, 38.

252 **distracted** threw into confusion

254 **balmy slumbers** Having just heard that Othello and Desdemona are bride and groom (14, 171), are we really to believe in their balmy slumbers?

244.1] *F (after 245); Enter* Desdemona, *with others. Q (opp. 245, 246)* 248 dear] *F; not in Q* now] *Q; not in F* 250 SD] *as Capell; not in QF* 252 vile] *Q*; vil'd *F* 254 SD] *Exit Moore*, Desdemona, *and attendants. Q (after 255); Exit. F*

CASSIO Ay, past all surgery.

IAGO Marry, God forbid!

CASSIO Reputation, reputation, reputation! O, I have lost my reputation, I have lost the immortal part of myself – and what remains is bestial. My reputation, Iago, my reputation!

IAGO As I am an honest man I thought you had received some bodily wound; there is more of sense in that than in reputation. Reputation is an idle and most false imposition, oft got without merit and lost without deserving. You have lost no reputation at all, unless you repute yourself such a loser. What, man, there are ways to recover the general again. You are but now cast in his mood, a punishment more in policy than in malice, even so as one would beat his offenceless dog to affright an imperious lion. Sue to him again, and he's yours.

CASSIO I will rather sue to be despised, than to deceive so good a commander with so slight, so drunken, and

257 **God forbid** common in the Bible (Genesis 44.7, Joshua 22.29, Romans 3.4, 6, 31, etc.): usually a pious person's phrase

259ff. Cf. *R2* 1.1.177–8, 'The purest treasure mortal times afford / Is spotless reputation'; Dent, C817, 'He that has lost his credit is dead to the world.' Usually one's *soul* is 'the immortal part'.

263 **sense** capability of feeling

264 **idle** baseless, useless

265 **imposition** something imposed (by others)

266–7 **You . . . loser** Cf. Dent, M254, 'A man is weal or woe as he thinks himself so.'

267 **repute** consider
man Cf. 40.

268 **recover** regain (possession of), win back

269 **cast . . . mood** cast off in his (passing) mood of anger

270 **malice** ill-will, enmity

270–1 **as . . . lion** Cf. Dent, D443, 'Beat the dog (whelp) before the lion.' Also proverbial in French: Cotgrave glossed 'To punish a mean man in the presence of and for an example to the mighty'. Here the 'lion' is either the Venetian army or the Cypriots (Othello has to establish his authority with both).

271 **offenceless** unoffending
Sue petition (him to pardon you)

274 **slight** worthless

257 God] *Q;* Heauen *F* 258–61] *as F; Q lines* my reputation: / selfe, / reputation, / reputation. / 258 Reputation] *twice Q; three times F* O, I have] *F;* I ha *Q* 259 have] *F;* had *Q* part] *F;* part sir *Q* 262 thought] *Q;* had thought *F* 263 of sense] *Cam 1892 (anon.);* offence *Q;* sence *F* 268 ways] *Q;* more wayes *F* 274 slight] *F;* light *Q*

so indiscreet an officer. Drunk? and speak parrot? and squabble? swagger? swear? and discourse fustian with one's own shadow? O thou invisible spirit of wine, if thou hast no name to be known by, let us call thee devil!

IAGO What was he that you followed with your sword? What had he done to you?

CASSIO I know not.

IAGO Is't possible?

CASSIO I remember a mass of things, but nothing distinctly; a quarrel, but nothing wherefore. O God, that men should put an enemy in their mouths, to steal away their brains! that we should with joy, pleasance, revel and applause, transform ourselves into beasts!

IAGO Why, but you are now well enough: how came you thus recovered?

CASSIO It hath pleased the devil drunkenness to give place to the devil wrath; one unperfectness shows me another, to make me frankly despise myself.

IAGO Come, you are too severe a moraler. As the time, the place and the condition of this country stands, I could heartily wish this had not befallen; but since it is as it is, mend it for your own good.

275 **indiscreet** lacking in sound judgement; inconsiderate
Drunk? F often uses? where we would put! (as perhaps here).
speak parrot babble senselessly. Cf. Dent, P60, 'To speak (prate) like a parrot'.
276 **swagger** quarrel, squabble
fustian nonsense
287 **pleasance** pleasure, enjoyment
288 **transform . . . beasts** perhaps alluding to the Circe story
289–90 **how . . . recovered** How did it come about that you have thus recovered?
291–2 Cf. Ephesians 4.27, 'Neither give place to the devil'. Drunkenness (= gluttony?) and wrath could be two of the seven deadly sins. 'The whole of Cassio's apostrophe . . . finds a close parallel in Ecclus. 31.25–31' (Noble, 217).
292 **wrath** could mean anger with himself (273ff.), and that he has not recovered, because still angry; or, anger with Roderigo
unperfectness (unique in Shakespeare) imperfection
293 **frankly** undisguisedly; unreservedly
294 **moraler** moralizer (a coinage)
297 **mend** rectify

275 so] *F; not in Q* 275–7 Drunk? . . . shadow?] *F; not in Q* 285 God] *Q; not in F* 287–8 pleasance, revel] *F;* Reuell, pleasure *Q* 289 Why,] *Q;* Why? *F* 295 and] *F; not in Q* 296 not] *F;* not so *Q*

CASSIO I will ask him for my place again, he shall tell me I am a drunkard: had I as many mouths as Hydra, such an answer would stop them all. To be now a sensible man, by and by a fool, and presently a beast! O strange! – Every inordinate cup is unblest, and the ingredience is a devil.

IAGO Come, come, good wine is a good familiar creature, if it be well used: exclaim no more against it. And, good lieutenant, I think you think I love you.

CASSIO I have well approved it, sir. I drunk?

IAGO You, or any man living, may be drunk at some time, man. I'll tell you what you shall do. Our general's wife is now the general. I may say so in this respect, for that he hath devoted and given up himself to the contemplation, mark and denotement of her parts and graces. Confess yourself freely to her, importune her help to put you in your place again.

299 **Hydra** The many-headed monster of Greek mythology, which it was one of Hercules' tasks to destroy; 'as each head was cut off, two more grew in its place' (Ridley). Cf. Dent, H278, 'As many heads as Hydra'.
300 **stop** plug, close. Cf. Dent, M1264, 'To stop one's mouth'.
301 **by and by** soon afterwards
presently in a little while
beast Cf. Dent, B152.1, 'A drunken man is a beast.'
302 **inordinate** immoderate. Only found three times in Shakespeare: *Luc* 94, *1H4* 3.2.12 both read *in-*, so F is likely to be right here.
303 **ingredience** that which enters into a mixture (*OED*); cf. *Mac* 1.7.11, 4.1.34.
304 **familiar** friendly; 'punning on the sense of "familiar spirit", with an emphasis on *good*; he half admits that wine may be a devil, but good wine well used is a *good* devil' (Ridley)
304–5 See LN.
305 **well** properly
307 **approved** proved by experience
sir Cassio senses that Iago puts pressure on him.
309–10 **Our . . . general** Cf. 2.1.74; Ovid, *Heroides*, 9.114, 'you are victor over the beast, but she over you'.
311 **for that** that
312 **mark** marking, observation
***denotement** Cf. 3.3.126. Here = nothing(?); Q 'deuoted . . . to the . . . deuotement' must be wrong. F followed Q; the corruption may involve more than a turned letter (u/n).
313 **parts** personal qualities. Cf. *MA* 5.2.60, 'for which of my bad parts didst thou first fall in love with me?'
graces pleasing qualities

300 them] *F;* em *Q* 302 O strange!] *F; not in Q* inordinate] *F;* vnordinate *Q* 303 ingredience] *Q;* Ingredient *F* 308 some] *Q;* a *F* 309 man] *F; not in Q* I'll] *Q;* I *F* 311 hath] *F;* has *Q* 312 mark] *Q;* marke: *F* denotement] *Q2;* deuotement *QF* 314 help] *F;* shee'll helpe *Q*

She is of so free, so kind, so apt, so blest a disposition that she holds it a vice in her goodness not to do more than she is requested. This broken joint between you and her husband entreat her to splinter – and my fortunes against any lay worth naming, this crack of your love shall grow stronger than it was before.

CASSIO You advise me well.

IAGO I protest, in the sincerity of love and honest kindness.

CASSIO I think it freely, and betimes in the morning I will beseech the virtuous Desdemona to undertake for me. I am desperate of my fortunes if they check me here.

IAGO You are in the right. Good-night, lieutenant, I must to the watch.

CASSIO Good-night, honest Iago. *Exit.*

IAGO

And what's he then that says I play the villain?
When this advice is free I give and honest,
Probal to thinking and indeed the course

315 **free** generous; ready, willing (to grant) (*OED* 4, 20)
apt fit, ready
blest a disposition He appropriates a thought he had previously ridiculed (2.1.249–51).

317–18 **This . . . splinter** Cf. Dent, B515, 'A broken bone is the stronger when it is well set'; *2H4* 4.1.220, 'like a broken limb united, / Grow stronger for the breaking'; *splinter* = apply splints to.

319 **lay** wager
crack partial fracture (*OED* 7b)

323 **kindness** natural inclination; affection

324 **freely** unreservedly
betimes early

325–6 **undertake for me** take my case in hand

326 **I . . . of** I have lost hope concerning
check stop

328 **You . . . right** You are right; also hinting 'you have justice on your side', i.e. you have been badly treated.

331 He picks up where he left off at 2.1.308, but now *knavery* sees clearly how to proceed. Note his alertness to possible reactions.

332 **free** frank and open; honourable; freely given

333 **Probal** probable; or, 'such as approves itself' (from Lat. *probo*, I prove, make credible). A nonce word. Cf. *admiral* = admirable (Dekker, *Patient Grissill*, 2.2.91). Iago has a habit of weighing probabilities: 2.1.282ff., 5.1.11ff.

315 of so] *F;* so *Q* 316 that] *Q; not in F* 317 broken joint] *F;* braule *Q* 320 it was] *F;* twas *Q* 324–5 I will] *F;* will I *Q* 327 here] *Q; not in F* 331] *as Q; F lines* then, / Villaine? /

To win the Moor again? For 'tis most easy
Th'inclining Desdemona to subdue
In any honest suit. She's framed as fruitful
As the free elements: and then for her
To win the Moor, were't to renounce his baptism,
All seals and symbols of redeemed sin,
His soul is so enfettered to her love
That she may make, unmake, do what she list,
Even as her appetite shall play the god
With his weak function. How am I then a villain
To counsel Cassio to this parallel course
Directly to his good? Divinity of hell!
When devils will the blackest sins put on
They do suggest at first with heavenly shows
As I do now. For whiles this honest fool
Plies Desdemona to repair his fortune,
And she for him pleads strongly to the Moor,
I'll pour this pestilence into his ear:

334 **win** regain the favour of
335 **inclining** mentally inclining (to be helpful); perhaps physically leaning (towards a suitor)
subdue win
336 **framed** made, fashioned
fruitful beneficial; generous
337 **As . . . elements** It is her nature to be as beneficial (to others) as the unrestrained elements are there to be used.
338 **win** win over
339 **seals** tokens. Cf. Ephesians 4.30, 'the holy spirit of God, by whom ye are sealed unto the day of redemption' (i.e. the Anglican doctrine of baptism: Noble, 218).
redeemed redeemed (Christ as Redeemer delivers us from sin); paid for, ransomed
341 **list** likes
342 **her appetite** 'his desire for her' (Ridley); or, her fancy, inclination
343 **weak** enslaved
function natural instincts (Ridley); or perhaps 'functioning (of mental and moral powers)'
344 **parallel course** i.e. it seems to lead straight to his advantage but in fact takes him in the opposite direction, to his destruction.
345 **Divinity of hell!** 'O, the theology of hell!' Or, he addresses Satan, 'O god of hell!' Cf. 1.3.358.
346 **devils** (including himself!). Cf. Dent, D231, 'The devil can transform himself into an angel of light.'
put on incite
347 **suggest** prompt, tempt
349 **Plies** solicits
351 **pestilence** that which is morally pernicious. Cf. *Ham* 1.5.63–4, 'in the porches of my ears did pour / The leprous distillment'.

334] *as Q; F lines* againe. / easie / 335 Th'] *F;* The *Q* 338 were't] *Q;* were *F* 346 the] *F;* their *Q* 348 whiles] *F;* while *Q* 349 fortune] *F;* fortunes *Q*

That she repeals him for her body's lust.
And by how much she strives to do him good
She shall undo her credit with the Moor—
So will I turn her virtue into pitch
And out of her own goodness make the net
That shall enmesh them all.

Enter RODERIGO.

How now, Roderigo?

RODERIGO I do follow here in the chase not like a hound that hunts, but one that fills up the cry. My money is almost spent, I have been tonight exceedingly well cudgelled, and I think the issue will be I shall have so much experience for my pains: and so, with no money at all, and a little more wit, return again to Venice.

IAGO
How poor are they that have not patience!
What wound did ever heal but by degrees?
Thou know'st we work by wit and not by witchcraft,
And wit depends on dilatory time.
Does't not go well? Cassio hath beaten thee
And thou by that small hurt hast cashiered Cassio.

352 **repeals** tries to get him restored to his former position (*OED* 3d); lit. recalls
354 **credit** reputation; trustworthiness
355 **pitch** suggests blackness and foulness, and 'a snaring substance, like birdlime . . . leading on to the *net*' (Ridley)
357 **enmesh** catch or entangle, as in a net (unique in Shakespeare). Cf. 2.1.168 *ensnare*.
359 **cry** pack, 'the hounds who merely give tongue as they follow those who are really running the scent' (Ridley)
361 **cudgelled** Cf. 143n.
361–2 **I . . . pains** Cf. Dent, L1, 'He has his labor for his pains'; i.e. so much experience and nothing more.
363 **wit** sense
365 Cf. Dent, P103, 'He that has no patience has nothing.'
367 **we** How much wit has Roderigo contributed?
wit cleverness, good judgement
370 **cashiered** (succeeded in having Cassio) dismissed; cf p. 338 (to 'cass' = to cashier).

357] *QF lines* all: / *Roderigo?* / enmesh them] enmesh em *Q;* en-mash them *F* SD] *opp.* all 357 *Q; after 357 Rodorigo F* 360 have] *F;* ha *Q* 361 and] *F; not in Q* 362–4 pains . . . Venice] *as F;* paines, as that comes to, and no money at all, and with that wit returne to *Venice. Q* 365 have] *F;* ha *Q* 367 know'st] *F;* knowest *Q* 369 Does't] Do'st *Q;* Dos't *F* hath] *F;* has *Q* 370 hast] *Q;* hath *F*

Though other things grow fair against the sun
Yet fruits that blossom first will first be ripe;
Content thyself a while. By the mass, 'tis morning:
Pleasure and action make the hours seem short.
Retire thee, go where thou art billeted,
Away, I say, thou shalt know more hereafter:
Nay, get thee gone. *Exit Roderigo.*
Two things are to be done:
My wife must move for Cassio to her mistress,
I'll set her on.
Myself the while to draw the Moor apart
And bring him jump when he may Cassio find
Soliciting his wife: ay, that's the way!
Dull not device by coldness and delay! *Exit.*

[3.1] *Enter* CASSIO *and some* Musicians.

CASSIO
Masters, play here, I will content your pains;

371–2 'Though other plants grow vigorously when exposed to (= *against*) the sun, yet fruit trees that blossom first will bear ripe fruit first' (NB this is not always true); i.e. though others thrive in Desdemona's favour, we'll succeed in bringing our plots to fruition. In this false analogy blossom = Cassio's cudgelling!

373 **By the mass** a mild oath, hence changed in F, found also in plays with Protestant settings (*Ham* 2.1.50, 3.2.378, etc.). Cf. 3.3.74n.

374 Cf. Dent, H747, 'Hours of pleasure are short.'

375 **billeted** assigned quarters (troops, or others)

378 **My wife** Do husbands think of 'my wife', or think of her by name? Here *my wife* helps the audience. Cf. 5.2.95–6.
move solicit

379 Short lines in Iago's soliloquies suggest pauses, as he thinks of a new stratagem (cf. 1.3.400, 3.3.323).

380 ***the while** in the meantime

381 **jump** precisely (at the moment when)

383 **Dull** an imperative, addressed to himself: 'don't let the plot lose its momentum'
device plot, stratagem; pleasure, desire (*OED* 3, 6)
coldness lack of enthusiasm

3.1.1–20 Cf. *RJ* 4.5.102ff., *AYL* 5.3.34ff.: the Clown's baiting of the Musicians was a 'comic turn'.

1 **content your pains** reward you for taking the trouble

372 Yet] *F;* But *Q* 373 By the mass] *Q;* Introth *F* 377] *as Q; F lines* gone. / done: / SD] *F; not in Q* Two] *F;* Some *Q* 379–80] *as Q; one line F* 380 Myself the while] *Theobald;* My selfe awhile, *Q;* my selfe, a while, *F* 383 SD] *F; Exeunt. Q* **3.1**] *Actus Tertius. Scena Prima. F; not in Q* 0.1] *Enter* Cassio, *with Musitians and the Clowne. Q; Enter Cassio, Musitians, and Clowne. F*

Something that's brief, and bid 'Good morrow,
general.'

They play. Enter CLOWN.

CLOWN Why, masters, have your instruments been in Naples, that they speak i'th' nose thus?

1 MUSICIAN How, sir? how?

CLOWN Are these, I pray you, wind instruments?

1 MUSICIAN Ay marry are they, sir.

CLOWN O, thereby hangs a tail.

1 MUSICIAN Whereby hangs a tail, sir?

CLOWN Marry, sir, by many a wind instrument that I know. But, masters, here's money for you, and the general so likes your music that he desires you, for love's sake, to make no more noise with it.

1 MUSICIAN Well, sir, we will not.

CLOWN If you have any music that may not be heard, to't again. But, as they say, to hear music the general does not greatly care.

1 MUSICIAN We have none such, sir.

2 **Good morrow** the traditional *aubade* to wake bride and groom after the wedding night. Cf. Donne's 'The Good-Morrow' (morrow = morning).

2.1 CLOWN *Clown* could = peasant, countryman; ignorant or rude fellow; fool or jester (in a great house or in the theatre). Here the theatre clown plays a clown (a comic servant). Shakespeare gave names to most of his clowns and fools, but not in *Oth* and *KL*.

3–4 See LN.

8 **tail** i.e. a penis (or animal tail?). Cf. *AYL* 2.7.28; Dent, T48, 'Thereby hangs a tale' (= there's a story about that).

10 **wind instrument** 'Podex – or *ars musica*' (Partridge). A joke about flatulence.

12–13 **for love's sake** So Philemon, 1.9, 'Yet for love's sake I rather beseech thee'; for Q's *of all loues*, cf. *MND* 2.2.154.

13 **noise** could mean 'an agreeable or melodious sound' (*OED* 5): the clown specializes in ambiguous insults

18 **none such** perhaps a quibble: 'None-such' was the name of a popular tune (R. King, as in 3–4n.)

2.1] *as Q2 (They play, and enter the Clowne.); not in QF* 3 have] *F;* ha *Q* in] *F;* at *Q* 4 i'th'] *F;* i'the *Q* 5 SP] *Boy Q (throughout); Mus. F (throughout)* 6 pray you,] *F;* pray, cald *Q* 12–13 for . . . sake] *F;* of all loues *Q* 18 have] *F;* ha *Q*

CLOWN Then put up your pipes in your bag, for I'll away. Go, vanish into air, away! *Exeunt Musicians.*

CASSIO Dost thou hear, mine honest friend?

CLOWN No, I hear not your honest friend, I hear you.

CASSIO Prithee keep up thy quillets; there's a poor piece of gold for thee – if the gentlewoman that attends the general's wife be stirring, tell her there's one Cassio entreats her a little favour of speech. Wilt thou do this?

CLOWN She is stirring, sir; if she will stir hither, I shall seem to notify unto her.

Enter IAGO.

CASSIO
Do, good my friend. (*Exit Clown.*) In happy time,
Iago.

IAGO
You have not been a-bed then?

CASSIO
Why no, the day had broke before we parted.
I have made bold, Iago, to send in
To your wife: my suit to her is that she will

19 **put . . . pipes** could = desist, 'shut up' (*OED* pipe 1e), or pack up your pipes

19–20 perhaps alluding to the practice of carrying away a tedious Fool in a cloak-bag (cf. Leslie Hotson, *Shakespeare's Motley*, 1952, ch. 4); i.e. put your pipes, not me, in your bag, for I'll go away on my own

22 To 'mistake the word' (*TGV* 3.1.284) was a regular clown routine.

23 **keep up** refrain from
quillets quibbles

24 **gentlewoman** originally, a woman of good birth; then, a female attendant on a lady of rank

26 **entreats . . . speech** begs the favour of briefly speaking with her (here *little* looks like a transferred epithet)

28 **stirring** He understands it as 'sexually exciting' (cf. *OED* stirring 3, quoting Dekker, 'Capon is a stirring meate'; Partridge, stir).

28–9 **I . . . her** i.e. I shall have notified her

29 The Clown makes fun of Cassio's courtliness or accent (cf. Iago, 2.1.166ff.), and perhaps quibbles on *stir–steer*.

30 **In happy time** well met; *happy* = fortunate

31–9 These lines could be prose or verse (see p. 367).

19 up] *F; not in Q* 20 into air] *F; not in Q* SD] *Exit Mu. F; not in Q* 21 hear, mine] heare my *Q;* heare me, mine *F* 22] *as Q; F lines* Friend: / you. / 25 general's wife] *Q;* Generall *F* 30 Do, . . . friend] *Q; not in F* SD] *F (Exit Clo., after 29); not in Q* 31, 33 have] *F;* ha *Q* 32–6 Why . . . access] *Q lines* parted: / her, / *Desdemona*, / accesse. /; *F lines* parted. / wife: / *Desdemona* / accesse. /

To virtuous Desdemona procure me
Some access.

IAGO I'll send her to you presently,
And I'll devise a mean to draw the Moor
Out of the way, that your converse and business
May be more free.

CASSIO
I humbly thank you for't. *Exit* [*Iago*.]
I never knew
A Florentine more kind and honest.

Iago- contradictory w/ his true character.

Enter EMILIA.

EMILIA Iago's wife
Good morrow, good lieutenant. I am sorry
For your displeasure, but all will sure be well.
The general and his wife are talking of it,
And she speaks for you stoutly; the Moor replies
That he you hurt is of great fame in Cyprus
And great affinity,
And that in wholesome wisdom he might not but
Refuse you; but he protests he loves you
And needs no other suitor but his likings
To take the safest occasion by the front

37 **mean** opportunity

41 **Florentine** Did Shakespeare delete 1.1.19–20 (*Texts*, 36)? If he did, Cassio is naively ignorant that Florence, the home of Machiavelli, was not generally thought a centre of honesty; if not, he praises Iago as if a fellow countryman, and also misunderstands him.

43 **displeasure** loss of favour
all . . . well Cf. 3.4.19, 4.2.173, *RJ* 4.2.40: a common saying.

45 **stoutly** vigorously (stronger than today)

47 **great** important, powerful
affinity kindred, family. This half-line may have been deleted and printed in error (*Texts*, 37). Cf. Ruth 2.20, 'The man is nigh unto us, and of our affinity.'

48 **wholesome** beneficial; health-giving: i.e. wisdom that restores the well-being of Cyprus
he . . . but he could only; or, he was forced to

49 **Refuse** dismiss; decline to reappoint; i.e. he had (earlier or now) no choice except to *refuse* you
loves is fond of

51 **front** forelock. The proverb (Dent, T311, 'To take time (occasion) by the forelock') refers to the classical *Occasio*, long-haired in front, bald behind.

40 for't] *F;* for it *Q* SD] *opp. 39 QF* 41.1] *Enter* Emilia. *Q; Enter Æmilia. F* 43 sure] *F;* soone *Q* 46–9] *QF lines Cypres,* / wisedome, / loues you, / 51] *Q; not in F*

To bring you in again.

CASSIO Yet I beseech you,
If you think fit, or that it may be done,
Give me advantage of some brief discourse
With Desdemon alone.

EMILIA Pray you come in,
I will bestow you where you shall have time
To speak your bosom freely.

CASSIO I am much bound to you.

Exeunt.

[**3.2**] *Enter* OTHELLO, IAGO *and* Gentlemen.

OTHELLO
These letters give, Iago, to the pilot,
And by him do my duties to the Senate;
That done, I will be walking on the works,
Repair there to me.

IAGO Well, my good lord, I'll do't.

OTHELLO
This fortification, gentlemen, shall we see't?

1 GENTLEMAN
We'll wait upon your lordship. *Exeunt.*

[**3.3**] *Enter* DESDEMONA, CASSIO *and* EMILIA.

52 **in** into favour
54 **advantage** opportunity
55 **Desdemon** This form of the name occurs seven times, but never in Q. The speaker is mostly Othello, which makes it sound more intimate than 'Desdemona'. Perhaps Shakespeare wrote the full name and wanted final and initial *a* to be slurred: 'Desdemona alone'.
56 **bestow** place
57 **bosom** bosom thoughts
3.2 This scene gives us a glimpse of Othello at work, undistracted by thoughts of Desdemona.
2 **do my duties** pay my respects
3 **works** defensive fortification
4 **Repair** come, make your way
Well . . . do't an odd way of responding to an order?
6 **wait** attend
3.3 Location: Cassio has 'come in' (3.1.55), but the location is vague: 'yond marble heaven' (463) suggests that Shakespeare now thinks it an outdoor scene. On the 'unlocalized stage' such inconsistencies pass unnoticed.

55 Desdemon] *F; Desdemona Q* 57 I . . . you] *F; not in Q* SD] *Q; not in F* 3.2] *Scoena Secunda. F; not in Q* 0.1] *F; . . . and other Gentlemen. Q* 1 pilot] *F;* Pilate *Q* 2 Senate] *F;* State *Q* 4 Well] *QF; om. Pope* 6 We'll] *F2 (*Weel*);* We *Q;* Well *F* 3.3] *Scoena Tertia. F; not in Q*

DESDEMONA

Be thou assured, good Cassio, I will do
All my abilities in thy behalf.

EMILIA

Good madam, do, I warrant it grieves my husband
As if the cause were his.

DESDEMONA

O, that's an honest fellow. Do not doubt, Cassio,
But I will have my lord and you again
As friendly as you were.

CASSIO

Bounteous madam,
Whatever shall become of Michael Cassio,
He's never anything but your true servant.

DESDEMONA

I know't, I thank you. You do love my lord,
You have known him long, and be you well assured
He shall in strangeness stand no farther off
Than in a politic distance.

CASSIO

Ay, but, lady,
That policy may either last so long,
Or feed upon such nice and waterish diet,
Or breed itself so out of circumstance,
That, I being absent and my place supplied,
My general will forget my love and service.

DESDEMONA

Do not doubt that: before Emilia here

3 **warrant** be bound (common asseveration); monosyllabic (warr'nt), as in *Ham* 1.2.242, 'I warn't it will' (Q2), *MND* 5.1.320.

7 **Bounteous** good, virtuous (Fr. *bonté*, goodness, kindness)

9 **true** faithful, sincere

12 **strangeness** coldness, aloofness

13 **politic** sagacious, shrewd; i.e. than the distance required by judiciousness

14 **policy** sagacity, diplomacy; an expedient course of action

15 or feed on such a poor diet (i.e. as to fade away); *nice* = delicate, thin

16 or engender itself to such an extent from non-essential factors, i.e. depend so much on chance

17–18 Cf. Dent, F596, 'Long absent soon forgotten'.

17 **supplied** filled

19 **doubt** fear

3] *as Q; F lines* do: / Husband, / warrant] *F;* know *Q* 4 cause] *F;* case *Q* 10 I know't] *F;* O sir *Q* 12 strangeness] *F;* strangest *Q* 14 That] *F;* The *Q* 16 circumstance] *Q;* Circumstances *F*

I give thee warrant of thy place. Assure thee,
If I do vow a friendship I'll perform it
To the last article. My lord shall never rest,
I'll watch him tame and talk him out of patience,
His bed shall seem a school, his board a shrift,
I'll intermingle everything he does
With Cassio's suit: therefore be merry, Cassio,
For thy solicitor shall rather die
Than give thy cause away.

Enter OTHELLO *and* IAGO.

EMILIA
Madam, here comes my lord.

CASSIO
Madam, I'll take my leave.

DESDEMONA
Why, stay and hear me speak.

CASSIO
Madam, not now; I am very ill at ease,
Unfit for mine own purposes.

DESDEMONA
Well, do your discretion. *Exit Cassio.*

IAGO Ha, I like not that.

OTHELLO
What dost thou say?

IAGO
Nothing, my lord; or if – I know not what.

20 **warrant** assurance, pledge. This seems as impetuous as her elopement with Othello. **Assure thee** be certain

22 **article** item

23 **I'll . . . tame** a metaphor from the training of hawks (*watch* = keep awake, to make obedient). Cf. *TC* 3.2.43, 'you must be watch'd ere you be made tame, must you?' (Ridley).

24 **bed . . . board** Marriage was a 'bond of board and bed' (*AYL* 5.4.142: cf. *3H6* 1.1.248); *board* = table, *shrift* = place of confession. Without realizing it, she puts her marriage at risk.

26 **merry** happy

27 **solicitor** advocate

28 **give . . . away** abandon thy suit

34 **do your discretion** do as you think fit. Usually 'use your discretion' (*AYL* 1.1.146; Lyly, *Endymion*, 1.4.5).

28 thy cause away] *F;* thee cause: away *Q* 28.1] *F; Enter* Othello, Iago, *and Gentlemen. Q* 33 purposes] *F*; purpose *Q* 34 Ha,] *Q*; Hah? *F* 36 if –] *F;* if, *Q*

OTHELLO

Was not that Cassio parted from my wife?

IAGO

Cassio, my lord? no, sure, I cannot think it
That he would steal away so guilty-like
Seeing you coming.

OTHELLO I do believe 'twas he.

DESDEMONA

How now, my lord?
I have been talking with a suitor here,
A man that languishes in your displeasure.

OTHELLO

Who is't you mean?

DESDEMONA

Why, your lieutenant, Cassio. Good my lord,
If I have any grace or power to move you
His present reconciliation take:
For if he be not one that truly loves you,
That errs in ignorance and not in cunning,
I have no judgement in an honest face.
I prithee, call him back.

OTHELLO Went he hence now?

DESDEMONA

Yes, faith, so humbled
That he hath left part of his grief with me
To suffer with him. Good love, call him back.

OTHELLO

Not now, sweet Desdemon, some other time.

DESDEMONA

But shall't be shortly?

OTHELLO The sooner, sweet, for you.

39 **steal away** Cf. *Cor* 1.1.252 SD, '*Citizens steale away*'.
guilty-like unique in Shakespeare; his coinage
42 **suitor** petitioner
46 **grace** pleasing quality; privilege (OED 1, 8)
move influence
47 **present** immediate
reconciliation restoration to favour (*OED* 1c)
take accept, agree to
49 **in cunning** wittingly
50 **in** of

39 steal] *F;* sneake *Q* 40 you] *Q;* your *F* 52 Yes, faith] *Q;* I sooth *F* 53 hath] *F;* has *Q* grief] *F;* griefes *Q* 54 To] *F;* I *Q* 55 Desdemon] *F; Desdemona Q*

DESDEMONA

Shall't be tonight, at supper?

OTHELLO

No, not tonight.

DESDEMONA

Tomorrow dinner then?

OTHELLO

I shall not dine at home.
I meet the captains at the citadel.

DESDEMONA

Why then, tomorrow night, or Tuesday morn;
On Tuesday, noon or night; on Wednesday morn!
I prithee name the time, but let it not
Exceed three days: i'faith, he's penitent,
And yet his trespass, in our common reason
– Save that they say the wars must make examples
Out of their best – is not, almost, a fault
T'incur a private check. When shall he come?
Tell me, Othello. I wonder in my soul
What you would ask me that I should deny
Or stand so mamm'ring on? What, Michael Cassio
That came a-wooing with you? and so many a time
When I have spoke of you dispraisingly
Hath ta'en your part, to have so much to do
To bring him in? By'r lady, I could do much!—

58 **dinner** a midday meal at this time

64 **common reason** general way of thinking

65 **wars** i.e. the military profession

66 **their best** their best men. If *wars* = war generally, singular *her* (as in QF) is possible. But *their* (or *ther*) could be misread as *her*.
not, almost hardly. 'I have not breathed almost, since I did see it' (*CE* 5.1.181) (Ridley).

67 **check** rebuke

70 **mamm'ring** (1) hesitating, (2) stammering, muttering. Editors prefer (1), but (2) could be appropriate for 56ff. An unkind word, unique in Shakespeare, signalling her critical surprise. It echoes *Euphues*, 'neither stand in a mammering whether it be best to departe or not' (Lyly, 1.253) (Malone).

71 **That . . . you** Cf. 1.2.52n.

72 **dispraisingly** i.e. she has been critical of him before – 'of course, in order to hear Cassio praise him in reply' (Kittredge)

74 **bring him in** Cf. 3.1.52.
By'r lady a mild oath, changed by F, found also in 'Protestant' plays (e.g. *Ham* 3.2.133). Cf. 2.3.373n.

60 or] *Q;* on *F* 61 Tuesday, noon] Tuesday morne, *Q;* Tuesday noone, *F* on] *F;* or *Q* 63 i'faith] *Q;* Infaith *F* 65–6] (Saue . . . examples / . . . her best) *Q;* (Saue . . . example) / . . . her best, *F* 66 their best] *Rowe;* her best *QF* 67 T'] *F;* To *Q* 69 would] *F;* could *Q* 70 mamm'ring] *F (*mam'ring*);* muttering *Q* What,] What *Q;* What? *F* 74 By'r lady] *Q;* Trust me *F*

OTHELLO
Prithee, no more. Let him come when he will,
I will deny thee nothing.

DESDEMONA Why, this is not a boon,
'Tis as I should entreat you wear your gloves,
Or feed on nourishing dishes, or keep you warm,
Or sue to you to do a peculiar profit
To your own person. Nay, when I have a suit
Wherein I mean to touch your love indeed
It shall be full of poise and difficult weight
And fearful to be granted.

OTHELLO I will deny thee nothing.
Whereon I do beseech thee, grant me this,
To leave me but a little to myself.

DESDEMONA
Shall I deny you? No, farewell, my lord.

OTHELLO
Farewell, my Desdemona, I'll come to thee straight.

DESDEMONA
Emilia, come. – Be as your fancies teach you:
Whate'er you be, I am obedient.
Exeunt Desdemona and Emilia.

76 **I . . . nothing** Cf. Plautus, *Trinummus*, 357, 'I cannot keep refusing you anything you wish': 'Non edepol tibi pernegare possum quicquam quod velis.'
boon favour
77 **as** as if
gloves worn by the well-off as a sign of their importance; i.e. to do what is normal and natural
79–80 **do . . . person** i.e. do something that will be of special benefit to yourself
81 **touch** test
82 **poise** weight; balance
difficult weight difficult to weigh; i.e. it shall be so finely balanced (between the possible and impossible) that it will be a momentous thing for you to grant it. Cf. 2.3.120n. Or, more simply, it will be 'too heavy'.
83 **fearful** terrible (stronger than today)
84 **Whereon** almost = in return for which
87 **straight** immediately
88 **fancies** whims (another unkind word)
89 **obedient** Wives were expected to obey their husbands. She means, 'However good or bad you may be as a husband, I am a good wife.'

82 difficult weight] *F;* difficulty *Q* 87 to thee] *QF; om. Pope* 88 Be] *F;* be it *Q* 89 SD] *Exit* Desd. *and* Em. *Q; Exit. F*

OTHELLO

Excellent wretch! perdition catch my soul
But I do love thee! and when I love thee not
Chaos is come again.

IAGO

My noble lord –

OTHELLO What dost thou say, Iago?

IAGO

Did Michael Cassio, when you wooed my lady,
Know of your love?

OTHELLO He did, from first to last.
Why dost thou ask?

IAGO

But for a satisfaction of my thought,
No further harm.

OTHELLO Why of thy thought, Iago?

IAGO

I did not think he had been acquainted with her.

OTHELLO

O yes, and went between us very oft.

IAGO

Indeed?

OTHELLO

Indeed? Ay, indeed. Discern'st thou aught in that?

90 **wretch** could be a term of endearment, or the opposite. Perhaps meant to imply both, playfully. Cf. *RJ* 1.3.44, 'The pretty wretch left crying and said, "Ay".'
perdition destruction, i.e. damnation
catch take

91 **But** could = 'if . . . not', i.e. 'may I be damned if I don't love thee', almost 'may I be damned if I stop loving thee'. Yet *but* could be a fairly meaningless part of an asseveration (*MV* 2.6.52, 'Beshrow me but I love her heartily'). For *when* = if, see *OED* 8.

92 **Chaos** 'The allusion is to the classical legend that Love was the first of the gods to spring out of original chaos. Cf. Ben Jonson, *Love Freed from Ignorance*, 26–7: "without me / All again would Chaos be" ' (Sanders, quoting a speech by Love).

97 **satisfaction** information that answers a person's demands, removal of doubt; satisfying proof (*OED* 6b, first in 1601)

99 **he had** probably one syllable

100 **went between** *OED* first records *go-between* in *MW* 2.2.263.

102 **aught** i.e. anything strange

94–5 Did . . . love?] *Q; F lines Cassio* / loue? / you] *Q;* he *F* 95–6 He . . . ask?] *as F; one line Q* 97 thought] *F;* thoughts *Q* 100 oft] *F;* often *Q* 102 Ay] *F (I); not in Q*

Is he not honest?

IAGO

Honest, my lord?

OTHELLO

Honest? Ay, honest.

IAGO

My lord, for aught I know.

OTHELLO

What dost thou think?

IAGO

Think, my lord?

OTHELLO

Think, my lord! By heaven, thou echo'st me
As if there were some monster in thy thought
Too hideous to be shown. Thou dost mean something,
I heard thee say even now thou lik'st not that
When Cassio left my wife: what didst not like?
And when I told thee he was of my counsel
In my whole course of wooing, thou criedst 'Indeed?'
And didst contract and purse thy brow together
As if thou then hadst shut up in thy brain
Some horrible conceit. If thou dost love me
Show me thy thought.

IAGO My lord, you know I love you.

OTHELLO

I think thou dost.
And for I know thou'rt full of love and honesty
And weigh'st thy words before thou giv'st them breath,

110 **monster** prodigy; monstrosity; monstrous creature (cf. 168)

111 **hideous** ugly; repulsive; detestable

114 **of my counsel** i.e. in my confidence; or, he advised me

116 **purse** contract in wrinkles, 'suggesting the tightly drawn-in mouth of a purse' (*OED* 4, first here)

118 **conceit** idea, conception

119 **you . . . you** 'a horrible reminiscence of Peter's "thou knowest that I love thee" (John 21.15–17)' (Ridley)

119–21 For the emphasis on knowing and thinking here, cf. *MM* 5.1.203–4, 'Who thinks he knows that he ne'er knew my body, / But knows he thinks that he knows Isabel's'.

121 **for** because

109 By . . . echo'st] By heauen he ecchoes *Q;* Alas, thou ecchos't *F* 110 thy] *F;* his *Q* 111 dost] *F;* didst *Q* 112 even] *F;* but *Q* 115 In] *Q;* Of *F* 118 conceit] *F;* counsell *Q* 121 thou'rt] *F;* thou art *Q* 122 weigh'st] *F;* weighest *Q* giv'st them] *F;* giue em *Q*

Therefore these stops of thine fright me the more.
For such things in a false disloyal knave
Are tricks of custom, but in a man that's just
They're close delations, working from the heart,
That passion cannot rule.

IAGO
For Michael Cassio,
I dare be sworn, I think, that he is honest.

OTHELLO
I think so too.

IAGO
Men should be what they seem,
Or those that be not, would they might seem none.

OTHELLO
Certain, men should be what they seem.

IAGO
Why then I think Cassio's an honest man.

OTHELLO
Nay, yet there's more in this:
I prithee speak to me, as to thy thinkings,
As thou dost ruminate, and give thy worst of
thoughts
The worst of words.

IAGO
Good my lord, pardon me;

123 **stops** pauses
125 **tricks** stratagems; characteristic practices (*OED* 1, 7)
of custom customary
126 **close** secret
***delations** See LN.
127 **That . . . rule** i.e. (self-accusations or self-betrayals) that passion cannot control
128 **be sworn** Q's *presume* is attractive, creating uncertainty and confusion (Iago's aim in this scene).
***think,** The inserted comma makes Iago more doubtful.
129 **Men . . . seem** Tilley, S214, 'Be what thou would seem to be.'
130 'Or, those that be not (what they seem), would that they might not seem (honest) at all', taking *none* = by no means, not at all (*OED* adv. 3, first recorded 1651).
132 **then** (= in that case) hints at reservations
I think Cf. 128.
134 **thinkings** spoken as if in inverted commas, *thy 'thinkings',* picking up 108, 128, 132
135 **ruminate** lit. chew the cud; hence, 'just as thou dost turn them over in thy mind'

123 fright] *F;* affright *Q* 126 They're] *F;* They are *Q* delations] *Steevens;* dilations *F;* denotements *Q* 128 be sworn] *F;* presume *Q* think,] *this edn;* thinke *QF* 129 what] *F;* that *Q* 133 this:] *F* (this?) 134 as to] *F;* to *Q* 135 thy] *F;* the *Q* thoughts] *F;* thought *Q* 136 words] *F;* word *Q*

Though I am bound to every act of duty
I am not bound to that all slaves are free to –
Utter my thoughts? Why, say they are vile and false?
As where's that palace whereinto foul things
Sometimes intrude not? Who has a breast so pure
But some uncleanly apprehensions
Keep leets and law-days and in session sit
With meditations lawful?

OTHELLO

Thou dost conspire against thy friend, Iago,
If thou but think'st him wronged and mak'st his ear
A stranger to thy thoughts.

IAGO

I do beseech you,
Though I perchance am vicious in my guess
– As I confess it is my nature's plague
To spy into abuses, and oft my jealousy
Shapes faults that are not – that your wisdom
From one that so imperfectly conceits
Would take no notice, nor build yourself a trouble
Out of his scattering and unsure observance:

138 **that** what
free to not bound to (do). Dent, T244, 'Thought is free.'
142 **uncleanly** filthy
apprehensions ideas
143 **leets** special courts, held by some lords of the manor once or twice a year
law-days days for the meeting of a court of law; the session of such a court
145 **friend** He speaks in general terms but clearly sees himself as the friend, redefining their relationship. Cf. 5.2.150.
147ff. Two consecutive parentheses confuse Iago's thought, viz. 148 and 149–51 ('As . . . not'), interrupting 'I do beseech you that your wisdom'.
148 **Though** could = if (*OED* 4), but the sentence is deliberately serpentine
vicious wicked; blameworthy; faulty, mistaken (*OED* 2, 3, 6). It suits Iago to use elastic words.
149 **plague** affliction
150 **spy into** look out for; pry into
jealousy zeal (against abuses); devotion (to serve someone); vigilance (*OED* 1–3)
151 **Shapes** devises, imagines
152 **conceits** conceives, imagines; could be a misreading of Q's *coniects* (= conjectures), the 'harder reading', preferred by some editors
154 **scattering** scattered, i.e. disordered
observance observant care (*OED* 4); observation

138 that . . . to –] that all slaues are free to, *Q;* that: All Slaues are free: *F* 139 vile] *Q;* vild *F* 141 a] *Q;* that *F* 142 But some] *Q;* Wherein *F* 143 session] *Q;* Sessions *F* 146 think'st] *F;* thinkest *Q* mak'st] *F;* makest *Q* 150 oft] *Q;* of *F* 151 that your wisdom] *F;* I intreate you then *Q* 152 conceits] *F;* coniects *Q* 153 Would] *F;* You'd *Q* 154 his] *F;* my *Q*

It were not for your quiet nor your good
Nor for my manhood, honesty and wisdom
To let you know my thoughts.

OTHELLO Zounds! What dost thou mean?

IAGO
Good name in man and woman, dear my lord,
Is the immediate jewel of their souls:
Who steals my purse steals trash – 'tis something-nothing,
'Twas mine, 'tis his, and has been slave to thousands –
But he that filches from me my good name
Robs me of that which not enriches him
And makes me poor indeed.

OTHELLO By heaven, I'll know thy thoughts!

IAGO
You cannot, if my heart were in your hand,
Nor shall not whilst 'tis in my custody.

OTHELLO
Ha!

IAGO O beware, my lord, of jealousy!
It is the green-eyed monster, which doth mock

155 **were not for** would not be conducive to
quiet peace of mind

159 See LN.

160 **purse** (= money, 161). Cf. his advice to Roderigo, 1.3.340ff.
trash could = slang for money (*OED* 3d), as in *JC* 4.3.72ff., 'wring / From the hands of peasants their vile trash'
***something-nothing** (?)something trivial. Cf. Dent, S620.1, 'Something nothing', quoting Porter, *Two Angry Women* (1599), 'let me heare that something nothing then' (MSR 698), T. Powell, *Welch Bayte* (1603, C2b), 'newes of a something nothing'.

165 Cf. Dent, H331.2, 'To have someone's heart (leaping, panting) in one's hand', and 1.1.63. The hearts of traitors were ripped out and held up immediately after their execution. Here *if* = even if.

168 **green-eyed** Cf. *MV* 3.2.110, 'green-eyed jealousy'; *OED* green 3, 'of bilious hue, indicative of fear or jealousy', hence 'green with envy'.
monster Cf. *KL* 1.1.122, 'Come not between the dragon and his wrath': an emotion is externalized.
doth mock makes sport of, teases (*OED* 2b, 3) (perhaps as a cat with a mouse)

156 and] *F;* or *Q* 157 Zounds . . . mean?] Zouns. *Q;* What dost thou meane? *F* 158 woman, . . . lord,] woman's deere my Lord; *Q;* woman (deere my Lord) *F* 159 their] *F;* our *Q* 160] *as Q; F lines* trash: / nothing; / something-nothing] *this edn;* something, nothing *QF* 164 By heaven] *Q; not in F* thoughts] *F;* thought *Q* 167 OTHELLO Ha!] *Oth.* Ha? *F; not in Q* my lord, of] *F; not in Q* 168 mock] *as QF;* make *Hanmer (Theobald)*

The meat it feeds on. That cuckold lives in bliss
Who, certain of his fate, loves not his wronger,
But O, what damned minutes tells he o'er
Who dotes yet doubts, suspects yet strongly loves!

OTHELLO

O misery!

IAGO

Poor and content is rich, and rich enough,
But riches fineless is as poor as winter
To him that ever fears he shall be poor.
Good God, the souls of all my tribe defend
From jealousy.

OTHELLO

Why — why is this?
Think'st thou I'd make a life of jealousy
To follow still the changes of the moon
With fresh suspicions? No: to be once in doubt
Is once to be resolved. Exchange me for a goat
When I shall turn the business of my soul

169 **meat** food; i.e. suspicions. But the image of a self-devourer is also present, as in *Cor* 4.2.50, 'Anger's my meat; I sup upon myself.'
cuckold (refers to Othello indirectly, but still an explosive word)

170 **Who . . . fate** who, though sure that his wife is unfaithful
wronger = wife, or wife's lover. Othello probably spoke of his love for Cassio in Iago's presence (2.3.244).

171 'what accursed minutes does he suffer (count)'; *minutes* = dragging minutes, slow time

172 **dotes** is infatuated; hinting 'is weak-minded from age' (*OED* 2, 3), which points at Othello
strongly intensely

174 **Poor and content** Cf. 1.1.40ff. (Iago is not content to be poor), 2.1.129ff.; Dent, C629, 'Contentment is great riches.'

175 **fineless** boundless

177 **Good God** not the modern (devalued) exclamation but an appeal to God's goodness. Cf. Dent, J38.1, 'From jealousy the good Lord deliver us' (not recorded before Shakespeare).
tribe Cf. 1.1.180n.

180 **make** suffer (*OED* 64); i.e. that I would let jealousy take over my life

181 wax and wane (in suspicion) like the moon (Ridley), i.e. to act like a lunatic; *still* = always

183 **once** once for all. But F could be right: 'Is – to be resolved.'
resolved determined (on a course of action); freed from doubt
goat because a horned animal? Or because goats, highly sexed, spend too much time in lustful activity?

169 The] *F;* That *Q* 172 strongly] *Q;* soundly *F;* fondly *Knight* 177 God] *Q;* Heauen *F* 183 Is once] *Q;* Is *F*

To such exsufflicate and blown surmises,
Matching thy inference. 'Tis not to make me jealous
To say my wife is fair, feeds well, loves company,
Is free of speech, sings, plays and dances well:
Where virtue is, these are more virtuous.
Nor from mine own weak merits will I draw
The smallest fear or doubt of her revolt,
For she had eyes and chose me. No, Iago,
I'll see before I doubt, when I doubt, prove,
And on the proof there is no more but this:
Away at once with love or jealousy!

IAGO

I am glad of this, for now I shall have reason
To show the love and duty that I bear you
With franker spirit: therefore, as I am bound,
Receive it from me. I speak not yet of proof:

185 ***exsufflicate** = (?)inflated, i.e. improbable. *OED* records no other example, but cites exsufflation (sixteenth century) from Lat. *exsufflare* = blow up.
blown Editors suggest (1) fly-blown, (2) inflated, (3) rumoured.
surmises allegations (esp. if unfounded or unproved); suspicions; conjectures (*OED* 2–4)

186 **inference** 'It looks as though the unhappy confusion of "infer" and "imply" was as old as the Elizabethans' (Ridley, citing *2H4* 5.5.14, *R3* 3.7.12, *Tim* 3.5.72); or, conclusion, i.e. the conclusion you have drawn from the evidence (*OED* 2, first in 1612).
jealous F always has *iealious*, an alternative spelling.

187 **feeds well** could be an 'irrelevant interpolation', making this a long line. So Walker, citing Cinthio on women who 'with beauty of body and under a semblance of virtue, for instance in *singing, playing, dancing* lightly and *speaking* sweetly, hide an ugly and abominable soul' (Bullough, 7.240). But Othello's point is that a woman given over to sociable and physical pleasures need not have an 'ugly soul', so *feeds well* fits in. Cf. 343n.

188 **free** unreserved

190 **weak** deficient
draw deduce

191 **revolt** 'any "falling off" from allegiance or obedience'; can = revulsion, as in *TN* 2.4.99, 'their love may be called appetite . . . That suffer surfeit, cloyment, and revolt' (Ridley)

193 **prove** prove it one way or the other

194 **on the proof** when I have proof

195 i.e. either love or jealousy will be ruled out. *Away*: a gesture is needed. Cf. 266.

197 **love and duty** Cf. 1.1.58, 'not I for love and duty'!

198 **franker** more open, unreserved

199 **proof** proof of guilt. Othello spoke of proof of guilt *or innocence*.

185 exsufflicate] *Malone;* exufflicate *QF* blown] *Q;* blow'd *F* 188 well] *Q; not in F* 196 this] *F;* it *Q*

Look to your wife, observe her well with Cassio.
Wear your eyes thus, not jealous nor secure;
I would not have your free and noble nature
Out of self-bounty be abused: look to't.
I know our country disposition well –
In Venice they do let God see the pranks
They dare not show their husbands; their best conscience
Is not to leave't undone, but keep't unknown.

OTHELLO
Dost thou say so?

IAGO
She did deceive her father, marrying you,
And when she seemed to shake, and fear your looks,
She loved them most.

OTHELLO
And so she did.

IAGO
Why, go to then:
She that so young could give out such a seeming
To seel her father's eyes up, close as oak —

200 **Look to** echoing 1.3.293, 'Look to her, Moor'
Cassio a dangerous moment: he names Cassio (prepared for in 94ff.)
201 **Wear** present (the look of) (*OED* 7)
thus A gesture is needed.
secure free from apprehension
202 **free** generous
203 **self-bounty** Shakespeare's coinage. Many new 'self-' compounds appeared in the sixteenth and seventeenth centuries (see 2.3.198; *OED*). Here *self* = your own, as in *TC* 2.3.171–2, 'pride / That quarrels at self-breath'. For *bounty* (= kindness, goodness), cf. 7n.
abused abuse = take advantage of; cheat, deceive; injure, wrong
204 **our country** our country's. Implies that Iago, despite his Spanish name, is a Venetian. Cf. 5.1.89. He means 'I know, *but you cannot know* . . .'.
205 **In Venice** See pp. 22–3. He means 'they prefer to defy God rather than their husbands', a variant of a commonplace: cf. *R3* 1.4.197–8, 'Will you then / Spurn at his [God's] edict, and fulfill a man's?'; Acts 5.4.
pranks Cf. 2.1.142n.
206–7 i.e. the best their conscience aspires to is not to leave it (wickedness) undone, but to keep it unknown. Cf. *The Book of Common Prayer*, 'We have left undone those things which we ought to have done' (Noble, 219).
209 again echoing 1.3.293–4
211 **go to** there you are
212 **give out** give it out to be believed (that such a 'seeming' was the truth). Cf. 129–31.
213 **seel** Cf. 1.3.270n.
close as oak Cf. Dent, O1, 'As close as oak' (not recorded before Shakespeare). 'Usually explained by reference to the close grain of oak' (Ridley).

201 eyes] *F;* eie *Q* 205 God] *Q;* Heauen *F* 206] *as Q; F lines* Husbands. / Conscience, / 207 leave't] *F;* leaue *Q* keep't] *F (*kept*);* keepe *Q*

He thought 'twas witchcraft. But I am much to
blame,
I humbly do beseech you of your pardon
For too much loving you.

OTHELLO

I am bound to thee for ever.

IAGO

I see this hath a little dashed your spirits.

OTHELLO

Not a jot, not a jot.

IAGO

I'faith, I fear it has.
I hope you will consider what is spoke
Comes from my love. But I do see you're moved;
I am to pray you not to strain my speech
To grosser issues nor to larger reach
Than to suspicion.

OTHELLO

I will not.

IAGO

Should you do so, my lord,
My speech should fall into such vile success
As my thoughts aimed not at: Cassio's my worthy
friend.

214 **to** QF *too* may be a reading taken by F from Q (see *Texts*, 94ff.), but 'too blame' is found elsewhere.
215 **of** for
217 **bound** indebted; tied (cf. 482n.)
218 Iago's delight in Othello's alleged misfortune expresses itself in faked solicitude.
219 **Not a jot** a common phrase (e.g. *Ham* 5.1.113, 207)
221 F *your* could = my love of you
222 **am** have (*OED* be 16a)
223 'There is a suggestive undertone of our sense of "gross" and of the Elizabethan sense of "large" = "licentious", as in "some large jests he will make" (*Ado* 2.3.198)' (Ridley); *issues* = conclusions; *reach* = scope, extent of application (*OED* 9); *gross* could = flagrant.
225 **Should . . . lord** completes a pentameter with 224: 'I will not' is probably an interruption (cf. 1.1.101n.)
226 **fall . . . success** come to such a vile result; *success* = outcome (good or bad)
227 **aimed** F *aym'd* (without *at*) is probably correct (*OED* 3: to guess, conjecture).

214] *as Q; F lines* Witchcraft. / blame: / to] too *QF* 219 I'faith] *Q;* Trust me *F* 221] *as Q; F lines* Loue. / moou'd: / my] *Q;* your *F* you're] *F (*y'are*);* you are *Q* 226 vile] *Q;* vilde *F* 227] As my thoughts aime not at: *Cassio's* my trusty friend: *Q;* Which my Thoughts aym'd not. / *Cassio*'s my worthy Friend: / *F*

| My lord, I see you're moved. |

OTHELLO No, not much moved.
I do not think but Desdemona's honest. ↖ Lie.
IAGO ↳ HIS faith in her.
Long live she so; and long live you to think so. 230
OTHELLO
And yet how nature, erring from itself –
IAGO
Ay, there's the point: as, to be bold with you,
Not to affect many proposèd matches
Of her own clime, complexion and degree,
Whereto we see, in all things, nature tends – 235
Foh! one may smell in such a will most rank,
Foul disproportion, thoughts unnatural.
But pardon me, I do not in position
Distinctly speak of her, though I may fear
Her will, recoiling to her better judgement, 240
May fall to match you with her country forms,
And happily repent.
OTHELLO Farewell, farewell.

229 **but** but that: 'I do not think Desdemona is anything other than *honest*' (= chaste, honourable)

230 **and . . . so** 'and long may you live thinking so'. *Think* is meant to ring alarm bells, after 107ff., 132ff.

233–5 He follows up Othello's recollection of 1.3.63 by echoing Brabantio again (1.2.67–71).

233 **affect** like
 proposèd proposèd

234 of her own *clime* (= region, country), *temperament* (the combination of qualities that determines the nature of a person; or, *skin colour*), and *rank*

235 Cf. Tilley, L286, 'Like will to like.'

236 **smell** could = suspect. Cf. *KL* 1.1.16, 'Do you smell a fault?'
 will wilfulness; carnal desire. Cf. 240, and *Texts*, 16–18 (Shakespeare's wish to protect Desdemona from the charge of wilfulness).
 rank rebellious; excessive; lustful; (after smell) rancid, foul-smelling

237 **disproportion** lack of a sense of proportion

238–9 **in position / Distinctly** in (making this) proposition speak specifically of her

240 **recoiling to** i.e. giving way to

241 may come to compare you with the *forms* of her own country; *form* = body (in its outward appearance); example; behaviour. *Fall to* = come to, or sink (so low as) to.

242 **happily** perchance (with a hint of 'fortunately'?)

228 you're] *F* (*y'are); you are Q* 230] *as Q; F lines* so; / . . . so. / 232] *as Q; F lines* point: / you) / 236 Foh! one] *F;* Fie we *Q* 237 disproportion] *Q;* disproportions *F* 242–4] *Q lines* if more / set on / *Iago.* /; *F lines* farewell: / know more: / obserue. / *Iago.* /

If more thou dost perceive, let me know more:
Set on thy wife to observe. Leave me, Iago.

IAGO
My lord, I take my leave.

OTHELLO
Why did I marry?
This honest creature doubtless
Sees and knows more – much more – than he unfolds.

IAGO
My lord, I would I might entreat your honour
To scan this thing no farther. Leave it to time;
Although 'tis fit that Cassio have his place,
For sure he fills it up with great ability,
Yet if you please to hold him off a while
You shall by that perceive him, and his means:
Note if your lady strain his entertainment
With any strong or vehement importunity,
Much will be seen in that. In the meantime
Let me be thought too busy in my fears
– As worthy cause I have to fear I am –
And hold her free, I do beseech your honour.

OTHELLO
Fear not my government.

IAGO
I once more take my leave. *Exit.*

245 **Why . . . marry?** Cf. Thorello, the jealous husband, in *Every Man in His Humour* (1601), 3.3.15, 'what meant I to marrie?'

246 **creature** could = fellow, person (without contemptuousness) but here sounds unflattering. Othello speaks to himself.

247 **unfolds** reveals

249 Cf. Dent, T324, 'Time brings the truth to light.'

251 Cf. *JC* 3.2.99, 'And sure he is an honourable man' (Antony, like Iago, means the opposite of what he says).

253 **means** intermediaries; methods (*OED* 9, 10)

254 **strain his entertainment** press (insist on) his reinstatement

257 **busy** officious, meddlesome

258 **worthy** good

259 **hold her free** consider her innocent; or, let her have her freedom (to betray herself)

260 **government** self-government, management: 'don't be uneasy about the way I'll handle it (or, about my self-control)'

245–6 Why . . . doubtless] *as F; one line Q* 248 SP] *Qc, F; not in Qu* 249 farther] *F;* further *Q* 250 Although 'tis] *F;* Tho it be *Q* 252 hold] *Q; not in F;* put *F2* 254 his] *F;* her *Q* 261 SD] *Qc, F; not in Qu*

OTHELLO

This fellow's of exceeding honesty
And knows all qualities, with a learned spirit,
Of human dealings. If I do prove her haggard,
Though that her jesses were my dear heart-strings,
I'd whistle her off and let her down the wind
To prey at fortune. Haply for I am black
And have not those soft parts of conversation
That chamberers have, or for I am declined
Into the vale of years – yet that's not much –
She's gone, I am abused, and my relief
Must be to loathe her. O curse of marriage
That we can call these delicate creatures ours
And not their appetites! I had rather be a toad
And live upon the vapour of a dungeon

263 **qualities** characters, natures
264 **dealings** intercourse
haggard wild, untamed (lit. a wild female hawk caught in her adult plumage)
265 **Though that** even if
jesses straps, fastened round the legs of a hawk, attached to the falconer's wrist
heart-strings tendons or nerves supposed to brace and sustain the heart (in early anatomy)
266 Hawks were sent off with a whistle, against the wind in pursuit of prey, with the wind when turned loose; i.e. Desdemona is too wild to tame. Cf. Dent, W432, 'To go down the wind' = to go to ruin. N.B. He does not intend to kill Desdemona at this stage.
267 **To . . . fortune** to fend for herself; to prey as fortune wills
Haply for perhaps because
268–9 **soft . . . have** pleasing qualities in my social behaviour that drawing-room gallants have (*chamberers* here first in this sense). Cf. Romans 13.13, 'Let us walk honestly . . . not in rioting and drunkenness, neither in chambering and wantonness.'
270 **vale of years** Alluding to 'the valley of the shadow of death' (Psalms 23.4)?
271 **gone** ruined, undone (*OED* gone 1)
abused wronged
relief assistance in time of need; alleviation of a pain; 'deliverance (esp. in *Law*) from some . . . burden, or grievance' (*OED* 6, from 1616)
272 **O . . . marriage** *either* 'it is the curse of marriage that', *or* 'O, the curse of marriage! – that'
273 **ours** Upper-class English wives were, in effect, the property of their husbands and addressed them as 'my lord' (= my master): 1.3.184n.
274–7 Cf. 4.2.58ff. Kean spoke these lines 'with a peculiar, snarling, sardonic laugh, but yet extremely quiet in manner' (Rosenberg, 64).
274 **toad** a type of anything hateful or loathsome; pre-Shakespeare (*OED* 1b)

263 qualities] *Q;* Quantities *F* learned] *Q;* learn'd *F* 264 dealings] *F;* dealing *Q* 267 Haply] *F;* Happily *Q* 270 vale] *F;* valt *Q* 275 of] *F;* in *Q*

Than keep a corner in the thing I love
For others' uses. Yet 'tis the plague of great ones,
Prerogatived are they less than the base;
'Tis destiny unshunnable, like death –
Even then this forked plague is fated to us
When we do quicken.

Enter DESDEMONA *and* EMILIA.

Look where she comes:
If she be false, O then heaven mocks itself,
I'll not believe't.

DESDEMONA How now, my dear Othello?
Your dinner, and the generous islanders
By you invited, do attend your presence.

OTHELLO
I am to blame.

DESDEMONA Why do you speak so faintly?
Are you not well?

276 **corner** *keep a corner* = reserve a small place (*OED* 6c), here with secondary sexual sense. Cf. *Cambises* (1st edn, n.d., *c.* 1570), Bla-b: 'Where-soeuer I goe, in eche corner I will grope. *Ambidexter*. What and ye run in the corner of some prittie maide? *Snuf*. To grope there good fellow I will not be afraid.'
thing Cf. 306n.

277 **uses** Cf. 5.2.69n.

277–81 Ridley thought this nonsense: 'There is no question of the great being either less or more liable to be cuckolded than the base; every one is equal.' But Shakespeare may mean that great ones are in greater danger because their duties keep them from home.

277 **plague** affliction

278 **Prerogatived** privileged
base lower orders

279 **unshunnable** inescapable. A coinage (cf. *MM* 3.2.60, 'an unshunned consequence'; Dent, C889, 'Cuckolds come by destiny').

280 **forked** forkèd: horned

281 **do quicken** are conceived

282 **mocks** makes a mockery of; counterfeits, makes a false pretence of (*OED* 4b)

284 **generous** noble. We hear no more of the dinner, but perhaps should now hear laughter from a nearby room, voices, music?

285 **attend** await; give attendance to

286 **to blame** blameworthy, i.e. I'm wrong (*OED* blame 6)

276 the] *F;* a *Q* 277 of great ones] *Q;* to Great-ones *F* 281 SD] *after* beleeue it *283 Q; after 281 F* Look . . . she] *F; Desdemona Q* 282 O . . . mocks] *Q;* Heauen mock'd *F* 283 't] *F;* it *Q* 284 islanders] *F;* Ilander *Q* 286 do . . . faintly] *F;* is your speech so faint *Q* 286–7 Why . . . well?] *as F; one line Q*

OTHELLO

I have a pain upon my forehead, here.

DESDEMONA

Faith, that's with watching, 'twill away again.
Let me but bind it hard, within this hour
It will be well.

OTHELLO

Your napkin is too little.

[*She drops her handkerchief.*]

Let it alone. Come, I'll go in with you.

DESDEMONA

I am very sorry that you are not well.

Exeunt Othello and Desdemona.

EMILIA

I am glad I have found this napkin,
This was her first remembrance from the Moor.
My wayward husband hath a hundred times
Wooed me to steal it, but she so loves the token
– For he conjured her she should ever keep it –
That she reserves it evermore about her
To kiss and talk to. I'll have the work ta'en out
And give't Iago: what he will do with it
Heaven knows, not I,

288 Cf. Thorello (as in 245n.), 1.4.191, 'Troth my head akes extreamely on a suddaine': he fears horns. Othello *may* have a headache, but 287 gives him an excuse for claiming one.

289 **watching** i.e. not sleeping enough

291 **napkin** handkerchief
*SD See LN.

292 **in** i.e. to join the others. Or are they out of doors (cf. 3.3n)?

293 SD The F SD may mean that Othello sweeps out without listening to Desdemona's last line, or it may be misplaced.

295 **remembrance** keepsake

296 **wayward** self-willed; wrong-headed; perverse. Might be confused with *weird*, which could be spelt *weyward* (as in *Mac* 1.3.33).

297 **token** love token

298 **conjured** conjùred: earnestly entreated

299 **reserves** preserves

300 **To . . . to** For Desdemona's age see p. 96.
work pattern; embroidery
ta'en out copied (*OED* 85e). From Cinthio: see pp. 386, 390; cf. 3.4.180, 4.1.153.

302 Cf. Dent, G189.1, 'God he knows, not I' (cf. *R3* 3.1.26). She implies 'I don't want to know.'

289 Faith] *Q;* Why *F* 290 it hard] *F;* your head *Q* 291 well] *F;* well againe *Q* SD] *Rowe; not in QF* 293 SD] *Ex.* Oth. *and* Desd. *(opp. 294) Q; Exit. (opp. 292) F* 300 have] *F;* ha *Q* 301 he will] *F;* hee'll *Q*

I nothing, but to please his fantasy.

Enter IAGO.

IAGO
How now! What do you here alone?

EMILIA
Do not you chide, I have a thing for you –

IAGO
You have a thing for me? it is a common thing –

EMILIA Ha?

IAGO
To have a foolish wife.

EMILIA
O, is that all? What will you give me now
For that same handkerchief?

IAGO What handkerchief?

EMILIA
What handkerchief?
Why, that the Moor first gave to Desdemona,
That which so often you did bid me steal.

IAGO
Hast stolen it from her?

EMILIA
No, faith, she let it drop by negligence
And, to th'advantage, I being here, took't up.

303 **I nothing** 'I am nothing (in his eyes; he thinks I'm here) only to please his whims'; or, 'I know nothing, except to please . . .'. See p. 48.
fantasy could = habit of deluding oneself (*OED* 3)

305 **a thing** could = something (*Ham* 5.2.90)

306 **thing** Iago pretends to misunderstand *thing* as pudendum: cf. *TGV* 3.1.351, *1H4* 3.3.115ff.
common free to be used by everyone; undistinguished, ordinary (*OED* 6, 11)

310 **handkerchief** This is F's form throughout; Q always reads *handkercher*, and this may be what Shakespeare wrote (*Texts*, 70).

312 **that** that which

316 **to th'advantage** i.e. seizing the opportunity

303 but to please] *F;* know, but for *Q* 303.1] *as F; opp. 302 Q* 306] *as Q; F lines* me? / thing – / You have] *F; not in Q* 308 wife] *F;* thing *Q* 310 handkerchief] *F (throughout);* handkercher *Q (throughout)* 314 stolen] *F (*stolne*);* stole *Q* 315 No, faith,] *as Q;* No: but *F* 316 th'] *F;* the *Q*

Look, here it is.

IAGO A good wench, give it me.

EMILIA

What will you do with't, that you have been so earnest
To have me filch it?

IAGO [*Snatching it*] Why, what's that to you?

EMILIA

If it be not for some purpose of import
Give't me again. Poor lady, she'll run mad
When she shall lack it.

IAGO Be not acknown on't,
I have use for it. Go, leave me. *Exit Emilia.*
I will in Cassio's lodging lose this napkin
And let him find it. Trifles light as air
Are to the jealous confirmations strong
As proofs of holy writ. This may do something.
The Moor already changes with my poison:
Dangerous conceits are in their natures poisons
Which at the first are scarce found to distaste
But with a little art upon the blood

317 **A good wench** good girl. *Wench* (girl, young woman) could be 'an endearing form of address' (*OED* 1c).

318 **you have** elide: *you've*

319 **filch** pilfer (something of small value) (originally slang)

*SD Some Iagos snatch the handkerchief, others get it by coaxing (Sprague, 197).

Why . . . you Dent, W280.4, 'What is that to you?'

320 **import** weighty significance

321 **run mad** Cf. *1H4* 3.1.209, 'Nay, if you melt, then will she run mad.' We would say 'go frantic'.

322 **lack** miss; need

acknown unique in Shakespeare; usually acknown *of (OED* 4d). Seems to mean 'acknowledged'; in effect, don't acknowledge that you have a part in it, keep out of it.

323 **leave me** Cf. 85, Othello's request to *his* wife to leave: the two marriages are brought into focus.

325 **Trifles . . . air** Cf. Dent, A90, 'As light as air'. Perhaps he toys with the handkerchief (blows it into the air? Cf. 448).

327 **As . . . writ** alluding to the Bible as Holy Writ, i.e. holy writing

329 **conceits** thoughts

330 **distaste** cause disgust, offend the taste (*OED*, first here)

331 **art** skill. Iago prides himself on his 'art' elsewhere: cf. 'double knavery' (1.3.393 and 400), 'we work by wit' (2.3.367–8).

upon the blood to arouse passion

317 it is] *Q;* 'tis *F* 318–9] *verse Q (*bin/*); prose F* 318 't] *F;* it *Q* 319 SD] *Rowe; not in QF* what's] *Q;* what is *F* 321 Give't me] *F;* Giue mee't *Q* 322–3 Be . . . me] *as F; one line Q* 322 acknown] *F;* you knowne *Q* 328] *F; not in Q* 329 natures] *QF;* nature *Pope* 331 art] *Q;* acte *F*

Burn like the mines of sulphur.

Enter OTHELLO.

I did say so:
Look where he comes. Not poppy nor mandragora
Nor all the drowsy syrups of the world
Shall ever medicine thee to that sweet sleep
Which thou owedst yesterday.

OTHELLO
Ha! Ha! false to me?

IAGO
Why, how now, general? No more of that.

OTHELLO
Avaunt, be gone, thou hast set me on the rack!
I swear 'tis better to be much abused
Than but to know't a little.

IAGO
How now, my lord?

OTHELLO
What sense had I of her stolen hours of lust?
I saw't not, thought it not, it harmed not me,
I slept the next night well, fed well, was free and merry;

332 Cf. Pliny, quoted Hart: 'Sulphur . . . is engendered within the Islands of Aeolia, which lie between Italy and Sicily . . . [which] do always burn by reason thereof' (i.e. are difficult to put out).

333 **poppy** opium
mandragora (the juice of the) mandrake plant, a soporific. Cf. *AC* 1.5.4–5, 'Give me to drink mandragora . . . That I might sleep out this great gap of time', and Marlowe, *Jew of Malta*, 5.1.80–1.

334 **drowsy** inducing sleepiness

335 **medicine** bring by medicine (nonce use)

336 **owedst** didst own or possess
Ha! Ha! *Ha*, like *O*, was a signal to the actor to make the appropriate noise: cf. *OED* 1, 4.2.56n.

337 **how now** what's this

338 **Avaunt** away!
rack Cf. *KL* 4.7.45–6, 'I am bound / Upon a wheel of fire'.

339 **abused** wronged, deceived

340 **Than . . . little** than only to know a little of what has happened

341 Othello's imagination has persuaded him of Desdemona's guilt (in Iago's absence!).
sense feeling, consciousness
stolen secret

342 Cf. Dent, K179.1, 'What one does not know does not hurt.'

343 **fed well** Cf. *feeds well*, 187.
free unreserved in behaviour; (?)carefree

332 mines] *F;* mindes *Q* SD] *opp. 331 Q; after 332 F* 336 owedst] *Q;* owd'st *F* to me?] *F;* to me, to me? *Q* 340 know't] *F;* know *Q* 341 of] *Q;* in *F* 343 fed well] *F; not in Q*

Iago: Venice' women - (Desdemona) - do and don't talk about it.

I found not Cassio's kisses on her lips;
He that is robbed, not wanting what is stolen,
Let him not know't, and he's not robbed at all.

IAGO

I am sorry to hear this.

OTHELLO

I had been happy if the general camp,
Pioneers and all, had tasted her sweet body,
So I had nothing known. O now for ever
Farewell the tranquil mind, farewell content!
Farewell the plumed troops and the big wars
That makes ambition virtue! O farewell,
Farewell the neighing steed and the shrill trump,
The spirit-stirring drum, th'ear-piercing fife,
The royal banner, and all quality,
Pride, pomp and circumstance of glorious war!

345–6 Cf. Ovid, *Amores*, 3.14, 'That you should not err, since you are fair, is not my plea, but that I be not compelled, poor wretch, to know it . . . let me think you honest though you are not'; *Son* 138; Dent, L461, 'He that is not sensible of his loss has lost nothing.'

345 **wanting** missing

348 **camp** i.e. army

349 **Pioneers** the lowest kind of soldier; carried spades, pickaxes, etc., to dig trenches – perhaps relevant, in view of Othello's inflamed imagination

and all Cf. *KL* 3.6.62, 'The little dogs and all'.

tasted handled, explored by touch; had carnal knowledge of (*OED* 1, 3b, citing *Cym* 2.4.57–8, 'make't apparent / That you have tasted her in bed', as first example).

350 **So** so long as

350–60 The 'farewell' speech was a commonplace (e.g. Ovid, *Heroides*, 9.165ff.). Shakespeare's version was much echoed by other dramatists, esp. Beaumont and Fletcher (in *Bonduca; The Loyal Subject; The Prophetess*, 'farewell Pride and Pomp / And circumstance of glorious Majestie, / Farewell for ever' (4.6.72–4, quoted Malone).

351 **tranquil** serene, peaceful (*OED*, from Lat. *tranquillus*, first here)

352 **plumed** plumèd: decked with feathers

big mighty; violent

353 **makes** Cf. 1.1.148–9n.

354–5 perhaps an echo of Lyly's *Campaspe*, 2.2.35; Alexander the Great, in love, neglects 'the warlike sound of *drumme* and *trumpe* . . . the *neighing* of barbed *steeds*'. *Trump* = trumpet.

356 **royal** magnificent (*OED* 8–10): Othello did not proclaim his own royal descent (1.2.19ff.).

quality essential nature

357 **Pride, pomp** usually deplored, not admired (as here). Cf. L. Wright, *Summons for Sleepers* (1589), A4a: 'pomp, pride, and superfluity'; Plutarch, *Lives* (1579), '[he] brought all the pride and pompe of those Courts into GRÆCE' ('Agis and Cleomenes', p. 850); *Homilies*, 280, 282.

circumstance formality, ceremony. See Parker (as in 126n.).

glorious possessing glory; eager for glory; ostentatious, boastful (*OED* 1–5)

347 this.] *Q;* this? *F* 352 troops] *F;* troope *Q* 355 th'] *F;* the *Q*

And, O you mortal engines whose rude throats
Th'immortal Jove's dread clamours counterfeit,
Farewell: Othello's occupation's gone.

IAGO

Is't possible? my lord?

OTHELLO

Villain, be sure thou prove my love a whore,
Be sure of it, give me the ocular proof,
[*Catching hold of him*]
Or by the worth of man's eternal soul
Thou hadst been better have been born a dog
Than answer my waked wrath!

IAGO

Is't come to this?

OTHELLO

Make me to see't, or at the least so prove it
That the probation bear no hinge nor loop
To hang a doubt on, or woe upon thy life!

IAGO

My noble lord –

358 **mortal** deadly
engines machines, i.e. cannons
rude rough, rugged

359 **clamours** (Lat. *clamor*, a shout), i.e. thunder

360 **occupation** employment, hence life, because life has lost all meaning for him. Hulme (124) thinks Othello refers to his military role but 'must refer also to his loss of Desdemona' (since *occupy* could = cohabit with). Iago spoke of the *trade* of war (1.2.1).

361 'Is it possible that you should feel like this?'

362ff. close to Cinthio: cf. p. 385. Brabantio flared up more quickly (1.1.116). Barton Booth took Iago by the throat during this speech; other actors did so later (371) – an action authenticated by 5.2.353.

362 **my love** Does he still love her?

363 **ocular proof** Cf. *Cynthia's Revels* (1600), 2.3.11ff., 'You shall now, as well be the ocular, as the eare-witnesse'; *Poetaster* (1601), 4.5.75, 'wilt thou suffer this ocular temptation?'

364 See LN.

366 **answer** have to answer to, or defend yourself against

368–9 **That . . . on** 'that the proof permits of no support to attach a doubt to'. *Hinge* = pivot (*OED* 4, first here); *loop* = looped string or cord. Cf. *OED* hang 9b, 'to be supported or suspended at the side, as on a hinge or pivot, so as to be free to turn or swing horizontally': i.e. the proof must be so secure that doubts will not move it.

358 you] *F;* ye *Q* rude] *F;* wide *Q* 359 Th'] *F;* The *Q* dread clamours] *F;* great clamor *Q* 361 possible? my] *Capell subst.;* possible my *QF* 362 thou] *Qc, F;* you *Qu* 363 SD] *Rowe; not in QF* 364 man's] *Q;* mine *F*

OTHELLO

If thou dost slander her and torture me
Never pray more, abandon all remorse;
On horror's head horrors accumulate,
Do deeds to make heaven weep, all earth amazed,
For nothing canst thou to damnation add 375
Greater than that!

IAGO O grace! O heaven forgive me!
Are you a man? have you a soul, or sense?
God buy you, take mine office. O wretched fool *"I x want lieutant anymore*
That lov'st to make thine honesty a vice!
O monstrous world! Take note, take note, O world, 380
To be direct and honest is not safe. ← *Talking bout himself.*
I thank you for this profit, and from hence
I'll love no friend, sith love breeds such offence.

OTHELLO

Nay, stay, thou shouldst be honest. *Contradictory*

IAGO

I should be wise, for honesty's a fool *ppl don't get* 385
 Iago's statements (money, I am not what I am, honesty)

371ff. Cf. *KJ* 4.3.117–34, 'Beyond the infinite and boundless reach / Of mercy, if thou didst this deed of death, / Art thou damn'd'.
372 **remorse** repentance (because you cannot win forgiveness for what you have done); compassion
373 **head** perhaps = summit (*OED* 12)
 accumulate heap up. Cf. a similar image in *Ham* 5.1.280ff., 'let them throw / Millions of acres on us'.
374 **heaven weep** Cf. *MM* 2.2.122: man 'makes the angels weep'.
 amazed stronger than today: 'paralyzed with horror' (Kittredge)
376 **forgive** i.e. for daring to be 'honest': more subtle than Q *defend*
377 **sense** consciousness; intelligence
378 **God buy you** here = (God be with you, i.e.) God help you, I wash my hands of you
 office his position of trust, *either* as ensign,

or as Othello's 'friend' and informer
378–9 **O . . . vice** He addresses himself; vice = defect, fault.
380 could be punctuated 'O monstrous! world, take note . . .' Cf. *KL* 4.1.10, 'World, world, O world!'; *TC* 5.10.36.
381 **direct** straightforward
 honest honourable
382 **profit** profitable lesson (Sanders). Cf. Montaigne, bk 3, ch. 1, 'Of profit and honesty'.
 from hence henceforth
383 **sith** since (archaic)
 breeds begets
 offence hurt; pain; disgrace
384 **stay** *Either* Iago is about to slip away, *or* Othello asks him not to proceed in that way of thinking.
 shouldst be appear to be, or, ought to be
385 **should be** ought to be

376 forgive] *F*; defend *Q* 378 buy you] *F*; buy, you *Q* mine] *Qc, F*; thine *Qu* 379 lov'st] *F*; liuest
Q thine] *Qc, F*; mine *Qu* 383 sith] *F*; since *Q*

237 ** Em is moral only when she realizes how serious it is.*

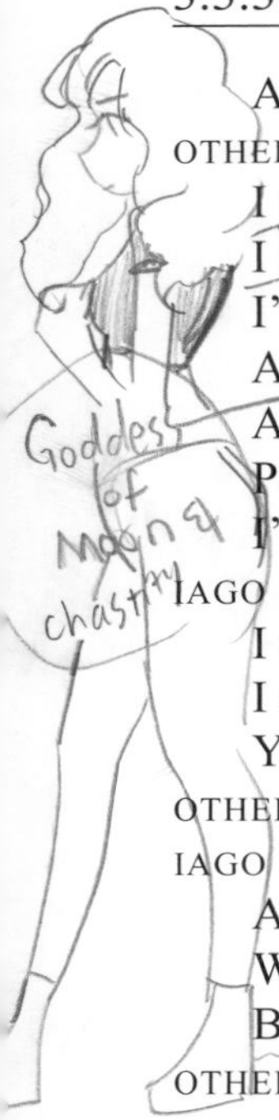

And loses that it works for.

OTHELLO By the world,
I think my wife be honest, and think she is not,
I think that thou art just, and think thou art not.
I'll have some proof. Her name, that was as fresh
As Dian's visage, is now begrimed and black
As mine own face. If there be cords or knives,
Poison, or fire, or suffocating streams,
I'll not endure it. Would I were satisfied!

IAGO
I see, sir, you are eaten up with passion.
I do repent me that I put it to you.
You would be satisfied?

OTHELLO Would? nay, and I will!

IAGO
And may – but how? how satisfied, my lord?
Would you, the supervisor, grossly gape on?
Behold her topped?

OTHELLO Death and damnation! O!

386 **By the world** common asseveration, as in *LLL* 4.3.17, 5.1.102, 105; *R3* 4.4.375; but more meaningful here, after 380 (cf. also 90–2, 4.3.63–9)
387–8 elide: 'she's', 'thou'rt not' (*Texts*, 119)
388 **just** honourable (in what you say)
389 **I'll have** I must have
***Her name** Ridley defends F: 'Othello is maddened by the befoulment of his own honour.' But the comparison with Diana (the moon goddess, patron of chastity) points to a woman and *her* chastity, not to a man.
390 **begrimed** *grime* = soot, smut, coal dust. The actor's face was *begrimed*: he had to be careful to keep his makeup off Desdemona's clothes (Lois Potter in *The Arts of Performance*, ed. Murray Biggs [1991], 118). A curious way to speak of his own face?
391–3 Is he thinking of suicide (Sanders)? In *Faerie Queene*, 1.9.50, Despair offers 'swords, ropes, poison, fire, / And all that might him to perdition [i.e. suicide] draw'. But Othello may have in mind murder, not suicide: cf. 445, 4.1.175.
393 **satisfied** set free from doubt, satisfied one way or the other. Iago plays with the word to suggest a voyeur's satisfaction. Cf. *WT* 1.2.232ff.
394 **eaten up** devastated. Cf. *gnaw my inwards* (2.1.295).
395 **put** suggested
398 **supervisor** onlooker, spectator (*OED* 2, first here; previously 'one who directs the work of others')
grossly indelicately, brutally
399 **topped** Cf. 1.1.88n., 5.2.134.

386–93 By . . . satisfied!] *F; not in Q* 389 Her] *Q2;* My *F* 394 sir] *Q; not in F* 396 Would? . . . and] *as F;* Would, nay *Q* 398 supervisor] *Q;* super-vision *F* 399 topped] topt *Q;* top'd *F;* tupp'd *Theobald*

IAGO

'Tis a shrewd doubt, though it be but a dream,
And this may help to thicken other proofs
That do demonstrate thinly.

OTHELLO

I'll tear her all to pieces!

IAGO

Nay, yet be wise, yet we see nothing done,
She may be honest yet. Tell me but this,
Have you not sometimes seen a handkerchief
Spotted with strawberries, in your wife's hand?

OTHELLO

I gave her such a one, 'twas my first gift.

IAGO

I know not that, but such a handkerchief,
I am sure it was your wife's, did I today
See Cassio wipe his beard with.

OTHELLO

If it be that—

431 This line could be Othello's, as in F. Alexander and Sisson prefer Q. Othello 'does not entangle himself; he is entangled [by Iago]' (Sisson).
shrewd strongly indicative; vexatious; sharp
doubt suspicion; fear

432 **thicken** i.e. confirm

433 **demonstrate** establish the truth (*OED* 4, first intransitive use); accent on second syllable
thinly weakly. Cf. 1.3.109, *thin* evidence.

434 Is the urge to *tear her* a sign of his 'primitiveness'? Not necessarily: cf. *RJ* 5.3.35, 'I will tear thee joint by joint', *Cym* 2.4.147, 'tear her limb-meal', and also Psalms 50.22.

435 [1]**yet** If we retain F *yet*, the third *yet* (436) in two lines receives a special emphasis: 'She may be honest – yet' (i.e. even if not for long).
[2]**yet** up to now
wise Cf. 4.1.233.
done Perhaps a quibble on *do* = copulate: cf. *Tit* 4.2.76, 'I have done thy mother'; *MM* 1.2.87–8, 'what has he done? *Pompey*. A woman.'

436 **yet** still; nevertheless; after all
Tell . . . this The same words occur, in a scribe's hand, in *Sir Thomas More*, Addition II, 237 (usually assigned to Shakespeare).

438 **Spotted** decorated
strawberries might suggest a hidden evil, or the purity of the Virgin (L. J. Ross, in *Studies in the Renaissance*, 7 [1960], 225–40). Or drops of blood?

439 **first gift** Cf. 295.

440 **I . . . that** He validates his lies by refusing to say more than he knows.

441 **today** As Iago has only just received it (319), he takes a risk in saying this. Othello could have seen it if it was Desdemona who dropped it: cf. 291 SD n.

431 SP] *Q; not in F*   432 And] *Q; Iago*. And *F*   435 [1]yet] *F*; but *Q*   442 it] *F*; 't *Q*

IAGO

If it be that, or any that was hers,
It speaks against her with the other proofs.

OTHELLO

O that the slave had forty thousand lives!
One is too poor, too weak for my revenge.
Now do I see 'tis true. Look here, Iago,
All my fond love thus do I blow to heaven:
'Tis gone!
Arise, black vengeance, from the hollow hell,
Yield up, O love, thy crown and hearted throne
To tyrannous hate! Swell, bosom, with thy fraught,
For 'tis of aspics' tongues!

IAGO

Yet be content!

OTHELLO

O blood, blood, blood! *Othello kneels.*

IAGO

Patience, I say, your mind perhaps may change.

OTHELLO

Never, Iago. Like to the Pontic sea

443 *[2]**that** could be written 'y[t]' and misread as *yt* (it), hence Malone's emendation
444 **proofs** What proofs?
445 Cf. 4.1.175. The *slave* = Cassio.
447–8 Some action is required ('Look *here*', '*thus*'), but what? He blows something upwards, then looks down and addresses 'vengeance' in hell.
448 **fond** foolish; affectionate
450 **black vengeance** Cf. *A Larum for London* (1602; SR: 27 May 1600), A4b, 'send blacke vengeance to that hated towne'.
hollow hell See LN.
451 **hearted** fixed in the heart (*OED* 5, first here; but cf. 1.3.367)
452 **fraught** burden
453 **aspics'** (*aspic* = asp, a small venomous serpent, found in Egypt and Libya): cf. 3.4.58
content calm; satisfied in mind (a harmless word, yet calculated to infuriate him). Cf. *satisfied*, 396–9.
454 SD SDs placed in the margin (as in Q) are not always placed precisely in manuscripts: the kneel could be intended for 457 or 463. For revengers who kneel, cf. *Tit* 4.1.87ff.; *Arden of Faversham* (Revels), 9.37, 'Then he kneels down and holds up his hands to heaven'; Marlowe, *Edward II*, 3.1.127, *Jew of Malta*, 1.2.165.
456–9 Cf. Pliny (see pp. 15–17). The Pontic Sea, Propontic and Hellespont = Black Sea, Sea of Marmora and the Dardanelles.

443 [2]that] *Malone;* it *QF* 447 true] *F;* time *Q* 448–9] *one line QF* 450 the . . . hell] *F;* thy . . . Cell *Q* 453 Yet] *F;* Pray *Q* 454] *F;* O blood, *Iago*, blood. *Q* SD] *Q (he kneeles. opp. 453); not in F* 455 perhaps] *Q; not in F* 456–63 Iago . . . heaven] *F; not in Q*

Whose icy current and compulsive course
Ne'er keeps retiring ebb but keeps due on
To the Propontic and the Hellespont:
Even so my bloody thoughts with violent pace
Shall ne'er look back, ne'er ebb to humble love
Till that a capable and wide revenge
Swallow them up. Now by yond marble heaven
In the due reverence of a sacred vow
I here engage my words.

IAGO Do not rise yet. *Iago kneels.*
Witness, you ever-burning lights above,
You elements that clip us round about,
Witness that here Iago doth give up
The execution of his wit, hands, heart,
To wronged Othello's service. Let him command
And to obey shall be in me remorse

457 **compulsive** caused by compulsion, compelled; or, compelling

458 See LN.

461 **humble** The lover is usually humble; appropriate here because Lat. *humilis* (from *humus*, earth) could = low-lying. Olivier paused after *humble* and then 'forced himself to say the word "love" ' (J. R. Brown, quoted Hankey, 253).

462 **capable** able to receive, contain; capacious (*OED* 1, 2)
wide vast, spacious

463 **marble** indifferent to the sufferings of others. Malone compared *Antonio and Mellida* (printed 1602, acted 1599 or 1600), 'pleased the marble heavens' (Revels, 2.1.230). Cf. *Tim* 4.3.191, 'the marbled mansion all above', *Cym* 5.4.87, 'Peep through thy marble mansion' (both = heaven).

464 **due** proper; necessary

465 **engage** pledge

466 **Witness** Such formal invocations were more often addressed to God or heaven: cf. *TGV* 2.6.25, *2H6* 4.8.62.
ever-burning Cf. 2.1.15, *ever-fired*. Implies 'ever-watchful' and 'never-ending'.

467 **elements** heavenly bodies (*OED* 10); or, powers of nature (Ridley)
clip clasp; encompass

469 **execution** performance; implying the 'execution' of Cassio
wit mind

470 **Othello's** Speaking of 'Othello' to his face, Iago takes a liberty acknowledged by 472, *thy love*. Cf. 4.1.48n.
service At 1.1.41ff. he saw himself as Othello's servant; now, despite his assurances, Othello is almost the ventriloquist's dummy.

471 **remorse** glossed as 'a solemn obligation' by *OED* (4c, first here, citing no other instance). But the usual sense (= pity, compassion) is possible: 'to obey shall be an act of pity (for "wronged Othello") whatever bloody task I have to undertake'.

458 keeps] *F;* feels *Q2*; Never retiring ebbs, but keeps due on *Sisson* 465 SD] *Q (* Iago *kneeles.) opp. 467; not in F* 469 execution] *F;* excellency *Q* hands] *F;* hand *Q* 471 in me] *F; not in Q*

What bloody business ever.

OTHELLO I greet thy love
Not with vain thanks but with acceptance bounteous,
And will upon the instant put thee to't. *Agree..*
Within these three days let me hear thee say 475
That Cassio's not alive.

IAGO My friend is dead,
'Tis done – at your request. But let her live. *Desd.*

Iago feels
OTHELLO *sorry for*
Damn her, lewd minx: O damn her, damn her! *her*
Come, go with me apart; I will withdraw *(Repetition.)*
To furnish me with some swift means of death 480 *his vengeance*
For the fair devil. Now art thou my lieutenant. *is d*

IAGO I am your own for ever. *Exeunt.*

only for
[3.4] *Enter* DESDEMONA, EMILIA *and* CLOWN. *Cassio .*

DESDEMONA Do you know, sirrah, where lieutenant
Cassio lies?

472 **ever** soever
 greet welcome; salute
473 **vain** empty
 bounteous 'normally used of the giver rather than the receiver' (Ridley). Cf. 203n. Implies 'whole-hearted', or perhaps a bounteous reward?
474 **to't** to the test
476 **My . . . dead** Cf. 2.3.161, *he dies!*
477 **But . . . live** He means the opposite, noticing that Othello seems preoccupied with Cassio.
478 **lewd** (a richer word than now) base, worthless; wicked; lascivious
 minx wanton (woman), trull: cf. 4.1.152
479 **apart** aside, away from here
480 **some . . . death** He has not decided on the *means*.
481 **Now . . . lieutenant** The first sign that he knows of Iago's wish for promotion.
482 **for ever** Cf. 1.3.365, 3.3.217: a special

emphasis on *for ever*. Cf. LN, 1.1.8. Othello welcomes Iago as '*my* lieutenant'; Iago acknowledges this, 'I am your own – for ever' (also implying the opposite: '*you* belong to *me* through all eternity'. So Faustus belongs to his servant–master Mephistopheles).

3.4.1–22 This clown episode was once regularly omitted in performance (Sprague, 202). The Clown, like the Porter in *Macbeth* (2.3), arrests the play as it gathers tragic momentum, and is equally self-absorbed.

1 **sirrah** term of address used for servants or social inferiors
 lieutenant Othello dismissed him, but she gives him his title.
2ff. **lies** Cf. the quibbles on *hear* (3.1.22), and on *lives* in *TN* 3.1.1ff. The clowns in *TN* and *Oth* were probably played by the same actor, Robert Armin.

472 business] *F;* worke so *Q* 477] *as Q; F lines* Request. / liue. / at your request.] *F;* as you request, *Q* 478] *one line Q; F lines* Minx: / her. / ³damn her] *F; not in Q* 481] *as Q; F lines* Diuell. / Lieutenant. / 3.4] *Scoena Quarta. F; not in Q* 1 lieutenant] *F;* the Leiutenant *Q*

CLOWN I dare not say he lies anywhere.

DESDEMONA Why, man?

CLOWN He's a soldier, and for me to say a soldier lies, 'tis stabbing.

DESDEMONA Go to, where lodges he?

CLOWN To tell you where he lodges is to tell you where I lie.

DESDEMONA Can anything be made of this?

CLOWN I know not where he lodges, and for me to devise a lodging and say he lies here, or he lies there, were to lie in mine own throat.

DESDEMONA Can you enquire him out and be edified by report?

CLOWN I will catechize the world for him, that is, make questions and by them answer.

DESDEMONA Seek him, bid him come hither, tell him I have moved my lord on his behalf, and hope all will be well.

CLOWN To do this is within the compass of man's wit, and therefore I will attempt the doing it. *Exit.*

6 **stabbing** i.e. to run the risk of being stabbed. Cf. Raleigh, *The Lie*: 'Because, to give the lie, / Deserves no less than stabbing'.

9 **I lie** *Lie* could = dwell, as in *MW* 2.1.179–80, 'Does he lie at the Garter?' The Clown quibbles 'To tell you where *he* lies is to tell you where *I* lie (because I don't know)'.

12 **devise** invent; guess (*OED* 5, 10)

13 **lie . . . throat** to lie foully or infamously (*OED* throat 3c). In the finely graded art of giving the lie (for which see *AYL* 5.4.68ff.), to say that someone lied in his throat was a stronger reproof than simply to say he lied: cf. *R3* 1.2.93, *TN* 3.4.156, Dent, T268.

14 **edified** informed, instructed, often in religious sense. Cf. *TN* 5.1.290, 'Look then to be well edified when the fool delivers the madman.'

16 **catechize** Cf. *TN* 1.5.62ff., '*Clown*. I must catechize you for it, madonna': perhaps joking at a 'clown routine' (cf. 2n., 14n.).

17 **questions . . . answer** (as in the Catechism) **by them** 'i.e. and by them, when answered, form my own answer to you' (Malone)

19 **moved** urged

21 **compass** due limits: so *RJ* 4.1.47, 'It strains me past the compass of my wits.'

5 SP] *F; not in Q* He's] *F;* He is *Q* me] *F;* one *Q* 6 'tis] *F;* is *Q* 8–10] *F; not in Q* 12 here . . . there] *F;* there *Q* 13 mine own] *F;* my *Q* 17 by] *QF;* bid *Theobald* 19 on] *F;* in *Q* 21 man's wit] *F;* a man *Q* 22 I will] *F;* I'le *Q* it] *F;* of it *Q*

DESDEMONA
Where should I lose that handkerchief, Emilia?

EMILIA
I know not, madam.

DESDEMONA
Believe me, I had rather have lost my purse
Full of crusadoes; and but my noble Moor
Is true of mind, and made of no such baseness
As jealous creatures are, it were enough
To put him to ill-thinking.

EMILIA
Is he not jealous?

DESDEMONA
Who, he? I think the sun where he was born
Drew all such humours from him.

EMILIA
Look where he comes.

Enter OTHELLO.

DESDEMONA
I will not leave him now till Cassio
Be called to him. How is't with you, my lord?

OTHELLO
Well, my good lady. [*aside*] O hardness to dissemble!—
How do you, Desdemona?

DESDEMONA
Well, my good lord.

23 **should I lose** could I have lost

25 **my purse** Cf. 3.3.160, 'Who steals my purse steals trash'.

26 **crusadoes** Portuguese coins, bearing the figure of the cross. Mentioned nowhere else by Shakespeare – why here? Perhaps to remind us that Christian Venice was threatened by Muslim states. A *crusado* was also a crusader.
but except that

27 **baseness** inferior quality

29 **Is . . . jealous** probably meant as a warning.

31 **humours** the four chief fluids of the body, which were thought to determine a person's mental and physical qualities; moods, whims

34 **O . . . dissemble** The stock formula was 'I must dissemble!' (as in *2H6* 5.1.13, *Per* 2.5.23); here = O how hard it is to dissemble!

23 that] *Q;* the *F* 25 have lost] *F*; loose *Q* 31.1] *F; opp. 31 Q* 32–3] *as Steevens 1793; Q lines* now, / Lord? /; *F lines* be / Lord? / 32 till] *F;* Tis *Qu*; Let *Qc* 33 is't] *F;* is it *Q* 34 SD] *Hanmer; not in QF*

OTHELLO

Give me your hand. This hand is moist, my lady.

DESDEMONA

It yet hath felt no age, nor known no sorrow.

OTHELLO

This argues fruitfulness and liberal heart:
Hot, hot, and moist. This hand of yours requires
A sequester from liberty, fasting and prayer,
Much castigation, exercise devout,
For here's a young and sweating devil, here,
That commonly rebels. 'Tis a good hand,
A frank one.

Alludes to Iago w/ conversation.

DESDEMONA You may indeed say so,
For 'twas that hand that gave away my heart.

OTHELLO

A liberal hand. The hearts of old gave hands
But our new heraldry is hands, not hearts.

DESDEMONA

I cannot speak of this. Come, now, your promise.

OTHELLO

What promise, chuck?

36 **moist** Cf. Tilley, H86, 'A moist hand argues an amorous nature'; *AC* 1.2.52–3, 'if an oily hand be not a fruitful prognostication'.
38 **argues** gives grounds for inferring
fruitfulness fertility in offspring
liberal bountiful; unrestrained, licentious. Here ambiguous near-synonyms (fruitful, liberal) can be taken favourably or unfavourably (Elliott, 30): so *frank*, 44.
39 **Hot** could = passionate; lustful, sexually excited
40 **sequester** sequestration, isolation; probably séquester, lib'rty
41 **castigation** corrective discipline
exercise devout exercises of devotion, religious discipline
42 **sweating** i.e. hot and moist; toiling (for Satan)
44 **frank** free (from restraint); generous, lavish
45 (in the troth-plighting or marriage ceremony)
46 **gave** perhaps with a quibble on *give* = display as armorial bearing (*OED* 24)
47 See LN.
heraldry heraldic practice
48 **I . . . this** Cf. 3.3.440, 'I know not that'.
49 **chuck** term of endearment (perhaps = chick). So Macbeth to Lady Macbeth (3.2.45), Antony to Cleopatra (4.4.2).

36] *as Q; F lines* your hand. / Lady. / 37 yet hath] yet has *Q;* hath *F* 39 Hot, hot] *F;* Not hot *Q* 40 prayer] *F;* praying *Q* 46 hearts . . . hands] *QF;* hands . . . hearts *Hanmer* 48] *as Q; F lines* this: / promise. / Come, now] *F;* come, come *Q*

DESDEMONA

I have sent to bid Cassio come speak with you.

OTHELLO

I have a salt and sullen rheum offends me,
Lend me thy handkerchief.

DESDEMONA

Here, my lord.

OTHELLO

That which I gave you.

DESDEMONA

I have it not about me.

OTHELLO

Not?

DESDEMONA

No, faith, my lord.

OTHELLO

That's a fault. That handkerchief
Did an Egyptian to my mother give,
She was a charmer and could almost read
The thoughts of people. She told her, while she kept it
'Twould make her amiable and subdue my father
Entirely to her love; but if she lost it
Or made a gift of it, my father's eye
Should hold her loathed and his spirits should hunt
After new fancies. She, dying, gave it me
And bid me, when my fate would have me wive,

51 **salt** vexatious
sullen unyielding; F *sorry* would = painful, grievous
rheum offends running cold that troubles
57–8 Cf. 5.2.215n.
58 **Egyptian** probably a true Egyptian (see pp. 49–51), not a Gipsy
59 **charmer** one who uses spells and enchantments
59–60 **and . . . people** N.B. the importance of reading 'the thoughts of people' in *Othello*!
61 **amiable** lovable
62–5 This sounds like superstition but (if not fabricated by Othello) the prediction later comes true, in so far as Othello and Desdemona are concerned.
64 **loathed** perhaps loathèd
spirits perhaps an error for *spirit*
65 **fancies** amorous inclinations, loves

51 sullen] *Q;* sorry *F* 56 Not?] *F;* Not. *Q* 57 faith] *Q;* indeed *F* 62] *line repeated Q from foot of* $H4^v$ *to top of I1* 64 loathed] *F;* lothely *Q* 66 wive] *Q;* Wiu'd *F*

To give it her. I did so, and – take heed on't!
Make it a darling, like your precious eye! –
To lose't or give't away were such perdition
As nothing else could match.

DESDEMONA Is't possible?

OTHELLO
'Tis true, there's magic in the web of it.
A sibyl that had numbered in the world
The sun to course two hundred compasses,
In her prophetic fury sewed the work;
The worms were hallowed that did breed the silk,
And it was dyed in mummy, which the skilful
Conserved of maidens' hearts.

DESDEMONA I'faith, is't true?

OTHELLO
Most veritable, therefore look to't well.

DESDEMONA
Then would to God that I had never seen't!

OTHELLO
Ha! wherefore?

DESDEMONA
Why do you speak so startingly and rash?

67 **her** i.e. my wife
take heed on't pay attention; or, look after it
68 Cf. Dent, E249.1, 'To love as one's own eye'.
69 **perdition** loss; ruin; echoing 3.3.90
71 **web** woven fabric
72–3 See LN.
74 **prophetic fury** Perhaps Ariosto's 'furor profetico' (*Orlando Furioso*, c. 46, st. 80); if so, Shakespeare knew Ariosto in the original, as the English translation had no 'prophetic fury'. But he may have found the phrase in the writings of Joshua Sylvester (Muir, 183, 305n.).
fury inspired frenzy
sewed The fabric was woven but the embroidered *work* (3.3.300n.) was sewn.
75 **worms** T. Moffett's *The Silkewormes* was published in 1599. A matter of topical interest?
hallowed consecrated
breed produce
76 **mummy** medicinal liquid, supposedly made from embalmed bodies
77 **Conserved of** made or preserved from
maidens' virgins'
78 **veritable** unique in Shakespeare
81 **startingly** (?)disconnectedly (Ridley); or, jumpily (*OED* start 5); startlingly
rash hastily, urgently

67 so,] *Q;* so; *F* 68 eye!] eye, *Q;* eye: *F* 69 lose't] *F;* loose *Q* 73 course] *F;* make *Q* 76 which] *F;* with *Q* 77 Conserved] *F;* Conserues *Q* I'faith] *Q;* Indeed? *F* 79 God] *Q;* Heauen *F* seen't] *F;* seene it *Q* 80 Ha!] Ha, *Q;* Ha? *F* 81 rash] *F;* rashly *Q*

OTHELLO
Is't lost? Is't gone? Speak, is't out o'the way?
DESDEMONA
Heaven bless us!
OTHELLO
Say you?
DESDEMONA
It is not lost, but what an if it were?
OTHELLO
How?
DESDEMONA
I say it is not lost.
OTHELLO Fetch't, let me see't.
DESDEMONA
Why, so I can, sir; but I will not now.
This is a trick to put me from my suit.
Pray you, let Cassio be received again.
OTHELLO
Fetch me the handkerchief, my mind misgives.
DESDEMONA
Come, come,
You'll never meet a more sufficient man.
OTHELLO
The handkerchief!
DESDEMONA I pray, talk me of Cassio.

82 **out . . . way** lost, missing. Cf. 1.3.359–60.
83 **Heaven bless us** expresses surprise, but could be ironical = what's all the fuss about (*OED* bless 9)
84 **Say you**? 'do you say so!' or 'what do you say?' Cf. *Ham* 4.5.28, *MM* 5.1.274, *Cym* 4.2.379.
85 This sounds like a lie, because *we* know that she has lost it (cf. 23); but *she* may believe that, though missing, it will turn up again; *an if* = if.
88 **sir** This word creates distance between them.
90 **received** readmitted to his post as lieutenant; received as guest
91–9 **misgives** has misgivings. Cf. *RJ* 1.4.106, 'my mind misgives / Some consequence yet hanging in the stars'.
93 **sufficient** capable
94 F's omission could be caused by eye-skip. Equally, the Q compositor might have 'cast off badly and invented these words to fill a gap: *talk me* is unusual (*Texts*, 47).

82 is't] *F;* is it *Q* o'the] *Q;* o'th' *F* 83 Heaven bless] *Q;* Blesse *F* 86 How?] *F;* Ha. *Q* 87 see't] *F;* see it *Q* 88 sir] *Q; not in F* 90 Pray you] *F;* I pray *Q* 91] *as Q; F lines* Handkerchiefe, / mis-giues. / the] *F;* that *Q* 92–3] *one line QF* 94] *Q; not in F*

OTHELLO

The handkerchief!

DESDEMONA A man that all his time
Hath founded his good fortunes on your love,
Shared dangers with you –

OTHELLO

The handkerchief!

DESDEMONA I'faith, you are to blame.

OTHELLO

Zounds! *Exit.*

EMILIA

Is not this man jealous?

DESDEMONA

I ne'er saw this before,
Sure there's some wonder in this handkerchief;
I am most unhappy in the loss of it.

EMILIA

'Tis not a year or two shows us a man.
They are all but stomachs, and we all but food:
They eat us hungerly, and when they are full
They belch us.

Enter IAGO *and* CASSIO.

Look you, Cassio and my husband.

IAGO

There is no other way, 'tis she must do't,

96 i.e. has relied on your affection for his advancement in the world
98 **to blame** at fault, in the wrong (to treat me like this)
99 **Zounds** F *Away* looks like a substitution for Q's profanity.
100 **Is . . . jealous** Cf. 29.
102 **wonder** marvellous quality (because the Egyptian's prediction is coming true?)
103 **unhappy** unfortunate; miserable
104 i.e. a year or two does not fully reveal to us (women) what (a monster) a man is
105 **but** nothing but
stomachs i.e. appetites
106 **hungerly** greedily. So *TS* 3.2.175, *Tim* 1.1.253. Variant of *hungrily*, which is not found in Shakespeare.
107 **belch** vomit

98 I'faith] *Q;* Insooth *F* 99 Zounds] *Q (Zouns);* Away. *F* 103 the] *Qc, F;* this *Qu* of it] *F; not in Q* 107 SD] *as F; after 103 Q* 108 do't] *F;* doe it *Q*

And lo, the happiness! go and importune her.

DESDEMONA

How now, good Cassio, what's the news with you?

CASSIO

Madam, my former suit. I do beseech you
That by your virtuous means I may again
Exist, and be a member of his love
Whom I, with all the office of my heart
Entirely honour. I would not be delayed:
If my offence be of such mortal kind
That nor my service past nor present sorrows
Nor purposed merit in futurity
Can ransom me into his love again,
But to know so must be my benefit;
So shall I clothe me in a forced content
And shut myself up in some other course
To fortune's alms.

DESDEMONA Alas, thrice-gentle Cassio,
My advocation is not now in tune;
My lord is not my lord, nor should I know him
Were he in favour as in humour altered.
So help me every spirit sanctified

109 **happiness** lucky chance (happy = lucky). Cf. Lyly, *Sapho*, 5.3.2, 'And loe how happilye shee sitteth in her caue.'
importune sue to; probably impòrtune

112 **by . . . means** by your good (or efficacious) help; or, 'by means of you, virtuous madam' (Kittredge)

113 **Exist** be myself (as Lieutenant Cassio)
member of one who participates in

114 **office** duty (Lat. *officium*)

115 **I . . . be** I don't want to be

116 **mortal** fatal

117 that neither my (military) service in the past nor my regrets now (for misbehaving)

119 **ransom** elliptical: set me free (from his displeasure, and bring me back) into his love

120 merely to know that must be my gain (because I'll know the worst)

121 so I shall invest myself with enforced contentment (*OED* clothe 7b, citing Job 39.19)

122–3 and commit myself to some other course (leading) to fortune's charitable relief. Cf. *Mac* 2.1.16, 'shut up / In measureless content'; *KL* 1.1.277–8, 'receiv'd you / At fortune's alms'.

123 **thrice-gentle** unique in Shakespeare

124 **advocation** (unique in Shakespeare) advocacy

125 **My . . . lord** Cf. 1.1.64, 'I am not what I am.'

126 **favour** appearance
humour mood

127 Cf. 'so help me God'.

114 office] *F;* duty *Q* 117 nor my] *F;* neither *Q* 122 shut] *F;* shoote *Q*

As I have spoken for you all my best
And stood within the blank of his displeasure
For my free speech. You must awhile be patient:
What I can do I will, and more I will
Than for myself I dare. Let that suffice you.

IAGO
Is my lord angry?

EMILIA He went hence but now,
And certainly in strange unquietness.

IAGO
Can he be angry? I have seen the cannon
When it hath blown his ranks into the air
And like the devil, from his very arm,
Puffed his own brother – and can he be angry?
Something of moment then. I will go meet him,
There's matter in't indeed, if he be angry.

DESDEMONA
I prithee do so. (*Exit* [*Iago*.]) Something sure of state
Either from Venice, or some unhatched practice
Made demonstrable here in Cyprus to him,
Hath puddled his clear spirit, and in such cases
Men's natures wrangle with inferior things

128 **all my best** to the best of my ability

129 **blank** once explained as 'the white spot in the centre of a target' (so *OED*). But J. R. Hale shows that *blank* here = 'point-blank range' ('The true Shakespearian blank', *SQ*, 19 [1968], 33–40).

130 **free** frank, unreserved

134 **unquietness** disquiet, perturbation

135 **Can . . . angry**? Iago knows that he can be angry (3.3.434ff.). Elliptical: 'I have seen his ranks blown into the air . . . *and meanwhile have seen him cool and unruffled*. And can he now be angry?' (Malone).

138 **brother** In this scene we hear of Othello's father, mother, brother, of the Egyptian, the sibyl – i.e. his background.

139 **moment** importance

140 **There's . . . indeed** some importance attaches to it (*OED* matter 11c)

141 **Something . . . state** surely some affair of state

142 **unhatched practice** plot that is still hatching

143 **demonstrable** known, 'capable of being proved' (unique in Shakespeare)

144 **puddled . . . spirit** muddied or confused his (usually) clear mind

145–6 **wrangle . . . object** dispute angrily about (or with) less important things though important ones are their real concern. She appears to class herself with the less important things, taking for granted that Othello's business comes first.

138 can . . . be] *Q;* is he *F* 141 SD] *F (opp. 140); not in Q*

Though great ones are their object. 'Tis even so,
For let our finger ache and it indues
Our other healthful members even to that sense
Of pain. Nay, we must think men are not gods
Nor of them look for such observancy
As fits the bridal. Beshrew me much, Emilia,
I was, unhandsome warrior as I am,
Arraigning his unkindness with my soul,
But now I find I had suborned the witness
And he's indicted falsely.

EMILIA Pray heaven it be
State matters, as you think, and no conception
Nor no jealous toy, concerning you.

DESDEMONA
Alas the day, I never gave him cause.

EMILIA
But jealous souls will not be answered so:
They are not ever jealous for the cause,

147 **indues** (?)brings to a certain state (*OED* 4b, first here, no other instance cited). At this time *indue* and *endue* were interchangeable, and included 'all the senses of *endow*' (*OED*).

148 **members** limbs or parts of the body
to i.e. with

149 **think** keep in mind
men . . . gods Cf. Dent, M593, 'We are but men, not gods.'

150 **observancy** respectful attention; observance of forms (unique in Shakespeare)

151 **As . . . bridal** as befits the wedding
Beshrew me evil befall me (mild oath)

152 **unhandsome** unskilful (*OED* 3, first here, no other instance cited); could = unseemly, discourteous (*OED* 4, from 1645; handsome = seemly, recorded 1597); or, unsoldierly (handsome = soldierly, first in 1665)
warrior Cf. 2.1.180, 'O my fair warrior!'

153 **Arraigning** accusing, calling to account
unkindness (a richer word than now) unnatural conduct; lack of natural affection; unkind action
with my soul i.e. from my heart and soul

154 **suborned** corrupted
witness i.e. herself

156 **conception** mere fancy

157 **jealous** F *Iealious* could be two syllables (as in 159) or three
toy fantastic notion; unreasoning dislike; trifle (*OED* 4, 5)

158 **Alas the day** Cf. 4.2.43.

159–62 an indirect comment on Iago's 'motivelesss malignity' (see pp. 57–8), not really true of Othello?

146–9] *as F; Q lines* obiect, / ake, / members, / thinke, / gods, / 146 their] *F;* the *Q* 148 that] *Q;* a *F* 150 observancy] *F;* obseruances *Q* 155–7] *as F; Q lines* thinke, / toy / you.

But jealous for they're jealous. It is a monster
Begot upon itself, born on itself.

DESDEMONA
Heaven keep that monster from Othello's mind!

EMILIA
Lady, amen.

DESDEMONA
I will go seek him. Cassio, walk here about,
If I do find him fit I'll move your suit
And seek to effect it to my uttermost.

CASSIO
I humbly thank your ladyship.

Exeunt Desdemona and Emilia.

Enter BIANCA.

BIANCA
Save you, friend Cassio!

CASSIO
What make you from home?
How is't with you, my most fair Bianca?
I'faith, sweet love, I was coming to your house.

BIANCA
And I was going to your lodging, Cassio.
What, keep a week away? seven days and nights?
Eight score eight hours? and lovers' absent hours
More tedious than the dial, eight score times!

161 **monster** Cf. 3.3.168n.; *Cor* 5.3.36, 'As if a man were author of himself'. For a similar monster, cf. *Faerie Queene*, 4.10.41, 'She syre and mother is her selfe alone, / Begets and eke conceives, ne needeth other none.'
165 **here about** Othello and Desdemona talked in a private place (a garden?): Cassio now walks to a more public place, where Bianca finds him.
166 **fit** i.e. in a suitable mood
168.1 SD BIANCA Elizabethan prostitutes apparently wore red petticoats: cf. *1H4* 1.2.10, 'a fair hot wench in a flame-coloured taffeta' (Ard[2], n.).
169 **Save** God save, i.e. protect, as in 'God save the King'
make you are you doing
173–5 Bianca counts correctly (168 hours): has she been brooding about her wrongs?
175 **dial** clock

161 they're . . . It is] *F;* they are . . . tis *Q* 163 that] *Q;* the *F* 165 here about] *QF;* hereabout *F3* 168 SD] *as Q (opp. 166); Exit F (opp. 167)* 168.2] *F; opp. Cassio 169 Q* 169 Save] *Q;* 'Saue *F* 170 is't] *F;* is it *Q* 171 I'faith] *Q;* Indeed *F*

O weary reckoning!

CASSIO Pardon me, Bianca,
I have this while with leaden thoughts been pressed,
But I shall in a more continuate time
Strike off this score of absence. Sweet Bianca,
[*Giving her Desdemona's handkerchief*]
Take me this work out.

BIANCA O Cassio, whence came this?
This is some token from a newer friend!
To the felt absence now I feel a cause:
Is't come to this? Well, well.

CASSIO Go to, woman,
Throw your vile guesses in the devil's teeth
From whence you have them! You are jealous now
That this is from some mistress, some remembrance:
No, by my faith, Bianca.

BIANCA Why, whose is it?

CASSIO
I know not neither, I found it in my chamber.
I like the work well: ere it be demanded,
As like enough it will, I'd have it copied.
Take it, and do't, and leave me for this time.

176 **O weary reckoning** Cf. Ovid, *Heroides*, 2.7, 'Should you count the days, which we count well who love'.

177 **leaden** oppressive (cf. *R3* 5.3.105, 'leaden slumber')
pressed oppressed; harassed

178 **continuate** uninterrupted; long-continued. Cf. *Tim* 1.1.11, 'an untirable and continuate goodness'.

179 **Strike . . . score** i.e. pay my account, so that it can be struck out (cancelled); *score* = reckoning (quibbling on 174, 176).

180 **Take . . . out** the very words of Emilia (3.3.300)!

181 **friend** mistress

183 **Well, well** Cf. Dent, W269, 'Well, well is a word of malice.'
Go to get away with you!
woman Cf. 5.2.146n.

184 i.e. and not in *my* teeth. Cf. Dent, T429, 'To cast (hit) in the teeth'.

186 **remembrance** keepsake

188 **I know not** And yet Desdemona kept it 'evermore about her / To kiss and talk to' (3.3.299–300)!
neither used to strengthen a preceding negative (*OED* 3)

191 **leave me** Cf. 3.3.323n.

176 O] *F (*Oh*);* No *Q* reckoning] *Q;* reck'ning *F* 177 leaden] *F;* laden *Q* 178 continuate] *F;* conuenient *Q* 179 SD] *Rowe; not in QF* 182 felt absence now] *as Q;* felt-Absence: now *F* 183 Well, well.] *F; not in Q* Go to, woman] *QF;* Woman, go to! *Capell* 184 vile] *Q;* vilde *F* 187 by . . . faith] *Q;* in good troth *F* whose] *Q2;* who's *QF* 188] *as Q; F lines* neither: / Chamber, / neither] *F;* sweete *Q* 190 I'd] *Q;* I would *F*

BIANCA
Leave you? Wherefore?

CASSIO
I do attend here on the general
And think it no addition, nor my wish,
To have him see me womaned.

BIANCA
Why, I pray you?

CASSIO
Not that I love you not.

BIANCA
But that you do not love me.
I pray you, bring me on the way a little,
And say if I shall see you soon at night.

CASSIO
'Tis but a little way that I can bring you
For I attend here, but I'll see you soon.

BIANCA
'Tis very good: I must be circumstanced. *Exeunt.*

[**4.1**] *Enter* OTHELLO *and* IAGO.

IAGO
Will you think so?

OTHELLO
Think so, Iago?

IAGO
What,

193 **attend . . . on** wait for

194 **addition** usually = title, or additional title, as at 4.1.105, but here 'seems to be "credit" ' (Ridley). Or perhaps 'no (good) addition to have him see me with a woman (added)', quibbling on two kinds of addition.

195 **womaned** (encumbered) with a woman (unique in Shakespeare)

197 Bianca interrupts?

199 **soon at night** Cf. Dent, S639.1, 'Soon at night (i.e., tonight)'.

202 **circumstanced** unique in Shakespeare; 'subject to or governed by circumstance' or 'surrounded with conditions' (*OED*). Or, adapting the noun (*OED* circumstance III, 'That which is non-essential . . . or subordinate'), 'I must be treated as insignificant.'

4.1.0.1 Q may be right in making Iago lead, Othello follow.

1 As at 1.1.1, the opening words imply that the speakers have talked for a while. Othello now echoes Iago, reversing their roles (cf. 3.3.103ff.); Iago continues to work on Othello's visual imagination.

195–6] *F; not in Q* 202 SD] *Q; Exeunt omnes. F* **4.1**] *Actus.* 4. *Q; Actus Quartus. Scena Prima. F* 0.1] *F; Enter* Iago *and* Othello. *Q*

To kiss in private?

OTHELLO An unauthorized kiss!

IAGO

Or to be naked with her friend in bed
An hour or more, not meaning any harm?

OTHELLO

Naked in bed, Iago, and not mean harm?
It is hypocrisy against the devil:
They that mean virtuously, and yet do so,
The devil their virtue tempts, and they tempt heaven.

IAGO

So they do nothing, 'tis a venial slip;
But if I give my wife a handkerchief –

OTHELLO

What then?

IAGO

Why, then 'tis hers, my lord, and being hers
She may, I think, bestow't on any man.

OTHELLO

She is protectress of her honour too:
May she give that?

IAGO

Her honour is an essence that's not seen,

2 **unauthorized** i.e. not authorized by the conventions of polite society, which permitted some kissing (2.1.97ff.)

3–4 Early romances sometimes manoeuvred lovers into bed, 'not meaning any harm' (Chaucer's *Troilus*, bk 3, st. 157; Sidney's *Arcadia*, 1593 edn, fo. 190b), but not usually naked. See also A. S. Cairncross, 'Shakespeare and Ariosto', *RQ*, 29 (1976), 178–82.

6 **against** in front of, in full view of (*OED* 1; cf. 2.3.365). Or, towards (if they really mean no harm, they try to dissimulate with the devil); 'to cheat the devil' (Johnson).

8 **tempts** puts to the test; incites to evil. Cf. Matthew 4.1, 7: Jesus went into the wilderness 'to be tempted of the devil', and said to him 'Thou shalt not tempt the Lord thy God' (Henley, in Malone).

9 **So** as long as

do nothing Cf. 2.1.142, and *R3* 1.1.99–100, 'He that doth naught with her (excepting one) / Were best to do it secretly alone.'

venial slip A venial sin is a pardonable sin, admitting of remission; a *venial slip* would be less serious (*slip* = fault).

16 **essence** something that *is*, an entity; that by which anything subsists; foundation of being (*OED* 2, 5)

3, 5 in bed] *F;* abed *Q* 9 So] *Q;* If *F*

They have it very oft that have it not.
But for the handkerchief –

OTHELLO

By heaven, I would most gladly have forgot it!
Thou said'st – O, it comes o'er my memory
As doth the raven o'er the infectious house
Boding to all – he had my handkerchief.

IAGO

Ay, what of that?

OTHELLO That's not so good now.

IAGO

What if I had said I had seen him do you wrong?
Or heard him say – as knaves be such abroad
Who, having by their own importunate suit
Or voluntary dotage of some mistress
Convinced or supplied them, cannot choose
But they must blab –

OTHELLO Hath he said anything?

IAGO

He hath, my lord, but be you well assured
No more than he'll unswear.

OTHELLO What hath he said?

IAGO

Faith, that he did – I know not what. He did –

17 'One of Iago's cryptic remarks, meaning . . . that many people are erroneously credited with the possession of this invisible essence' (Ridley).

21–2 **As . . . all** Cf. Dent, R33, 'The croaking raven bodes misfortune.'

21 **infectious** presumably infected with the plague

22 **Boding** predicting (ominously)

23 **That's . . . now** Cf. Dent, G324.1, 'That's not so good (now).' A characteristic understatement. A nine-syllable line: perhaps *That's* should be *That is* (see *Texts*, ch. 12), a more ruminative line.

24 **I had** = I'd (twice)

25 **abroad** at large

27 **voluntary dotage** self-induced infatuation

28 **Convinced** (convincèd) overcome
supplied satisfied a need or want (*OED* 5). '*Supplied* relates to the words *voluntary dotage*, as *convinced* does to *their own importunate suit*. "Having by their importunacy *conquered* the resistance of a mistress, or, in compliance with her own request . . . *gratified her desires*" ' (Malone).

29 **blab** chatter; tell (what should be concealed)

32 ***He did** – I repunctuate, and assume that Iago pauses tantalizingly (*Texts*, 132). Cf. 2.1.158n.

21 infectious] *F;* infected *Q* 27 Or] *F;* Or by the *Q* 28 Convinced] *Qc, F;* Coniured *Qu* 32 Faith] *Q;* Why *F* what. He did –] *this edn;* what he did. *QF*

OTHELLO
What? what?

IAGO
Lie.

OTHELLO With her?

IAGO With her, on her, what you will.

OTHELLO Lie with her? lie on her? We say lie on her when they belie her! Lie with her, zounds, that's fulsome! – Handkerchief! confessions! handkerchief! – To confess, and be hanged for his labour! First to be hanged, and then to confess: I tremble at it. Nature would not invest herself in such shadowing passion without some instruction. It is not words that shakes me thus. Pish! Noses, ears, and lips. Is't possible? Confess! handkerchief! O devil!

[*He*] *falls in a trance.*

34 **what you will** Cf. Dent, W280.5, 'What you will'. A poisonous phrase: it implies 'anything you like to think (or do with her)'.

35–43 Othello's fit in some ways resembles the 'pill' episode in *Poetaster*, 5.3.465ff. (performed 1601), and the raging of the hero in Greene's *Orlando Furioso* (printed 1594). With his loss of control, cf. also Cassio's drunkenness (2.3.60ff.).

35–6 He worries at the meaning of lying *with* and *on* her (cf. 34). *Lie on* could = tell lies about (*OED* 2), therefore 'We say lie *on* her when they (i.e. people) tell lies about (belie) her.' But he cannot reason away lie *with* her (= copulate with her).

37 **fulsome** nauseating; obscene

38–9 **First . . . confess** Cf. Dent, C587, 'Confess and be hanged' (a proverbial phrase meaning, roughly, 'You lie' [*OED* confess 10]), L590, 'First hang and draw, then hear the cause.' Cf. also 2.3.105ff. (Cassio on the correct sequence of things): tragedy teetering on the edge of comedy.

39–42 He tries to rationalize his trembling before he falls. 'Nature would not clothe (or endue) herself in such an all-enfolding passion without some special information (i.e. instinctive knowledge of the truth of what Iago has said, expressed in my trembling).' (*OED* invest 3; shadow 6b; instruction 3.)

41 **words** mere words

42 **Noses . . . lips** surrogate genital images. The thought is filled out later ('I see that nose of yours . . .'); or, as Steevens proposed, Othello imagines 'the familiarities which he supposes to have passed between Cassio and his wife' (as in *WT* 1.2.285–6).

43 SD *trance* J. P. Emery has shown that Othello suffers from several specific epileptic symptoms (in *Psychoanalysis and the Psychoanalytic Review*, 46 (1959), 30–2).

33 What? what?] *F;* But what? *Q* 36 zounds] *Q; not in F* 37 Handkerchief . . . handkerchief!] *as F;* handkerchers, Confession, hankerchers. *Q* 38–43 To . . . devil!] *as F; not in Q* 43 SD] *F subst.; not in Qu; He fals downe. Qc* (*after 37*)

IAGO

Work on,
My medicine, work! Thus credulous fools are caught,
And many worthy and chaste dames even thus,
All guiltless, meet reproach. – What ho! my lord!
My lord, I say! Othello!

Enter CASSIO.

How now, Cassio?

CASSIO

What's the matter?

IAGO

My lord is fallen into an epilepsy;
This is his second fit, he had one yesterday.

CASSIO

Rub him about the temples.

IAGO

No, forbear:
The lethargy must have his quiet course,
If not, he foams at mouth, and by and by
Breaks out to savage madness. Look, he stirs;
Do you withdraw yourself a little while,
He will recover straight. When he is gone
I would on great occasion speak with you.

[*Exit Cassio.*]

45 **medicine** i.e. poison. Cf. 2.1.292ff.
work F *workes* is possible.

47 **reproach** disgrace; censure. 'Almost always in Shakespeare stronger than our sense, e.g. "black scandal or foul-faced reproach" (*R3* 3.7.231)' (Ridley).
What . . . lord He calls when he hears someone approaching.

48 **Othello** He addresses Othello by name, perhaps because Othello is still unconscious.

50 **epilepsy** also known as 'the falling sickness' (*JC* 1.2.254). Here it is *petit mal*, a milder form of the illness (cf. 43n.), but still a most difficult, exhausting episode for the actor. In *Look About You* (1600, acted by the Admiral's Men) a pursuivant has a similar fit (F1b): this could have given Shakespeare the idea to stage a seizure.

53 **lethargy** morbid drowsiness (here, coma)
his its

54 **by and by** immediately; or, soon afterwards

55 **savage** enraged

58 **on great occasion** about an important matter

44–8] *as F; prose Q* 45 work] *Q;* workes *F* 48 SD] *as F; opp. Cassio 48 Q* 52 No, forbear] *Q; not in F* 58 SD] *Q2 (after* mocke me? *60); not in QF*

How is it, general? have you not hurt your head?

OTHELLO

Dost thou mock me?

IAGO

I mock you? no, by heaven!
Would you would bear your fortune like a man!

OTHELLO

A horned man's a monster, and a beast.

IAGO

There's many a beast then in a populous city,
And many a civil monster.

OTHELLO

Did he confess it?

IAGO

Good sir, be a man,
Think every bearded fellow that's but yoked
May draw with you. There's millions now alive
That nightly lie in those unproper beds
Which they dare swear peculiar: your case is better.
O, 'tis the spite of hell, the fiend's arch-mock,

59 **hurt your head** i.e. in falling. Othello thinks by sprouting horns.

60 **Dost . . . me?** so Lyly, *Mother Bombie*, 2.1.24, 'Doest thou mocke me, *Dromio*?'
no For final *-t* variants (*no:not*), see *Texts*, 85.

61 **Would** I wish
fortune bad fortune (but Iago, being Iago, also hints gleefully at 'good fortune'; cf. 'satisfaction', 3.3.404n.)

62 Cf. Dent, C876.2, 'A cuckold is a beast (monster)'; *beast* = horned beast.

64 **civil** civilized, courteous; city-dwelling (from Lat. *civis*, a citizen). Monsters were not usually *civil*: for the same pleasantry, cf. *Tem* 2.2.89, 'a most delicate monster'.

65 **be a man** Cf. 1.3.336: Iago has gained an ascendancy very like his hold on Roderigo. The phrase helps to *unman* Othello.

66 **bearded fellow** Cassio has a beard (3.3.442). This could mean that Othello is bearded as well.
yoked yoked in marriage; suggesting, yoked like an ox (a horned beast)

67 **draw** pull (like an ox)

68 **unproper** 'not (solely) his own; *proper* often means little more than *own*' (Ridley). Also = improper, not in accordance with decorum. Unique in Shakespeare.

69 **peculiar** restricted to themselves. Cf. 3.3.79n.
your . . . better i.e. because you know the truth

70 **spite** envious malice
arch-mock a coinage. Note how the fiend Iago mocks throughout this scene (4.1.2ff., 61, 67–8, 102n.).

60 you? no, by heaven] *Q;* you not, by Heauen *F* 61 fortune] *F;* fortunes *Q* 65 confess it] *F;* confesse *Q* Good] *Qc, F;* God *Qu* 68 lie] *F;* lyes *Q*

To lip a wanton in a secure couch
And to suppose her chaste. No, let me know,
And, knowing what I am, I know what she shall be.

OTHELLO

O, thou art wise, 'tis certain.

IAGO

Stand you a while apart,
Confine yourself but in a patient list.
Whilst you were here o'erwhelmed with your grief
– A passion most unsuiting such a man –
Cassio came hither. I shifted him away
And laid good 'scuse upon your ecstasy,
Bade him anon return and here speak with me,
The which he promised. Do but encave yourself
And mark the fleers, the gibes and notable scorns
That dwell in every region of his face;

71 ***To . . . couch** roughly = to kiss an unchaste woman in a bed free from anxiety (transferred epithet). But the words are more suggestive, esp. *lip*, which could = kiss obscenely (cf. *WT* 1.2.286); also, because the *wanton* points to Desdemona.

72–3 a slippery comparison of one who *supposes* with one who *knows*, for 'knowing what I am' (viz. an imperfect creature) only leads to another supposition, 'I know what she shall be' (i.e. she's bound to be unchaste). Cf. 1.3.350ff., and *Ham* 4.5.43–4, 'we know what we are, but know not what we may be'.

74 **'tis certain** *Either* it is certain that Iago is wise, *or* that Desdemona is unchaste.

75 **Stand . . . apart** A comedy routine: a victim is tricked into overhearing what others want him to hear. Cf. Plautus, *Miles Gloriosus*, 1175ff., *MA* 2.3.40ff., 3.1, 3.3.144ff.

76 i.e. only keep yourself within the boundary of patience. Cf. *TN* 1.3.8, 'confine yourself within the modest limits of order'.

77 **o'erwhelmed** o'erwhelmèd; *ere while, mad* is one of Q's clearest instances of misreading: *Texts*, 41–2, 89.

78 **unsuiting** unique in Shakespeare. The Q press-corrector probably consulted the manuscript, otherwise he would not have changed *vnfitting*.

79 **I . . . away** I got him out of the way (*OED* shift 16, first here).

80 **'scuse** i.e. explanation (implying that Othello's fit was somehow shameful)
ecstasy state of unconsciousness (swoon, trance, etc.)

81 **anon** soon; or, immediately

82 **encave** a coinage = conceal. Cf. *Cym* 4.2.138, 'Cave here, hunt here' (= to lurk, as in a cave).

83 **fleers** sneers
notable striking, noticeable

84 **dwell** abide; persist
region part or division of the body (*OED* 6)

71 couch] *F (*Cowch*);* Coach *Q* 73 she shall] *QF;* shall *Steevens conj.* 74 wise,] *Q;* wise: *F* 77 o'erwhelmed] *F;* ere while, mad *Q* 78 unsuiting] vnsuting *Qc;* vnfitting *Qu;* resulting *F* 80 'scuse] *Q (*scuse*);* scuses *F* 81 Bade] *F;* Bid *Q* return] *F;* retire *Q* 82 Do] *F; not in Q* 83 fleers] *F;* leeres *Q*

For I will make him tell the tale anew
Where, how, how oft, how long ago, and when
He hath and is again to cope your wife.
I say, but mark his gesture; marry, patience,
Or I shall say you're all in all in spleen
And nothing of a man.

OTHELLO Dost thou hear, Iago?
I will be found most cunning in my patience
But – dost thou hear? – most bloody.

IAGO That's not amiss,
But yet keep time in all. Will you withdraw?
[*Othello withdraws.*]
Now will I question Cassio of Bianca,
A housewife that by selling her desires
Buys herself bread and clothes: it is a creature
That dotes on Cassio – as 'tis the strumpet's plague
To beguile many and be beguiled by one.
He, when he hears of her, cannot refrain
From the excess of laughter. Here he comes.

Enter CASSIO.

87 **hath** A teasing pause is effective (cf. 32n.), and helps to explain the change of construction.
cope encounter, come into contact with, i.e. copulate with. A *cope(s)mate* is a paramour (*OED* 3).
88 **gesture** bearing, deportment; expression
89 [1]**all . . . spleen** altogether turned into spleen (the seat of melancholy and sudden or violent passion)
91 Cf. *TC* 5.2.46, the comedy routine of the impatient man swearing patience.
92 **not amiss** quite in keeping with the object in view (*OED* 2). A strangely detached remark.
93 **keep time** Cf. Dent, T308.1, 'Keep time in all'; = maintain control (Ridley); or, everything in good time. SD In fact he *hides* (becoming more like Iago, who habitually 'hides').
94 **of** about
95 **housewife** Perhaps we should read hussy (a woman of light character, or prostitute: cf. 1.3.273n.).
97–8 Cf. Dent, D179, 'He that deceives (beguiles) another is oft deceived himself', and 'Wily beguiled' (Tilley, W406). *Plague* = affliction; *beguile* = deceive; charm.
99 **refrain** F *restraine* is possible (*OED* 7 = refrain). Q or F misreads.
100 **Here he comes** Cassio's opportune arrival suggests that everything plays into Iago's hands.

87 hath] *F;* has *Q* 89 you're] *F (*y'are*);* you are *Q* 93 SD] *Rowe; not in QF* 96 clothes] *Q;* Cloath *F* 99 refrain] *Q;* restraine *F* 100.1] *as F; opp. 98 Q*

As he shall smile, Othello shall go mad.
And his unbookish jealousy must construe
Poor Cassio's smiles, gestures and light behaviour
Quite in the wrong. How do you now, lieutenant?

CASSIO

The worser, that you give me the addition 105
Whose want even kills me.

IAGO → *So that Othello doesn't hear it.*
Ply Desdemona well, and you are sure on't.
[*Speaking lower*] Now if this suit lay in Bianca's power
How quickly should you speed!

CASSIO Alas, poor caitiff!

OTHELLO

Look how he laughs already! *Seperate* 110
 them far apart.
IAGO

I never knew a woman love man so.

CASSIO

Alas, poor rogue, I think i'faith she loves me.

OTHELLO

Now he denies it faintly, and laughs it out.

IAGO

Do you hear, Cassio?

OTHELLO Now he importunes him

102 **unbookish** a coinage. Cf. 1.1.23: Iago is equally scornful about the bookish and unbookish!
 ***construe** interpret. See *Texts*, 83.
103 **light** frivolous
104 **in the wrong** erroneously
105 **addition** title
106 **want** lack
107 **Ply** handle; keep working on
 sure on't i.e. sure to get what you want
108 **power** Sisson thinks Iago has Bianca's 'marriage to Cassio in mind' and reads *dower* (= F). A turned letter (*p:d*)?
109 **speed** succeed
 caitiff wretch
112 **rogue** could be a term of endearment
113 **faintly** i.e. without expecting to carry conviction
 out away

102 construe] *Rowe;* conster *Q;* conserue *F* 103 behaviour] *Q;* behauiours *F* 104 now] *Q; not in F* 108 SD] *Rowe; not in QF* power] *Q;* dowre *F* 110–57] *all Othello's speeches marked 'Aside', Theobald; not in QF* 111 a] *Q; not in F* 112 i'faith] *Q;* indeed *F* 114–15 him . . . o'er] *as F;* him to tell it on, *Q*

To tell it o'er; go to, well said, well said.

IAGO

She gives it out that you shall marry her;
Do you intend it?

CASSIO

Ha, ha, ha!

OTHELLO

Do ye triumph, Roman, do you triumph?

CASSIO I marry! What, a customer! prithee bear some charity to my wit, do not think it so unwholesome. Ha, ha, ha!

OTHELLO So, so, so, so: they laugh that win.

IAGO Faith, the cry goes that you shall marry her.

CASSIO Prithee say true!

IAGO I am a very villain else.

OTHELLO Have you stored me? Well.

CASSIO This is the monkey's own giving out. She is

115 **o'er** i.e. over again
well said = well done (sarcastic). Often said when no words have been spoken (e.g. 5.1.98; *Poetaster*, 3.4.345).

118 **Ha, ha, ha** a signal for the actor to laugh, for as long as he sees fit: cf. 5.1.62n.

119 **triumph** prevail (over an enemy); exult; celebrate a triumph (a ceremonial entry by a victorious general). 'Othello calls him *Roman* ironically. *Triumph*, which was a Roman ceremony, brought Roman into his thoughts' (Johnson).

120 **customer** one who purchases (sexual services) (= Cassio); or, a prostitute (= Bianca) (*OED* 3, 4)

120–1 **bear . . . wit** think more kindly of my judgement

121 **unwholesome** unhealthy, defective

123 **they . . . win** Cf. Dent, L93, 'He laughs that wins', i.e. they that laugh last laugh best.

124 **cry goes** rumour is current

126 I am a true villain if it's not so. Cf. 2.1.114n.

127 **stored** could mean to provide for the continuance of a stock or breed, or to produce offspring (cf. Heywood, *Golden Age* [1611], H2, 'from your own blood you may store a prince / To do those sacred rights', quoted *OED* 2): i.e. 'Have you begotten children for me?' F's *scoar'd* (= wounded) is less likely.

128 **monkey's** 'Used as a term of playful contempt, chiefly of young people' (*OED* 2b), more usually of boys than girls. Cf. *Mac* 4.2.59, 'God help thee, poor monkey!'; *Tem* 3.2.45.

115 [2]well said] *F; not in Q* 119 ye] *F;* you *Q* 120–2] *QF line as verse* wit / ha. / *Q;* beare / it / ha. *F* 120 marry!] *as F;* marry her? *Q* What . . . customer!] *F; not in Q* prithee] *F;* I prethee *Q* 123 they] *F; not in Q* win] *F4;* wins *QF* 124 Faith] *Q;* Why *F* that you shall] you shall *Q;* that you *F* 127 Have] *F;* Ha *Q* stored] *Q(*stor'd*);* scoar'd *F* me? Well] *F;* me well. *Q* 128–30] *prose Q; F lines* out: / marry her / promise. /

persuaded I will marry her, out of her own love and flattery, not out of my promise.

OTHELLO Iago beckons me: now he begins the story.

CASSIO She was here even now, she haunts me in every place. I was the other day talking on the sea-bank with certain Venetians, and thither comes the bauble and, by this hand, falls me thus about my neck –

OTHELLO Crying 'O dear Cassio!' as it were: his gesture imports it.

CASSIO So hangs and lolls and weeps upon me, so shakes and pulls me! Ha, ha, ha!

OTHELLO Now he tells how she plucked him to my chamber. O, I see that nose of yours, but not that dog I shall throw it to.

CASSIO Well, I must leave her company.

IAGO Before me! look where she comes!

Enter BIANCA.

130 **flattery** in the sense of 'she flatters herself that' (Ridley)

131 **beckons** makes a signal to. Could be spelled *becon* (*OED*); F probably misread *becon(e)s*.

133 **sea-bank** sea coast or shore

134 **bauble** a childish or foolish person (*OED* 5b, first here): originally a child's toy or childish foolery

135 **by this hand** probably omitted from F by Crane (*Texts*, 166)
me ethic dative

137 **imports** implies

138 **lolls** hangs down, dangles

139 **shakes** Q *hales* = hauls, drags

141 **chamber** private room; bedroom **nose** Cf. Martial: 'Husband, you have disfigured the wretched gallant, and his countenance, deprived of nose and ears, regrets the loss of its original form' (2.83; cf. 3.85); also 42 above: 'Noses, ears, and lips.' Hulme, 135, thinks *nose* suggests penis.

141–2 **but . . . to** Cf. Exodus 22.30, 'neither shall ye eat any flesh that is torn of beasts in the field, but shall cast it to a dog'.

143 **company** could mean 'sexual connection', as in Caxton, 'Thamar, that had company with her husbondes fader' (*OED* 2)

144 **Before me** perhaps formed on the analogy of 'before God' (= by God). So *TN* 2.3.178, 'Before me, she's a good wench'; *Cor* 1.1.120.

131 beckons] *Q;* becomes *F* 133 the other] *F;* tother *Q* 134 the] *F;* this *Q* 135 and . . . me] by this hand she fals *Q*; and falls me *F* 138–9] *prose Q; F lines* vpon me: / ha. / 139 shakes] *F;* hales *Q* 140–2] *prose F; Q lines* Chamber, / to. / 141 O] *F; not in Q* 142 it] *F;* 't *Q* 144.1] *as F; opp. 143 Q*

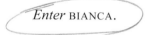

CASSIO 'Tis such another fitchew; marry, a perfumed one. What do you mean by this haunting of me?

BIANCA Let the devil and his dam haunt you! What did you mean by that same handkerchief you gave me even now? I was a fine fool to take it – I must take out the work! A likely piece of work, that you should find it in your chamber and know not who left it there! This is some minx's token, and I must take out the work? There, give it your hobby-horse; wheresoever you had it, I'll take out no work on't!

CASSIO How now, my sweet Bianca, how now, how now?

OTHELLO By heaven, that should be my handkerchief!

BIANCA If you'll come to supper tonight, you may; if you will not, come when you are next prepared for. *Exit.*

IAGO After her, after her!

CASSIO Faith, I must, she'll rail in the streets else.

IAGO Will you sup there?

CASSIO Faith, I intend so.

IAGO Well, I may chance to see you, for I would very fain speak with you.

CASSIO Prithee come, will you?

IAGO Go to, say no more. *Exit Cassio.*

145 **such another** another of the same sort (*OED* 1c); like all the rest of them (Ridley)
fitchew polecat, notoriously malodorous and lecherous. Cf. *OED* polecat 2: a vile person; prostitute.

145–6 **marry . . . one** F's punctuation could imply 'Do they think that I'll marry a perfumed fitchew?!'

147 Cf. Dent, D225, 'The devil and his dam'; *dam* = mother (dame).

149 **even** just

149–50 **I must . . . work** Cf. 3.4.180n.

150 **A . . . work** i.e. a likely story! *A piece of work* was a set phrase, as in *Ham* 2.2.303, 'What a piece of work is a man'.

152 **minx's** Cf. 3.3.478n.
token pledge, present

153 **hobby-horse** loose woman, prostitute

154 **on't** from it

155 **How now** (meant to soothe or restrain)

156 **should** i.e. must

158 **when . . . for** when next I make preparations for you, i.e. never

164 **fain** gladly

145 SP] *F; not in Q* 145–6 fitchew; marry, . . . one.] ficho; marry a perfum'd one, *Q;* Fitchew: marry a perfum'd one? *F* 150 the] *F;* the whole *Q* 151 know not] *F;* not know *Q* 153 your] *F;* the *Q* 155] *as Q; F lines Bianca*? / now? / 157 If] *F;* An *Q* if] *F;* an *Q* 160 Faith] *Q; not in F* in . . . streets] *F;* i'the streete *Q* 162 Faith] *Q;* Yes *F* 166 SD] *Q; not in F*

OTHELLO How shall I murder him, Iago?

IAGO Did you perceive how he laughed at his vice?

OTHELLO O Iago!

IAGO And did you see the handkerchief?

OTHELLO Was that mine?

IAGO Yours, by this hand: and to see how he prizes the foolish woman your wife! She gave it him, and he hath given it his whore.

OTHELLO I would have him nine years a-killing. A fine woman, a fair woman, a sweet woman!

IAGO Nay, you must forget that.

OTHELLO Ay, let her rot and perish and be damned tonight, for she shall not live. No, my heart is turned to stone: I strike it, and it hurts my hand. O, the world hath not a sweeter creature: she might lie by an emperor's side and command him tasks.

IAGO Nay, that's not your way.

OTHELLO Hang her, I do but say what she is: so delicate with her needle, an admirable musician. O, she will sing the savageness out of a bear! of so high and plenteous wit and invention!

IAGO She's the worse for all this.

167ff. For the first time Iago and Othello converse in prose.

172–4 **Yours . . . whore** Q's omission comes at the end of a page (K1a), an error in 'casting off' (*Texts*, 46–7).

172 **prizes** esteems

175 **a-killing** in the killing, i.e. I'd have him die a very slow death (unique in Shakespeare)

175–6 **A . . . [3]woman** Here, and in the next speeches, with their sudden flip-over from hate to love, tragedy comes close to farce: cf. *MV* 3.1.97ff.

179–80 **my . . . stone** Dent, H311, 'A heart of (as hard as a) stone'. Cf. Job 41.15, 'His heart is as hard as a stone, and as fast as the stithy that the smith smiteth upon.'

181 **creature** any created being; person

181–2 **she . . . tasks** i.e. (if she had been chaste) her sweetness would have had an irresistible power over an emperor. An image inspired by folk tale or romance? Normally the lady commanded tasks *before* marriage.

183 **your way** 'like you' or 'the best course'

185–6 **O . . . bear** like Orpheus?

186 **high** superior

187 **wit and invention** even if taken as 'understanding and imagination', unexpected attributes

167 murder] *Q;* murther *F* 172–4] *F; not in Q* 175–6] *prose Q; F lines* killing: / woman? / 177 that] *F; not in Q* 178 Ay] *F (I); And Q* 181 hath] *F;* has *Q*

OTHELLO O, a thousand, a thousand times: and then
of so gentle a condition. 190

IAGO Ay, too gentle.

OTHELLO Nay, that's certain. But yet the pity of it, Iago
– O, Iago, the pity of it, Iago!

IAGO If you are so fond over her iniquity, give her patent
to offend, for if it touch not you it comes near 195
nobody.

OTHELLO I will chop her into messes! Cuckold me!

IAGO O, 'tis foul in her.

OTHELLO With mine officer! *Cassio*.

IAGO That's fouler. 200

OTHELLO Get me some poison, Iago, this night. I'll
not expostulate with her, lest her body and beauty
unprovide my mind again. This night, Iago.

IAGO Do it not with poison, strangle her in her bed –
even the bed she hath contaminated. 205

Iago tries to avoid getting poison

→ I hate Iago.

190 **so . . . condition** probably 'so sweet-natured a disposition', but could = so well bred in social background. Cf. 2.1.247–8.

191 **gentle** mild; yielding, pliant

192 **the . . . it** Cf. *MM* 2.3.42, ' 'Tis pity of him' (*of* = in respect of: *OED* pity 3b). Othello appeals as the weaker to the stronger.
pity Cf. 1.3.162, ' 'Twas pitiful, 'twas wondrous pitiful', 169: pity plays a significant part in their relationship.

193 **O . . . Iago!** Cf. 2.3.260–1, 'My reputation, Iago'.

194–5 If you be so doting as regards her wickedness, give her a licence to sin (*OED* over *prep.* 4c: concerning).

194 **patent** licence; a papal licence or indulgence. Malone compared *E3* 2.1.422

(1596 edn, D1b), 'Why then giue sinne a pasport to offend' (meaning a sexual offence, in both plays).

195–6 **if . . . nobody** if it doesn't hurt you it hurts nobody. See p. 385; Holland's *Livy* (1600): 'In this last speech he came neere unto the LL. of the Senat, and touched them to the quick' (quoted *OED*, near, 12b).

197 **messes** (servings of) meat; we might say 'chop her into mincemeat'. The 'Barbarian' has many European cousins: cf. Plautus, *Truculentus*, 613, 'I'll take this blade and here hew thee into gobbets!'

199 **officer** an act of whoredom and insubordination!

202 **expostulate** set forth my grievances, argue

203 **unprovide** i.e. disarm

189–90] *as Q; F lines* times: / condition? 189 O . . . thousand] *F;* A thousand thousand *Q* 192–3] *as Q; F lines* certaine: / 192 Nay] *F;* I *Q* 193 O, Iago . . . Iago!] *F;* the pitty. *Q* 194 are] *F;* be *Q* 195 touch] *F;* touches *Q* 199 officer!] Officer? *F* 201 night. I'll] *F;* night I'le *Q* 204–9] *prose Q; F lines* bed, / contaminated. / good: / very good. / vndertaker: / midnight. /

OTHELLO Good, good, the justice of it pleases; very good!

IAGO And for Cassio, let me be his undertaker. You shall hear more by midnight.

OTHELLO Excellent good. *A trumpet within.* What trumpet is that same?

IAGO I warrant something from Venice.

Enter LODOVICO, DESDEMONA *and Attendants.*

'Tis Lodovico, this, comes from the duke.
See, your wife's with him.

LODOVICO God save you, worthy general.

OTHELLO With all my heart, sir.

LODOVICO
The duke and senators of Venice greet you.
[*Gives him a letter.*]

OTHELLO
I kiss the instrument of their pleasures.
[*Opens the letter and reads.*]

DESDEMONA
And what's the news, good cousin Lodovico?

206–7 **Good . . . good** Some repetitions in this scene suggest that Othello's mind is half tranced. Cf. Marston, *Antonio and Mellida* (Revels), 3.2.30, 'Good, very good, very passing, passing good'. There are comic overtones, as in *AYL* 5.1.27, ' "So, so" is good, very good, very excellent good'.

206 **justice of it** Cf. 193, 'the pity *of it*'.

208 **undertaker** one who (1) carries out work for another; (2) takes up a challenge; (3) 'takes on' something. *OED* first records 'one who makes arrangements for funerals' in 1698, but this sense may be glanced at.

212.1 Though not named, Gratiano probably enters here.

216 **With . . . heart** (I thank you) with all my heart, or, (I wish it) with all my heart. One expects Othello to return the wish. He merely accepts it.

218 **instrument** formal document in which they express their commands (*OED* pleasure 2)

219 **cousin** could = kinsman. Gratiano is Desdemona's uncle (5.2.252): Shakespeare reminds us that she is well connected in Venice.

210 SD] A Trumpet. *Q (opp. 209); not in F* 212–14] *F;* Something from *Venice* sure, tis *Lodouico*, / Come from the Duke, and see your wife is with him. *Q;* 'Tis Lodovico – this comes from the Duke. *Sisson* 212.1] *QF (after 209)* 215 God save] *Q;* Saue *F* you] *F;* the *Q* 217 and] *Q;* and the *F* SD] *Rowe; not in QF* 218 SD] *Capell subst.; not in QF*

IAGO

I am very glad to see you, signior.
Welcome to Cyprus.

LODOVICO

I thank you. How does Lieutenant Cassio?

IAGO

Lives, sir.

DESDEMONA

Cousin, there's fallen between him and my lord
An unkind breach, but you shall make all well –

OTHELLO

Are you sure of that?

DESDEMONA

My lord?

OTHELLO [*Reads.*]

This fail you not to do, as you will –

LODOVICO

He did not call, he's busy in the paper.
Is there division 'twixt my lord and Cassio?

DESDEMONA

A most unhappy one: I would do much
T'atone them, for the love I bear to Cassio.

OTHELLO

Fire and brimstone!

DESDEMONA My lord?

OTHELLO Are you wise?

220 Iago butts in, as often elsewhere.
223 Cf. Plautus, *Curculio*, 235, '*quid agis? – Vivo* (How are you? – Living [lit. I live])'; *Persa*, 17; also *2H4* 3.2.200.
225 **unkind** unnatural; strange
breach disagreement, quarrel; a breaking of relations (*OED* 5, first recorded 1605)
229 **in** in reading
230 **division** disagreement
231 **unhappy** unfortunate
232 **atone** reconcile
love affection, goodwill (Othello thinks sexual love)
233 **Fire and brimstone** first recorded by *OED* as ejaculation in *TN* 2.5.50, but biblical in origin (Genesis 19.24, Revelation 19.20). *Fire* is disyllabic here (Abbott, 480). Traditionally associated with hell (*Faerie Queene*, 1.9.49).
wise in your right mind, sane (*OED* 4)

220–1] *as F; prose Q* 226] (Aside) *Theobald* 228 SD] *Theobald; not in QF* 230 'twixt my] *F;* betweene thy *Q* 232 T'] *F;* To *Q*

DESDEMONA
What, is he angry?
LODOVICO Maybe the letter moved him.
For, as I think, they do command him home,
Deputing Cassio in his government.
DESDEMONA
By my troth, I am glad on't.
OTHELLO Indeed!
DESDEMONA My lord?
OTHELLO
I am glad . . . to see you mad.
DESDEMONA Why, sweet Othello?
OTHELLO
Devil! [*Striking her*]
DESDEMONA
I have not deserved this.
LODOVICO
My lord, this would not be believed in Venice
Though I should swear I saw't. 'Tis very much;
Make her amends, she weeps.
OTHELLO O devil, devil!
If that the earth could teem with woman's tears
Each drop she falls would prove a crocodile:

236 **Deputing** appointing (not necessarily as deputy)
government appointment as governor (*OED* 3b, first in 1617); tenure of office (*OED* 4b, first in 1603)
237 **on't** of it
Indeed as at 3.3.101, but with different implications
238 He echoes or mimics Desdemona's 'I am glad', i.e. to see you so foolish (mad) (as to admit your love for Cassio). But *mad* may be corrupt.
Why, sweet Othello? This could be an exclamation of surprise or remonstrance, rather than a question. Cf. *AYL* 4.3.157, 'Why, how now, Ganymed, sweet Ganymed'.
239 *SD Some actors strike her with the letter, but 272 suggests that he strikes her with his hand. Calderwood thinks that the letter 'arouses his passion' but Desdemona's innocent remarks are surely the cause.
241–2 Cf. Dent, E264.1, 'To believe one's (own) eyes'.
242 **'Tis very much** it goes too far
244 **teem** give birth, bring forth (as a result of women's tears)
245 **falls** lets fall. Cf. Dent, C831, 'Crocodile tears'.
prove turn out to be

234 the letter] *Q;* thLetter *F* 237 By . . . troth] *Q;* Trust me *F* Indeed!] Indeed. *Q;* Indeed? *F* 238 glad . . .] *this edn;* glad *QF* Why] *F;* How *Q* 239 SD] *Theobald; not in QF* 244 woman's] *F;* womens *Q*

Out of my sight!

DESDEMONA I will not stay to offend you.

LODOVICO

Truly, an obedient lady.
I do beseech your lordship, call her back.

OTHELLO

Mistress!

DESDEMONA

My lord?

OTHELLO

What would you with her, sir?

LODOVICO Who, I, my lord?

OTHELLO

Ay, you did wish that I would make her turn.
Sir, she can turn, and turn, and yet go on
And turn again. And she can weep, sir, weep.
And she's obedient: as you say, obedient,
Very obedient. – Proceed you in your tears. –
Concerning this, sir – O well-painted passion! –
I am commanded home. – Get you away.
I'll send for you anon. – Sir, I obey the mandate
And will return to Venice. – Hence, avaunt! –

[*Exit Desdemona.*]

249 **Mistress** not the normal way of addressing one's wife. Cf. 1.3.178, 5.2.181.

250 **My lord?** her fourth 'My lord?' since 227, part of the crescendo effect here

252–3 **turn** turn back; be fickle (turn = change); also implying 'the best turn i'th' bed' (*AC* 2.5.59). A. Shickman compared 'turning pictures', which could show different images of a person at the same time (weeping, a devil, etc.) (*N&Q*, 223 [1978], 145–6).

255 **obedient** yielding to desires or wishes; compliant (*OED* 3): he means sexually compliant.

256 **Proceed . . . tears** This could be a question (Warner, in Malone, 1821).

257 **this** i.e. the letter from Venice
well-painted well-pretended

258 **home** might = Venice or Mauretania (4.2.226), but 260 proves that he understands it as Venice. Q *here* looks like misreading but is possible (giving an unfinished sentence).

259 **mandate** command

260 **avaunt** (usually expresses loathing or horror) away! be off!

247 an] *Q; not in F* 258 home] *F;* here *Q* 260 SD] *Rowe; not in QF*

Cassio shall have my place. And, sir, tonigh
I do entreat that we may sup together.
You are welcome, sir, to Cyprus. Goats and monkey

LODOVICO

Is this the noble Moor whom our full senate
Call all in all sufficient? This the nature
Whom passion could not shake? whose solid virtue
The shot of accident nor dart of chance
Could neither graze nor pierce?

IAGO He is much changed.

LODOVICO

Are his wits safe? Is he not light of brain?

IAGO

He's that he is: I may not breathe my censure
What he might be; if what he might, he is not,
I would to heaven he were!

LODOVICO What! strike his wife!

IAGO

Faith, that was not so well; yet would I knew

261 **Cassio . . . place** This may be shouted at Desdemona as or after she leaves; *place* = his place as commander; perhaps, his place as lover (cf. *KL* 5.1.10–11, 'have you never found my brother's way / To the forfended place?').

263 **Goats and monkeys** Cf. 'as prime as goats, as hot as monkeys' (3.3.406–7n.). 'These words, we may suppose, still ring in the ears of Othello' (Malone).

264 **full** complete

265 **sufficient** competent, capable
***This the nature** Q *noble* and F *Is* look like unconscious repetitions.

266 **shake** upset. (Has Othello been shaking with passion? Cf. 39ff., 5.2.44.)
solid substantial (*OED* 13, first in 1601)
virtue (moral) excellence; manliness

267 (neither) accidental shot nor a chance spear (thrust), i.e. no unforeseen misfortune

269 **safe** in sound health

270–2 Cf. 2.3.117–24, where Iago also draws attention to a change (in Cassio) that he has brought about.

270 **breathe** whisper
censure opinion; criticism

271–2 'Perhaps the most cryptic of all Iago's similar remarks' (Ridley). *Might* seems to change its meaning: first, Othello might be at fault (therefore to be censured); second, he might be unchanged (hence 'would to heaven he were'). Or, 'if he isn't of unsound mind, then it might be better to wish he were in fact insane, since only that could excuse his wild behaviour' (Bevington).

273 **that . . . well** Cf. 23, 'That's not so good now.'

263] *as Q; F lines* Cyprus. / Monkeys. / SD] *Qc, F; not in Qu* 265 This the nature] *as Pope*; This the noble nature *Q;* Is this the Nature *F* 270 is:] *F;* is, *Q* censure] *(see Furness);* censure, *Q;* censure. *F* 271 be: if what] *F;* be, if as *Q*

That stroke would prove the worst.

LODOVICO Is it his use?
Or did the letters work upon his blood
And new-create this fault?

IAGO Alas, alas!
It is not honesty in me to speak
What I have seen and known. You shall observe him,
And his own courses will denote him so
That I may save my speech. Do but go after
And mark how he continues.

LODOVICO
I am sorry that I am deceived in him. *Exeunt.*

[**4.2**] *Enter* OTHELLO *and* EMILIA.

OTHELLO
You have seen nothing, then?

EMILIA
Nor ever heard, nor ever did suspect.

OTHELLO
Yes, you have seen Cassio and . . . she together.

EMILIA
But then I saw no harm, and then I heard
Each syllable that breath made up between them.

OTHELLO
What, did they never whisper?

274 **stroke** blow; (?)masterstroke (first recorded in later seventeenth century)
use custom
275 **blood** passion
279 **courses** habitual actions
denote be the outward visible mark of (*OED* 3), reveal
282 **I am** . . . **I am** read 'I'm . . . I am'; or 'I am sorry that I'm'
deceived mistaken
4.2 Location: this scene starts indoors (cf. 28), and in some productions in Desdemona's bedroom. Later Roderigo wanders in (174n.), and it seems to be outdoors: one of the advantages of unlocalized staging.
1–11 Note the abrupt opening. And the tug between prose and verse rhythms, coming to rest in 'That's strange'.
2 **suspect** Othello may interrupt before she can finish.
3 ***seen** . . . **she** While *she* was sometimes used as object, I assume that Othello hesitates to use Desdemona's name. Cf. *AC* 3.13.98 (repunctuated), 'So saucy with the hand of – she here, what's her name'.

276 this] *Q;* his *F* 4.2.1 then?] *F;* then. *Q* 3 you] *F;* and you *Q* and . . . she] *this edn;* and she *QF* 5 them] *F;* 'em *Q*

EMILIA Never, my lord.

OTHELLO
Nor send you out o'th' way?

EMILIA
Never.

OTHELLO
To fetch her fan, her gloves, her mask, nor nothing?

EMILIA
Never, my lord.

OTHELLO
That's strange.

EMILIA
I durst, my lord, to wager she is honest,
Lay down my soul at stake: if you think other
Remove your thought, it doth abuse your bosom.
If any wretch have put this in your head
Let heaven requite it with the serpent's curse,
For if she be not honest, chaste and true
There's no man happy: the purest of their wives
Is foul as slander.

OTHELLO Bid her come hither; go. *Exit Emilia.*
She says enough; yet she's a simple bawd
That cannot say as much. This is a subtle whore,
A closet, lock and key, of villainous secrets;

9 **mask** Venetian ladies wore masks during the Carnival.
12 **honest** chaste
13 **at stake** at hazard (after *wager*); at the stake (like a martyr dying for his faith)
14 **abuse** deceive; wrong
bosom breast (considered as the seat of secret thoughts and feelings: *OED* 6a). Cf. 3.1.57.
15 She contradicts her earlier view that jealousy is self-begotten (3.4.159–62). This prepares for 132ff.
16 **serpent's curse** Cf. Genesis 3.14, where God curses the serpent.
20 **enough** elliptical: enough to sound plausible
simple naive, artless, feeble
bawd procuress
21 **This** seems to refer to Emilia, but *kneel and pray* to Desdemona
22 **closet** private room; safe, cabinet (as in *Mac* 5.1.6)
lock and key with lock and key. But cf. *Homilies*, 385, 'this article . . . is even the very lock and key of all our Christian religion'.

7 o'th'] *F;* o'the *Q* 9 gloves, her mask] *F;* mask, her gloues *Q* 15 have] *F;* ha *Q* 16 heaven] *F;* heauens *Q* requite] *Q;* requit *F* 18 their wives] *F;* her Sex *Q* 19 SD] *F; opp.* slander *Q* 21 subtle] *Q;* subtile *F* 22 closet, . . . key,] *Q;* Closset Locke and Key *F;* closset-lock and key *Rowe*

And yet she'll kneel and pray, I have seen her do't.

Enter DESDEMONA *and* EMILIA.

DESDEMONA
My lord, what is your will?
OTHELLO Pray, chuck, come hither.
DESDEMONA
What is your pleasure?
OTHELLO Let me see your eyes.
Look in my face.
DESDEMONA What horrible fancy's this?
OTHELLO [*to Emilia*]
Some of your function, mistress,
Leave procreants alone and shut the door;
Cough, or cry hem, if anybody come.
Your mystery, your mystery: nay, dispatch! *Exit Emilia.*
DESDEMONA
Upon my knees, what doth your speech import?
I understand a fury in your words
But not the words.
OTHELLO
Why, what art thou?
DESDEMONA
Your wife, my lord: your true and loyal wife.
OTHELLO
Come, swear it, damn thyself,

23 **she'll** (special emphasis: he avoids naming Desdemona as at 3, but may mean Emilia here)
24 **chuck** Cf. 3.4.49.
25 **pleasure** wish, will
27 **function** the action proper to a person who is the holder of an office. He treats Emilia as if she has a function in a brothel: 'behave as a bawd should, leave us alone'.
28 **procreants** procreators (usually an adjective, as in *Mac* 1.6.8)
29 **cry hem** give a warning cough
30 **mystery** trade; here, facetiously, your trade as bawd
dispatch hurry
31 **Upon my knees** Kneeling in submission was not unusual.

23 have] *F;* ha *Q* 24 Pray] *Q;* Pray you *F* 27 SD] *Hanmer; not in QF* 30 nay] *Q;* May *F* 31 knees] *Q;* knee *F* doth] *F;* does *Q* 33 But . . . words] *Q; not in F* 36–9 Come . . . honest!] *as Q; prose F*

Lest, being like one of heaven, the devils themselves
Should fear to seize thee: therefore be double-damned,
Swear thou art honest!

DESDEMONA Heaven doth truly know it.

OTHELLO
Heaven truly knows that thou art false as hell.

DESDEMONA
To whom, my lord? with whom? how am I false?

OTHELLO
Ah, Desdemon, away, away, away!

DESDEMONA
Alas the heavy day, why do you weep?
Am I the motive of these tears, my lord?
If haply you my father do suspect
An instrument of this your calling back,
Lay not your blame on me: if you have lost him
Why, I have lost him too.

OTHELLO Had it pleased heaven
To try me with affliction, had they rained
All kinds of sores and shames on my bare head,

37–8 **Lest . . . thee** Devils may only carry off to hell those who spiritually belong to them. *Lest* = for fear that.

38 **double-damned** (1) for adultery, (2) for perjury

40 **false as hell** Cf. Dent, H398, 'As false as hell' (not recorded before Shakespeare).

42 **away** *Either* she clings to him and he pushes her away, *or* he wants to get away, *or* he means 'let's get away from this pointless talk': cf. *TC* 5.3.88, *KL* 1.4.89–91, *Cor* 1.1.12.

43 **heavy** sorrowful. Cf. 3.4.158.

44 **motive** cause

45 **haply** by chance

46 **instrument** usually 'a person made use of by another person for the accomplishment of a purpose' (*OED* 1b); here 'as instrumental in'
calling back recall (to Venice)

47 **lost him** lost him as a friend

48–54 Referring to the *afflictions* of Job: God *rained* these (sores, poverty, etc.) upon him: Job 2.7, 20.23.

48–9 **heaven . . . they** Should we read *he* for *they* (cf. *Texts*, 83), *God* for *heaven*?

49 **rained** Note the 'water' imagery: *rained, Steeped, drop, fountain, current, dries up, cistern.*

41] *as Q; F lines* Lord? / false? / 42 Ah, Desdemon] *F;* O *Desdemona Q* 44 motive . . . these] *F;* occasion . . . those *Q* 45 haply] *Q;* happely *F* 47, 48 lost] *F;* left *Q* 48 Why] *Q; not in F* 49 they rained] *F;* he ram'd *Q* 50 kinds] *Q;* kind *F* bare head] *Q;* bare-head *F*

Steeped me in poverty to the very lips,
Given to captivity me and my utmost hopes,
I should have found in some place of my soul
A drop of patience; but, alas, to make me
The fixed figure for the time of scorn
To point his slow and moving finger at!
Yet could I bear that too, well, very well:
But there where I have garnered up my heart,
Where either I must live or bear no life,
The fountain from the which my current runs
Or else dries up – to be discarded thence!
Or keep it as a cistern for foul toads
To knot and gender in! Turn thy complexion there,

51 perhaps alluding to Tantalus, who was punished in hell with intense thirst and placed in water up to the chin, but unable to drink

52 **utmost** lit. 'farthest from the centre'; greatest; latest. Perhaps referring to his *utmost* descendants.

55 Perhaps we should read 'The fixed figure, for the time, of scorn', i.e. the fixed target of scorn for the whole age (*OED* time 4) to point its (his) slow and (relentlessly) moving finger at. Or does 'the time of scorn' merely = the scornful time?
fixed fixèd
figure Cf. Hebrews 10.33, 'ye were made a gazing stock both by reproaches and afflictions'.

56 Cf. Dent, D321, 'To move as does the dial hand, which is not seen to move'. Perhaps referring to 'the finger of God' (Exodus 8.19 and Luke 11.20). 'The finger of the scornful world is slowly raised to the position of pointing; and then . . . it becomes *unmoving*' (Kittredge, defending Q). No: Othello sees himself as unmoving (the 'fixed figure'), so Q seems unlikely here. *Finger* (if F is correct) may be a collective noun.
*For Q *oh, oh*, cf. 5.1.62n.

58ff. The sequence *there where, where, from the which, thence, there, here*, 'helps the passage to cohere' (Elliott, 180).
garnered up stored (the products of the earth) as in a garner. Perhaps *heart* = all my emotions, or hopes.

60 See LN.

62 **cistern** an artificial reservoir for water; a pond (*OED* 3, first in *AC* 2.5.94–5, 'So half my Egypt were submerged and made / A cestern for scaled snakes').
toads Cf. 3.3.274n.

63 **knot . . . gender** i.e. copulate. A 'Marstonian' image: cf. *Antonio's Revenge* (1602), 'Clipping the strumpet with luxurious twines . . . clinged in sensuality' (Revels, 1.4.18, 31); also *TC* 2.3.158–9, 'I do hate a proud man, as I do the engend'ring of toads.'
complexion countenance, face (*OED* 4c, only this instance cited). The gloss 'Grow pale when that happens' (Sanders) is unlikely: after *there*, 58, *Turn* must mean 'switch', not 'change colour'. A corrupt line?

52 utmost] *F; not in Q* 53 place] *F;* part *Q* 55 The] *F;* A *Q* time] *QF;* hand *Rowe* 56 and moving] *F;* vnmouing *Q* finger at] *F;* fingers at – oh, oh *Q*

Patience, thou young and rose-lipped cherubin,
Ay, here look, grim as hell!

DESDEMONA

I hope my noble lord esteems me honest.

OTHELLO

O, ay, as summer flies are in the shambles,
That quicken even with blowing. O thou weed
Who art so lovely fair and smell'st so sweet
That the sense aches at thee, would thou hadst ne'er been born!

DESDEMONA

Alas, what ignorant sin have I committed?

OTHELLO

Was this fair paper, this most goodly book
Made to write 'whore' upon? What committed!

64 **Patience** 'Even Patience, that rose-lipped cherub, will look grim and pale at this spectacle' (Bevington). Cf. a near-contemporary personification, 'She sate like Patience on a monument, / Smiling at grief' (*TN* 2.4.114–15).
rose-lipped a coinage (with sexual overtones?)
cherubin survived in popular usage as a singular to the eighteenth century (*OED*)

65 ***here look,** First he speaks obliquely of Desdemona (58–64), now he turns on her: it is not some remote place he means, it is *here*, it is Desdemona! The difference between *here, look* and *here look*, is not huge. Both are possible, as is *there* (for *here*): *Texts*, 90.
grim unrelenting; cruel, savage

66 **honest** chaste, virtuous

67 **shambles** slaughter-house; meat market

68 **quicken** receive life, are inseminated, i.e. with the blowing of the wind

68–9 Weeds are neither lovely nor sweet-smelling: he means, 'thou weed, pretending to be a beautiful flower'. But weed could = any herb or small plant (*OED* 2: 'chiefly poetical'). He perhaps savours the sweet smell, anticipating 5.2.15ff.

70 a regular verse line if we read 'would thou'dst ne'er been born!' (*Texts*, 119)
aches 'the keenness and intensity of the pleasure becomes even painful' (Kittredge)

71 **ignorant** unknowing (transferred epithet: she, not the sin, is ignorant); or, unknown (*OED* 4). Cf. Middleton, *The Witch* (MSR 752), 'What secreat syn haue I committed'.

72 For the loved one as a book, cf. *RJ* 1.3.87, 'This precious book of love, this unbound lover', *KJ* 2.1.485.

73 **committed** 'Othello's furious iteration of Desdemona's unhappily chosen word depends on its Elizabethan use absolutely as = "commit adultery"; "commit not with man's sworn spouse" (*KL* 3.4.81)' (Ridley). Cf. *OED* 6c.

64 thou] *F;* thy *Q*   65 here look,] *this edn;* here looke *QF;* there look *Theobald;* there, look *Capell*   67 as] *Q, Fc;* as a *Fu*   summer] *F (*Sommer*);* summers *Q*   68–70] O . . . faire? / at thee, / borne. *Q;* weed: / sweete, / at thee, / borne. *F*   68–9 thou weed / Who] *F;* thou blacke weede, why *Q*   69 and] *F;* Thou *Q*   70 thou hadst] *QF;* thou'dst *F4*   ne'er] *Q;* neuer *F*   73 upon] *F;* on *Q*

Committed? O thou public commoner!
I should make very forges of my cheeks
That would to cinders burn up modesty
Did I but speak thy deeds. What committed!
Heaven stops the nose at it, and the moon winks,
The bawdy wind that kisses all it meets
Is hushed within the hollow mine of earth
And will not hear't. What committed!
Impudent strumpet!

DESDEMONA By heaven, you do me wrong.

OTHELLO
Are not you a strumpet?

DESDEMONA
No, as I am a Christian.
If to preserve this vessel for my lord
From any hated foul unlawful touch
Be not to be a strumpet, I am none.

OTHELLO
What, not a whore? He calls her a whore.

DESDEMONA No, as I shall be saved.

74 **public commoner** common whore

75 **forges** A forge consisted of an open hearth with bellows attached, used for heating iron: here the *cheeks* are the bellows, her *modesty* is tough as iron.

78 **Heaven . . . it** Cf. Ezechiel 39.11, 'those that travel thereby, shall stop their noses'.
moon (symbol of chastity)
winks shuts its eye(s)

79 Cf. Dent, A88, 'As free as the air (wind)'; John 3.8, 'The wind bloweth where it listeth'; *MV* 2.6.16, 'the strumpet wind'.

80 **mine** cave. In Virgil (*Aeneid*, 1.52), Aeolus, controller of the winds, keeps the winds in a vast cavern. Cf. *2H6* 3.2.89, 'he that loos'd them [winds] forth their brazen caves'.

81 **will not** refuses to

82 **Impudent** (shockingly) shameless: stronger than now

85 **vessel** body. Cf. 1 Thessalonians 4.3ff., 'abstain from fornication: That every one of you should know how to possess his vessel in holiness and honour'; 1 Peter 3.7, let the husband give honour to his wife, 'as unto the weaker vessel'. Cf. jokes in other plays about woman as 'the weaker vessel' (*AYL* 2.4.6), 'the emptier vessel' (*2H4* 2.4.60).

86 **hated** F *other* might imply that Othello's touch is foul and unlawful.
touch Cf. Plautus, *Amphitruo*, 831ff. (a wife to her suspicious husband), 'I swear . . . no mortal man, save you only, has taken me to him as a wife' (*corpus corpore contigit* = has touched my body with his).

74–7 Committed? . . . committed!] *F; not in Q* 80 hollow] *F;* hallow *Q* 81 hear't] *QF;* hear it *Steevens* 82 Impudent strumpet] *Q; not in F* 86 hated] *Q;* other *F*

OTHELLO

Is't possible?

DESDEMONA

O heaven, forgive us!

OTHELLO

I cry you mercy then,
I took you for that cunning whore of Venice
That married with Othello. You! Mistress!

Enter EMILIA.

That have the office opposite to Saint Peter
And keep the gates of hell – you, you, ay you!
We have done our course, there's money for your pains,
I pray you turn the key and keep our counsel. *Exit.*

EMILIA

Alas, what does this gentleman conceive?
How do you, madam? how do you, my good lady?

DESDEMONA

Faith, half asleep.

EMILIA

Good madam, what's the matter with my lord?

89 **Is't possible**? Note how this question echoes through the play: 2.3.283, 3.3.361, 3.4.70, 4.1.42.

90 **O . . . us** With Q, compare *R2* 5.5.90, 'Forgiveness, horse!' But as Desdemona has done no wrong, *forgive us* (i.e. for misunderstanding and hurting each other?) seems more appropriate. Perhaps she now collapses, and Othello rants as she lies insensible, coming out of a state of shock at 99 (hence Emilia's concern). This would then be her equivalent to Othello's fit.

90–1 **I . . . for** 'I beg your pardon, I mistook you for' (sarcastic). Cf. *KL* 3.6.52, 'Cry you mercy, I took you for a join-stool' (the same pretence of misunderstanding).

93–4 Cf. Matthew 16.18–19, 'the gates of hell shall not prevail . . . I will give unto thee the keys of the kingdom of heaven' (Noble, 276).

95 **course** the rush together of two combatants, bout, i.e. sexual encounter

96 **keep our counsel** i.e. don't give us away

97 **this gentleman** Cf. 3.4.100, 'this man'. **conceive** imagine

99 **asleep** stunned, numb (*OED* 4)

90 forgive us] *F;* forgiuenesse *Q* then] *F; not in Q* 92.1] *as F; opp.* saued *88 Q* 94 keep] *Rowe;* keepes *QF* gates] *Q;* gate *F* of] *F;* in *Q* [1]you . . . [3]you] *F;* I, you, you, you *Q* 95 have] *F;* ha *Q* 100] *as Q; F lines* Madam, / Lord? /

DESDEMONA
With whom?

EMILIA
Why, with my lord, madam.

DESDEMONA
Who is thy lord?

EMILIA
He that is yours, sweet lady.

DESDEMONA
I have none. Do not talk to me, Emilia;
I cannot weep, nor answers have I none
But what should go by water. Prithee, tonight
Lay on my bed my wedding sheets; remember,
And call thy husband hither.

EMILIA
Here's a change indeed!

Exit.

DESDEMONA
'Tis meet I should be used so, very meet.
How have I been behaved that he might stick
The small'st opinion on my greatest misuse?

Enter IAGO *and* EMILIA.

IAGO
What is your pleasure, madam? How is't with you?

DESDEMONA
I cannot tell. Those that do teach young babes

101 ***whom** For omitted *m*, see *Texts*, 89.
106 **go by water** be conveyed by tears. There was much traffic 'by water' on the River Thames.
107 **wedding sheets** to remind Othello of their former love (but, according to 'short time', their wedding sheets were used the previous night: see pp. 51–3). Also ominous, as wives were sometimes buried in their wedding sheets.
109 **meet** fitting
used treated
110–11 i.e. 'how have I misbehaved myself that he thinks it right to attach the smallest (adverse) judgement to my greatest fault?' Walker paraphrased F, 'how enormous my smallest fault must have been that the least significance could be attached to it'.
112 **How . . . you?** so *Ham* 3.4.116

101 whom] *F2;* who *QF* 103] *F; not in Q* 104 have] *F;* ha *Q* 105 answers] *F;* answer *Q* 107 [2]my] *F;* our *Q* 108 Here's] *F;* Here is *Q* 109 [2]meet] *F;* well *Q* 111 small'st] *F;* smallest *Q* greatest] *Q;* least *F* misuse] *F;* abuse *Q* 112] *as* QF*; Q lines* Madam, / you? /

Do it with gentle means and easy tasks.
He might have chid me so, for, in good faith,
I am a child to chiding.

IAGO
What is the matter, lady?

EMILIA
Alas, Iago, my lord hath so bewhored her,
Thrown such despite and heavy terms upon her
That true hearts cannot bear it.

DESDEMONA
Am I that name, Iago?

IAGO
What name, fair lady?

DESDEMONA
Such as she said my lord did say I was.

EMILIA
He called her whore. A beggar in his drink
Could not have laid such terms upon his callat.

IAGO
Why did he so?

DESDEMONA
I do not know; I am sure I am none such.

IAGO
Do not weep, do not weep: alas the day!

EMILIA
Hath she forsook so many noble matches,
Her father, and her country, and her friends,

114 **tasks** perhaps = reproofs, from *task* (*OED vb* 5) = chide, censure. Cf. *KL* 1.4.343, 'much more at task for want of wisedome, / Then prai'sd for harmefull mildnesse' (F).
117 **bewhored** i.e. berated her as if she were a whore; a coinage, from the verb 'to whore' (as in *Ham* 5.2.64, 'whor'd my mother'), to make a whore of, with prefix *be-* (= thoroughly)
118 **despite** outrage; anger; abuse
heavy angry; violent; distressing
terms words
122 **whore** She feels Desdemona's pain, yet adds to it by repeating the word.
in . . . drink when drinking or drunk
123 **laid . . . upon** applied to
callat slut
127 **forsook** declined, given up
matches marriages; husbands

115 have] *F;* ha *Q* 116 to] *F;* at *Q* 119 That . . . bear it] *Fc (*heart *Fu);* As true hearts cannot beare *Q* 121 said] *F;* sayes *Q* 127–8] *punctuated as Q; F punctuates* Matches? . . . Father? . . . Country? . . . Friends? 127 Hath] *F;* Has *Q* 128 [2]and] *F;* all *Q*

To be called whore? would it not make one weep?

DESDEMONA

It is my wretched fortune.

IAGO

Beshrew him for't,
How comes this trick upon him?

DESDEMONA

Nay, heaven doth know.

EMILIA

I will be hanged if some eternal villain
Some busy and insinuating rogue,
Some cogging, cozening slave, to get some office,
Have not devised this slander, I'll be hanged else!

IAGO

Fie, there is no such man, it is impossible.

DESDEMONA

If any such there be, heaven pardon him.

EMILIA

A halter pardon him, and hell gnaw his bones!
Why should he call her whore? who keeps her company?
What place, what time, what form, what likelihood
The Moor's abused by some most villainous knave,

130 **Beshrew** evil befall (a refined oath)

131 **trick** a freakish or stupid act
heaven doth know (only) heaven knows

132 **I will** let me
eternal 'Used to express extreme abhorrence' (*OED* 7, citing *JC* 1.2.159–60, 'There was a Brutus once that would have brooked / Th'eternal devil to keep his state in Rome'); or, used as an intensive (Hart). Cf. 15–16. An *eternal villain* almost = a devil.

133 **busy** meddlesome
insinuating wriggling into favour, subtly penetrating (as in *1H6* 2.4.35, 'base insinuating flattery')

134 some cheating, deceiving scoundrel, to obtain some position. Emilia senses that someone like Iago is responsible, and may suspect him.

138 **A halter** the hangman's noose. Cf. T. Harman, *Groundworke of Conny-catching* (?1592), C1b, 'a halter blesse him for mee'.
hell . . . bones Cf. Middleton, *Your Five Gallants* (?1608), D4a, 'Hel gnawe these dice'.

140 **form** manner, way. Presumably Shakespeare knew that his 'short time' allowed no *time* or *likelihood* for adultery, and trusted his audience not to notice.

141 **abused** deceived

130 for't] *F;* for it *Q* 135 I'll] *Q;* I will *F* 138–40] *as Q; F lines* him: / bones. / Whore? / companie? / Time? / liklyhood? / 141 most villainous] *F;* outragious *Q*

Some base notorious knave, some scurvy fellow.
O heaven, that such companions thou'dst unfold
And put in every honest hand a whip
To lash the rascals naked through the world
Even from the east to th' west.

IAGO Speak within doors.

EMILIA
O fie upon them! some such squire he was
That turned your wit the seamy side without
And made you to suspect me with the Moor.

IAGO
You are a fool, go to.

DESDEMONA O God, Iago,
What shall I do to win my lord again?
Good friend, go to him, for, by this light of heaven,
I know not how I lost him. Here I kneel:
If e'er my will did trespass 'gainst his love
Either in discourse of thought or actual deed,

142 **notorious** gross (Johnson: but *OED* 6 first records in 1666)
scurvy contemptible, worthless

143 **companions** fellows (contemptuous)
unfold expose

145 Cf. 4.3.37–8, her other geographical fantasy: the guilty have to travel huge distances in some discomfort.
lash Sexual and minor offenders were lashed in public. Cf. *KL* 4.6.160–1, 'Thou rascal beadle, hold thy bloody hand! / Why dost thou lash that whore?'

146 Cf. Dent, E43.1, 'as far as (from) the east from (to) the west'.
within doors less loudly (*OED* door 5: speak so as not to be heard outside the door). Or perhaps 'keep your thoughts to yourself.

147 **squire** used contemptuously (*OED* 1d)

148 **the . . . without** inside out. The *seamy side* of a garment = the worst or roughest side. Cf. 2.3.49, 1.3.385–7, 2.1.289ff.

150 **go to** Cf. 194n.
***God** F *Alas* looks like expurgated profanity: cf. 2.3.147, 5.2.116, where F *alas* is clearly expurgated. Q *Good* could be an error for *God* (cf. 4.1.65 t.n.; *good* was not normally capitalized). Cf. *Ham* 5.2.344, 'O *god* Horatio, what a wounded name' (Q2; *good* F).

151 **win** regain the affection of

154 **trespass** sin (noun or verb)

155 **discourse** process. Noble (34–5) notes that here Q2 has independent support from the Liturgy: 'sins (committed) by thought, word, and deed' (taking discourse = word).

143 heaven] *Q;* Heauens *F* thou'dst] thoudst *Q;* thou'd'st *F* 145 rascals] *F;* rascall *Q* 146 to th'] *F;* to the *Q* doors] *Q;* doore *F* 147 them] *F;* him *Q* 150 O God] *this edn;* O Good *Q;* Alas *F* 153–66 Here . . . me.] *F; not in Q* 155 of] *F;* or *Q2*

Or that mine eyes, mine ears or any sense
Delighted them in any other form,
Or that I do not yet, and ever did,
And ever will – though he do shake me off
To beggarly divorcement – love him dearly,
Comfort forswear me! Unkindness may do much,
And his unkindness may defeat my life
But never taint my love. I cannot say whore:
It does abhor me now I speak the word;
To do the act that might the addition earn
Not the world's mass of vanity could make me.

IAGO
I pray you, be content, 'tis but his humour;
The business of the state does him offence
And he does chide with you.

DESDEMONA
If 'twere no other –

IAGO 'Tis but so, I warrant.
[*Trumpets*.]
Hark how these instruments summon to supper:
The messengers of Venice stay the meat,

156 **that** if (= 158)
157 **form** (human) body; person
158 **Or . . . yet** or if I do not still
159 **shake me off** Cf. 3.3.266, 'I'd whistle her off'.
161 **Comfort** may relief or aid (in want or distress)
forswear abandon
Unkindness absence of affection; unnatural conduct; hostility
162 **defeat** destroy
163 **taint** corrupt
164 **It . . . me** I feel abhorrence. A quibble, as in 'Abhorson' (*MM* 4.2.19), though *abhor* comes from Lat. *abhorreo* and *whore* from OE *hore*. Cf. *Homilies*, 109 ('against Whoredom'), 'whoredom . . . ought to be abhorred'.
165 **addition** title
166 **mass** greater part (*OED* 6)
vanity vain or worthless things (treasure? fine clothes?). Cf. Ecclesiastes 1.2, 'Vanity of vanities . . . all is vanity.'
167 **be content** don't worry
humour temporary state of mind (*OED* 5)
168 **does him offence** displeases him, gives him pain
169 **And** and therefore
chide quarrel (*OED* 2b)
170–1 Q has *you* in 170 and 171, both omitted by F. Perhaps *you* was a later addition for 170 (where *warrant* could be a monosyllable), marked unclearly, and so wrongly inserted in 171.
172 **stay** stay for, await
meat food

157 them in] *Q2;* them: or *F* 169] *Q; not in F* 170 'Tis] Tis *Q;* It is *F* warrant] *F;* warrant you *Q* SD] *Rowe (after 171); not in QF* 171 summon] *F;* summon you *Q* 172 The . . . meat] *as F (*staies the meate*);* And the great Messengers of *Venice* stay *Q*

Go in, and weep not; all things shall be well.

Exeunt Desdemona and Emilia.

Enter RODERIGO.

How now, Roderigo?

RODERIGO I do not find that thou deal'st justly with me.

IAGO What in the contrary?

RODERIGO Every day thou doff'st me with some device, Iago, and rather, as it seems to me now, keep'st from me all conveniency than suppliest me with the least advantage of hope. I will indeed no longer endure it; nor am I yet persuaded to put up in peace what already I have foolishly suffered.

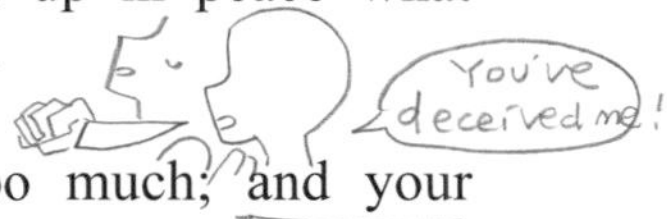

IAGO Will you hear me, Roderigo?

RODERIGO Faith, I have heard too much; and your words and performances are no kin together.

IAGO You charge me most unjustly.

RODERIGO With nought but truth. I have wasted myself out of my means. The jewels you have had from me to deliver to Desdemona would half have corrupted a votarist. You have told me she hath received them,

173 **all . . . well** a common saying (cf. 3.1.43, 3.4.19–20)

175 a verse line (it follows a verse passage) or prose (it begins a passage of prose)?

177 **doff'st** dost put me off, get rid of me
device trick

179 **conveniency** opportunity (*OED* 4c, first in 1645)

180 **advantage** opportunity, favourable occasion

181 **put up** put up with

184–5 ***Faith . . . together** For the misplaced 'And hell gnaw his bones' (t.n.), see Walton, 215–27.
your . . . together Cf. Dent, P602, 'Great promise small performance'.

190 **votarist** one bound by vows to a religious life (and to renounce fornication)

173 SD] *as F; Exit women. Q* 173.1] *F; opp. 174 Q* 175] *as Q; F lines* finde / me. / 177–82] *prose F; Q lines Iago*; / from me, / least / indure it, / already / sufferd. / 177 doff'st] dofftst *Q;* dafts *F* 178 now, keep'st] *F;* thou keepest *Q* 184–5 RODERIGO . . . words and] *as Q, Fc;* And hell gnaw his bones, *Fu* 184 Faith] *Q; not in F* 185 performances] *F;* performance *Q* 187 With . . . truth.] *F; not in Q* 188 my means] *F;* meanes *Q* 189 deliver to] *Q;* deliuer *F* 190 hath] *F;* has *Q* them] *F;* em *Q*

and returned me expectations and comforts of sudden respect and acquittance, but I find none.

IAGO Well, go to; very well.

RODERIGO 'Very well,' 'go to'! I cannot go to, man, nor 'tis not very well. By this hand, I think it is scurvy, and begin to find myself fopped in it.

IAGO Very well.

RODERIGO I tell you, 'tis not very well! I will make myself known to Desdemona: if she will return me my jewels I will give over my suit and repent my unlawful solicitation; if not, assure yourself I will seek satisfaction of you.

IAGO You have said now.

RODERIGO Ay, and said nothing but what I protest intendment of doing.

IAGO Why, now I see there's mettle in thee, and even from this instant do build on thee a better opinion than ever before. Give me thy hand, Roderigo. Thou hast taken against me a most just exception – but yet

191–2 **returned . . . acquittance** sent back favourable promises and encouragements (implying) imminent consideration and repayment. F *acquaintance* is possible.

194 [2]**go to** Roderigo takes Iago's all-purpose phrase (= be quiet; come, come; yes, yes; or, leave me alone) as 'copulate'. Cf. Montaigne, 1.97, 'Married men, because . . . they may go to it when they list, ought never to press'; *AC* 1.2.63–4, 'O, let him marry a woman that cannot go, sweet Isis'; *Per* 4.6.74.

196 **scurvy** shabby

fopped fobbed, cheated; made a fool

198–9 [2]**I . . . known** I will introduce myself (to Desdemona and ask for an explanation).

200 **repent** a curious repentance, standing on conditions!

201 **solicitation** petition; sexual soliciting

202 **satisfaction** repayment; atonement for an offence; the opportunity of satisfying one's honour by a duel (*OED* 4, first in 1602)

203 **said** said your say (statement or question)

204–5 **protest intendment** solemnly declare my intention

206 **mettle** spirit, courage; quibbling on *metal*, after *satisfaction*, with its hint of a duel

209 **taken . . . exception** made objection, found fault

191 expectations] *F;* expectation *Q* 192 acquittance] *Q;* acquaintance *F* 193 well] *F;* good *Q* 194–5 nor 'tis] *F;* it is *Q* By this hand] *Q;* Nay *F* think it is] *F;* say tis very *Q* 196 fopped] fopt *QF;* fob'd *Rowe* 198 I . . . 'tis] *F;* I say it is *Q* 201 I will] *F;* I'le *Q* 204 and said] *F;* and I haue said *Q* 207 instant] *F;* time *Q* 209 exception] *F;* conception *Q*

I protest I have dealt most directly in thy affair. 210

RODERIGO It hath not appeared.

IAGO I grant indeed it hath not appeared, and your
suspicion is not without wit and judgement. But,
Roderigo, if thou hast that in thee indeed which I
have greater reason to believe now than ever – I mean 215
purpose, courage, and valour – this night show it. If
thou the next night following enjoy not Desdemona,
take me from this world with treachery and devise
engines for my life. *Iago – "Honest" 36 times*

RODERIGO Well – what is it? Is it within reason and 220
compass? ®️ *convinced by what Iago says → this time,*

IAGO Sir, there is especial commission come from *flattering*
Venice to depute Cassio in Othello's place.

RODERIGO Is that true? Why, then Othello and
Desdemona return again to Venice. 225

IAGO O no, he goes into Mauretania and taketh away
with him the fair Desdemona, unless his abode be
lingered here by some accident – wherein none can
be so determinate as the removing of Cassio.

RODERIGO How do you mean, removing of him? 230

IAGO Why, by making him uncapable of Othello's place:
knocking out his brains.

RODERIGO And that you would have me to do!

IAGO Ay, if you dare do yourself a profit and a right.

210 **directly** straightforwardly; correctly
 affair business
216 **purpose** determination
219 **engines** plots, snares; engines of torture
 (*OED* 5b)
221 **compass** the bounds of possibility
223 **depute** appoint
226 **Mauretania** the homeland of the north
 African Moors. If this is a lie (cf. 4.1.235),
 what does Iago gain by it? In Mauretania

Desdemona will be out of Roderigo's
reach, so he must act now.
227 **abode** abiding, stay
228 **lingered** prolonged
229 **determinate** decisive
 removing See 2.1.274–5, 'the *displanting*
 of Cassio'; and *KL* 5.1.64–5, 'Let him who
 would be rid of him devise / His speedy
 taking off.
234 **profit** benefit

210 affair] *F;* affaires *Q* 214 in] *F;* within *Q* 217 enjoy] *F;* enioyest *Q* 220 what is it?] *F; not in
Q* 222 especial] *QF;* a special *(Malone)* commission] *F;* command *Q* 222–8] *prose F; Q lines as if
verse Venice, / place. / Desdemona / Venice. / him / linger'd* 226 taketh] *F;* takes *Q* 230 removing of] *Q;*
remouing *F* 231–2] *prose F; Q lines as if verse* place, / braines. / 234 if] *F;* and if *Q* a right] *F;* right *Q*

He sups tonight with a harlotry, and thither will I go to him. He knows not yet of his honourable fortune: if you will watch his going thence – which I will fashion to fall out between twelve and one – you may take him at your pleasure. I will be near to second your attempt, and he shall fall between us. Come, stand not amazed at it, but go along with me: I will show you such a necessity in his death that you shall think yourself bound to put it on him. It is now high supper time, and the night grows to waste: about it.

RODERIGO I will hear further reason for this.

IAGO And you shall be satisfied. *Exeunt.*

promise..

[**4.3**] *Enter* OTHELLO, LODOVICO, DESDEMONA, EMILIA *and Attendants.*

LODOVICO

I do beseech you, sir, trouble yourself no further.

235 **harlotry** harlot (so *RJ* 4.2.14, *1H4* 2.4.395).

236 **He . . . fortune** Iago cannot know this for certain. It implies that Cassio will not be attended, as the new governor might be, and can be struck down more easily.

238 **fashion** arrange, contrive
fall out happen

239 **take** strike; come upon suddenly (*OED* 5, 8b); i.e. kill
second support

240 **fall between us** fall down (or, be wounded; or, die) by our joint action. Deliberately vague.

241 **go along** walk; join in

241–3 **I . . . him** Iago (or Shakespeare) sometimes shrugs off explanations (3.3.322–3, 5.2.301–2, 320); in this instance the explanations follow off stage (5.1.8–10).

243 **put** *Put*, like *removing* (229) and *take* (239), is vague, screening the suggestion of murder. Cf. *Ham* 5.2.383, 'deaths put on by cunning and forced cause', *WT* 3.3.34–5.
high well advanced (as in high noon, high time)

244 **grows to waste** approaches its end (*OED* waste 10c); implies 'we're wasting our time (talking)'
about it i.e. bestir yourself, make a move!

246 **satisfied** content (with satisfactory reasons); convinced

4.3.0.1–2 Q's entry, two lines before the end of 4.2, looks like another misplaced or misinterpreted marginal SD. The scene seems to be a public room or place, but later becomes a more private place where Desdemona unpins.

1–8 prose or verse? The short lines confuse the issue. See p. 367.

235 harlotry] *F;* harlot *Q* 246 SD] *Ex.* Iag. *and* Rod. *Q; Exeunt. F* **4.3**] *Scena Tertia. F; not in Q* 0.1–2 SD] *as F;* Enter *Othello, Desdemona, Lodouico, Emillia*, and Attendants. *Q (after 4.2.244)*

OTHELLO
O, pardon me, 'twill do me good to walk.

LODOVICO
Madam, good night: I humbly thank your ladyship.

DESDEMONA
Your honour is most welcome.

OTHELLO
Will you walk, sir?
O, Desdemona –

DESDEMONA
My lord?

OTHELLO
Get you to bed
On th'instant, I will be returned forthwith.
Dismiss your attendant there: look't be done.

DESDEMONA
I will, my lord.

Exeunt Othello, Lodovico and Attendants.

EMILIA
How goes it now? He looks gentler than he did.

DESDEMONA
He says he will return incontinent,
And hath commanded me to go to bed
And bid me to dismiss you.

EMILIA
Dismiss me?

DESDEMONA
It was his bidding; therefore, good Emilia,
Give me my nightly wearing, and adieu.
We must not now displease him.

EMILIA
Ay. – Would you had never seen him!

6 **returned** back

10 **incontinent** at once. Could also mean 'wanting in self-restraint: chiefly with reference to sexual appetite' (*OED* 1), therefore an odd word here. Cf. *AYL* 5.2.38–9.

14 **wearing** apparel

15 **We** Associating Emilia with herself, Desdemona unconsciously indicates that she needs help.

16 ***Ay** 'I' was a normal spelling for 'Ay', and F's comma suggests a stop after *Ay*. Heard in the theatre, 'I' and 'Ay' would be indistinguishable, hence Desdemona's reply (*Texts*, 132–3).

2 'twill] *F;* it shall *Q* 4–7] *prose QF* 6 On th'] *F;* o'the *Q* 7 Dismiss] *F;* dispatch *Q* 't] *F;* it *Q* 8.1] *Exeunt. Q; Exit. F (opp. 7 QF)* 11 And] *F;* He *Q* 12 bid] *F;* bad *Q* 16 Ay. – Would] *this edn;* I would *Q;* I, would *F;* Would *Q2*

DESDEMONA

So would not I: my love doth so approve him
That even his stubbornness, his checks, his frowns
– Prithee unpin me – have grace and favour.

EMILIA

I have laid those sheets you bade me on the bed.

DESDEMONA

All's one. Good faith, how foolish are our minds!
If I do die before thee, prithee shroud me
In one of these same sheets.

EMILIA Come, come, you talk.

DESDEMONA

My mother had a maid called Barbary,
She was in love, and he she loved proved mad
And did forsake her. She had a song of 'willow',
An old thing 'twas, but it expressed her fortune
And she died singing it. That song tonight

17 **approve** commend

18 **stubbornness** roughness: cf. 1.3.228.
checks reprimands

19, 33 **unpin** The word occurs nowhere else in Shakespeare. It refers to the unpinning of Desdemona's dress or hair. Ellen Terry wrote 'Hair' in her text (Hankey, 297), but editors and stage histories give little help. Either way, the unpinning brings the two women intimately together.

19 **grace and favour** So *Homilies*, 469, *R3* 3.4.91, *KL* 1.1.229; *favour* = charm, attractiveness.

20 **those sheets** Perhaps the bed is already visible (see pp. 51–3), and she points to those sheets. But beds were less easy to bring on stage than chairs: *those* probably means 'those sheets you asked for' (4.2.107).

21 **All's one** It's all the same, it doesn't matter.
***faith** F's misreading, *Father*, is also found in *RJ* 4.4.21 (Q2), 'good father (= faith) tis day'. See *Texts*, 169.
foolish i.e. in thinking about death (a half-apology)

23 **you talk** i.e. how you talk! She speaks almost as if to a child; Desdemona's reference to her mother continues this redefinition of their roles.

24 **Barbary** Cf. 1.1.110. The name suggests the Barbary coast, home of the Moors. Did her mother have a maid who was a Moor? Not necessarily: the name was in use in England. Shakespeare's lawyer, Francis Collins, had a daughter called 'Barbery', named in his will, 1617.

25 **proved** turned out to be
mad lunatic; or 'wild' (Johnson)

26 **willow** F's *Willough* was probably Crane's spelling (*Texts*, 66).

27 **fortune** fate

28 **And . . . it** Desdemona's attendant, Emilia, also dies singing the Willow Song (5.2.245ff.).

18 [3]his] *F;* and *Q* 19 favour] *F;* fauour in them *Q* 20 those] *F;* these *Q* 21 one. Good faith,] one good faith: *Q;* one: good Father, *F* 22 before thee] *Q;* before *F* 23 these] *F;* those *Q* 26 had] *F;* has *Q* willow] *Q;* Willough *F (throughout)*

Will not go from my mind. I have much to do
But to go hang my head all at one side
And sing it like poor Barbary. Prithee dispatch.

EMILIA Shall I go fetch your night-gown?

DESDEMONA No, unpin me here.

EMILIA This Lodovico is a proper man. A very handsome man.

DESDEMONA He speaks well.

EMILIA I know a lady in Venice would have walked barefoot to Palestine for a touch of his nether lip.

DESDEMONA [*Sings.*]

The poor soul sat sighing by a sycamore tree,
Sing all a green willow:
Her hand on her bosom, her head on her knee,
Sing willow, willow, willow.
The fresh streams ran by her and murmured her moans,
Sing willow, willow, willow:

29–30 **I** . . . **But** it is all I can do not to (Ridley)
30 **hang my head** let my head droop (in despondency)
31 **dispatch** hurry
32 **night-gown** dressing-gown
34–5 ***This** . . . **man** F prints 'This . . . proper man' as one line, as if it is verse (which it may be). I follow Ridley's conjecture in moving the SP. For Desdemona to praise Lodovico at this point seems out of character. Shakespeare sometimes omitted SPs or added them later (cf. his pages in *STM*), so misplaced SPs are understandable: but see S. N. Garner, 'Shakespeare's Desdemona' (*SSt*, 9 [1976], 233ff.).
34 **proper** good-looking; admirable; complete
37–8 This suggests a penitential pilgrimage: the chastest kiss would have required a considerable mortification of the flesh! But pilgrims normally went from Venice to Palestine by sea (as in *The Book of Margery Kempe*, ch. 28).
38 **nether lip** Cf. 5.2.43, 'Alas, why gnaw you so your nether lip?'
39ff. For the song, see LN.
39 **sycamore** a species of fig tree. 'It was not traditionally associated with the forsaken in love (except perhaps by the punning "sick-amour"); but it is in a grove of sycamore that the love-sick Romeo is found wandering by Benvolio (*RJ* 1.1.121)' (Sanders).
40 **a** of. Steevens quoted a ballad printed in 1578 with the refrain 'Willow, willow, willow, sing all of green willow'.
willow symbol of grief for unrequited love or the loss of a mate

29–52 I have . . . next.] *F; not in Q* 34 SP] *Ard*^{2}*; before* A very *F* 39 SD] *as Q2; not in F* 39ff.] *song in italics F 39* sighing] *Q2; singing Fc; sining Fu*

Her salt tears fell from her and softened the stones,
Sing willow, willow, willow.
[*Speaks*.] Lay by these.
Willow, willow –
[*Speaks*.] Prithee hie thee: he'll come anon.
Sing all a green willow must be my garland.
Let nobody blame him, his scorn I approve –
[*Speaks*.] Nay, that's not next. Hark, who is't that knocks?

EMILIA
It's the wind.

DESDEMONA [*Sings*.]
I called my love false love; but what said he then?
Sing willow, willow, willow:
If I court moe women, you'll couch with moe men.
[*Speaks*.] So, get thee gone; good night. Mine eyes do itch,
Doth that bode weeping?

EMILIA 'Tis neither here nor there.

DESDEMONA
I have heard it said so. O, these men, these men!
Dost thou in conscience think – tell me, Emilia –
That there be women do abuse their husbands
In such gross kind?

EMILIA There be some such, no question.

45 Cf. Dent, D618, 'Constant dropping will wear the stone.'
47 **Lay by these** put these things aside
49 **hie** haste
51–2 **Let . . . next** a Freudian slip (unconsciously she wants to shield Othello from blame)?
56 **moe** more
couch lie.
57–8 **Mine . . . weeping** 'I find in MacGregor's *Folklore of North-East Scotland* that "An itching in the eyes indicated tears and sorrow" ' (Hart).
58 Cf. Dent, H438, 'It is neither here nor there.'
60 **in conscience** truly
62 **gross kind** disgusting manner

47, 49, 52, 57SD] *this edn* 49 hie] high *F* 52 who is't] *F;* who's *Q* 53 It's] *F;* It is *Q* 54–6] *F; not in Q* 57–8] *F; Q lines* night; / weeping? / 57 So] *F;* Now *Q* 58 Doth] *F;* does *Q* 59–62 DESDEMONA . . . question.] *F; not in Q*

DESDEMONA
Wouldst thou do such a deed for all the world?

EMILIA
Why, would not you?

DESDEMONA
No, by this heavenly light!

EMILIA
Nor I neither, by this heavenly light:
I might do't as well i'th' dark.

DESDEMONA
Wouldst thou do such a deed for all the world?

EMILIA
The world's a huge thing: it is a great price
For a small vice.

DESDEMONA
Good troth, I think thou wouldst not.

EMILIA By my troth, I think I should, and undo't when I had done. Marry, I would not do such a thing for a joint-ring, nor for measures of lawn, nor for gowns, petticoats, nor caps, nor any petty exhibition. But for all the whole world? ud's pity, who would not make

63–6 ***Why** . . . **dark** See *Texts*, 34–5. I think that these lines were cancelled by Shakespeare, who reused 63 as 67. Emilia knows, after 4.2, that Desdemona's chastity is not a joking matter.

63 Cf. Matthew 16.26, 'For what doth it profit a man if he win all the whole world and lose his own soul?'
do . . . **deed** = have sexual intercourse (Partridge, citing *LLL* 3.1.198–9, 'one that will do the deed / Though Argus were her eunuch and her guard')
for . . . **world** resumes 4.2.165–6 (as 'by this heavenly light' picks up 'by this light of heaven', 4.2.152). She and Othello both think each other, and 'honesty', worth the whole world.

64 **by** . . . **light** an oath not used elsewhere by Shakespeare (but cf. 4.2.152, 'by this light of heaven'); adapted from 'by this light' or '[God]'s light'

68 **price** price to be paid; or, prize (variant spelling)

72 **joint-ring** a finger-ring formed of two separable halves to make one, like husband and wife. Often given by lovers. She perhaps implies 'for a mere promise of marriage'.
measures of lawn quantities of fine linen

73 **petty** trivial; inferior
exhibition gift, present

74 **ud's** God's. Cf. 5.2.69.

74–5 **who** . . . **monarch** Her 'easy virtue' is in character, but her willingness to do anything for Iago less so. Is she joking?

66 do't] *F;* doe it *Q* i'th'] *F;* in the *Q* 67 Wouldst] *F;* Would *Q* deed] *F;* thing *Q* 68–9] *as Q; F lines* thing: / vice. / 68 world's] *F;* world is *Q* 69 Good troth] *Q;* Introth *F* 70 By my troth] *Q;* Introth *F* 71 done] *F;* done it *Q* 72 [1]nor] *F;* or *Q* 73 petticoats] *F;* or Petticotes *Q* petty] *F;* such *Q* 74 all] *F; not in Q* ud's pity] *Q;* why *F*

her husband a cuckold to make him a monarch? I should venture purgatory for't.

DESDEMONA

Beshrew me, if I would do such a wrong
For the whole world!

EMILIA Why, the wrong is but a wrong i'th' world; and having the world for your labour, 'tis a wrong in your own world, and you might quickly make it right.

DESDEMONA I do not think there is any such woman.

EMILIA Yes, a dozen, and as many to th' vantage as would store the world they played for.

But I do think it is their husbands' faults
If wives do fall. Say that they slack their duties
And pour our treasures into foreign laps;
Or else break out in peevish jealousies,
Throwing restraint upon us; or say they strike us,

76 **venture** risk
purgatory a reminder that the play is set in a Catholic world

77 **Beshrew me** Cf. 3.4.151n.

82 Cf. 4.2.136.

83–4 A prose beginning for a verse speech is unusual, but 85–102 are more likely to be a cut in Q than an afterthought in F: see *Texts*, 12.

83 **a dozen** a facetious understatement, cancelled out by what follows. Cf. Falstaff, who 'went to a bawdy-house not above once in a quarter – of an hour' (*1H4* 3.3.16–17).
to th' vantage over and above

84 **store** stock
played gambled; sported amorously

85–102 She resumes 3.4.104–7. Though she begins by thinking of Othello, it is soon clear that she refers to her own marriage. Such protests against 'double standards' were not uncommon: cf. *CE* 2.1.10ff.

86 **fall** fall from virtue
slack neglect; cease to prosecute in a vigorous manner (*OED* 1, 2)
duties The *Book of Common Prayer* ('Of matrimony') explained 'the duty of husbands toward their wives, and wives toward their husbands', but sexual duties were treated less explicitly than in some bibles. Cf. 1 Corinthians 7.2–3, 'But because of fornication let every man have his own wife . . . Let the husband render his debt to the wife'. (This is the Catholic 'Rheims' bible of 1582; for *debt* Protestant bibles read 'due benevolence'.)

87 perhaps alluding to the myth of Danaë, who was impregnated by Zeus disguised as a shower of gold. But *treasure* = seed was not uncommon: cf. *1H4* 2.3.45, 'my treasures and my rights of thee' (Lady Hotspur to Hotspur); *Son* 20, 'Mine be thy love, and thy love's use their treasure'.
foreign another woman's
laps lap could = pudendum (*OED* 2b)

88 **peevish** foolish; mad; spiteful; perverse; irritable (a word that has narrowed in meaning)

89 **Throwing . . . us** i.e. restricting our freedom

76 for't] *F;* for it *Q* 79 i'th'] *F;* i'the *Q* 83 to th'] *F;* to the *Q* 85–102 But . . . so.] *F; not in Q* 89 upon] *F;* on *Rowe*[3]

Or scant our former having in despite,
Why, we have galls: and though we have some grace
Yet have we some revenge. Let husbands know
Their wives have sense like them: they see, and smell,
And have their palates both for sweet and sour
As husbands have. What is it that they do
When they change us for others? Is it sport?
I think it is. And doth affection breed it?
I think it doth. Is't frailty that thus errs?
It is so too. And have not we affections?
Desires for sport? and frailty, as men have?
Then let them use us well: else let them know,
The ills we do, their ills instruct us so.

DESDEMONA

Good night, good night. God me such usage send
Not to pick bad from bad, but by bad mend! *Exeunt.*

[5.1] *Enter* IAGO *and* RODERIGO.

IAGO

Here, stand behind this bulk, straight will he come.
Wear thy good rapier bare, and put it home;

90 or reduce what we had before (our 'treasures') out of spite

91 **we have galls** i.e. we can feel resentment
grace mercy

93 **sense** sensation, or sensual appetite (Malone); or, emotional consciousness (*OED* 16)

96 **change** exchange
sport recreation, fun

97 **affection breed** passion (or lust) produce

98 **frailty** moral weakness

101 **use us well** Cf. 1.3.292, 'use Desdemona well', and 5.2.69n.

102 **ills** wicked or sinful acts
so i.e. so to do (Malone). Cf. *MV* 3.1.71–2, 'The villainy you teach me, I will execute'. This speech (Shylock's 'Hath not a Jew eyes?') is close to Emilia's here.

103 **usage** treatment; behaviour

104 not to select (and copy) bad from what is bad, but to improve by (knowing what is) bad

5.1.1 ***Here, stand** So F (no comma Q). Or, 'Here stand,'. In *Arden of Faversham* killers also wait for their victim outside a shop when it is 'very late' ('stand close, and take your fittest standing', Revels, 3.39).
bulk stall, a framework projecting from the front of a shop

2 **bare** ready, drawn
home i.e. as far as it will go

103] *as Q; F lines* good night: / send, / God] *Q;* Heauen *F* usage] *Q;* vses *F* **5.1**] *Actus.* 5. *Q; Actus Quintus. Scena Prima. F* 1] *as Q; F lines* Barke, / come: / bulk] *Q;* Barke *F*

Quick, quick, fear nothing, I'll be at thy elbow.
It makes us or it mars us, think on that
And fix most firm thy resolution.

RODERIGO

Be near at hand, I may miscarry in't.

IAGO

Here, at thy hand: be bold, and take thy stand.

[*Retires.*]

RODERIGO

I have no great devotion to the deed
And yet he hath given me satisfying reasons:
'Tis but a man gone. Forth, my sword: he dies.

IAGO

I have rubbed this young quat almost to the sense
And he grows angry. Now, whether he kill Cassio
Or Cassio him, or each do kill the other,
Every way makes my gain. Live Roderigo,
He calls me to a restitution large
Of gold and jewels that I bobbed from him
As gifts to Desdemona:
It must not be. If Cassio do remain

3 **at thy elbow** Cf. Dent, EE5, 'To be at one's elbow'; D243.1, 'The devil is at one's elbow.'
4 **It . . . ^{2}us** Dent, M48, 'To make or mar'.
5 **resolution** five syllables
7 **stand** position. Cf. *JC* 2.4.25, 'I go to take my stand, / To see him pass.'
8 **devotion** enthusiasm for; incongruous, suggesting religious devotion (to commit murder)
9 **reasons** Cf. 4.2.245–6, 5.2.305–9. We do not hear the reasons: Shakespeare sometimes states that there are reasons without giving them (*KL* 4.3.51 ff., *Tem* 1.2.266). Scan 'he'th giv'n'.
10 **Forth** Only now does he manage to draw his sword!
11 **quat** pimple, small boil, 'which rubbing irritates' (Ridley). Note that Iago, aged 28, thinks Roderigo *young*: he may be a boy in his teens (cf. 1.3.341n.).
to the sense to the quick
12 **angry** could = inflamed (*OED* 8: 'sores with often touching waxe angry')
14 **gain** profit. Q *game* = 'gives me the game' (Ridley; so Kittredge).
Live should Roderigo live
16 **bobbed** diddled (more playful than 'cheated')
18 **It . . . be** metrically 'amphibious', because these words could also complete 17 (*Texts*, 105–6)

4 on] *F;* of *Q* 7 stand] *F;* sword *Q* SD] *as Capell; not in QF* 8 deed] *F;* dead *Q* 9 hath] *F;* has *Q* 11 quat] *F;* gnat *Q* 12 angry. Now,] *F;* angry now: *Q* 14 gain] *F;* game *Q* 16 Of] *F;* For *Q*

He hath a daily beauty in his life
That makes me ugly; and besides, the Moor
May unfold me to him – there stand I in much peril.
No, he must die. Be't so! I hear him coming.

Enter CASSIO.

RODERIGO
I know his gait, 'tis he. Villain, thou diest!
[*Makes a thrust at Cassio.*]

CASSIO
That thrust had been mine enemy indeed
But that my coat is better than thou know'st:
I will make proof of thine.
[*Draws, and wounds Roderigo.*]

RODERIGO
O, I am slain!
[*Iago from behind wounds Cassio in the leg, and exit.*]

CASSIO
I am maimed for ever! Help, ho! murder! murder!

Enter OTHELLO.

OTHELLO
The voice of Cassio. Iago keeps his word.

19 **daily beauty** i.e. an ever-present attractiveness. Does this suggest searing self-contempt (so Rosenberg, 174) on the part of Iago? Or is he describing the conventional view of Cassio's beautiful manners (cf. 2.1.98ff.) compared with his own bluntness (2.1.164ff.)?

21 **unfold** expose. Scan 'May 'nfold me to'm' (*Texts*, 121).

25 **coat** undercoat (of proof armour)

26 **make proof** test (the proof of)
[2]SD Iago wounds him in the leg, having heard that his *coat* protects his upper body (Malone).

27 **maimed** For Q *maind*, cf. 1.3.100n.

27.1 Othello usually enters 'above'. Does he arrive by chance, or did Iago tell him that Cassio would be killed here?

19 hath] *F;* has *Q* 21 much] *F; not in Q* 22 Be't] *Q;* But *F* hear] *Q;* heard *F* 23 SD] *Rowe subst. (He runs at* Cassio, *and wounds him.); not in QF* 24 mine] *F;* my *Q* 25 know'st] *F;* think'st *Q* 26 [1]SD] *this edn; not in QF* [2]SD] *Theobald subst. (Fight. Iago cuts Cassio behind in the Leg, and* Exit.*); not in QF* 27ff. murder] *Q;* murther *F throughout scene* 27] *as Q; F lines* euer: / murther. / maimed] *F;* maind *Q* Help] *F;* light *Q* 27.1] *QF; Enter* Othello, *above at a Window / Rowe*

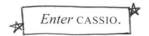

RODERIGO

O, villain that I am!

OTHELLO

It is even so.

CASSIO

O, help ho! light! a surgeon!

OTHELLO

'Tis he. O brave Iago, honest and just,
That hast such noble sense of thy friend's wrong!
Thou teachest me. Minion, your dear lies dead,
And your unblest fate hies; strumpet, I come.
Forth of my heart those charms, thine eyes, are blotted,
Thy bed, lust-stained, shall with lust's blood be spotted. *Exit.*

Enter LODOVICO *and* GRATIANO.

CASSIO

What ho, no watch, no passage? murder, murder!

GRATIANO

'Tis some mischance, the voice is very direful.

They can't say them.

CASSIO

O help!

LODOVICO

Hark!

29 **O . . . am** Cf. Romans 7.24, 'O wretched man that I am'.
It . . . so Q *Harke* implies that Othello can hear but not see. He does not know about Roderigo, cannot see him, and thinks Cassio speaks. *Even* = just.
31 **brave** worthy, good; courageous
32 **sense** Cf. 4.3.93n.
friend's Having called himself 'thy friend' (3.3.145) to get information from Iago, while thinking of him as 'This . . . creature' (3.3.246), he now *thinks* Iago a friend.
33 **Minion** hussy (contemptuously, addressing the absent Desdemona); more usually 'darling' (endearingly)
34 **unblest** unholy (i.e. she is damned)
hies makes haste, hurries nearer
35 **Forth** out
blotted obliterated
36 **blood** Cf. 3.3.454 ('O blood, blood, blood!'), 4.1.201ff., 5.2.3. Is it Shakespeare or Othello who cannot decide how she should be killed?
spotted stained
37 **passage** i.e. people passing
38 **mischance** mishap
direful dreadful, terrible

29 It is] *F;* Harke tis *Q* 34 unblest fate hies] *F (*highes*);* fate hies apace *Q* 35 Forth] *Q;* For *F* 37] *as Q; F lines* passage?/Murther. / 38 voice] *F;* cry *Q*

RODERIGO

O wretched villain!

*2'o clock in the am
describe to the audience.

LODOVICO

→ dark, cannot see

Two or three groan. It is a heavy night;
These may be counterfeits, let's think't unsafe
To come in to the cry without more help.

RODERIGO

Nobody come? then shall I bleed to death.

Enter IAGO, *with a light.*

enters so he looks innocent.

LODOVICO

Hark!

GRATIANO

Here's one comes in his shirt, with light and weapons.

IAGO

Who's there? Whose noise is this that cries on murder?

LODOVICO

We do not know.

IAGO

Did not you hear a cry?

CASSIO

Here, here! for heaven's sake help me!

IAGO

What's the matter?

GRATIANO

This is Othello's ancient, as I take it.

42 **heavy** overcast, dark
44 **come in to** approach(?); or, Cassio and Roderigo staggered into the *bulk* (1) and he fears to follow. Cf. 59.
45 This could be two questions.
47 **in his shirt** in his night attire; without his outer garments (*OED* 2b)
48 **noise** *Q noise* could be a misreading of *voice*, leading to a 'common error' in F: 'whose noise is this, that cries' sounds odd. Cf. 5.2.85 t.n.
cries on exclaims against
50 **heaven's** F *heauen* could be the old genitive, as in *KJ* 4.1.77, 'For heauen sake', or Chaucer, *Wife of Bath's Tale*, 325, 'Jesus, hevene king', or *-s* dropped before *s*, as in *MV* 4.1.379, Q, 'for Godsake'. Cf. *Barnavelt* (a Crane manuscript; MSR 1383), 'for heaven-sake'.

42 groan. It is a] grones, it is a *Q;* groane. 'Tis *F* 44 in to] *Capell;* into *QF* 45.1] *as Q; Enter Iago. F* 47 light] *F;* lights *Q* 49 We] *F;* I *Q* Did] *Q;* Do *F* 50 heaven's] *Q;* heauen *F*

LODOVICO

The same indeed, a very valiant fellow.

IAGO

What are you here that cry so grievously?

CASSIO

Iago? O, I am spoiled, undone by villains!
Give me some help.

IAGO

O me, lieutenant! What villains have done this?

CASSIO

I think that one of them is hereabout
And cannot make away.

Go over to him

IAGO

O treacherous villains!
What are you there? Come in, and give some help.

to: Lodovico Gratiano

RODERIGO

O, help me here!

CASSIO

That's one of them.

IAGO

O murderous slave! O villain!

[*Stabs Roderigo.*]

Iago attacks R

RODERIGO

O damned Iago! O inhuman dog!

IAGO

Kill men i'th' dark? Where be these bloody thieves?
How silent is this town! Ho, murder, murder!

52 **fellow** They do not remember his name (he is a social inferior), but he remembers theirs (67, 93).

53 **grievously** piteously, wretchedly

54 **spoiled** destroyed. Cf. *CE* 5.1.37.

56 **O me** A 'genteel' exclamation: cf. *RJ* 1.1.173.

58 **make** i.e. get

59 **What . . . there?** What kind of men are you there? This seems to anticipate 65, but might also be printed 'What, are you there?' (addressing supposed villains). **Come in** Iago has entered the *bulk* (1) to help Cassio.

62 **[1]O . . . dog!** Q's 'o, o, o' is a signal to the actor to groan or make whatever noise is appropriate; more common in F than in Q texts. See Honigmann, 'Stage direction'.

64 Iago enjoys uproar: cf. 1.1.66ff., 2.3.153.

56] *as Q; F lines* Lieutenant! / this? / me,] *F (*mee,*);* my *Q* 57 that] *F;* the *Q* 60 here] *Q;* there *F* 61 them] *F;* em *Q* murderous] *Q;* murd'rous *F* SD] *as Q2, Rowe; not in QF* 62 dog!] *as F;* dog, – o, o, o. *Q* 63] *as Q; F lines* darke? / Theeues? / men i'th'] *F;* him i' the *Q* these] *F;* those *Q*

What may you be? Are you of good or evil?

LODOVICO

As you shall prove us, praise us.

IAGO

Signior Lodovico?

LODOVICO

He, sir.

Iago ~ cowardly way, doesn't stab Cassio.

IAGO

I cry you mercy: here's Cassio hurt by villains.

R.

GRATIANO

Cassio?

IAGO

How is't, brother?

CASSIO My leg is cut in two.

IAGO

Marry, heaven forbid!
Light, gentlemen, I'll bind it with my shirt.

Enter BIANCA.

BIANCA

What is the matter, ho? who is't that cried?

IAGO

Who is't that cried?

BIANCA O my dear Cassio!
My sweet Cassio! O Cassio, Cassio, Cassio!

65 Lodovico and Gratiano have kept their distance, and now step forward. **of** on the side of. The idea is familiar (Joshua 5.13, 'Art thou on our side, or on our adversaries'?') but the phrasing is odd.

66 **prove** find or prove (us to be)
praise appraise, value. Cf. Dent, P614.2, 'Prove (assay, try) ere you purpose (. . . praise)'; i.e. as you prove our value, so esteem us.

69 **I . . . mercy** I beg your pardon (*you* is indirect object): a 'genteel' phrase.

71 **brother** From Cinthio: discovering the wounded Cassio, Iago grieved 'as if he had been his own brother' (cf. p. 391), the words of the narrator. Shakespeare gives the word to Iago, who wants to impress the Venetians.

72 **heaven forbid** Cf. 2.3.257n.

73 **Light** Iago has put down his own light, to bind Cassio's wounds.

75 **Who . . . cried** Iago has a dangerous tendency to mock others by echoing them: cf. 1.1.116, 2.1.249, 3.3.104ff., 306, 443.
Cassio three syllables, for emphasis. Two in 76.

71 is't] *F;* is it *Q* 76 My] *F;* O my *Q* O] *F; not in Q*

IAGO
O notable strumpet! Cassio, may you suspect
Who they should be that have thus mangled you?

CASSIO
No.

GRATIANO
I am sorry to find you thus;
I have been to seek you.

IAGO
Lend me a garter. So. – O for a chair
To bear him easily hence!

BIANCA
Alas, he faints! O Cassio, Cassio, Cassio!

IAGO
Gentlemen all, I do suspect this trash
To be a party in this injury.
Patience awhile, good Cassio. Come, come,
Lend me a light. Know we this face, or no?
Alas, my friend and my dear countryman,
Roderigo? No – yes sure! – O heaven, Roderigo!

GRATIANO
What, of Venice?

IAGO
Even he, sir. Did you know him?

GRATIANO
Know him? Ay.

IAGO
Signior Gratiano? I cry you gentle pardon:
These bloody accidents must excuse my manners

77 **notable** known, conspicuous
strumpet Cf. *R3* 3.4.71, 74, where another murderer's moral outrage at a strumpet is equally hypocritical.
77–8 **may . . . be** have you any idea who they are
78 **mangled** hacked; wounded
80–1 Even with elision (I'm, I've) this would be an irregular verse line.
82 **garter** a band, worn as a sash or belt
85 **trash** Cf. 2.1.301, 3.3.160.
87 **Cassio** three syllables
89 **countryman** fellow countryman
93 **I . . . pardon** a 'genteel' turn of phrase, again! A variant of 'I cry you mercy' (69n., 4.2.90).
94 **accidents** unforeseen happenings

78 have thus] *F;* thus haue *Q* 80–3] *divided as F* 82–3] *F; not in Q* 86 be] *F;* beare *Q* party . . . injury] *F;* part in this *Q* 87 Come, come] *F; not in Q* 90 O heaven] *Q;* Yes, 'tis *F* 93 you] *Q;* your *F*

That so neglected you.

GRATIANO I am glad to see you.

IAGO

How do you, Cassio? O, a chair, a chair!

GRATIANO

Roderigo?

IAGO

He, he, 'tis he. [*A chair is brought in.*] O, that's well said, the chair.
Some good man bear him carefully from hence,
I'll fetch the general's surgeon. [*To Bianca.*] For you, mistress,
Save you your labour. – He that lies slain here, Cassio,
Was my dear friend. What malice was between you?

CASSIO

None in the world, nor do I know the man.

IAGO [*to Bianca*]

What, look you pale? – O, bear him out o'th' air.
– Stay you, good gentlemen. – Look you pale, mistress?
– Do you perceive the gastness of her eye?
– Nay, if you stare we shall hear more anon.
– Behold her well, I pray you, look upon her:

95 **neglected** ignored, paid no attention to
96 **chair** i.e. a seat (or litter?) to carry Cassio to the surgeon
98 **well said** Cf. 4.1.115n.
the chair F *the* presupposes 82–3, Q *a* doesn't (Q omits 82–3). Revision?
99 **man** Emend to *men*?
100 **For** as for
101 **Save . . . labour** don't trouble yourself, i.e leave him alone
102 **malice** ill-will
104 **O . . . air** Cf. Tilley, A93, 'Fresh air is ill for the diseased or wounded man.'
106 **gastness** dread, terror; ghastliness
107 **Nay . . . anon** i.e. if you stare (it is a sign of guilt) we'll soon hear more (we'll make you confess). Q *stirre* (= try to get away) would imply much the same. Cf. 5.2.184, 'Nay, stare not'.

98] *as Q; F lines* 'tis he / Chaire. / He, he] *F;* He *Q* SD] *Capell subst.; not in QF* the] *F;* a *Q* 100 SD] *Johnson; not in QF* 102 between] *F;* betwixt *Q* 104 out] *Q; not in F* 105 gentlemen] *F;* Gentlewoman *Q* 106 gastness] *F;* ieastures *Q* 107 if] *F;* an *Q* stare] *F;* stirre *Q* hear] *F;* haue *Q*

Do you see, gentlemen? nay, guiltiness will speak
Though tongues were out of use.

Enter EMILIA.

EMILIA 'Las, what's the matter?
What's the matter, husband?

IAGO
Cassio hath here been set on in the dark
By Roderigo and fellows that are 'scaped:
He's almost slain, and Roderigo dead.

EMILIA
Alas, good gentleman! alas, good Cassio!

IAGO
This is the fruits of whoring. Prithee, Emilia,
Go know of Cassio where he supped tonight.
What, do you shake at that?

BIANCA
He supped at my house, but I therefore shake not.

IAGO
O, did he so? I charge you, go with me.

EMILIA
O fie upon thee, strumpet!

BIANCA I am no strumpet
But of life as honest as you, that thus
Abuse me.

EMILIA As I? Foh, fie upon thee!

109–10 **nay . . . use** i.e. guilt will betray itself, even if we were all struck dumb (*out of use* = not used). Dent, M1315, 'Murder will out.'

114 **dead** Cf. 5.2.326.

115 She seems to think the two men equally 'good'. This brings out her failure to look below the surface.

116 **This . . . whoring** Cf. *R3* 2.1.135, 'This is the fruits of rashness', and 77n.

117 **know** learn

120 **charge** order

121–3 *sometimes printed as irregular verse lines, but can be spoken as verse if *I am* is slurred as *I'm*, and heavy stress on *you*: see *Texts*, 123

122 **honest** i.e. sexually honest. In a more general sense she is indeed more honest than Emilia, who lied about the handkerchief (3.4.24).

123 **Foh** signifies disgust, *fie* disapproval. Cf. *Ham* 2.2.587, 'Fie upon't, foh!'

109–10] *as F; Q lines* guiltinesse / vse. / 110 SD] *Q (Enter* Em.*) opp.* vse; *not in F* 'Las, what's] *Q;* Alas, what is *F* 111 What's] *Q;* What is *F* 112 hath] *F;* has *Q* 114 dead] *Q;* quite dead *F* 116 fruits] *F;* fruite *Q* Prithee] *F;* pray *Q* 121 O fie] *F;* Fie, fie *Q* 121–3] *this edn;* QF *lines* honest, / me. / thee. / 123 Foh, fie] *Q (*fough*);* Fie *F*

IAGO

Kind gentlemen, let's go see poor Cassio dressed.
Come, mistress, you must tell's another tale.
Emilia, run you to the citadel
And tell my lord and lady what hath happed.
– Will you go on afore? – This is the night
That either makes me or fordoes me quite.

Exeunt.

[5.2] *Enter* OTHELLO, *with a light.* DESDEMONA *in her bed* [*asleep*].

OTHELLO

It is the cause, it is the cause, my soul!
Let me not name it to you, you chaste stars,
It is the cause. Yet I'll not shed her blood
Nor scar that whiter skin of hers than snow

124 **Kind** almost = good (but more ingratiating) **dressed** bandaged

125 Cf. Dent, T49, 'To tell another tale'; *tell's* = tell us.

127 **and lady** Should Iago register that he thinks the lady already dead, perhaps by the slightest hesitation after *lord*?

128–9 **This . . . quite** He fails to realize that the night may make *and* 'fordo' him.

129 **makes me** i.e. brings me success **fordoes me quite** ruins, undoes me completely (*quite* = completely, *OED* 1). He repeats 5.1.4.

5.2 For the staging, see LN. For 5.2.1–20 see also pp. 370–4.

1 **cause** could = ground for action; the case of one party in a law suit; a matter before a court for decision. How characteristic of Othello that he does not define the cause (= chastity? purity? the good of the world in general?)! See J. Money, in *SS*, 6 (1953), 94–105. **my soul** Addressing one's soul is common in the Bible (Genesis 49.6, Psalms 16.2, etc.) and in classical literature. For the biblical imagery of this speech, see J. E. Hankins, *Shakespeare's Derived Imagery* (1953); also J. Tobin, in *N and Q*, NS 24 (1977), 112; and in *SS*, 31 (1978), 33–43.

2 **stars** any celestial bodies, including the chaste moon (*MND* 2.1.162). In classical myth reluctant ladies pursued by Zeus were changed into stars.

4 Cf. Dent, S591, 'As white as (the driven) snow'. Snow, though, was connected with chastity (Money, as in In., citing *Cym* 2.5.13, 'As chaste as unsunn'd snow'), so contradicts the charge of Desdemona's unchastity. Shakespeare also reanimates the cliché by *not* writing 'that skin of hers whiter than snow'.

124] *as Q; F lines* Gentlemen: / drest. / 127 hath] *F;* has *Q* 128 afore] *F;* I pray *Q* 129 makes] *F;* markes *Q* quite] *Q; F* (quight) **5.2**] *Scoena Secunda. F; not in Q* 0.1–2] *Enter* Othello *with a light. Q; Enter Othello, and Desdemona in her bed. F*

And smooth as monumental alabaster:　　　　　　　　5
Yet she must die, else she'll betray more men.
Put out the light, and then put out the light!　*Repetition.*
If I quench thee, thou flaming minister,
I can again thy former light restore　*metaphor,*　*Euphemism*
Should I repent me. But once put out thy light,　　　10
Thou cunning'st pattern of excelling nature,
I know not where is that Promethean heat
That can thy light relume! when I have plucked the rose
I cannot give it vital growth again,
It needs must wither. I'll smell thee on the tree;　　　15
O balmy breath, that dost almost persuade

There's (physically) a candle.

resolved that she must die

5 **monumental** i.e. as used for monuments; here referring to funeral monuments (where effigies often lie on their backs, heads resting on a stone 'pillow', hands pressed together in prayer, as if awaiting the resurrection. A hint for staging? The 'church' tableau is also suggested by Othello's candle).
alabaster often spelt alablaster *c.* 1600 (= QF). Cf. *Luc* 419, 'her alablaster skin', Dent, A95.2, 'As white as alabaster'.

6 **betray** prove false to; cheat (*OED* 2, 3)
more men His motives are as confused as Iago's. Does he really care what happens to *more men*?

7 **and . . . light** i.e. extinguish her life. Cf. Sidney's *Arcadia* (1593 edn, fos 231b, 237, of killing a princess), 'so soone may the fayrest light in the world be put out', 'become not the putters out of the worlds light' (from Steevens); C. A., *A Fig for Fortune* (1596), B3b, 'Out with thy candle [= life], let it burne no more', *Mac* 5.5.23, 'Out, out, brief candle!' A commonplace.

8 **flaming minister** Cf. Psalms 104.4, 'God maketh his angels spirits: and his ministers

a flaming fire', Hebrews 1.7; *minister* = servant.

10 **repent me** (reflexive verb) regret it, change my mind
But once but if I once

11 **thou most skilful instance** (or specimen, image, design, model) of nature excelling herself. Cf. 2.1.63–5, 'One that excels . . .'.

12 **Promethean** 'Shakespeare seems to be combining two separate Greek myths about Prometheus, one in which Prometheus gave fire to human-kind and one in which he was the creator of human-kind' (Folger).

13 **relume** relight (*OED*, first here, from late Lat. *reluminare*)

14 **vital** living

15 **needs** necessarily, inevitably

16 **O** Q *A* could = Ah.
balmy deliciously fragrant; cf. 20, 'So sweet'. Q's SD, '*He kisses her*', may refer to three kisses but, as the sense of smell is so important to him, I think he smells at 17, again at 19, here finishing with a kiss, as is also suggested by the placing of Q's SD. Q2 and later editors moved the SD, without authority.

5 alabaster] *QF (*Alablaster*)*　7 then put] *QF;* then – put *Hanman*　10 thy light] *F;* thine *Q*　11 cunning'st] *F;* cunning *Q*　13] *as Q; F lines* re-Lume. / Rose, / relume] *F;* returne *Q*　the] *Q;* thy *F*　15 needs must] *F;* must needes *Q*　thee] *F;* it *Q*　16 O] *F; A Q*　dost] *F;* doth *Q*

Justice to break her sword! Once more, once more:

Kisses ← (?)

Be thus when thou art dead and I will kill thee

And love thee after. Once more, and that's the last.

He [smells, then] kisses her.

So sweet was ne'er so fatal. I must weep, 20

But they are cruel tears. This sorrow's heavenly,

It strikes where it doth love. She wakes.

DESDEMONA

Who's there? Othello?

OTHELLO Ay, Desdemona.

DESDEMONA

Will you come to bed, my lord?

we see their connection – it's hard to watch.

OTHELLO

Have you prayed tonight, Desdemon?

He's about to kill her.

DESDEMONA Ay, my lord. 25

OTHELLO

If you bethink yourself of any crime

Unreconciled as yet to heaven and grace,

Solicit for it straight.

Kills her

DESDEMONA

Alack, my lord, what may you mean by that?

bc/

Othello cheating → kills her → insecurity, sense of inferiority

17 **Justice . . . sword** The sword and scales were emblems of Justice (traditionally female). The scales weighed the evidence (not here!), the sword punished.

17, 19 **Once** Either *one* or *once* looks like a minim error, common in Shakespeare generally (*Texts*, 82). Each is possible; I prefer *once more* since he refers, initially, to smelling, not kissing. But Shakespeare could have revised this speech (see p. 373).

20 **fatal** destructive; fateful

21 **cruel tears** 'meaning, I think, that the tears

are no sign of faltering purpose' (Ridley)

21–2 **This . . . love** Cf. Proverbs 3.12, 'For whom the Lord loveth, him he chasteneth', Hebrews 12.6.

23 **Ay** Note this word in this scene: at first quietly menacing (here, 33, 41, 70), then still resolute (139, 143), finally exhausted (295). Here it could be the pronoun: '(Yes, it is indeed) I, Desdemona.' *pride*

26 **bethink yourself** call to mind **crime** sin

27 **grace** (the source of grace, i.e.) God. So *AW* 1.3.220.

28 **Solicit** pray for pardon

17] Iustice her selfe to breake her sword once more, *Q; Iustice her selfe to breake her Sword. One more, one more: F* 19 Once] *Q;* One *F* that's] *F;* this *Q.* SD] *Q (opp. 19, 20); not in F* SD *smells, then] this edn; not in QF* 22 where it doth] *F;* when it does *Q* She wakes] *QF; as* SD *(Cam anon.)* 23 Ay] *QF (I)* 25 Desdemon] *F; Desdemona Q* 29] *as Q; F lines* Lord, / that? / Alack] *F;* Alas *Q*

OTHELLO

Well, do it, and be brief; I will walk by.
I would not kill thy unprepared spirit,
No, heaven forfend, I would not kill thy soul.

DESDEMONA

Talk you of killing?

OTHELLO

Ay, I do.

DESDEMONA

Then, heaven,
Have mercy on me!

OTHELLO

Amen, with all my heart.

DESDEMONA

If you say so, I hope you will not kill me.

OTHELLO Hum!

DESDEMONA

And yet I fear you, for you're fatal then
When your eyes roll so. Why I should fear I know not,
Since guiltiness I know not. But yet I feel I fear.

OTHELLO

Think on thy sins.

DESDEMONA

They are loves I bear to you.

OTHELLO

Ay, and for that thou diest.

DESDEMONA

That death's unnatural that kills for loving.

30 **by** i.e. aside

31–2 If he killed her *unpreparèd spirit* he would 'kill' her soul by sending it to hell (cf. *Ham* 3.3.73–95). Cf. Matthew 10.28, 'fear ye not them which kill the body, but are not able to kill the soul . . . fear him which is able to destroy both body and soul in hell'.

32 **heaven forfend** Cf. 182. Already a set phrase (as in *1H6* 5.4.65); *forfend* = forbid.

33–4 **Then** . . . **me!** Cf. 'Lord have mercy upon us!', a frequent response in the *Book of Common Prayer*. Cf. 57.

34 **Amen** a liturgical response, as at 57

36 **Hum!** probably our 'hmm!', a threatening sound

38 **Why** . . . **not** Cf. Ovid, *Heroides*, 1.71 'quid timeam, ignoro' (what – or how, why – I am to fear I know not).

40 **They** . . . **you** 'An allusion to the sin of loving a human being more than God' (Sanders). Yet she does not say she loves him more than God. Did Shakespeare write *bore*, misread *bere?* Then Othello would mean 'you die because you have stopped loving me'.

42 **That death's** i.e. that killing is

32 heaven] *Q;* Heauens *F* 33–4 Then . . . me] *as Cam³; one line QF* 35 so] *Q; not in F* 36 Hum] *Q; F (*Humh*)* 37 you're] *F;* you are *Q* 38] *as Q; F lines* so. / not, / 41 Ay] *F (*I*); not in Q*

Alas, why gnaw you so your nether lip?
Some bloody passion shakes your very frame,
These are portents: but yet I hope, I hope
They do not point on me.

OTHELLO Peace, and be still.

DESDEMONA
I will. So: what's the matter?

OTHELLO That handkerchief
Which I so loved and gave thee, thou gavest
To Cassio.

DESDEMONA No, by my life and soul:
Send for the man and ask him.

OTHELLO Sweet soul, take heed,
Take heed of perjury. Thou art on thy death-bed.

DESDEMONA
I? – but not yet to die!

OTHELLO Yes, presently.
Therefore confess thee freely of thy sin,
For to deny each article with oath
Cannot remove nor choke the strong conception

43 Cf. *R3* 4.2.27, 'The King is angry, see, he gnaws his lip.' Burbage played both Richard and Othello.

44 **bloody** portending bloodshed
frame body

45 **portents** omens

46 **They . . . me** i.e. they are not portents for me.
Peace . . . still Cf. Mark 4.39, 'he arose, and rebuked the wind, and said unto the sea, Peace, and be still'.

47 ***I will. So**: 'I will so' (as in most editions) is odd. 'Be still' implies that she is agitated: she becomes still ('I will'), then adds 'So' = So, I have done as you asked. Cf. 5.1.82, 'Lend me a garter. So.'

48 strong accusing stress on *thou*

50 **Sweet soul** usually an expression of tenderness (*MV* 5.1.49, *H5* 4.6.17)

51 **Thou art** scan 'Thou'rt'

52 ***I**? could be 'Ay,', but a strange reply either way; *but not yet to die* is a cry, an appeal, not a statement
presently immediately

53 confess your sin unreservedly, without holding anything back. He seems to mean 'confess to heaven *and to me*'.

54 **article** item (in the accusation)

55 **choke** smother, silence
strong grievous; irresistible (*OED* 11, 16)
conception notion. But could = embryo, offspring: this submerged image makes Othello the mother who *groans* and wants to *remove* an unwanted child (the notion of her adultery). For similar images, cf. 1.3.402–3, 2.1.127–8.

45 [2]I hope] *F; not in Q* 47 will. So:] *this edn;* will, so, *Q;* will so: *F* 47–52] *Q lines* gaue thee, / *Cassio.* / soule, / him. / periury, / death-bed. / die. / presently: /; *F lines* Handkerchiefe / *Cassio.* / man, / him. / Periury, / 48 gavest] *Q;* gau'st *F* 52 I? – but] *this edn;* I, but *QF* die!] *this edn;* die. *QF* Yes] *Q; not in F* 55 conception] *F;* conceit *Q*

That I do groan withal. Thou art to die.

DESDEMONA

Then Lord have mercy on me.

OTHELLO

I say amen.

DESDEMONA

And have you mercy too. I never did
Offend you in my life, never loved Cassio
But with such general warranty of heaven
As I might love: I never gave him token.

OTHELLO

By heaven, I saw my handkerchief in's hand!
O perjured woman, thou dost stone my heart
And makest me call what I intend to do
A murder, which I thought a sacrifice!
I saw the handkerchief.

DESDEMONA

He found it then,
I never gave it him. Send for him hither,
Let him confess the truth.

OTHELLO

He hath confessed.

DESDEMONA

What, my lord?

OTHELLO

That he hath – ud's death! – used thee.

57 Cf. 33–4n., and Psalms 6.2, 9.13, 27.7.
59 **Offend** wrong, sin against
60 **warranty** authorization
61 **might** am allowed to
token i.e. love token
63 **stone** turn to stone, make hard like stone (*OED* 2, first here). Repeating 4.1.179–80.
my Johnson defended Q *thy*: thou dost harden thy heart, leaving this life 'in the state of the *murdered* without preparation for death, when *I intended* that thy punishment should have been *a sacrifice* atoning for thy crime'.
65 Cf. *JC* 2.1.166.
68 **confess** declare, testify to
***the truth** a 'common error' (*Texts*, 95)? That is, F followed Q. At 126 *Q* again misprints *a* (for *the*) *truth*.
69 **That . . . thee** As F normally softens or omits profanity, and Q has lost something leading up to 'How, vnlawfully?', I retain both Q *vds death* and F *vs'd thee*, even though *vds* and *vsd* consist of the same three letters (which suggests transposition in Q or F). To retain Q profanity and eke out obvious Q omissions from F is normal procedure, and here yields regular metre.
used had sexual intercourse with (*OED* 10b). Cf. 3.3.277; *Tim* 4.3.84, 'Be a whore still. They love thee not that use thee', *Son* 20.14.

57 Then Lord] *Q;* O Heauen *F* 58–9] *as F; Q lines* too: / *Cassio,* / 62 in's] *F;* in his *Q* 63 my] *F;* thy *Q* 64 makest] *Q;* makes *F* 65ff. murder] *Q;* Murther *F throughout scene* 68 Let] *F;* And let *Q* the] *this edn;* a *QF* 69 hath] *F;* has *Q* ud's death! – used thee] *Alexander;* vds death. *Q;* vs'd thee. *F*

DESDEMONA
How? unlawfully?

OTHELLO
Ay.

DESDEMONA
He will not say so.

OTHELLO
No, his mouth is stopped. Honest Iago
Hath ta'en order for't.

DESDEMONA
O, my fear interprets!
What, is he dead?

OTHELLO
Had all his hairs been lives
My great revenge had stomach for them all.

DESDEMONA
Alas, he is betrayed, and I undone.

OTHELLO
Out, strumpet, weep'st thou for him to my face?

DESDEMONA
O, banish me, my lord, but kill me not!

OTHELLO
Down, strumpet!

DESDEMONA
Kill me tomorrow, let me live tonight!

OTHELLO
Nay, if you strive –

70 **He will not** i.e. surely he will not.
71 **mouth is stopped** Cf. 2.3.300.
72 **ta'en order** taken measures
interprets i.e. guesses the worst
73 **Had . . . lives** Cf. Dent, H30, 'As many as there are hairs on the head'; Psalms 40.15, 'my sins . . . are more in number than the hairs of my head'.
74 **had stomach** would have had appetite (to consume them all). Cf. 3.3.462–3.
75 **betrayed** treacherously destroyed by his enemies; Othello thinks 'revealed (as her lover)' (*OED* 6)
76 **Out** exclamation of abhorrence or reproach
weep'st . . . him He misinterprets again.
77 **banish** send or drive away
78 **Down** The stage image (a man forcing a woman down on a bed) is suggestive. Note that his three speeches in Q make up a pentameter: 'Downe strumpet. – Nay, an you striue. – It is too late.'
80 **strive** struggle, resist

71–2] *this edn;* QF *lines* stop'd, / for't. / 72–4] *this edn; Q lines* dead? / liues, / all. /; *F lines* dead? / Reuenge / all. / 72 O . . . interprets] *F;* My feare interprets then *Q* 74 them] *F;* 'em *Q* 76 Out] *F;* O *Q* weep'st] *F;* weepest *Q* 80 if] *F;* an *Q*

DESDEMONA

But half an hour!

OTHELLO Being done, there is no pause –

DESDEMONA

But while I say one prayer!

OTHELLO It is too late.

DESDEMONA

O Lord! Lord! Lord! [*He*] *smothers her.*

EMILIA (*within*)

My lord, my lord! what ho, my lord, my lord!

OTHELLO

What noise is this? Not dead? not yet quite dead?
I that am cruel am yet merciful,
I would not have thee linger in thy pain.
So, so.

EMILIA (*within*) What ho! my lord! my lord!

OTHELLO Who's there?

EMILIA [*within*]

O good my lord, I'd speak a word with you.

OTHELLO

Yes. 'Tis Emilia. – [*to Emilia.*] By and by. – She's dead.

81 **But** only
Being . . . pause perhaps = (while it is) being done, there must be (room for) no pause (stopping or hesitation)

82 **But . . . prayer** a common request: cf. Marlowe, *Massacre*, 301, 'O let me pray before I dye'. Othello's disregard of it reflects on his Christianity. I assume that she cries 'O Lord . . .' before he begins to smother her: it is more a prayer than a shriek.

83 **O** . . . [3]Lord! Granville-Barker defended Q's line, omitted by some editors. 'Imagine it: Desdemona's agonised cry to God, and as the sharp sound of it is slowly stifled, Emilia's voice at the door rising through it, using the same words in another sense. A macabre duet' (*Othello* [1945], p. 122).
SD See LN.

85 In some productions Emilia knocks on the door, with an effect like that of the 'knocking at the gate in *Macbeth*' (see De Quincey's famous essay).

88 **So, so** Cf. 4.1.123. Some actors and critics think Othello now stabs Desdemona (see M. Ware, in *ES*, 45 [1964], 177–80; Furness, 302ff.; Hankey, 319): I think it unlikely.

90 **By and by** soon. Common in Shakespeare and the Bible.

81 OTHELLO Being . . . pause] *F; not in Q* 82 It is] *F;* Tis *Q* 83 O . . . [3]Lord] *Q; not in F* SD] *he stifles her. Q; Smothers her. F (*QF *place* SD *after* too late *82)* 84 SD] Emillia *calls within. Q; Aemilia at the doore. F* 84] *as Q; F lines* hoa? / Lord. / 85 noise] *F;* voyce *Q* 86 that am] *Q, Fc;* am that *Fu* 88 SD] *F; not in Q* 89 SD] *Malone; not in QF* I'd] *Q;* I would *F* 90] *this edn;* Yes, tis *Emillia*, by and by: shee's dead: *Q;* Yes: 'Tis *Aemilia*: by and by. Shee's dead. *F*

'Tis like she comes to speak of Cassio's death,
The noise was high. Ha, no more moving?
Still as the grave. Shall she come in? were't good?
I think she stirs again. No – what's best to do?
If she come in, she'll sure speak to my wife.
My wife, my wife! what wife? I have no wife.
O insupportable, O heavy hour!
Methinks it should be now a huge eclipse
Of sun and moon, and that th'affrighted globe
Should yawn at alteration.

EMILIA [*within*] I do beseech you
That I may speak with you! O good my lord!

OTHELLO
I had forgot thee: O come in, Emilia.
Soft, by and by. Let me the curtains draw.
Where art thou? What's the matter with thee now?
[*He unlocks the door.*]

Enter EMILIA.

EMILIA
O my good lord, yonder's foul murders done!

91 **like** likely
92 **high** loud. The brawl outside was audible indoors (which explains the arrival of Lodovico and Gratiano in 5.1).
93 **Still . . . grave** Dent, D133.1, 'As dumb (silent, still) as death (the grave)'.
93, 95 **she** Emilia
94 **she** Desdemona
95 **my wife** Cf. 2.3.378n., 4.2.104.
97 **insupportable** unendurable. Could be an exclamation on its own (= O insupportable loss!) or an adjective qualifying *hour*. Cf. 1.3.259n. and *JC* 4.3.151, 'O insupportable and touching loss!'
heavy sorrowful
98–100 See LN.
99 **globe** earth
100 **yawn** gape (i.e. chasms should open in response to the changed appearance of sun and moon). Hart quoted Pliny, 2.80, 'Of the Gaping Chinks of the Earth': 'They [earthquakes] fortune also to be when the Sun and Moon are eclipsed.'
alteration this change (brought about by Desdemona's death). A limp last word: could it be an error?
103 **curtains** bed curtains
104 **What's . . . now**? What do you want now?

92 high] *F;* here *Q* moving?] *F;* mouing, *Q* 94 best to do?] *F;* the best *Q* 96 what . . . have] *F;* my wife; I ha *Q* 97 insupportable,] *this edn;* insupportable: *Q;* insupportable! *F* 99 th'] *F;* the *Q* 100] Should *Q;* Did *F* SD] *not in QF* 101 That] *F; not in Q* O] *F; not in Q* 104.1] *as Theobald; not in QF* 104.2] *as F; opp. 103 Q*

OTHELLO

What? now?

EMILIA

But now, my lord.

OTHELLO

It is the very error of the moon,
She comes more nearer earth than she was wont
And makes men mad.

EMILIA Cassio, my lord, hath killed
A young Venetian, called Roderigo.

OTHELLO

Roderigo killed? and Cassio killed?

EMILIA

No, Cassio is not killed.

OTHELLO Not Cassio killed?
Then murder's out of tune, and sweet revenge
Grows harsh.

DESDEMONA O falsely, falsely murdered!

EMILIA

O lord, what cry is that?

OTHELLO

That? what?

106 **What? now?** I prefer F to Q: it better conveys his sense of shock.

107 **But now** just now, only this moment (*OED* but 6b)

108 **very** *either* 'solely' (adverb), *or* 'indeed' (intensive) (Elliott, 104)
error mistake; wandering off course (Lat. *erro*, I wander)

109 **She** *Luna*, the moon, is feminine in Latin. Cf. 17n.
more nearer double comparative, common in Shakespeare

110 **makes men mad** The word lunacy shows how long and firmly men have believed in a connection between the moon and madness (Ridley).

111 **Venetian** (four syllables)

113 **Not . . . killed**? more disorientated than 'Cassio not killed!'

114–15 **and . . . harsh** and (the sweet music of) revenge grows harsh

115 **falsely** wrongly, mistakenly. She seems to reply to 114. See also 325–6n., and *Warning for Fair Women* (1599), Fla, 'What sound was that? it was not he that spake' (a 'dead' person speaks).
murdered disyllabic, which gives a nine-syllable line. The verse can be divided differently but, however we rearrange it, always breaks down. The broken lines highlight the speakers' tension.

116 **cry** utterance (not necessarily loud). Desdemona is concealed behind the bed curtains.

106 What? now?] *F;* What, now? *Q* 109 nearer] *F;* neere the *Q* 110 hath] *F;* has *Q* 113–15] *this edn;* QF *lines* tune, / harsh. / murdered. / 116 O lord] *Q;* Alas *F*

EMILIA

Out and alas, that was my lady's voice:

[*She draws the bed-curtains.*]

Help, help, ho, help! O lady, speak again,
Sweet Desdemona, O sweet mistress, speak!

DESDEMONA

A guiltless death I die.

EMILIA

O, who hath done
This deed?

DESDEMONA Nobody. I myself. Farewell.
Commend me to my kind lord – O, farewell! *She dies.*

OTHELLO

Why, how should she be murdered?

EMILIA

Alas, who knows?

OTHELLO

You heard her say herself it was not I.

EMILIA

She said so; I must needs report the truth.

OTHELLO

She's like a liar gone to burning hell:
'Twas I that killed her.

EMILIA

O, the more angel she,
And you the blacker devil!

OTHELLO

She turned to folly, and she was a whore.

EMILIA

Thou dost belie her, and thou art a devil.

118 **Out and alas** Cf. 76n. Usually 'out alas' (*Tit* 2.3.258, *MW* 4.5.63, *WT* 4.4.110); 'Out and' may be for emphasis.

121–2 Dividing as here, 'done / This deed', is unusual, but gives two consecutive pentameters instead of short lines. A slight pause after *done* mirrors Emilia's consternation. See *Texts*, 108.

124 **how . . . be** how should she come to be

127–8 Perhaps he thinks also of 58ff., though primarily of 122–3.

130 **folly** wickedness; unchastity (*OED* 2, 3). Cf. Deuteronomy 22.21, 'She hath wrought folly in Israel, to play the whore in her father's house.'

131 **Thou** Cf. *you* 129. Her indignation carries her away. *Belie* = slander.

118 that was] *F;* it is *Q* SD] *Cam² subst.; not in QF* 121 hath] *F;* has *Q* 121–2 O . . . deed?] *as Capell; one line QF* 123 SD] *Q; not in F* 125 heard] *Q;* heare *F* 126 the truth] *F;* a truth *Q* 127 burning] *QF;* burne in *Q3* 128–9 O . . . devil] *as Q; prose F*

OTHELLO
She was false as water.

EMILIA
Thou art rash as fire to say
That she was false. O, she was heavenly true!

OTHELLO
Cassio did top her: ask thy husband else.
O, I were damned beneath all depth in hell
But that I did proceed upon just grounds
To this extremity. Thy husband knew it all.

EMILIA
My husband?

OTHELLO
Thy husband.

EMILIA
That she was false?
To wedlock?

OTHELLO
Ay, with Cassio. Had she been true,
If heaven would make me such another world
Of one entire and perfect chrysolite,
I'd not have sold her for it.

EMILIA
My husband?

132 **false as water** Cf. Dent, W86.1, 'As unstable (false) as water' (from Genesis 49.4).
rash as fire Cf. Dent, F246.1, 'As hasty as fire'. Scan 'wat'r / Thou'rt' (Abbott, 464, 465).

133 **heavenly true** Cf. Dent, G173, 'As false as God is true'. True = true to you; virtuous.

134 **top** Cf. 1.1.88n.
else i.e. if you don't believe me (*OED* 4c)

135 Cf. Psalms 86.13, 'thou hast delivered my soul from the nethermost hell'.

137 **extremity** utmost penalty; extreme rigour or measure (*OED* 3b, 6, 9)

138, 142, 145 **My husband?** 'Emilia's repeated astonishment at Iago's complicity is the argument in favour of her not having suspected him to be the "eternal villain" [of 4.2.132]' (Hart). Hart, however, interpreted QF '?' as '!' in all three lines. If we retain '?', she could speak quietly at first, adjusting to an explanation that she had already suspected (a different kind of surprise).

138–9 Cf. 121–2: an unusual line division again gives 'regular' metre (*Texts*, 120).

140 **such another** (*OED* 1c) another of the same sort (but made of chrysolite)

141 Cf. *Faerie Queene*, 1.7.33 (Arthur's shield), 'But *all of Diamond perfect* pure and cleene / It framed was, one massy *entire* mould.'
entire complete, perfect, pure
chrysolite See LN.

142 **sold** exchanged. Cf. *2H6* 3.1.92, 'Or sell my title for a glorious grave'.

132–3 Thou . . . true] *as F; Q lines* fire, / true. / 132 art] *F;* as *Q* 134 top] *QF;* tup *Pope*[2] 138–9 That . . . wedlock] *this edn; one line QF* 139 Had] *as F;* nay, had *Q*

OTHELLO

Ay, 'twas he that told me on her first;
An honest man he is, and hates the slime
That sticks on filthy deeds.

EMILIA

My husband!

OTHELLO

What needs
This iterance, woman? I say thy husband.

EMILIA

O mistress, villainy hath made mocks with love!
My husband say she was false?

OTHELLO

He, woman;
I say thy husband: dost understand the word?
My friend thy husband, honest, honest Iago.

EMILIA

If he say so, may his pernicious soul
Rot half a grain a day! he lies to th' heart:
She was too fond of her most filthy bargain!

OTHELLO

Ha!

EMILIA

Do thy worst:
This deed of thine is no more worthy heaven
Than thou wast worthy her.

OTHELLO

Peace, you were best!

143 **on** of; *tell on* = play the informer (*OED* 16)
144 **slime** suggests sexual slime: *filthy* (= obscene) *deeds* are sexual here (cf. 4.2.72ff., 4.3.63ff.)
146 **iterance** repetition. Shakespeare's coinage; Q *iteration* was common.
146 **woman** deliberately discourteous, as often in the Bible (John 2.4, 'Jesus sayth unto her, Woman, what have I to do with thee?')
147 **made mocks with** usually *at* or *of*: 'made a mock(ery) of'
150 **friend** Cf. 3.3.145, 5.1.32n.
151 **pernicious** destructive; evil
152 **grain** particle. A slow death is the worst: cf. 4.1.175, 'nine years a-killing'.
lies . . . heart lies down to his very heart, i.e. he's an out-and-out liar. More emphatic than the proverbial 'To lie in one's throat' (Dent, T268).
153 **filthy** a 'racist' jibe, provoked by his *filthy* 145
156 **worthy** worthy of. She returns to 127ff., their dispute about the *angel* and *devil*.
157 **you were best** it would be best for you

143 on her] *F; not in Q* 145–6 What . . . husband] *one line Q; F lines* Woman? / Husband. / 146 iterance, woman?] *F subst.;* iteration? woman, *Q* 147–50] *F; not in Q* 147] *F lines* Mistris, / loue: /*; one line Q2* 154 Ha!] *QF (*Ha?*)*

EMILIA

Thou hast not half that power to do me harm
As I have to be hurt. O gull, O dolt,
As ignorant as dirt! Thou hast done a deed
[*He threatens her with his sword.*]
– I care not for thy sword, I'll make thee known
Though I lost twenty lives. Help, help, ho, help!
The Moor hath killed my mistress! Murder, murder!

Enter MONTANO, GRATIANO *and* IAGO.

MONTANO

What is the matter? How now, general?

EMILIA

O, are you come, Iago? you have done well
That men must lay their murders on your neck.

GRATIANO

What is the matter?

EMILIA

Disprove this villain, if thou be'st a man;
He says thou told'st him that his wife was false,
I know thou didst not, thou'rt not such a villain.
Speak, for my heart is full.

IAGO

I told him what I thought, and told no more
Than what he found himself was apt and true.

EMILIA

But did you ever tell him she was false?

158–9 **Thou . . . hurt** i.e. she can endure more than he can inflict (*harm* = hurt). Cf. *H8* 3.2.387ff., 'able . . . To endure more miseries . . . Than my weak-hearted enemies dare offer'.

159 **gull** dupe
dolt block-head, i.e. slow thinker

160 **dirt** resuming *filthy* (153), a jibe that went home. *OED* 1 glosses dirt as 'ordure = excrement', so this is another racist jibe at Othello's colour.

161 **care not for** don't fear
make thee known expose you

164 **How now** could be a question or interjection (*OED* how 4: modern equivalent 'What?' or 'What!')

166 **on your neck** to your charge

173 **apt** likely

158 that] *F;* the *Q* 160 SD] *not in QF* 161 known] *F;* know *Q* 162 ho] *F (*hoa*);* O *Q* 163 hath] *F;* has *Q* 163.1] *F; Enter* Montano, Gratiano, Iago, *and others. Q* 166 murders] *F (*Murthers*);* murder *Q* 167 SP] *as F; All Q* 170 thou'rt] *F;* thou art *Q* 172] *as Q; F lines* thought, / more / 174] *as Q; F lines* him, / false? /

IAGO

I did.

EMILIA

You told a lie, an odious, damned lie!
Upon my soul, a lie, a wicked lie!
She false with Cassio? Did you say with Cassio?

IAGO

With Cassio, mistress. Go to, charm your tongue.

EMILIA

I will not charm my tongue, I am bound to speak:
My mistress here lies murdered in her bed.

ALL

O heavens forfend!

EMILIA

And your reports have set the murder on.

OTHELLO

Nay, stare not, masters, it is true indeed.

GRATIANO

'Tis a strange truth.

MONTANO

O monstrous act!

EMILIA

Villainy, villainy, villainy!
I think upon't, I think I smell't, O villainy!
I thought so then: I'll kill myself for grief!
O villainy, villainy!

176 **odious, damned** *either* 'o-di-ous damn'd', *or* 'od-yus dam-nèd'

177 **Upon my soul** by the salvation of my soul (more deeply felt than the later ' 'pon my soul')
wicked evil, depraved, malicious (a richer word than today)

179 **charm** control. Cf. *TS* 4.2.58, *2H6* 4.1.64.

180 **bound** duty-bound; compelled, obliged (*OED* 7)

183 **set . . . on** incited

184 **masters** Cf. 2.3.116n.

185 **a strange truth** Cf. *MND* 5.1.2, *MM* 5.1.44.

187 **Villainy** a richer word than now, ranging from boorishness to discourtesy to extreme wickedness (*OED* 1, 6)

188 **think upon** remember, call to mind (*OED* 5c).
smell suspect, detect

178] *as Q; F lines Cassio? / Cassio? /* 179] *as Q; F lines* Mistris? / tongue. / 180] *as Q; F lines* Tongue; / speake, / 181–90] *F; not in Q* 181 murdered] *F (*murthered*)* 182 heavens] *F (*Heauens,*)* 184] *Q2; F lines* Masters, / indeede. / 188 think I smell't, O] *this edn;* thinke: I smel't: O *F*

IAGO
What, are you mad? I charge you, get you home.
EMILIA
Good gentlemen, let me have leave to speak.
'Tis proper I obey him – but not now.
Perchance, Iago, I will ne'er go home.
OTHELLO
O! O! O! *Othello falls on the bed.*
EMILIA
Nay, lay thee down and roar
For thou hast killed the sweetest innocent
That e'er did lift up eye.
OTHELLO
O, she was foul.
I scarce did know you, uncle: there lies your niece
Whose breath, indeed, these hands have newly
stopped;
I know this act shows horrible and grim.
GRATIANO
Poor Desdemon, I am glad thy father's dead;
Thy match was mortal to him, and pure grief
Shore his old thread in twain. Did he live now
This sight would make him do a desperate turn,

193 Cf. Ephesians 5.24, 'as the Church is subject unto Christ, likewise the wives to their own husbands in all things'.

195 a prolonged *roar*, not three separate sounds. Cf. 5.1.62n. A 'Herculean' feature: 'so did he with his roarings smite the stars' (Seneca, *Hercules Oetaeus*, 801ff.).

196 **Nay** used as an introductory word, without any negation (*OED* 1d); almost = yes

198 **lift up eye** Cf. Luke 6.20 and Psalms 121.1, 'I will lift up mine eyes unto the hills'; perhaps implying that she usually kept her eyes modestly down.

199 **uncle** i.e. Desdemona's uncle, presumably Brabantio's brother: cf. 1.1.173.

200 **these hands** He speaks as if his hands, not he, killed Desdemona. Cf. Macbeth's 'detached' hands, 2.2.56, 'What hands are here? Hah! they pluck out mine eyes.'

201 **shows** appears
grim merciless, cruel

203 **mortal** fatal
pure (intensive: *OED* 3b) utter

204 **Shore** sheared. Cf. *MND* 5.1.340, 'you have shore / With shears his thread'.
thread i.e. thread of life, 'which it was the prerogative of the Fate Atropos to sever with her shears' (Ridley)

205 **turn** act

191] *as Q; F lines* mad? / home. / 195 SD] *Q; not in F* 201 horrible] *F;* terrible *Q* 202] *as Q; F lines Desdemon*: / dead, / Desdemon] *F; Desdemona Q* 204 in twain] *F;* atwane *Q*

Yea, curse his better angel from his side
And fall to reprobance.

OTHELLO

'Tis pitiful; but yet Iago knows
That she with Cassio hath the act of shame
A thousand times committed. Cassio confessed it,
And she did gratify his amorous works
With that recognizance and pledge of love
Which I first gave her: I saw it in his hand,
It was a handkerchief, an antique token
My father gave my mother.

EMILIA

O God, O heavenly God!

IAGO

Zounds, hold your peace!

EMILIA

'Twill out, 'twill out! I peace?
No, I will speak as liberal as the north.
Let heaven and men and devils, let them all,
All, all cry shame against me, yet I'll speak.

206 **better angel** Cf. the Good and Bad Angel in Marlowe, *Doctor Faustus*, and *Son* 144, 'Tempteth my better angel from my side'.

207 **reprobance** a coinage: the state of being a reprobate, a sinner rejected by God. With QF *reprobation–Reprobance*, cf. QF *iteration–itterance* (146) and *Texts*, 86.

208 **pitiful** Cf. 4.1.192–3.

209 **act of shame** Cf. 2.1.225, 'the act of sport'.

211 **gratify** reward
works acts, deeds (*OED* 1), i.e. caresses

212 **recognizance** token

214 **antique** olden, belonging to former times; or, old-fashioned (*OED* 3, first in 1647). Perhaps stressed on first syllable.

215 This contradicts 3.4.57ff. Some think that he wanted to frighten Desdemona in 3.4, but the contradiction may be an oversight.

217–18 These lines may be revised in F: see *Texts*, 18.

217 **'Twill out** i.e. the facts will come out. But is there a hint that Emilia has bottled up a guilty secret, which now bursts forth? Cf. *Look About You* (1600), D4a, 'Twill out, twill out, my selfe my selfe can ease'.

218 **as . . . north** as freely as the north wind speaks (or blows), Cf. 2.1.5, 'the wind hath spoke aloud', *TC* 1.3.253, 'Speak frankly as the wind'.

220 **shame** because she defies her husband?

207 reprobance] *F;* reprobation *Q* 212 that] *F;* the *Q* 216 [1]God] *Q;* Heauen *F* [2]God] *Q;* Powres *F* Zounds] *Q;* Come *F* 217–18] *F;* 'Twill out, 'twill: I hold my peace sir, no, / I'le be in speaking, liberall as the ayre, *Q* 219 them] *F;* em *Q*

IAGO
Be wise and get you home.

EMILIA
I will not. [*Iago tries to stab Emilia.*]

GRATIANO Fie! Your sword upon a woman?

EMILIA
O thou dull Moor, that handkerchief thou speak'st of
I found by fortune and did give my husband,
For often, with a solemn earnestness
– More than indeed belonged to such a trifle –
He begged of me to steal't.

IAGO Villainous whore!

EMILIA
She give it Cassio? No, alas, I found it
And I did give't my husband.

IAGO Filth, thou liest!

EMILIA
By heaven I do not, I do not, gentlemen!
O murderous coxcomb, what should such a fool
Do with so good a wife?
[*Othello runs at Iago. Iago stabs his wife.*]

OTHELLO Are there no stones in heaven
But what serves for the thunder? Precious villain!

GRATIANO
The woman falls, sure he hath killed his wife.

222 **Your sword upon** use your sword against
223 **dull** obtuse, stupid
224 **fortune** chance
225 **solemn** imposing
226 **belonged** was appropriate
231 **coxcomb** (a cap worn by a professional fool, hence) fool, simpleton
232 **Do** have to do (*OED* 40), i.e. what business has he to have so good a wife?
SD ***runs at*** either 'rushes at', or 'runs his sword at, strikes at' (*OED* 5, 14, 48). Apart from entrances and exits, this is the only centred SD in Q, and it is unusually specific. Note the sequence: Othello attacks, Iago dodges away and, doing so, stabs Emilia.
stones thunderbolts or 'thunder-stones' (*JC* 1.3.49), to punish offenders; cf. *Cym* 5.5.240. 'Has not heaven one supernumerary bolt, to hurl directly at . . . this atrocious villain? Must all . . . of its arsenal be reserved for . . . ordinary thunder?' (Malone).
233 **Precious** (intensive) egregious

222 SD] *as Rowe (*Iago *offers to stab his wife); not in QF* 223] *as Q; F lines* Moore, / of / of] *F;* on *Q* 227 't] *F;* it *Q* 228 give] *F;* gaue *Q* 232 wife] *F;* woman *Q* SD] *The Moore runnes at* Iago. Iago *kils his wife. Q; not in F* 233] *as Q; F lines* Thunder? / Villaine. / Precious] *QF;* pernitious *Q2* 234] *as Q; F lines* falles: / Wife. / hath] *F;* has *Q*

EMILIA
Ay, ay; O lay me by my mistress' side. *Exit Iago.*
GRATIANO
He's gone, but his wife's killed.
MONTANO
'Tis a notorious villain. Take you this weapon
Which I have here recovered from the Moor;
Come, guard the door without, let him not pass
But kill him rather. I'll after that same villain,
For 'tis a damned slave. *Exeunt Montano and Gratiano.*
OTHELLO I am not valiant neither,
But every puny whipster gets my sword.
But why should honour outlive honesty?
Let it go all.
EMILIA What did thy song bode, lady?
Hark, canst thou hear me? I will play the swan
And die in music. [*Sings.*] Willow, willow, willow.
– Moor, she was chaste, she loved thee, cruel Moor,
So come my soul to bliss as I speak true!

237 **notorious** obvious, evident (*OED* 3, first in 1608)
238 **recovered** obtained, got hold of (*OED* 6); not 'taken back from'
239 **without** from the outside
241 **damned** damnable, accursed. Probably 'damnèd', although 'damn'd' and 'I'm' would give a pentameter.
neither 'used to strengthen a preceding negative: = either' (*OED* 3). He seems to voice an unspoken train of thought: I am a 'dull Moor', I have failed to kill Iago, I am a failure – and 'I am not valiant either'. He is no longer the 'valiant Othello' of 1.3.48–9. A process of self-assessment has begun.
242 **whipster** an insignificant person; one who wields a whip. This is not to disparage Montano: he means 'every whip can defeat my sword'.
gets = takes
sword The Moors in other plays carry a scimitar: not Othello.
243 **honour** esteem (from others), an honourable reputation
honesty integrity
244 **Let . . . all** more emphatic than 'Let it all go.' But *all* may be an adverb = entirely.
bode forebode; mean
245 **Hark . . . me** alluding to the belief that the souls of the dead linger near the body for a while
swan Cf. Dent, S1028, 'Like a swan, he sings before his death', *MV* 3.2.44, *KJ* 5.7.21.

235 SD] *Q; not in F* 237 you this] *F;* your *Q* 238 here] *Q; not in F* 241 SD] *Exit* Mont. *and* Gratiano. *Q; Exit. F* 244–6 What . . . [3]willow] *F; not in Q* 246 SD] *as Dyce; not in QF* Willow] *F (Willough)*

So speaking as I think, alas, I die. *She dies.*

OTHELLO

I have another weapon in this chamber,
It is a sword of Spain, the ice-brook's temper;
O, here it is. Uncle, I must come forth.

GRATIANO [*within*]

If thou attempt it it will cost thee dear;
Thou hast no weapon, and perforce must suffer.

OTHELLO

Look in upon me then, and speak with me,
Or, naked as I am, I will assault thee.

[*Enter* GRATIANO.]

GRATIANO

What is the matter?

OTHELLO Behold, I have a weapon,
A better never did itself sustain
Upon a soldier's thigh. I have seen the day
That with this little arm and this good sword
I have made my way through more impediments
Than twenty times your stop: but, O vain boast,
Who can control his fate? 'Tis not so now.
Be not afraid, though you do see me weaponed:
Here is my journey's end, here is my butt

249 Cf. Dent, S725, 'To speak as one thinks'. **alas** sometimes substituted for profanity in F (e.g. 2.3.154, 5.2.116) so Q *I die* may be corrupt. *I die, I die* sounds uncomfortably like *MND* 5.1.306, 'Now die, die, die, die, die'.

251 See LN.

252 **Uncle** Cf. 199n.

254 **suffer** i.e. be injured or killed

256 **naked** without weapon (or armour) (*OED* 4)

258 **sustain** maintain its position (*OED* 11e)

259 **I . . . day** Cf. Dent, D81.1, 'I have seen the day'; *RJ* 1.5.21, *KL* 5.3.277.

262 **your stop** the obstruction you offer **vain** empty; vainglorious

263 **control** command, exercise control over **fate** Cf. Dent, F83, 'It is impossible to avoid fate'. He blames fate, the stars, luck, etc. (270, 339) to minimize his own guilt.

264 **weaponed** armed. Cf. *wived, womaned* (2.1.60, 3.4.195).

265 **Here** Desdemona? Or, here in this place? **butt** terminal point; that towards which his efforts are directed, end

249 alas, I die] *F;* I die, I die *Q* SD] *Q; not in F* 251 is] *Q;* was *F* ice-brook's] *F (*Ice brookes*);* Isebrookes *Q* 253 SD] *Q (*Gra. *within.) opp. 252* 255 with] *F;* to *Q* 256.1] *as Theobald; not in QF* 262 your] *F;* you *Q* 264–70] *F; not in Q*

And very sea-mark of my utmost sail.
Do you go back dismayed? 'tis a lost fear:
Man but a rush against Othello's breast
And he retires. Where should Othello go?
Now: how dost thou look now? O ill-starred wench,
Pale as thy smock. When we shall meet at compt
This look of thine will hurl my soul from heaven
And fiends will snatch at it. Cold, cold, my girl,
Even like thy chastity. O cursed, cursed slave!
Whip me, ye devils,
From the possession of this heavenly sight!
Blow me about in winds, roast me in sulphur,
Wash me in steep-down gulfs of liquid fire!

266 **sea-mark** the boundary or limit of the flow of the sea; a conspicuous object which guides sailors in navigation
utmost farthest; last (*OED* 1, 3). Cf. *MM* 2.1.36, 'that's the utmost of his pilgrimage'.
267 **dismayed** appalled (stronger than today)
lost groundless
268 **Man . . . against** use a mere rush as a weapon against. Cf. *KJ* 4.3.129–30, 'a rush will be a beam / To hang thee on'.
270 **ill-starred** ill-fated. A coinage, like 'star-crossed' (*RJ* Prol. 6). Perhaps alluding to Disdemona's name (= the unfortunate one, to which Cinthio drew attention: p. 395).
wench Cf. 3.3.317n.
271 **Pale . . . smock** Cf. Dent, C446, 'As pale as a clout (= piece of cloth)'.
compt the Day of Judgement ([ac]compt = account); cf. *AW* 5.3.57, 'the great compt'. This was a popular subject with Renaissance painters, who depicted the damned being hurled from heaven and seized in mid-air by devils: also found in bibles, stained-glass windows, emblem books, etc.
273–4 **Cold . . . chastity** Cf. Dent, I1, 'As chaste as ice (snow)'. Cf. 3.4.39, 'Hot, hot, and moist', 5.2.4.
274 **O . . . slave** He curses himself (or possibly Iago). Placed in the same line with *Even . . . chastity* in both Q and F (Q has only one *cursed*, = cursèd; F has two, = curs'd, curs'd). Some editors move the words down one line and print 'O cursèd, cursèd slave! Whip me, ye devils /'.
276 **possession** i.e. having, enjoying (he does not deserve to enjoy a 'heavenly sight': his rightful place is hell)
heavenly a word associated with 'the divine Desdemona': cf. 4.3.65, 5.2.133
277–8 See LN.
277 **roast . . . sulphur** Cf. 3.3.332n.
278 **steep-down** precipitous (unique in Shakespeare)
gulfs perhaps influenced by Luke 16.19ff.: the rich man, tormented by flames in hell, looks up and sees Lazarus in Abraham's bosom. Between them is a 'great gulf'.
liquid fire Cf. Revelation 19.20, 'cast quick into a pond of fire, burning with brimstone'.

271 compt] *F;* count *Q* 274 [2]cursed] *F; not in Q* 275 ye] *F;* you *Q*

O Desdemon! dead, Desdemon. Dead! O, O!

Enter LODOVICO, MONTANO, *Officers with* IAGO, *prisoner, and* CASSIO *in a chair.*

LODOVICO
Where is this rash and most unfortunate man?

OTHELLO
That's he that was Othello? here I am.

LODOVICO
Where is that viper? bring the villain forth.

OTHELLO
I look down towards his feet, but that's a fable.
If that thou be'st a devil, I cannot kill thee.
[*Wounds Iago*.]

LODOVICO
Wrench his sword from him.

IAGO
I bleed, sir, but not killed.

OTHELLO
I am not sorry neither, I'd have thee live:
For in my sense 'tis happiness to die.

279 Like Lear's 'Never, never . . .' (5.3.309), this line can be spoken in many ways. F's punctuation is not likely to be Shakespeare's.
O, O! probably a single prolonged moan or cry: cf. 195n.

281 **That's . . . Othello** Some editors take this as a statement. I prefer a question (*That's* = that's to say): 'You mean – he that was Othello?' He is on the verge of disowning himself. Cf. the *he–I* switch at 353–4, and, in a different context, *TN* 1.5.234, 'such a one I was this present'.

283 **his** Iago's. Othello means the fable that the devil has a cloven foot (Tilley, D252).

285 **Wrench** Others hold Othello now; he probably surrenders his sword without a struggle.
I . . . killed sarcastic: 'I bleed (like a human being), but I'm not killed (therefore I may be a devil).

287 for one who feels as I do would think it happiness to die

279] *F;* O *Desdemona, Desdemoua*, dead, O, o, o. *Q* 279.1–2] *Enter* Lodouico, Montano, Iago, *and Officers*, Cassio *in a Chaire. Q; Enter Lodouico, Cassio, Montano, and Iago, with Officers. F; . . .* Cassio *led in wounded*, Montano, *and* Iago *Prisoner, with Officers. Rowe* 280 unfortunate] *F;* infortunate *Q* 281 Othello?] *this edn; Othello, Q; Othello: F* 282] *as Q; F lines* Viper? / forth. / that] *F;* this *Q* 284 If that] *F;* If *Q* SD] *Rowe; not in QF* 285 Wrench] *F;* Wring *Q* 286 live] *Qc, F;* loue *Qu.*

LODOVICO

O thou Othello, that wert once so good,
Fallen in the practice of a cursed slave,
What shall be said to thee?

OTHELLO

Why, anything;
An honourable murderer, if you will,
For nought I did in hate, but all in honour.

LODOVICO

This wretch hath part confessed his villainy.
Did you and he consent in Cassio's death?

OTHELLO

Ay.

CASSIO

Dear general, I never gave you cause.

OTHELLO

I do believe it, and I ask your pardon.
Will you, I pray, demand that demi-devil
Why he hath thus ensnared my soul and body?

IAGO

Demand me nothing. What you know, you know.

288 **O thou Othello** a curious form of address, but common in this play, usually spoken to or by Othello: 'O thou foul thief', 'O thou weed', 'O thou public commoner', 'O thou dull Moor', 'O thou pernicious caitiff' (1.2.62; 4.2.68, 74; 5.2.223, 316). Less respectful than *you*.

289 **in the practice** through the treachery or intrigue

cursed cursèd

290 **What . . . thee?** What can we possibly say to you?

anything anything you like; or perhaps a question, 'why (say) anything?'

292 **in honour** with honourable intent. Is he deceiving himself?

293 **part** partly

294 **consent in** agree in planning

296 **Dear general** Othello can inspire strong affection, not only in Desdemona.

I . . . cause Cf. 3.4.158.

297 Cf. Hamlet's similar apology to Laertes, shortly before his death, 'Give me your pardon, sir. I have done you wrong' (5.2.226).

298 **demi-devil** apparently Shakespeare's coinage. Othello accepts that Iago bleeds, therefore is not a proper devil: cf. 284–5.

299 **and body** He foresees his own damnation. Cf. *Homilies*, 82, 'damnation both of body and soul', and 357; Matthew 10.28, quoted 31–2n.

288 wert] *Q;* was *F* 289 cursed] *F;* damned *Q* 290 shall] *F;* should *Q* 292 I did] *F;* did I *Q* 296 never gave] *F;* did neuer giue *Q* 297 your] *F;* you *Q* 298 I pray] *F;* pray *Q*

From this time forth I never will speak word.

LODOVICO
What, not to pray?

GRATIANO Torments will ope your lips.

OTHELLO
Well, thou dost best.

LODOVICO
Sir, you shall understand what hath befallen,
Which, as I think, you know not. Here is a letter
Found in the pocket of the slain Roderigo,
And here another: the one of them imports
The death of Cassio, to be undertook
By Roderigo.

OTHELLO
O villain!

CASSIO Most heathenish and most gross!

LODOVICO
Now here's another discontented paper
Found in his pocket too, and this, it seems,
Roderigo meant t'have sent this damned villain
But that, belike, Iago in the nick
Came in, and satisfied him.

301 For his refusal to explain, cf. Hieronimo in *The Spanish Tragedy*, 'Sufficeth I may not, nor I will not tell thee' (Revels, 4.4.182); 'I'll speak no more but "Vengeance rot you all!" ' (*Tit* 5.1.58). How does Iago bear himself from now on? Some actors make him 'switch off', as if he has lost interest; others make him gloat in triumph.

302 **Torments** tortures

303 Does he mean 'Thou dost best not to tell us'?

304ff. Such summaries of the action are common in plays of the period: cf. *Tit* (as in 301n.) and Friar Lawrence in *RJ* 5.3.229ff. Here Shakespeare focuses less on events than on reactions to events.

304 **befallen** happened

305 **a letter** Letters that conveniently help the plot are a convention of comedy: *TGV* 4.4.121ff., *LLL* 4.3.191ff., *TN* 5.1.330ff.

310 **gross** monstrous; obvious. Cf. J. Chamber, *A Treatise* (1601), Cla, 'so grosse and heathenish a superstition'.

311 **discontented** i.e. filled with grievances

313 **damned** damnèd

314 **belike** probably

in the nick at that point. Colloquial and 'low', hence 'sophisticated' in F (where *interim* gives a long line) or revised by Shakespeare. Cf. Dent, N160, 'In the nick (nick of time)'.

315 i.e. arrived and gave a satisfactory explanation

304 Sir,] *as Q; F lines* Sir, / befalne, / 308–9] *as F; one line Q* 313 t'] *F;* to *Q* 314 nick] *Q;* interim *F*

OTHELLO
O thou pernicious caitiff!
How came you, Cassio, by that handkerchief
That was my wife's?
CASSIO I found it in my chamber,
And he himself confessed but even now
That there he dropped it for a special purpose
Which wrought to his desire.
OTHELLO O fool, fool, fool!
CASSIO
There is besides in Roderigo's letter
How he upbraids Iago, that he made him
Brave me upon the watch, whereon it came
That I was cast; and even but now he spake,
After long seeming dead, Iago hurt him,
Iago set him on.
LODOVICO [*to Othello*]
You must forsake this room and go with us.
Your power and your command is taken off
And Cassio rules in Cyprus. For this slave,
If there be any cunning cruelty
That can torment him much and hold him long,

316 **caitiff** scoundrel, villain
317 In some productions (Hankey, 239, 333) the handkerchief now bandages Cassio's leg (a good idea, or too obvious?). If no handkerchief is visible, we may prefer Q 'a' to F 'that', since Cassio was not present when Emilia explained its significance (223ff.). But the audience knows its significance, which may be enough.
319 ***but** Q *it* was 'caught by the compositor's eye' from 318 or 320 (so Malone). This is a QF 'common error' (*Texts*, 90), if Malone is right.
320 **special purpose** Cf. 4.2.241–3n.
321 i.e. which had the effect he wanted
O . . . fool He sees only the least of his errors: contrast Roderigo, 'O, villain that I am!' (Heilman, 164–5). This cry is almost a reply to his own 'O, blood, blood, blood!' (3.3.454).
324 **Brave** defy
whereon it came whereupon (or, for which cause) it happened
325 **cast** dismissed
325–6 **and . . . dead** Cf. Desdemona (115–23).
328 **forsake** leave; i.e. he is under arrest
room could = employment, appointment (*OED* 12; Hulme, 273)
329 **taken off** withdrawn
330 **For** as for
332 **hold him long** keep him alive a long time before he dies

316 thou] *F;* the *Q* 317 that] *F;* a *Q* 319 but even] *Capell;* it euen *Q;* it but euen *F*

It shall be his. You shall close prisoner rest
Till that the nature of your fault be known
To the Venetian state. Come, bring him away.

OTHELLO

Soft you, a word or two before you go.
I have done the state some service, and they know't:
No more of that. I pray you, in your letters,
When you shall these unlucky deeds relate,
Speak of me as I am. Nothing extenuate,
Nor set down aught in malice. Then must you speak
Of one that loved not wisely, but too well;
Of one not easily jealous, but, being wrought,
Perplexed in the extreme; of one whose hand,
Like the base Indian, threw a pearl away
Richer than all his tribe; of one whose subdued eyes,
Albeit unused to the melting mood,
Drops tears as fast as the Arabian trees

333 **You** (to Othello)
close confined, shut up
rest remain

336 **Soft you** See LN.
word or two Note the understatement: *some service, unlucky, not wisely, Perplexed*, etc. He tries to 'rewrite the past'.

338 **No . . . that** Cf. 3.3.337.

340 **Speak of** i.e. in writing (*OED* 11)
extenuate lessen, tone down. The sense 'extenuate the guilt of' first recorded 1741: *OED* 7b.

342ff. **Of one** Is this *one* a way of shifting some of the blame? With repeated *of*, cf. 1.3.135–40.

342 **loved not wisely** So Ovid, *Heroides*, 2.27, 'non sapienter amavi' (I loved not wisely).

343 **wrought** agitated (hence 'over-wrought'), worked upon

344 **Perplexed** 'not so much "puzzled" as "distracted"' (Ridley). *We* know that the stronger 'distracted' is applicable, but *he* may mean bewildered by misleading evidence.

345 **base** lowly (with 'Indian'); depraved, despicable (if we read 'Judean')
Indian See LN.

346 **Richer** of more worth
tribe could be the tribes of Israel or an Indian tribe
subdued overcome

347 **unused** (unusèd, if *Albeit* is disyllabic). Not strictly true: cf. his weeping elsewhere.

348–9 **Arabian . . . gum** Pliny (see p. 15) wrote at length about trees and gums (bks 12, 13). J. O. Holmer thinks *Arabian trees* = not balsam but myrrh trees, since they alone correspond fully to Shakespeare's specifications (Arabian, medicinal uses, profuse 'weeping'): *SSt*, 13 (1980), 145ff.

335 him] *Q; not in F* 336 before you go] *F; not in Q* 340 me as I am] *F;* them as they are *Q* 341] *as Q; F lines* malice. / speake, / 345 Indian] *Q, F2;* Iudean *F* 348 Drops] *QF;* Drop *Q2*

Their medicinable gum. Set you down this,
And say besides that in Aleppo once,
Where a malignant and a turbanned Turk
Beat a Venetian and traduced the state,
I took by th' throat the circumcised dog
And smote him – thus! *He stabs himself.*

LODOVICO
O bloody period!

GRATIANO All that's spoke is marred.

OTHELLO
I kissed thee ere I killed thee: no way but this,
Killing myself, to die upon a kiss.
[*Kisses Desdemona, and*] *dies.*

CASSIO
This did I fear, but thought he had no weapon,
For he was great of heart.

LODOVICO [*to Iago*] O Spartan dog,

349 **medicinable** medicinal
Set . . . this He asks for a written report; Lodovico speaks of an oral report (368–9).

350 **Aleppo** Not mentioned before, Aleppo reminds us that much of Othello's past remains a closed book. It was an important staging post for trade between Europe and the East: an English factor lived there (as in Venice).

351 **turbanned** A turban was a symbol of Islam.

352 **traduced** *Malignant* and *traduced* refer obliquely to Iago, who slandered Venetian women. But Othello, stabbing himself, also identifies himself with the Turk: see pp. 32–6.

353 **took . . . throat** Cf. 3.3.362n., 5.2.200n.
circumcised See LN.

354 SD This was one of Salvini's most sensational moments as Othello: see pp. 72–4. N.B. Should Othello's fall here remind us of his fit (4.1.43)?

355 **period** conclusion; appointed end of a journey (cf. 265–6). In some productions the curtain came down after *period* (Hankey, 339).

356 **I . . . [2]thee** If *Judean* is right and not *Indian* (see 345 LN), this line refers to the kiss and suicide of Judas (Matthew 26.49, 27.5).
ere before
no . . . this Cf. Dent, W148, 'There is no way but one (i.e., death).'

357 **to . . . kiss** For the conventional 'last kiss', cf. also *RJ* 5.3.120, 'Thus with a kiss I die', *AC* 4.15.20.

358 SD Several Othellos 'died in attempting to reach the bed, or just after reaching it' (Sprague, 220–1, Hankey, 237–8), i.e. not 'upon a kiss'. But 'no way *but this*' seems to imply that he kisses her.

359 **great of heart** 'great-hearted' = high-spirited, proud (*OED*)
Spartan dog See LN.

349 medicinable] *F;* medicinall *Q* 351 malignant . . . Turk] *Malignant* and a *Turband Turke Q;* malignant, and a Turbond-Turke *F* 354 SD] *Q; not in F* 355 that's] *Q;* that is *F* 357 SD] *He dies. Q; Dyes F* 359 Spartan] *F (*Sparton*)*

More fell than anguish, hunger, or the sea,
Look on the tragic loading of this bed:
This is thy work. The object poisons sight,
Let it be hid. Gratiano, keep the house
And seize upon the fortunes of the Moor
For they succeed to you. To you, lord governor,
Remains the censure of this hellish villain,
The time, the place, the torture: O, enforce it!
Myself will straight aboard, and to the state
This heavy act with heavy heart relate. *Exeunt.*

FINIS.

360 **fell** savage, ruthless
anguish excruciating bodily or mental pain
361 This line suggests (cf. 358 SD n.) that both Desdemona and Othello lie on the bed.
362 **object** spectacle; the presentation of something to the eye. Cf. *Cor* 1.1.20, 'the object of our misery'.
363 **hid** i.e. by a sheet, or by pulling the bed curtains (thus concealing the actors' breathing)
keep guard
364 **seize upon** take possession of
fortunes possessions
365 **they . . . you** pass to you by succession (as Desdemona's uncle: 199n.)
to F *on* is possible, but awkward after *upon*.
lord governor He reminds Cassio, who is mildly ineffective when sober, to take charge firmly as governor; hence, too, *enforce it*, 367.
366 **censure** formal judgement; correction
367 **torture** i.e. to make Iago confess his motives (cf. 301n.). Notice how insistently the end of this scene focuses on motives: 292, 296, 298–9, 301–2, 317, 320, 341ff.
368 **straight aboard** immediately go on board ship
369 **heavy . . . heavy** distressful . . . sorrowful
act action, deed

361 loading] *F;* lodging *Q* 362] *as Q; F lines* worke: / Sight, / 365 to] *Q;* on *F* 369 SD] *F; Exeunt omnes. Q*

LONGER NOTES

LIST OF ROLES 'The Names of the Actors' was printed in the Folio, at the end of the play, in two columns (*Texts*, 70). It is one of seven such lists in F and may have been compiled by Ralph Crane, who is thought to have transcribed other F plays which have similar lists (*Tem, TGV, MM, WT*: see *Texts*, 70–2). The embellishment below 'The Names of the Actors', consisting of brackets, colons and asterisks, resembles similar ones found in other Crane manuscripts, but I have not seen one that is exactly the same in Crane's work or elsewhere. Apart from changing the heading and printing the names in capitals, the Arden 3 list adopts the sequence and layout of the Folio, and therefore places female parts separately. All additions to F's list are in square brackets.

Dramatists would have found such lists useful when they wrote their plays, or even before they began to write (Honigmann, *Stability*, 44–6). Did Crane copy his list from Shakespeare's own papers? It is curious that his list for *MM* begins '*Vincentio: the Duke.*', for the text of *MM* never mentions the Duke's name. Shakespeare had a weakness for naming his characters even when names are not strictly necessary: the *MM* list could be authorial. So, too, the *Othello* list calls Montano '*Gouernour of Cyprus*', an authorial intention that we may deduce from the dialogue (see *Texts*, 71–2), though not one spelt out in F. In Q *Othello*, however, occurs the SD '*Enter* Montanio, *Gouernor of* Cypres' (2.1.0), and Crane might have taken these words from Q. It follows that we cannot tell whether Crane copied or tidied such lists from Shakespeare's papers or whether Crane alone was responsible for them. It should be noted, though, that Crane usually placed the play-world's ruler first whereas in *Othello* the Duke is placed sixth, and that the *Othello* list differs from Crane's lists in other ways.

In Cinthio Shakespeare found only one name, Disdemona. In the French translation of Cinthio (1583) this became Disdemone. While Shakespeare's 'Desdemona' and 'Desdemon' (3.1.55, 3.3.55, etc.) may indicate that he knew the Italian and French versions (see p. 375), feminine names ending in -a lose the -a at times in other plays (Helena in *AW*, Isabella in *MM*). It is just possible, in view of the not uncommon *e:i* confusion in *Othello* (*Texts*, 88–9), that Shakespeare actually wrote Disdemon(a) and that Desdemona was a misreading that stuck (compare Imogen–Innogen in *Cym*). The misreading 'Montanio' likewise stuck in Q, where F has 'Montano', and the misreading 'Rodorigo' stuck in F, instead of Q's

'Roderigo'. As F adopted many 'common errors' from Q (*ibid.*, 95–8), 'Desdemona' for 'Disdemona' could be one as well.

On a different tack, how should we pronounce 'Othello'? The medial -th- in *Hecatommithi* must be sounded as -t-; Ben Jonson's 'Thorello' (*Every Man In*) derives from Italian 'torello', a young bull; 'Othoman' was an alternative spelling for 'Ottoman': it seems possible that Shakespeare wrote 'Othello' and meant 'Otello'. He might have heard of the Jesuit, Girolamo Otello of Bassano (1519–81); according to T. Sipahigil ('Othello's name, once again', *N&Q*, 18 (1971), 147–8), 'Jesuit historians invariably speak of the notoriety of Girolamo Otello as an over-ardent spirit, quick to follow zealous impulses', i.e. he had something in common with Othello. But Otello was an out-of-the-way name; if Shakespeare knew it he might still want to change it, as also in the case of Disdemona.

Several of the play's names were probably invented or adapted by Shakespeare. (1) Othello: from Otello, or from Otho, Othoman or Thorello (see F. N. Lees, 'Othello's name', *N&Q*, 8 (1961), 139–41; R. F. Fleissner, 'The Moor's nomenclature', *N&Q*, 25 (1978), 143). (2) Desdemona: from Disdemona. (3) Brabantio: cf. Brabant Senior in *Jack Drum's Entertainment* (1601) and the Duke of Brabant in *The Weakest Goeth to the Wall* (1600). (4) Montano: the name reappears in Q1 *Hamlet* (1603): see p. 350. (5) Michael Cassio: the only person in *Othello* with two names. Compare Cassius in *JC*. The verb 'to cass' was 'a frequent form of our word "cashier"' (Hart).

Several of the names have curious associations. Both Iago and Roderigo are Spanish forms (and Iago's 'Diablo!', 2.3.157, unique in Shakespeare, is the Spanish form of this word). The most famous Spanish Iago was Sant'Iago (St James of Compostella), known as 'Matamoros' ('the Moor-killer') (see Bullough, 217; Everett, '"Spanish" Othello'). Iago's 'I know our country disposition well' (3.3.204) nevertheless appears to refer to Italy (where Spain was a dominant power in the later sixteenth century).

Disdemona, said Cinthio (see p. 395), was 'a name of unlucky augury' (it meant 'unfortunate'). Bianca (= Blanche, white, i.e. pure), a name previously used by Shakespeare in *TS* for a less than perfect young lady, was the Christian name of the notorious Bianca Capello (1548–87), a Venetian courtesan whose story Middleton dramatized in *Women Beware Women* and Webster perhaps glanced at when he created his 'white devil'.

Iago is usually trisyllabic ('I-a-go'). Cassio is more often disyllabic, but can be trisyllabic (1.1.19). See *Texts*, 104.

1.1.8 **his lieutenant** The military ranks of an ancient (i.e. ensign, or standard-bearer), a lieutenant and a general may confuse readers because 'Elizabethan field-grade officers had also a different company rank' (Paul A. Jorgensen, *Shakespeare's Military World* (1956), 100–18: in this note I am indebted to Jorgensen's helpful discussion). Cinthio's 'Cassio' is a corporal, but Shakespeare made him a lieutenant, apparently lieutenant of a company: as such he would be superior to the ancient, though there would be 'a troublesome overlapping of the two offices, and an occasion for friction'. A company-rank captain personally chose his company's lieutenant, ensign and lower officers; Othello did so and, it seems, gave Cassio accelerated promotion, therefore we should recognize that Iago has 'what to him seem real grievances'. Yet when Othello is replaced as general in command of Cyprus the Venetians appoint 'Cassio in his government' and 'Cassio rules in Cyprus' as 'lord governor' (4.1.236, 5.2.330, 365). Towards the end of the play Shakespeare appears to think of Cassio not as a lieutenant of a company but as a staff officer, a lieutenant-general – two ranks that are incompatible (unlike Othello's two ranks as captain of a company and as general of an army). Shakespeare either forgot Cassio's junior rank as a mere company lieutenant or assumed that his audience would forget (just as he probably assumed that the audience would not notice the double time scheme). See also Julia Genster, 'Lieutenancy, standing in and *Othello*', *ELH*, 57 (1990), 785–805.

1.1.20 Furness cites several pages of explanation, including the following: 'he is not yet *completely damned*, because he is not *absolutely married*' (Steevens, referring to 4.1.124: but the later suggestion that Cassio is expected to marry Bianca does not help at 1.1.20); 'a man almost degraded into a woman (through feminine tastes and habits) . . . as when one says "A soldier wasted in a parson"' (Earl of Southesk); 'a fellow who is willing to go to perdition . . . for a beautiful woman' (Crosby). Cf. Sisson, *Readings*, 'he is given to women, practically married and likely therefore to be uxorious and distracted from soldierly virtue' (2.246). I prefer Johnson's candid admission that the line is obscure and/or corrupt.

1.3.322 **nettles** Pliny has a chapter 'Of the nettle' (22.13), which was cultivated for medicinal purposes. J. T. McCullen thinks each pair of herbs here contains an aphrodisiac and an anti-aphrodisiac, a combination used by physicians to treat love sickness. Ridley compared Lyly, *Euphues* (1.187), 'good Gardeiners . . . mixe Hisoppe wyth Time as ayders the one to the growth of the other, the one beeinge drye, the other moyste'.

2.1.12 **clouds** Perhaps an echo of Ovid, *Tristia*, 1.2.19ff., 'what vast mountains of water heave themselves aloft . . . you think, they will touch the highest stars . . . you think they will touch black Tartarus' (T. Sipahigil,

'Ovid and the Tempest in *Othello*', *SQ*, 44 (1993), 468–71). But cf. Psalms 107.25ff.: such poetical storms were widely copied.

2.1.15 **guards, pole** These stars gave navigators their bearings. Both *everfired* and *-fixed* are possible: cf. *KL* 3.7.61, 'quenched the stelled fires', where *stelled* = either 'starry' (from Lat. *stella*) or 'fixed' (from ME *stellen*). Cf. also *Oth* 3.3.466, 'you ever-burning lights above'.

2.1.26 **Veronessa** = from Verona. The feminine ending *-essa* (as in *contessa*) is wrong here: the Italian word is Veronese (four syllables, perhaps what Shakespeare wrote). Verona, though an inland city, had ships at the battle of Lepanto; Shakespeare may have meant 'a ship on the side of Venice, belonging to Verona'. QF punctuation (unlikely to be Shakespeare's) implies that *Veronessa* refers to Cassio!

2.1.155 **change** exchange; hence, 'to make a foolish exchange' (Ridley). Shakespeare no doubt knew that 'the taile-piece [of many fishes] is in greatest request' (Pliny, quoted Hart), and that the cod's head is worthless. Puns on *cod* (= penis) and *tail* (= pudenda). Balz Engler compared Tilley, H240, 'Better be the head of yeomanry than the tail of the gentry', and proverbs 'directed against foolish ambition' ('To change the cod's head for the salmon's tail', *SQ*, 35 (1984), 202–3).

2.1.173 **three fingers** i.e. one after the other. 'The kissing of his hand was a quite normal courteous gesture from a gentleman to a lady' (Ridley, citing *LLL* 4.1.146, 'To see him kiss his hand', *TN* 3.4.32, 'Why dost thou smile so, and kiss thy hand so oft?'). But both extracts refer to foppish, extravagant behaviour, as Iago does here.

2.1.301 ***trash** check a hound, hence, hold back, restrain. An easy misreading in Q (less easy in F), and agrees with Roderigo's later complaint that Iago has not advanced his cause (4.2.175ff.). F *trace* might = pursue, dog (*OED* 5), i.e. whom I dog in the hope that he will help me with quick hunting; or, 'whom I keep hungry so that he may hunt the more eagerly' (a hawking metaphor: Hulme, 254–6).

2.3.85ff. Iago's song is adapted from an early ballad known as 'Bell my wife' or 'Take thy old cloak about thee'. The ballad predated *Othello*, being quoted in Robert Greene's *Quip for an Upstart Courtier* (1592), 'it was a good and blessed time heere in Englane [*sic*], when k. *Stephen* wore a paire of cloth breeches of a Noble a paire, anf [*sic*] thought them passing costlye' (sig. C3b). A complete text was printed in Thomas Percy's *Reliques of Ancient English Poetry* (1765), eight eight-line stanzas, consisting of the words of Bell and of her husband. They have been together forty-four years; it is bitter winter weather, and she tells him to put on his old cloak and to go out and save the old cow. Her stanzas end 'man! put (or, take) thine old cloak about thee!', his – 'for I'll have a new cloak about me'. *He* wants to abandon his peasant life and seek advancement at court, *she* warns him against pride. Stanzas 6 and 7 leave us in no doubt that the ballad expresses impatience with privilege (appropriately for Iago):

O Bell my wiffe! why doest thou flyte?
  now is nowe, and then was then;
seeke all the world now throughout,
  thou kens not Clownes from gentlemen;
they are cladd in blacke, greene, yellow, and blew,
  soe ffarr aboue their owne degree;
once in my liffe Ile take a vew,* [*= ?give myself some licence]
  ffor Ile haue a new cloake about mee.

King Harry was a verry good K[*ing*;]
  I trow his hose cost but a Crowne;
he thought them 12^{d}. ouer to deere,
  therfore he called the taylor Clowne.
he was King and wore the Crowne,
  and thouse but of a low degree;
itts pride *that* putts this cumtrye downe;
  man! put thye old Cloake about thee![1]

We cannot be certain that Percy printed the ballad exactly as Shakespeare knew it: if he did, which is unlikely, Shakespeare introduced changes in every line, though apparently retaining the character of the original and its 'class' feeling. We may assume that Shakespeare's audience was familiar with the ballad, even if Italian Cassio seems not to be. The ballad tune associated with the song is found in Robert Bremner's *Thirty Scots Songs* (1770), reproduced in Sternfeld, 149, and below on p. 402. (See also the books on music in Shakespeare cited in the LN on 4.3.39ff.).

2.3.166–7 Cf. *MA* 3.4.57, 'and you be not turned Turk'; Dent, T609, 'To turn Turk'. To Elizabethans, Turks and Moors must have seemed much alike (see p. 341): 166–8 bring out Othello's 'otherness'. Chew (108) notes 'the well attested fact that Turkish soldiers, though they might bicker and squabble among themselves, never came to blows with each other'; see Rodney Poisson, 'Which heaven has forbid the Ottomites',

1 Reprinted from *Bishop Percy's Folio Manuscript*, ed. J. W. Hales and F. J. Furnivall, 3 vols (1867), 2.320ff.

SQ 18 (1967), 67–70. That is, 'do we fight amongst ourselves, which the Turks are forbidden to do by their religion?' Walker glossed 167 'by destroying their fleet'. Cf. also *Homilies*, 456, 'Surely it is a shame that Paynims [pagans] should be wiser than we.'

2.3.304–5 **creature** 1 Timothy 4.1–4 warns against seducing spirits that 'abstain from meats which God hath created to be received with giving thanks . . . For every *creature* of God is good'. Intoxicating drink was called a *creature* (facetiously) before Shakespeare, as also later by Dryden, 'My master took too much of the creature last night' (*OED* 1d); but *creature* could = any created thing (including food and drink).

3.1.3–4 He refers to the Neapolitan (venereal) disease (cf. *TC* 2.3.18), which could eat away the nose (*Tim* 4.3.157). He means that the instruments snuffle or scrape instead of ringing out musically; they 'must have double reeds (like modern oboe reeds) which produce a nasal sound' (R. King, '"Then murder's out of tune": the music and structure of *Othello*', *SS*, 39 (1987), 155).

3.3.126 ***delations** accusations; narrations; Q *denotements* = indications. 'Delate' and 'dilate' were interchangeable (cf. *Ham* 1.2.38, Q2, F): see Patricia Parker, 'Shakespeare and rhetoric: "dilation" and "delation" in *Othello*', in *Shakespeare and the Question of Theory*, ed. P. Parker and G. Hartman (1985), 54–74. Kittredge glossed *dilations* as swellings, i.e. 'emotions that make the heart swell'.

3.3.159 **immediate** i.e. dearest; of a relation between two things: existing without any intervening medium or agency (*OED* 2). Cf. Proverbs 22.1, 'A good name is more to be desired than great riches', Ecclesiasticus 41.12 (Noble, 218); Dent, N22, 'A good name is better than riches.' Perhaps influenced by *Homilies*, 127, 'there cometh less hurt of a thief, than of a railing tongue: for the one taketh away a man's good name; the other taketh but his riches, which is of much less value' (T. W. Craik, private communication). Compare Iago at 2.3.258ff.

3.3.291 *SD. It is not clear here whether he or she drops the handkerchief: but cf. 315. If she tries to bind his head from behind he can push her hand away without looking at the handkerchief; *let it alone* then = leave my headache alone. See 441n. and L. Hartley, 'Dropping the handkerchief: pronoun reference and stage direction in *Othello* III.iii', *ELN*, 8 (1970–1), 173–6.

3.3.364 **man's** (as opposed to a dog, which has no soul), i.e. he will consign Iago's soul to eternal damnation (375). Q may imply that Iago risks his soul, F that Othello risks his (because of what he will do to Iago); but 364 could be less specific, i.e. a vague oath. See also Matthew 26.24–5, 'woe unto that man by whom the son of man is betrayed: It had been good for that man if he had not been born. Then Judas . . . said, Master, Is it I?' Did Shakespeare think of Iago as a Judas figure?

3.3.406–7 **prime, hot, salt, in pride** all synonyms for lecherous, 'on heat' (Ridley). *Prime* is not recorded in this sense elsewhere. I suggest *primed* = ready to discharge (sexually). Cf. Dent, G167, 'As lecherous as a goat'; also *TC* 3.1.130, 'hot thoughts beget hot deeds, and hot deeds is love'; *Tim* 4.3.84–6, 'Be a whore still . . . Make use of thy salt hours'; *Luc* 438–9, 'Smoking with pride . . . to make his stand / On her bare breast.'

3.3.450 **hollow hell** Cf. Seneca, *Thyestes*, tr. Jasper Heywood, 'Where most prodigious vglye thynges, / the hollowe hell dothe hyde' (1560 edn, sig. E4: 4th scene, added by translator). Q *Cell* is not unlike *Ham* 5.2.364–5, 'O proud death, / What feast is toward in thine eternal cell', and *Luc*, 881–2. F *hollow hell* anticipates *Tem* 1.2.214–15, 'Hell is empty, / And all the devils are here'. Cf. also Tourneur, *Transformed Metamorphosis* (1600), B6b, 'blacke horrors cell', R. Armin, *Two Maids* (1609), E1b, 'Rouse the blacke mischiefe from thy ebben cell'. Both Q and F are possible.

3.3.458 ***keeps** It is possible that one *keeps* is a copyist's error, but which one? Editors who follow Q2 may have two errors in this line. Cf. a possible echo in T. Powell, *Virtue's Due* (1603), B6a, 'Her resolution was *Proponticke* right, / And forward stem'd against the Moones retreat', which suggests 'ne'er keeps retiring ebb but stems due on' (*stems* = heads, *OED v.* 3). But Shakespeare liked to repeat words in 'rhetorical' passages. Sisson thinks that the first *keeps* was an anticipation of the second (by Shakespeare or a scribe): 'we simply delete the first keeps, and read *ebbs* for *ebb*, no difficult misreading'.

3.4.47 i.e. we now give our hands (in marriage) without giving our love. Stressing *of old* and *our*, the actor can suggest 'a denial of Desdemona's assertion' in 45 (Capell).

'It is difficult . . . to escape from seeing here an allusion to the new order of baronetage instituted by King James in 1612, of which the badge was the addition of a hand gules to the coat of arms' (Ridley, from Warburton, etc.). But this would mean that the 'allusion' was later added to the Q and F manuscripts – unlikely. Others thought no allusion necessary. Dyce compared Warner's *Albion's England* (1596 edn, 282): 'My hand shall neuer giue my heart, my heart shall giue my hand'; Hart quoted Cornwallis, *Essays* (1600–1): people used to 'give their hands and their hearts together, but we think it a finer grace to look asquint, our hand looking one way, and our heart another'.

3.4.72–3 **sibyl** prophetess, as in ancient Greece and Rome. 'We say, *I counted the clock to strike four*; so she *numbred* the sun *to course*, to run . . . two hundred annual circuits' (Johnson); i.e. she had calculated that the sun would make two hundred (further) circuits, that the world would end in two hundred years (hence *prophetic*). Calculating the date of the end of the world was a Renaissance pastime.

4.2.60 **fountain** spring, well (Lat. *fons*). The imagery picks up from 3.3.274, and from Proverbs 5.15–18, 'Drink the water of thy cistern, and of the rivers out of the mids(t) of thine own well. Let thy fountains flow forth . . . let thy fountain be blessed, and rejoice with the wife of thy youth' (Genevan Bible, which heads the chapter 'Whoredom forbidden'; here *thy cistern, thine own well* = thy wife). Cf. also *Homilies*, 114: whoredom is 'that most filthy lake, foul puddle, and stinking sink, whereunto all kinds of sins and evils flow'.

4.3.39ff. Shakespeare adapted the Willow Song 'from a pre-existing text and probably intended that his version be sung to one of two pre-existing tunes' (B. N. S. Gooch and D. Thatcher, *A Shakespeare Music Catalogue*, 5 vols (Oxford, 1991), 2.1255). The song was printed from an old ballad in Percy's *Reliques* (1765), and reprinted with music by Furness, 278. We should not assume, however, that Percy's version gives the ballad verbatim as Shakespeare found it. If it did, Shakespeare changed the sex of the singer and adapted quite freely, as the following extracts show.

A poore soule sat sighing under a sicamore tree;
  'O willow, willow, willow!'
With his hand on his bosom, his head on his knee:
  'O willow, willow, willow!
  'O willow, willow, willow!
Sing, O the greene willow shall be my garlànd.'
. . .
My love she is turned; untrue she doth prove:
  O willow, &c.
She renders me nothing but hate for my love.
  O willow, &c.
Sing, O the greene willow, &c.

The cold streams ran by him, his eyes wept apace;
  O willow, &c.
The salt tears fell from him, which drowned his face;
  O willow, &c.
Sing, O the greene willow, &c.

The mute birds sate by him, made tame by his mones:
  O willow, &c.

The salt tears fell from him, which softened the stones.
  O willow, &c.
Sing, O the greene willow shall be my garlànd!

Let nobody blame me, her scornes I do prove;
  O willow, &c.
She was borne to be faire: I, to die for her love, . . .[1]

The earliest version of the tune is to be found in a 1583 manuscript lute book in the library of Trinity College Dublin. The version reproduced below on pp. 403–4 is the contemporary setting in BL Add. MS. 15117, fo. 118 as reprinted in Sternfeld, 43–4. See also Sternfeld, 23–52, for further discussion and other facsimiles and transcriptions of the music; J. H. Long, *Shakespeare's Use of Music* (1971), 153–61; and Gooch and Thatcher, *op. cit.* For Q's omission of the song, see *Texts*, 10–11.

5.2 The original staging of 5.2 has been explained in two different ways. (1) L. J. Ross suggested that a curtained structure was placed on the main stage, in front of the tiring-house façade ('The use of a "fit-up" booth in *Othello*', *SQ* 12 (1961), 359–70). The bed was concealed when the curtains were drawn (cf. 103, 363). The same structure would be useful elsewhere – e.g. for the 'discovery' of the Senate at 1.3.0.1, or as the *bulk* of 5.1.1. (2) R. Hosley held that 'the bed with Desdemona lying in it is "thrust out" of the tiring-house by stage-keepers . . . the bed curtains are manipulated as called for by the dialogue; and when Lodovico says "Let it be hid" the bed, on which are now lying the bodies of Desdemona, Emilia, and Othello, is "drawn in" to the tiring-house through one of its doors' ('The staging of Desdemona's bed', *SQ* 14 (1963), 57–65). Both kinds of staging were possible, and we must not suppose that staging at the Globe and, later, at the Blackfriars, was identical: but note the clear SD in *2H6* 3.2.146, '*Bed put forth*' (F). Othello's *light* (5.2.0.1) = a candle.

5.2.83 SD Q *stifles* could = throttles; F *Smothers* = suffocates (actors normally use a pillow). Cf. Marlowe, *Massacre* (1.400), SD, '*Now they strangle him*'; Dekker, *Old Fortunatus* (1600), where Andelocia is strangled on stage (1.191). In some productions Desdemona was smothered behind closed curtains (Rosenberg, 99, 113).

5.2.98–100 For supernatural manifestations before or after an important death, common in classical literature, cf. *JC* 2.2.13ff., *Mac* 2.4.1ff. Othello's apocalyptic vision here may be biblical in inspiration: 'lo, there was a great earthquake, and the sun was as black as sackcloth . . . and the

1 Reprinted from *Percy's Reliques*, ed. G. Gilfillan, 3 vols (Edinburgh, 1858), 1.158ff.

moon waxed all even as blood. And the stars of heaven fell unto the earth' (Revelation 6.12–13).

5.2.141 **chrysolite** sometimes glossed as topaz; 'a name formerly given to several different gems of a green colour' (*OED*). Lynda Boose thinks that Shakespeare meant a 'translucent white' gem, as in the Genevan Bible, Song of Solomon, Revelation 21.20 ('Othello's "chrysolite" and the Song of Songs tradition', *PQ*, 60 (1981), 427ff.). Cf. also *Weakest Goeth to the Wall* (1600), C3a, 'walles of purest Chrysolyte'.

5.2.251 Spain was famous for its fine swords (e.g. Toledo blades). To *temper* = to strengthen metal by repeatedly heating and cooling it: *ice-brook* (a coinage) could refer to the cooling process. 'Spanish rivers, such as the Tagus, being fed by melting snows, were considered to be partly responsible for the quality of Spanish blades' (Sanders). Q *Isebrookes* has been seen as a misreading of Innsbruck (which exported fine metal to England), and would be an easy misreading (*Texts*, 83–4); but this would be a poor exchange for the evocative *ice-brook*, a word perhaps connected with the 'tempering' that Othello imagines in 275–8.

5.2.277–8 The 'torment of the damned in hell' was another popular subject in Renaissance art. It may be thought that to be blown about in winds would be a pleasant change for anyone roasting in sulphur – but cf. the similar vision of hell in *MM* 3.1.121ff., 'To bathe in fiery floods . . . To be imprison'd in the viewless winds / And blown with restless violence round about / The pendent world'.

5.2.336 **Soft you** *Soft* and *But soft* are common in Shakespeare (*Ham* 1.1.126, 1.5.58, 3.2.392); *soft you* (= not so fast) is rare. In this speech Othello's sense of his own unquestioned superiority shows through in his attitude to the *base Indian* and the *Turk*: he adopts a 'European' view of darker-skinned races. Surprisingly the only reference to Desdemona is as the *pearl* (but see LN, 5.2.345, below): his speech is largely self-centred.

5.2.345 **Indian** Both Q *Indian* and F *Iudean* have strong support from discerning editors. *Indian* has been more popular with editors, though *Iudean* was preferred by Johnson and Malone. I list some of the arguments for and against each. (1) For *Iudean*. Judas Iscariot is so called because he was the Judaean disciple, unlike the others, who were Galileans. The kiss of Judas as a token of treachery was a commonplace (Matthew 26.49), hence 356; betraying Jesus, Judas threw away a 'precious pearl' (Matthew 13.46; in the Genevan Bible, 'a pearl of great price': see Noble, 92, 273). Judas, like Othello, committed suicide. Others think that *Iudean* could refer to Herod, who killed Mariamne, his 'pearl' of a wife (J. O. Holmer, 'Othello's Threnos: "Arabian trees" and "Indian" versus "Judean"', *SSt*, 13 (1980), 145–67).

(2) Against *Iudean*. The word 'Judean' was not in use in Shakepeare's time (R. F. Fleissner, 'A clue to the "base Judean" in *Othello*', *N&Q*, 28 [1981], 137–8). The metre of 345 requires Júdean, not Judéan. These objections are not decisive, as Shakespeare often invented words or changed their stress.

(3) For *Indian*. The wealth of India, and the ignorance of Indians, unaware of the value of their gold and precious stones, were commented on by Renaissance and earlier writers. Pliny (34.17) mentioned Indians who barter and undervalue pearls. For Shakespeare's knowledge of these commonplaces, cf. 'as bountiful / As mines of India' (*1H4* 3.1.166–7) and 'Her bed is India, there she lies, a pearl' (*TC* 1.1.100). Such passages mostly refer to Indian Indians (e.g. Pliny), but Shakespeare could have meant American Indians.

A different kind of evidence also supports Q *Indian*: the fact that the second Folio (1632) switched from *Iudean* to *Indian*. In general F2 followed the first Folio (F) closely, introducing some corrections that are clearly unauthorized (i.e. are based on neither Q nor F). F2 *Indian* shows that a near-contemporary, who was far less interfering as an editor than the Q2 editor of 1630 (see *Texts*, 170), was dissatisfied with F *Iudean*: this was one of his most striking corrections of his copy. On the other hand, the F scribe corrected Q *Indian* to *Iudean*; although F also miscorrected Q (*ibid.*, 100), F's correction must carry some weight.

(4) Against *Indian*. The widely shared conviction that the Folio is the 'better text' has no doubt influenced those who argue for F *Iudean*. I have suggested that editors overrated F's reliability and underrated Q's (*ibid.*, 146), which leaves the balance finely poised.

Conclusion. The best analysis is, I think, Richard Levin's 'The Indian/ Iudean crux in *Othello*' (*SQ*, 33 (1982), 60–7), which ends with a telling point. It is appropriate for Othello to compare himself with the Indian, whose action results from ignorance, and 'very inappropriate for him to compare himself to Judas, whose action was regarded as a conscious choice of evil'.

5.2.353 **circumcised** (?circumcisèd) Circumcision was a religious rite with Muslims, so Othello's contemptuous reference to it implies that he 'was not nor had ever been a Mohammedan' (Chew, 521n.). But it could be simply a term of abuse, like 'the uncircumcised' in the Bible. These lines may be influenced by 1 Samuel 17.26ff., 'what is this uncircumcised Philistine, that he should revile the host of the living God?' (David of Goliath); 'I caught him by the beard, and smote him, and slew him' (David to Saul); 'And the Philistine [Goliath] said unto David, Am I a dog . . .?'

5.2.359 **Spartan dog** a kind of bloodhound. Applied to men, bloodhound = a hunter for blood (*OED* 2). Envy, Iago's disease, was sometimes represented as a snarling dog; *Spartan* may = unmoved, impassive, inhumanely determined (like the Spartan boy who carried a fox under his tunic, was bitten, and gave no sign of pain). Cf. the hounds of Sparta that were used to hunt bears (*MND* 4.1.112ff.).

APPENDIX 1
Date

Othello must have been written at some time between 1601 and 1604. Holland's translation of Pliny's *Historie of the World* (dated 1601 on the title-page; SR entry 20 May 1600) almost certainly supplied Shakespeare with much of the play's 'foreign' and exotic material; a performance at court on 1 November 1604 provides the *terminus ante quem*. Can we date the play more precisely? E. K. Chambers thought in 1930 that a 'production in 1604 is consonant with the stylistic evidence',[1] and others have felt that *Othello* is 'Jacobean'. Useful as it is in assigning Shakespeare's plays to an approximate period, stylistic evidence gives less help with precise dating; the 'Jacobean' feeling, moreover, expresses itself chiefly through Iago, and one could argue that the romantic hero and heroine are thoroughly 'Elizabethan'. We are back where we started.

Alfred Hart offered a new suggestion in 1935:[2] the 'bad' Quarto of *Hamlet* seems to echo *Othello*, just as it garbles lines from many other plays. The bad Quarto was published in 1603, and its text may have come into being some time before 26 July 1602, the date on which James Roberts entered *Hamlet* in the Stationers' Register. Some editors accepted Hart's dating, others ignored it. *Othello*, said the Cambridge 2 editors, J. Dover Wilson and Alice Walker, 'can hardly be later than early 1603, and may even belong to 1602'.[3] The reason why others continued to date the play as before, in 1603 or 1604, must be that some of Hart's 'echoes' from *Othello* in the bad Quarto (Q1) of *Hamlet* are not convincing, being phrases in general

1 Chambers, *William Shakespeare*, 1.462.
2 Alfred Hart, 'The date of *Othello*', *TLS*, 10 October 1935, p. 631.
3 Cam^2, xv.

use. Some, but not all: at least two echoes have to be taken more seriously.

(1) 'To my unfolding lend your prosperous ear' (*Oth* 1.3.245) must be connected with 'to my vnfolding / Lend thy listning eare' (Q1 *Ham* C3b, C4a). (2) The adjective 'Olympus-high' appears in both texts (*Oth* 2.1.186; Q1 *Ham* I1b).

On their own these two echoes are arresting, though perhaps insufficiently so to qualify as proof positive that *Othello* influenced Q1 *Hamlet*. Hart, however, did not cite all the relevant echoes. More have now been added.[1]

(3) The unusual name Montano, which replaces Reynaldo in Q1 *Hamlet*. The only Montano in Shakespeare occurs in *Othello*. This looks like unconscious substitution, perhaps because the same actor played Montano in *Othello* and Reynaldo in *Hamlet*. (4) In the closing moments of the two tragedies almost the same thought is repeated: 'Look on the tragic loading of this bed' (*Oth* 5.2.361) and 'looke vpon this tragicke spectacle' (Q1 *Ham* I4a). Other echoes have also been located, but we need not waste time on them. Hart's case seems to me to have proved correct: *Othello* must have existed by early 1603, and probably before July 1602. As Holland's Pliny printed a prefatory epistle dated 'Iunij xij. 1601' I conclude that *Othello* was probably written at some point in the period from mid-1601 to mid-1602.

How does this fit in with the 'Shakespeare chronology'? *Othello* is always placed later than *Hamlet* (*c.* 1600) and earlier than *King Lear* (1605): the tragedies are so well spaced that any date from 1601 to 1604 seems possible for *Othello*. Again, *Othello* and *Measure for Measure* are sometimes seen as twin plays, being based on the same collection of stories, Cinthio's *Hecatommithi*, and are therefore dated close together, in 1603–4.

1 See Honigmann, 'Date of *Othello*', and J. C. Maxwell, 'Othello and the bad Quarto of *Hamlet*', *N&Q*, 21 (1974), 130.

Yet while editors believe that some plays based on the same source were written consecutively (e.g. *Antony and Cleopatra* and *Coriolanus*), we know that others must be years apart (e.g. *Julius Caesar* and *Antony and Cleopatra*). The date of *Measure for Measure*, itself far from certain, should not influence our dating of *Othello*; neither should the dates of other plays that may belong to the years immediately after the turn of the century (*Merry Wives, Twelfth Night, Troilus, All's Well*), for these too defy all efforts to date them precisely.

Twelfth Night, though, may give some help, being related to *Othello* in two ways. (1) *Casting*. The casting requirements of the two plays are remarkably alike. So many characters have an obvious counterpart in the second play that Shakespeare must have had the same actors in mind, intending to exploit their special talents. Thus: (a) Orsino–Othello (a specialist in passion, despair, poetic declamation); (b) Viola–Desdemona (a boy actor who excelled in gentleness, suffering, romantic love); (c) Sir Andrew Aguecheek–Roderigo (a comedian who played foolish young gentlemen who are lovers and cowards); (d) Maria–Emilia (a boy actor who was good in sharp exchanges and plain speaking; an unromantic attendant); (e) Feste–the Clown; (f) Sebastian–Cassio (the supporting romantic lead). It would follow that other parts, less obviously alike, were also intended for the same actor: (g) Sir Toby–Iago; (h) Olivia–Bianca; (i) Fabian–Duke of Venice; (j) Antonio–Montano. The only major character that fails to fit in as obviously as the rest is Malvolio. I think that Brabantio (and later Gratiano) might be taken by the Malvolio actor (k), an older man (a specialist in rebuke, anger, despair), or, just possibly, that the same 'star' (Burbage) played both Malvolio and Othello.[1] In that case some minor adjustments would follow in the casting lists: Malvolio–Othello; Orsino–Cassio; Sebastian–Montano.

1 I think it likely that the same actor (Heminges?) played Julius Caesar, Polonius, Malvolio and Brabantio. He seems to have been good as a performer of tiresome, self-important older men.

Even so, the special actor strengths of the two plays remain surprisingly close, closer than in *Othello* and the adjacent tragedies.

Sir Toby and Iago, less self-evidently written for one actor than most of the other parts, call for several similar talents. Actor (g) could sing, roister in a drinking-scene, use his sword, could play 'the smiler with the knife under the cloak'[1] and, partnering boy actor (d) in a number of scenes in each play, may have been the master to whom this boy was apprenticed. Charles Gildon recorded in 1694 that he had heard 'from very good hands, that the Person that Acted Jago was in much esteem for a Comoedian',[2] a piece of gossip that confirms my casting and also throws light on Shakespeare's conception of Iago. While all the plays performed by a professional company in the same season had to be put on by the same group of actors, new plays written by the company dramatist would naturally pay more attention to the special talents of these actors than one would expect in the case of revivals. This would apply particularly to the parts written for boy actors, who could only take leading roles for a very few years.

(2) *A singing boy actor*. The Willow Song, intended for a boy actor who could sing, appears in F *Othello* but not in Q. It was carefully removed from the Q text (which omits 4.3.29–52, 54–6, 59–62, and also 5.2.244–6) – why would any sensible person wish to cut this song, so beautifully expressive of Desdemona's mood? The usual explanation is that at the time of a later revival of *Othello* the leading boy actor could not sing.[3] As it chances, something similar happened to a song in *Twelfth Night*, except that it was not cut but transferred to a different actor.

1 For the less favourable view of Sir Toby, see *Twelfth Night*, ed. E. A. J. Honigmann (The Macmillan Shakespeare, 1971), 13–14.

2 See Chambers, *William Shakespeare*, 2.261.

3 Chambers, *op. cit.*, 1.460.

> It is almost certain from the insistence on Viola's musical accomplishments at I.ii.57–58 that she was meant to be a singer, and from the awkward opening of II.iv that the song 'Come away, come away death' has been transferred from her to Feste. We must therefore suppose that when the play was originally produced the company had a singing boy who was no longer available on the occasion of some revival.
>
> (Greg, 297)

Greg stated a widely shared view. If, however, *Othello* has been postdated and was composed between mid-1601 and mid-1602, the very period to which many assign *Twelfth Night*,[1] a simpler hypothesis now suggests itself. The boy actor of Viola and Desdemona lost his voice earlier than expected, when Shakespeare had recently completed the two plays, and adjustments were hurriedly made in both, at the same time. This hypothesis avoids a difficulty that Greg (358 n. 9) noticed and tried to explain away: if Q *Othello* derives from the author's foul papers, or rough draft of the play (see p. 359) – as Greg assumed and I have tried to corroborate – why should changes introduced in a later revival be marked in the author's foul papers? The alternative is to assume that the Willow Song and other proposed cuts were lightly marked in the foul papers when *Othello* was first prepared for performance, and that the Folio scribe was later instructed to prepare a version of the complete text, reinstating all cuts (see *Texts*, 101). On this hypothesis the Willow Song, so far from being a special case,

1 *Twelfth Night* has sometimes been dated 1599 (see *Texts*, 175 n. 19). If the performance of this play witnessed by John Manningham on 2 February 1602 (Chambers, *op. cit.*, 2.327) was not the very first one, it would still be very close in time to the proposed first performance of *Othello*; that is, the same boy actor will have played both Viola and Desdemona at this time, and this will have been the time when his voice broke and he could not sing the songs in the two plays that were intended for him.

fits into a general picture: the play's textual history, date and casting requirements all point to the same conclusion.

Boys able to sing and to take leading dramatic parts 'were not easily obtainable in the public theatres at the beginning of James's reign', observed Richmond Noble,[1] the author of *Shakespeare's Use of Song* (1923), citing the changes involving the songs in *Twelfth Night* and *Othello*. 'If more evidence were wanted, we could turn to *Cymbeline* and note in Act IV, scene 3 the clumsy device Shakespeare had to adopt because Guiderius and Arviragus could not sing.' He continued:

> I am convinced that the first performance of *Hamlet, Twelfth Night* (in its original form), and *Othello* (as in the Folio) were not widely separated in time. When these three plays were produced Shakespeare had at his disposal a boy who could take a leading part and also sing ballads or popular songs.

A boy fully trained to act and sing would be a competent performer 'perhaps for two years, but certainly not very much longer'. Boy actor (b), it seems, was capable of playing Ophelia in 1600; he was approaching the time when his voice would break, but Shakespeare hoped that it would last another season and wanted to exploit his special gifts by creating two even more important roles for him, Viola and Desdemona. The likelihood that Desdemona's character was partly determined by a boy actor's ability to sing and to play gentle, vulnerable roles (unlike the boy for whom Shakespeare created Beatrice and Rosalind a season or two earlier) is as interesting as Gildon's story that Iago was first performed by a comedian – where, again, Shakespeare seems to have exploited the actor's gifts, making Iago something of a humorist (quite unlike Cinthio's Ensign).

1 'The date of *Othello*', *TLS*, 14 December 1935, p. 859.

If, then, *Othello* belongs to the winter–spring of 1601–2, very much the same time as *Twelfth Night*, its relationship with other contemporary plays needs to be reconsidered. Heywood's *A Woman Killed With Kindness*, for which Henslowe paid £6 in February and March 1603, should be seen as a reply to *Othello* rather than as the domestic tragedy that prompted Shakespeare to move in this new direction. On the other hand, *Patient Grissel* by Dekker and others, probably first performed early in 1600, would be closer to *Othello* than has been supposed, and this could help to explain why Cinthio's Disdemona becomes a more pronounced 'patient Grissel' figure in *Othello*. Shakespeare added episodes in which Othello rages at Desdemona and she, not understanding his fury, reacts, some think, too patiently (the letter episode, when he strikes her, 4.1.240; the 'brothel' episode, 4.2.24ff.). A lost play about George Scanderbeg, entered in the SR in July 1601, may have influenced Shakespeare as well: Scanderbeg, a renegade Christian, led Turkish armies against Christians, and *Othello* could have been intended as a counter-attraction, with a Moor starring as a Christian general against the Turks.

James Roberts, who entered *Hamlet* in the SR on 26 July 1602, appears to have acted as the players' agent on a number of occasions.[1] After the publication of the 'bad' Quarto of *Hamlet* (Q1) in 1603, Roberts printed the 'good' Quarto of 1604–5 that replaced Q1. The SR entry of 1602, I deduce, was made to 'block' the publication of an unauthorized text, since Roberts allowed two years to pass before printing *Hamlet*, an immediately popular play. An unauthorized text, it seems, was known or rumoured to exist as early as 1602, and this text is likely (but not certain) to have been the one printed in

1 This view of Roberts has been challenged, but seems to me the correct one of Roberts and also of Edward Blount, who succeeded Roberts as the players' agent: see *Texts*, 174 n. 15.

1603 – the one that contained echoes of many other plays,[1] including *Othello*. There are some steps in this reasoning that cannot be proved but, all things considered, the evidence suggests that *Othello* had been performed by mid-1602. I am aware of no compelling evidence for a later date.

It is usually assumed that the 'bad' Quarto of *Hamlet* was put together by a minor actor who had only a hazy recollection of the text as a whole and who interpolated many scraps of dialogue from other plays in which he had acted. When could he have had a part in *Othello*? The years 1601 and 1602 were free of the plague. In 1603 playing was 'restrained during the illness of Elizabeth on 19 March and probably not resumed', as plague broke out in April and continued for the rest of the year.[2] *Othello*, then, would have been performed not later than March 1603, a *terminus ante quem* that again points to 1602 as the probable year of the play's first performance.

1 For the echoes of other plays in *Hamlet* Q1 see G. I. Duthie, *The 'Bad' Quarto of 'Hamlet'* (Cambridge, 1941), and Alfred Hart, *Stolne and Surreptitious Copies* (Melbourne and Oxford, 1942).

2 Chambers, *Elizabethan Stage*, 4.349.

APPENDIX 2

The Textual Problem

Two early texts of *Othello* were published some years after Shakespeare's death in 1616: a Quarto (known as Q) in 1622, and a version included in the First Folio collection of 1623 (known as F). They differ in many hundreds of readings – in single-word variants and in longer passages, in spelling, verse lineation and punctuation. Ever since the second Quarto of 1630 (Q2) editors have conflated Q and F, that is, they have chosen readings from both, blending them together as they saw fit. Although I have not checked every recorded edition of the play, I think it probable that no two editions are exactly alike and that no edition prints the play exactly as Shakespeare wrote it.

Before I try to explain these extraordinary differences, here is a brief description of Q and F. Q collates A^2, $B{=}MM^4$, N^2, and contains forty-eight leaves. The title-page reads 'THE Tragoedy of Othello, The Moore of Venice. *As it hath beene diuerse times acted at the* Globe, and at the Black-Friers, by *his Maiesties Seruants*. *Written by* William Shakespeare. [Ornament] *LONDON*, Printed by *N.O.* for *Thomas Walkley*, and are to be sold at his shop, at the Eagle and Child, in Brittans Bursse. 1622.' After an epistle, 'The Stationer to the Reader', signed 'Thomas Walkley', the text follows on pages numbered 1 to 99. Walkley had previously entered his 'copy' in the Stationers' Register: '**Thomas Walkley** Entred for his copie vnder the hands of Sir GEORGE BUCK, and Master **Swinhowe** warden, *The Tragedie of OTHELLO, the moore of Venice* . . . vj^{d}.'[1]

1 See Charlton Hinman, *Othello 1622*, Shakespeare Quarto Facsimiles, 16 (Oxford, 1975), v.

The F text of *Othello* was placed near the end of the volume followed by only two more plays (*Antony and Cleopatra* and *Cymbeline*). It occupies thirty pages, printed in double columns; on the last page, after 'FINIS', it adds a list of 'The Names of the Actors'.

According to Charlton Hinman's Through Line Numbering,[1] F consists of 3,685 lines, about 160 lines more than Q. F's additional lines include more than thirty passages of 1 to 22 lines (all recorded in the textual notes); amongst F's more interesting additions we may mention Roderigo's account of Desdemona's elopement (1.1.119–35), Desdemona's Willow Song (4.3.29–52, 54–6, 59–62 and 5.2.244–6) and Emilia's speech on marital fidelity (4.3.85–102). On the other hand, F's omissions 'are trifling', said E. K. Chambers, chiefly a few half-lines here and there, 'and doubtless due to error'.[2]

Both Q and F were press-corrected. Many of the corrections merely adjusted loose type or spacing, and these are not recorded by Arden 3. I have recorded all corrections that affect meaning: such press-corrections do not necessarily restore authoritative manuscript readings, since press-correctors did not always refer back to the manuscript. Each correction has to be judged on its merits.

More than fifty instances of 'profanity', printed by Q, were deleted in F or replaced by less offensive words (e.g. 1.1.4, 32, 85, 107). Editors once assumed that F was purged because of the Act of Abuses (1606), which prohibited profanity and swearing on the stage, yet we now know that some scribes and perhaps compositors omitted profanity for other reasons (*Texts*, 77ff.). The censor of *Othello* was unusually cautious if he deleted *Tush* (1.1.1) and worried about other harmless expletives

1 See Charlton Hinman's Norton Facsimile of *Shakespeare's First Folio* (New York, n.d.), xxiv.

2 Chambers, *William Shakespeare*, 1.459.

(2.2.10, 4.1.239), yet he also overlooked some profanity; nevertheless the evidence of purging is clear enough. Editors think that the profanity was Shakespeare's (he wrote the play before 1606), and revert to Q's readings.

Q and F divide the play into acts and scenes. Q only numbers Acts 2, 4 and 5, and one scene (2.1); F numbers the acts and scenes as in Arden 3, except that F's 2.2 combines two scenes (2.2 and 2.3). Q, however, marked scene endings with the usual *Exeunt*, and in effect initiated the divisions adopted by later texts. As Q was the first of Shakespeare's 'good quartos' to be divided into acts, its act divisions – like F's – may have no authority.

Q stage directions are often fuller and more informative than F's (cf. 1.1.157; 1.3.0.1; 2.1.0.1; 5.2.195, 232), the opposite of what one would expect if F was printed from a prompt-copy, as was once supposed (Greg, 370). The Q directions, said W. W. Greg (360), 'might all have been written by the author', i.e. though fuller than F's they do not look like the essential information sometimes added in prompt-books. In fact, both Q and F omit many necessary stage directions.

Aware of so many differences between Q and F, how should an editor proceed? He must try to account for the differences: examining the detail of each text, he must explain its provenance and transmission. 'Provenance' refers to the manuscript origin of the printed text: it could be the author's rough draft or 'foul papers', or an authorial fair copy, or a scribal copy prepared for the theatre or for a private patron or for the printer. Clearly 'provenance' already involves transmission; an editor, however, also wants to know how many scribes and compositors copied and set the text, and, if possible, their working habits. Both scribes and compositors normally changed spelling and punctuation at this time, and took other liberties with the texts they 'transmitted'. When William Jaggard, later to be the printer of the First Folio, produced a reprint of *The Merchant of Venice* in 1619, 'the total number of variants introduced [by Jaggard's men] is something like 3,200', about one per line, mostly changes of spelling and punctuation.[1]

The 1619 text of *The Merchant of Venice*, being a reprint, gives the editor a less baffling challenge than the two texts of *Othello*. All or almost all of its 3,200 variants can be explained as conscious or unconscious compositorial substitutions. In the case of *Othello* we have to ask whether Q and F derive from a single authorial arch-text or from two (e.g. foul papers and authorial fair copy); if from two, some QF variants could be seen as Shakespeare's first and second thoughts. Again, since Q preceded F by a year, could F have been printed from a corrected copy of Q? Or could the F scribe or compositor have occasionally consulted Q, perhaps because the F copy was illegible, thus transplanting 'common errors' from Q to F? Editors agree that some weak or nonsensical readings found in both Q and F must be common errors: if so, other readings vouched for by both Q and F, even though not self-evidently corrupt, could also be Q mistakes taken over by F.

All the possibilities outlined in the preceding paragraph have been backed by recent editors, and each one accounts for the transmission of Q and F *Othello* in a different way. Every theory of transmission, again, has its own implications for editorial policy. It would not be easy to do justice to all the editorial problems and suggested solutions in this short appendix: instead of attempting the impossible, I have prepared a companion volume, *The Texts of 'Othello'*, where there is enough space for a systematic study of the textual detail. I propose, next, to summarize the conclusions of the companion volume, and then to indicate how they affect editorial decisions in Arden 3.

1 D. F. Mackenzie, quoted *Texts*, 51.

CONCLUSIONS

Soon after writing the foul papers of *Othello* (I call this version manuscript A), Shakespeare made a fair copy (manuscript B), changing some words and phrases but not undertaking large-scale revision; that is, the longer passages found in F and not in Q were not later additions, but were present in A and subsequently cut. Professional scribes copied out A and B, and their scribal manuscripts (Aa, Bb) were used as printer's copy for Q and F. The sequence of the six early texts of *Othello* can be shown as follows.

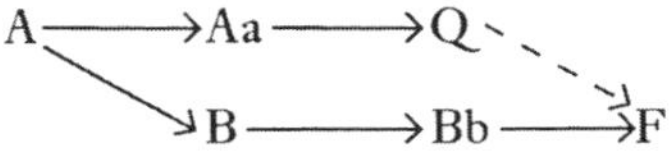

The broken arrow indicates that some Q readings also found their way into F.

EDITORIAL DECISIONS

Misreading

So many QF variants disagree in only one or two letters that misreading must account for the difference. Many such words would be easily confused in Secretary hand, which was used by Shakespeare in his six surviving signatures and, as all editors assume, in writing his plays.[1] A careful analysis of these variants suggests, further, that Shakespeare's hand was often almost illegible, much more so than in the three pages of *Sir Thomas More*, which were probably written eight or nine years earlier. The final letters of some words must have been an indistinct scribble, sometimes a superscript scribble (e.g. you^{r} = your), making it impossible to tell whether or not a letter was intended.

1 See the reproductions of Secretary-hand minuscules and capitals in the Arden 3 *King Henry V* (ed. T. W. Craik), pp. 103–4, which show how easily letters could be confused and misreading could occur.

Hence the frequent omission or addition of final *r* and *t* in *Othello*: you:your (1.1.79; 1.2.35; 3.3.40, 477; 5.2.262, 297); the:their (2.1.24, 45; 2.3.346; 3.4.146: viz. *their* spelt *ther*, as in *Sir Thomas More*, D, 260); worse:worsser (1.1.94), etc.; ouer:ouert (1.3.108); againe:again't (2.1.274); began:began't (2.3.213); of:oft (3.3.150); leaue . . . keepe:leaue't . . . kept (3.3.207); know:know't (3.3.340); loose:loose't (3.4.69); no:not (4.1.60), etc. Almost as commonly, initial and medial letters were omitted or confused, suggesting that Shakespeare's writing was difficult to read throughout and tailed off illegibly at the ends of many words.

Other letters often confused or misread in *Othello* include (1) minims (m, n, u, i, c, r, w); (2) a:minim; (3) e:d; (4) e:o; (5) o:a; (6) t:e; (7) t:c; (8) th:y; (9) h:th; (10) medial r; (11) the tilde, a suspension mark for m and n; (12) final y:e(e); (13) final s – the commonest cause of misreading, with more than one hundred variants in *Othello*. This is not a complete list, but gives some idea of the scale of the problem (for documentation, see *Texts*, ch. 8).

Since Q and F suffer from the same kinds of misreading we may deduce that Shakespeare himself was the source of the trouble. F has fewer obvious misreading errors, which is what one would expect if Q derives from foul papers and F from an authorial fair copy.

The Folio scribe

The hypothesis that it was Shakespeare's own writing that caused so much confusion is reinforced by the identification of the scribe who copied out manuscript Bb. A number of unusual spellings and his characteristic apostrophes, hyphens, colons, etc. make it as certain as such things can be that the scribe was Ralph Crane, who is generally accepted as the scribe responsible for five other Folio texts. Many dramatic and nondramatic manuscripts survive in Crane's hand, some with his signature: his spelling and punctuation were so distinctive that other printed plays are now recognized as 'Crane transcripts', apart from the five Folio texts (e.g. *The Duchess of Malfi*, 1623). For our purposes the all-important point is this: Crane, a professional scribe, wrote in a beautifully clear hand, therefore the misreading in F *Othello* cannot be blamed on an illegible manuscript (Bb) that defeated the Folio compositors. It was Crane, not the Folio compositors, who had to struggle to decipher a difficult manuscript – a manuscript that led to the same kinds of misreading as we find in Q. Again: the source of the trouble seems to have been Shakespeare's handwriting.

One arch-text or two?

Is it possible, though, that Q and F originated in the same manuscript, rather than in two different authorial manuscripts? Two reasons persuade me that we have to reckon with two autographs. (1) Short alternative passages in Q and F, too different to qualify as instances of misreading, are accepted by many editors as authorial revision. Such revision could conceivably survive in a single authorial manuscript, except for one factor. W. W. Greg, who analysed these passages and who did not subscribe to the 'two arch-texts' hypothesis, concluded in several instances that 'The impression is of deliberate revision in F rather than of corruption in Q', 'Everything therefore points to F's version having been reached by way of Q's, rather than Q's being a corruption of F's' (364ff.). Greg was impressed by the 'Shakespearian quality of both versions', with Q always the earlier and F the better one. Is this not strange? If Q and F both derive from a single authorial manuscript and it was obvious to the F scribe that one set of superior short passages replaced others that were inferior, why was it not obvious to the Q scribe? The simplest answer is that the Q scribe did not have access to the superior passages, because he copied from a different manuscript.

(2) F's inferior variants prompt a second argument on similar lines. Since the F scribe certainly had access to Q, as we know from common errors and common mislineation (*Texts*, 95ff.),

why did he prefer inferior manuscript variants which look like corruptions, when Q supplied him with readings that later editors have thought undoubtedly superior? Had this happened just once or twice one might attach little significance to it, pleading in his defence that he need not have compared every word in the two texts. But it happened many times, and, as we have seen, he was copying a difficult manuscript, one that often forced him to resort to guesswork because he could not make out what Shakespeare had written: all the more reason, then, for checking Q's reading, if only to save himself time. Why should he waste his time attempting to decipher an illegible manuscript when the correct reading lay at hand in Q? The answer must be, I think, that Heminges and Condell had directed him to do so. Handing Crane manuscript B (Shakespeare's fair copy), they would have expressed their wishes roughly as follows. 'We need a clearly written manuscript of *Othello* for the Folio printer. Transcribe *this* manuscript. It is not easy to read – if you can make nothing of it, check the passage in this printed version [Q]. But keep in mind that the printed version is full of errors: it is a badly printed, unauthorized text [see *Texts*, 48–9]. Our manuscript has a much more reliable text. Follow the manuscript, as far as you can.' Crane did as he was told: when he thought that the scribble in the manuscript should be read as *worser* or *comes* (1.1.94, 114), not *worse* or *come*, as in Q, he preferred the manuscript reading. And, because the manuscript was so difficult, he sometimes thought he could make out words, indistinctly written, that were not there (e.g. *tongued, chances*, instead of Q's *toged, changes*: 1.1.24, 71).

The 'better text'?

Assuming, as above, that Crane knew Q to be an inferior text and that he took some trouble to produce a better one, an editor may want to treat F as the 'better text', and therefore to follow F whenever Q and F readings are equally acceptable. Yet this is a dangerous policy, for several reasons. (1) Though he did his best, Crane clearly misread some words, some F variants being very unlikely (e.g. *super-vision*, 3.3.398, for Q *superuisor*). Consequently other words, which are not so self-evidently wrong, could be misreadings as well. (2) If Crane transcribed from an authorial fair copy and Q was printed from a scribal copy of the foul papers, we are not entitled to assume that, when Q and F disagree, one or the other must be corrupt. Where there are variant readings Shakespeare could have written both: we know from Thomas Middleton's holographs, and from other authorial texts, that many poets replace words when they transcribe their own work, either consciously or unconsciously. Even quite trivial changes were common, and many 'indifferent variants' in *Othello* may be instances of such authorial instability (1.1.16 chosen:chose; 42 be all:all be; 53 those:these). (3) Crane, and the Folio compositors, regarded some contractions and the uncontracted alternative as interchangeable, even when this appears to damage the metre (e.g. *Ile* and *I will, you've* and *you have, 't* and *it*). An editor who retains F's contracted or uncontracted form must warn readers that it may have to be lengthened or shortened or slurred, when spoken aloud, to suit the metre. I have in general chosen to follow F, not to correct the verse, because the alternative would be to force the verse into a metrical straitjacket. But when Q offers a variant that scans correctly (either the contracted or the uncontracted form), Arden 3 adopts the Q reading. In my view, Q rather than F is the 'better text' in some respects – in its punctuation, in retaining profanity, and in at least some of its stage directions and verbal variants.

Copy-text?

Yet F is better than Q in other respects – in its verse lineation, and in being marred by fewer 'manifest errors' than Q. Would it be possible, then, to modify the traditional editorial policy, and to treat F as copy-text for lineation, and to make Q the copy-text for profanity and punctuation? I believe that we should lean towards whichever text seems better at lineation when we consider lineation, whichever seems better at punctuation when we consider punctuation, and so on: lean towards but not follow slavishly, since both Q and F are sometimes self-evidently corrupt even in the textual department in which they seem generally better. Adopting this editorial position, Arden 3 is less committed to either Q or F than previous editions, exercising more freedom of choice. Nevertheless, because F transmits the later authorial version and corrects many Q errors, Arden 3 leans towards F rather than Q in some instances of genuine perplexity, particularly in dealing with indifferent variants (a preference shared with most other editions of *Othello*). We must acknowledge, however, that even this lesser reliance on F is dangerous. Arden 3 follows F twenty-two times in printing *hath* where Q prints *has*: yet there are good reasons for suspecting that the F scribe, Ralph Crane, substituted *hath* for *has* in *Othello* as in other texts (see *Texts*, 68), and was responsible for many other indifferent variants in F (including F's regular *handkerchief* and *murther* for Q's regular *handkercher* and *murder*). In the present state of knowledge we cannot be certain about indifferent variants but it seems likely that Arden 3, though far less committed to F as 'copy-text' than previous editions, still prints scores – or perhaps hundreds – of F variants that are scribal or compositorial substitutions, not the words written by Shakespeare.

Syllabic changes

In Elizabethan English a large number of words could gain or lose a syllable as the metre required. Some could be either monosyllabic or disyllabic (notably words with -er- and -en- syllables: heav(e)n, stol(e)n; nev(e)r, wheth(e)r, etc., and also others: dev(i)l, spir(i)t; dear, fire, hour). Others had a variable syllable for the endings -(i)on, -(i)ous, -(i)an (e.g. jeal(i)ous, Venet(i)an). Arden 3 does not attempt to regularize, leaving it to the reader to try out the scansion and come to his or her own decisions, as with other contractions (p. 364 above, 'The "better text"?'). Readers may stumble here and there, as Shakespeare's actors no doubt did, yet at the same time they will learn an important lesson – that there is no single correct way of speaking Shakespeare's verse. The commentary offers help when this is needed.

Lineation

Arden 3 prints as verse a number of passages usually printed as prose. These are mostly short passages embedded in verse (preceded and/or followed by verse) which divide readily into lines consisting of ten or eleven syllables, Shakespeare's normal measure: e.g. 1.1.4–6; 3.3.316–19; 4.1.234; 5.1.121–3; 5.2.33–4, 68–70, 121–3. In a few cases the decision to print verse rather than prose is more problematic (3.1.32–41; 5.2.115, 138–9). It should be remembered, though, that as Shakespeare experimented with verse-like prose and prose-like verse, that the difference between the two could be slight (2.1.178–80; 2.3.12, 61, 116; 4.2.175), and that, at the time of *Othello*, Shakespeare was capable of writing odd-looking verse lines (e.g. 3.1.48; 4.2.70; 5.2.279). In addition readers should note that expletives, vocatives and interruptions were often treated as extra-metrical (e.g. 1.1.4, 101; 1.3.173). The rules or conventions governing dramatic verse – I have only touched on a few – may be explored at greater length in specialist studies.[1]

Since Q mislines so many undoubted verse passages as prose and vice versa, wrongly divides verse lines and is exceptionally insensitive to the verse measure, the textual notes do not record Q's variant lineation in every instance. Where Arden 3 diverges from F's lineation, this is recorded.

Intended cuts?

Several 'good' texts of Shakespeare's plays print lines that were clearly meant to be deleted (sometimes they reappear in the

1 See Abbott, or George T. Wright's more recent *Shakespeare's Metrical Art* (Berkeley, 1988).

same text in slightly altered form). Shakespeare's deletions, it seems, were marked very lightly or not at all. *Othello* includes lines and half-lines that are puzzling or metrically irregular, the removal of which does not damage the sense. They too could have been lightly marked deletions printed in error (e.g. 1.1.20; 1.3.17; 3.1.47). One four-line passage (4.3.63–6) looks like a false start immediately replaced by 4.3.67–9. If Q printed intended deletions, the F scribe could have copied them from Q.

Punctuation

On the evidence of Shakespeare's three pages in *Sir Thomas More* and of most of the 'good' quartos, editors believe that Shakespeare punctuated lightly, and very often omitted all punctuation. Both Q and F *Othello* punctuate more heavily than the 'good' texts published in Shakespeare's lifetime: Arden 3 repunctuates, distrusting the pointing of Q and F as post-Shakespearian (see *Texts*, ch. 11).

Modernization

Every Arden 3 text has been modernized – what does this mean? It does not mean that each text follows precisely the same principles of modernization. To take one example, modern texts almost certainly punctuate more heavily than Shakespeare did, yet punctuation is a notoriously personal matter, so it is unlikely that Arden 3 punctuation will be the same from play to play; indeed, the same editor may choose to punctuate more or less heavily in different passages of the same play. Punctuation is partly a matter of feeling; careful readers of *Othello* may feel – no, *should* feel – that, here and there, they disagree with the editor's pointing. And why not?

> The noise was high. Ha, no more moving?
> Still as the grave. Shall she come in? were't good?
> I think she stirs again. No – what's best to do?
>
> (5.2.92–4, Ard^3)

The noise was high. Ha! no more moving.
Still as the grave . . . Shall she come in, were't good?
I think she stirs again . . .? – No. What's best to do?

Both are possible, and readers should remember that the editor's choice of punctuation often rests on grounds that could not be defended in a court of law.

Inevitably, the editor's modernized punctuation affects the 'feeling' of the whole play, in particular the flow of thought from sentence to sentence. It could be that we should not adopt the same pointing for dialogue and for soliloquy (where the thinking process, more elliptical, may need more dashes); or that the very different speech habits of Othello and Iago require different kinds of punctuation. Be that as it may, two things are clear. First, that the function of Shakespeare's dramatic words is often impossible to define with certainty. A question mark, in his texts, could indicate a question or an exclamation; the absence of a question mark, on the other hand, does not imply that no question is intended. There are questions and half-questions (as, perhaps, at 5.2.94, above), just as there are asides and half-asides:[1] Shakespeare's language breaks all the rules of grammar and precedent. Second, because he wrote performance scripts for actors, and because the actors must have spoken quickly, Shakespeare did not have to worry about the grammatical connections of words and sentences: in the theatre the verbal flow rushes past us like a fast-flowing river, and individual words are sometimes scarcely more identifiable than drops of water in a rippling current.

For these reasons a modernized text imposes a sharper focus than Shakespeare probably wanted – for example, by dividing dramatic speech into either prose or verse (see p. 367). A modern editor tidies the text, standardizing speech prefixes and stage directions, eliminating Shakespeare's first or second thoughts, normalizing his famously unstable spelling. Some editors even

1 For half-asides see Honigmann, 'Stage direction', 119–20, and *Oth* 2.1.213–15.

distinguish between 'Oh' and 'O' where, again, there is no evidence that Shakespeare did so (compare Othello's 'Oh, oh, oh' and 'O, o, o' in the Quarto at 5.2.195, 279). Such tidying introduces new difficulties: should we read 'O insupportable, O heavy hour!' (5.2.97) or 'Oh, insupportable! Oh, heavy hour!'? As with other forms of modernization, this question will seem more important to editors and readers than to actors in the theatre.

The editor of Arden 3 *Othello* modernizes reluctantly, with many reservations. Modern spelling and punctuation make Shakespeare more accessible, at a cost – namely, that we lose the Elizabethan flavour and suggestiveness of his language, making Shakespeare our contemporary even though his every word is around four hundred years old. It is like cleaning an old picture and slightly changing all the colours. In a few cases I refuse to modernize, since the modern form of some words will positively mislead. 'Count' now has different connotations and will not mean the Day of Judgement, therefore I retain F 'compt' (5.2.271); God is not an engineer, therefore remains an 'inginer' (2.1.65).

A sample passage

Having summarized the textual policy of this edition, I shall try to show how it affects editorial thinking in a sample passage, 5.2.0ff. (see pp. 370–4). (1) The opening stage direction differs in Q and F. Both texts omit essential information: Arden 3 reprints both, and adds one word to F, 'desdemona *in her bed* [*asleep*]'. Q supplies one other stage direction, '*He kisses her*', opposite lines 19 and 20, omitted by F; Arden 3 expands this (see [8], p. 373). (2) Though Q and F sometimes agree in their punctuation, they frequently differ (six times in the first five lines). Arden 3 modernizes and repunctuates, on the assumption that both Q and F are more heavily pointed than Shakespeare's manuscripts would have been. (3) F, in line with its practice elsewhere, introduces many more 'emphasis capitals' than Q.

Even if Arden 3 were not a modernized text, we would have to drop these capitals as post-Shakespearian.

Proceeding, next, to the verbal variants in the dialogue, we notice (4) that many are graphically related, i.e. would look very similar in Shakespeare's hand (see p. 361 above, 'Misreading') – e.g. (citing Q first, then F) returne:re-Lume (13), once:One

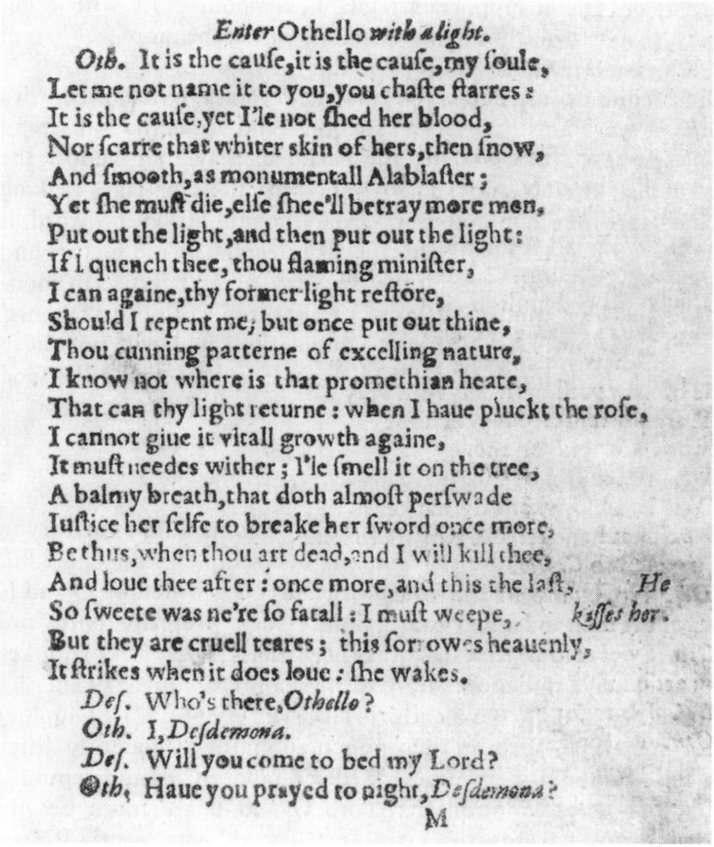

Enter Othello *with a light.*

Oth. It is the cauſe,it is the cauſe,my ſoule,
Let me not name it to you,you chaſte ſtarres:
It is the cauſe,yet I'le not ſhed her blood,
Nor ſcarre that whiter skin of hers,then ſnow,
And ſmooth,as monumentall Alablaſter;
Yet ſhe muſt die,elſe ſhee'll betray more men,
Put out the light,and then put out the light:
If I quench thee, thou flaming miniſter,
I can againe,thy former light reſtore,
Should I repent me; but once put out thine,
Thou cunning patterne of excelling nature,
I know not where is that promethian heate,
That can thy light returne: when I haue pluckt the roſe,
I cannot giue it vitall growth againe,
It muſt needes wither; I'le ſmell it on the tree,
A balmy breath,that doth almoſt perſwade
Iuſtice her ſelfe to breake her ſword once more,
Be thus,when thou art dead,and I will kill thee,
And loue thee after: once more,and this the laſt, *He*
So ſweete was ne're ſo fatall: I muſt weepe, *kiſſes her.*
But they are cruell teares; this ſorrowes heauenly,
It ſtrikes when it does loue: ſhe wakes.

Deſ. Who's there,*Othello*?
Oth. I,*Deſdemona.*
Deſ. Will you come to bed my Lord?
Oth. Haue you prayed to night,*Deſdemona*?

M

22 Quarto text of *Othello* 5.2.1–25

(17, 19), when:where (22). (5) In two instances the variants are graphically alike but differ in their endings – cunning:cunning'st (11), *Desdemona:Desdemon* (25) – which may mean that Shakespeare's writing tailed off into an indistinct squiggle, one which might be misinterpreted (a) as standing for illegible

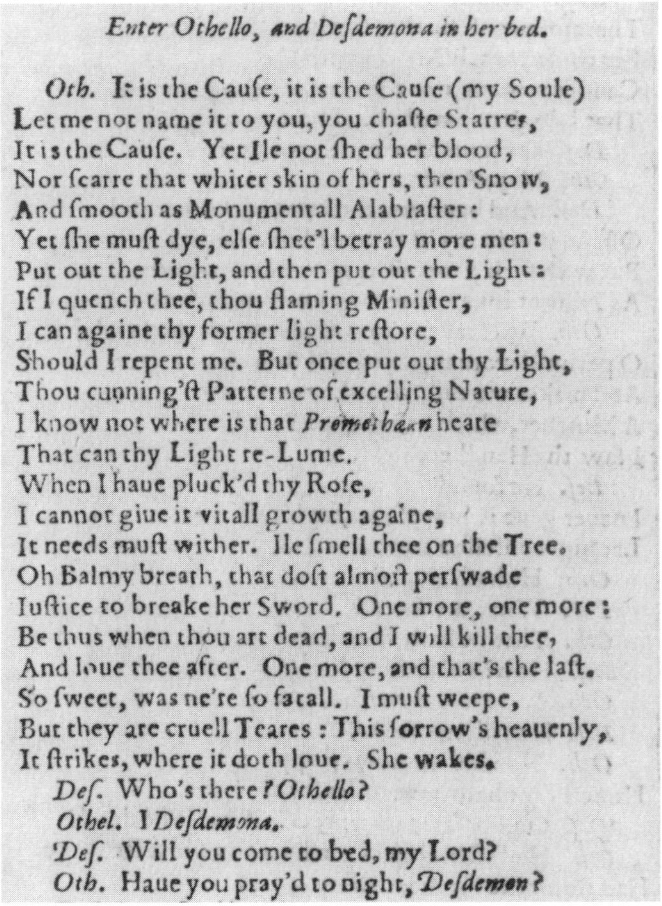

Enter Othello, and Deſdemona in her bed.

Oth. It is the Cauſe, it is the Cauſe (my Soule)
Let me not name it to you, you chaſte Starres,
It is the Cauſe. Yet Ile not ſhed her blood,
Nor ſcarre that whiter skin of hers, then Snow,
And ſmooth as Monumentall Alablaſter:
Yet ſhe muſt dye, elſe ſhee'l betray more men:
Put out the Light, and then put out the Light:
If I quench thee, thou flaming Miniſter,
I can againe thy former light reſtore,
Should I repent me. But once put out thy Light,
Thou cunning'ſt Patterne of excelling Nature,
I know not where is that *Promethæan* heate
That can thy Light re-Lume.
When I haue pluck'd thy Roſe,
I cannot giue it vitall growth againe,
It needs muſt wither. Ile ſmell thee on the Tree.
Oh Balmy breath, that doſt almoſt perſwade
Iuſtice to breake her Sword. One more, one more:
Be thus when thou art dead, and I will kill thee,
And loue thee after. One more, and that's the laſt.
So ſweet, was ne're ſo fatall. I muſt weepe,
But they are cruell Teares: This ſorrow's heauenly,
It ſtrikes, where it doth loue. She wakes.
Deſ. Who's there? *Othello*?
Othel. I *Deſdemona.*
Deſ. Will you come to bed, my Lord?
Oth. Haue you pray'd to night, *Deſdemon*?

23 Folio text of *Othello* 5.2.1–25

letters; or (b) as having no significance, even though the writer intended it as one or two letters. Arden 3 adopts the F readings, taking Q's '*Desdemona*' as an instance of (a) and 'cunning' as one of (b).

But should we ascribe all the variants to the misreading of a difficult hand? (6) Some variants in both Q and F appear to be connected with other readings in the same text. Q's *it* and *doth* (15, 16) go together (third person), as do F's *thee* and *dost* (second person). If Shakespeare revised these lines, perhaps he also omitted Q *her selfe* (17) and added *one more* to the same line in F. Or is it conceivable that the Q scribe or compositor misread his manuscript, and was responsible for these and other Q variants?

(7) Not all of F's variants are clearly improvements. 'When I haue pluck'd *thy* Rose' (F) is less pleasing than '. . . *the* rose' (Q), and looks like final *e:y* misreading (*Texts*, 85). 'It *needs must* wither' (F) and 'It *must needes* wither' (Q) could both be right. '*Oh* Balmy breath' (F) may seem preferable to '*A* balmy breath' (Q) – until we recall that 'A' could stand for 'Ah', which again means that there is little to choose between Q and F.

(8) A more striking difference occurs at lines 17 and 19, where Q reads 'once more . . . once more', and F 'One more, [one more . . .] One more'. This is less likely to be revision than minim-misreading, common in both Q and F. Most editors have followed F, at the same time moving Q's '*He kisses her*' from line 19 to line 15. Yet there is no textual evidence for a kiss at 15, though Othello's words reveal that another action is needed at this point – 'I'll smell thee on the tree; / O balmy breath . . .'. 'Once more' refers back to this action, and to Othello's highly developed sense of smell. 'One more [kiss]' would be acceptable if a kiss had preceded, 'one more [smell]' or 'one more [sniff]' less so, for reasons that are not easy to explain. Here an editor may choose to move Q's stage direction, as editors do elsewhere in *Othello*, and read 'One more' (with F) or may prefer Q's 'once more'. Arden 3 follows Q and adapts the stage direction at line 19 to include smelling and kissing.

(9) It will be agreed, I think, that more of Q's variants are inferior than F's. Are all of Q's inferior readings corruptions, though, or could some be Shakespeare's 'first thoughts', which he improved upon when he prepared his fair copy? That is not so clear, and the question cannot be decided from a single passage, as other passages that may be revised occur in other scenes, and reinforce one another (e.g. 1.3.261ff., 277ff.; 5.2.217–18). All local decisions depend on other local decisions, and on the resulting 'editorial policy'.

The textual notes

As will now be obvious, many of the textual problems of *Othello* have not yet been solved. While we may think that we can explain some – the disappearance of profanity from F, 'Crane' spellings, anomalous lineation, misreading errors – we cannot always distinguish between authorial revision and scribal or compositorial substitutions: indeed, the more trivial the variants the more difficult it becomes to guess who was responsible and to make a reasoned choice (compare 1.1.4 you will:you'l, 16 chosen:chose, 26 the:th', 34 But:Why). Readers are therefore urged to pay special attention to the textual notes: these record all significant QF variants, and are printed conveniently below the text and commentary, on the same page. The editor has done his best, but editors are fallible. The small type at the foot of the page may after all transmit the best reading. Here, as elsewhere in this transitory life, the true men may lie low while impostors parade themselves more openly.

N.B. The textual notes include unusual spellings and other oddities that look like hangovers from the distinctive writing habits of Shakespeare and of Ralph Crane. These clues as to textual provenance are so numerous that it was not possible to explain each one in the commentary, but they are discussed in *Texts*, pp. 158ff. (Shakespearian spellings), 63ff. (Crane's spellings), and 68ff. (compositor E's retention of copy-spellings).

APPENDIX 3

Cinthio and Minor Sources

The principal source of *Othello* is the seventh *novella* in the third decade of Giraldi Cinthio's *Hecatommithi* (1565). A French translation by G. Chappuys appeared in 1583, and the first extant English translation not until 1753. Chappuys kept close to the Italian version except for a few details, and Shakespeare could have read one or the other, or perhaps a lost English translation. The details that point to his acquaintance with the Italian text consist of unusual words or phrases not replicated in Chappuys, and are listed in the commentary at 1.3.350 (*acerb*), 2.1.16 (*molestation*), 3.3.363 (*ocular proof*), and in the notes on Cinthio in this appendix. Similar details, not found in the Italian text, suggest Shakespeare's possible acquaintance with Chappuys: 1.3.220 (*heart pierced*), 3.3.300 (*take out the work*), 4.1.196 (*touch*). The Italian words are more striking, and the *Othello* 'echoes' of Chappuys could be explained as coincidence.[1] Yet a lost English version, one that perhaps made use of both the Italian and the French texts, cannot be ruled out. Lodowick Bryskett's translations of various works of Cinthio were published before and after *Othello* was written,[2] and a translation of Cinthio's story of the Moor of Venice could have reached Shakespeare in manuscript. Not very long after composing *Othello* Shakespeare returned to the *Hecatommithi* for one of the sources of *Measure for Measure*.

1 See Honigmann, '*Othello*, Chappuys and Cinthio', *N&Q*, 13 (1966), 136–7; and Naseeb Shaheen, 'Shakespeare's knowledge of Italian', *SS*, 47 (1994), 161ff., and below, pp. 396–7.

2 See *Barnabe Riche His Farewell to Military Profession*, ed. Donald Beecher (New York, Publications of the Barnabe Riche Society, vol. 1, 1992), 50–1.

M. R. Ridley said that 'there are a few verbal parallels which may be taken to suggest an acquaintance with the original [i.e. Cinthio], but I do not think that they are very significant' (Ard^2, xv). I have to disagree: whether we consider Cinthio or Chappuys or a lost English version as Shakespeare's original, a surprising number of verbal parallels found their way into the play from Cinthio, with or without intermediaries – many more than Bullough listed in his translation. Their significance grows as we piece together the full jigsaw of borrowings – words, phrases, episodes, ideas – for then we see that, even though Shakespeare felt free to change whatever did not suit him, Cinthio's narrative supplied so much detail that in effect Shakespeare allowed it to guide his view of crucial events.

The translation of Cinthio that follows has been reprinted, with kind permission, from Geoffrey Bullough's *Narrative and Dramatic Sources of Shakespeare*, vol. 7, pp. 241–52. The footnotes, listing Shakespeare's verbal and other debts, are new. While, inevitably, some of these debts are less compelling than others, their cumulative weight seems to me considerable.

Cinthio's *Hecatommithi*, modelled on Boccaccio's *Decameron*, consists of a series of short stories about different kinds of love, chiefly married love. After an introduction (ten stories) there follow ten decades, each of ten stories, where the story-tellers explain how husbands and wives should be chosen. In the introduction one man argues that appetite should be ruled by reason (*Oth* 1.3.262–3, 'not / To please the palate of my appetite'; 327–9, 'If the balance of our lives had not one scale of reason to poise another of sensuality'), and that before marrying we should consider 'the quality, manners, life and habits' of possible partners (3.3.233, 'Not to affect many proposed matches / Of her own clime, complexion and degree'). He denounces women who, pretending to be virtuous, hide their ugly souls in 'singing, playing, dancing . . . and speaking sweetly' (3.3.186–8, ''Tis not to make me jealous / To say my wife is fair, feeds well, loves company, / Is free of speech, sings, plays and dances well'). Although these are commonplaces, I think it likely that Shakespeare glanced at Cinthio's introduction and at the pages that precede and follow the story of the Moor of Venice.

Cinthio's third decade revolves around the infidelity of husbands and wives (cf. *Oth* 4.3.85–102). In the sixth story a husband discovers his wife committing adultery, and revenges himself by arranging her 'accidental' death. The seventh story, which now follows, deals with a husband's revenge for supposed adultery and, again, the wife's 'accidental' death. In short, Cinthio's stories are interlinked: the account of the Moor, Shakespeare's immediate source, which he read with concentrated attention, no doubt led him to other parts of the *Hecatommithi*.

THE THIRD DECADE, STORY 7

A Moorish Captain takes to wife a Venetian lady, and his Ensign accuses her to her husband of adultery; he desires the Ensign to kill the man whom he believes to be the adulterer; the Captain kills his wife and is accused by the Ensign. The Moor does not confess, but on clear indications of his guilt he is banished; and the scoundrelly Ensign, thinking to injure others, brings a miserable end on himself.

The ladies would have had great pity for the fate of the Florentine woman had her adultery not made her appear worthy of the severest punishment; and it seemed to them that the gentleman's patience had been unusually great. Indeed they declared that it would be hard to find any other man who, discovering his wife in such a compromising situation, would not have slain both of the sinners outright. The more they thought about it the more prudently they considered him to have behaved.

After this discussion, Curzio, on whom all eyes were turned as they waited for him to begin his story, said: *I do not believe that either men or women are free to avoid amorous passion,*[1] *for human nature is so disposed to it that even against our will it makes itself powerfully felt in our souls.*[2] Nevertheless, *I believe that a virtuous lady has the power, when she feels herself burning with such a desire, to resolve rather to die than through dishonourable lust to stain that modesty which ladies should preserve*[3] as untainted as white ermine. And I believe that they err less who, free from the holy bonds of matrimony, *offer their bodies to the delight of every man*[4] than does a married woman who commits adultery with one person only. But as this woman suffered well-deserved punishment for her fault, so *it sometimes happens that without any fault at all, a faithful and loving lady, through the insidious plots* [tesele] *of a villainous mind,*[5] and the frailty *of one who believes more than he need,*[6] is murdered by her faithful husband; as you will clearly perceive by what I am about to relate to you.

There was once in Venice a Moor, a very gallant man, who, because he was *personally valiant*[7] and had *given proof in warfare*[8] of great prudence and skilful energy, was *very dear to the Signoria,*[9] who in rewarding virtuous actions ever advance the interests of the Republic. It happened that *a virtuous Lady of wondrous beauty called Disdemona,*[10] *impelled not by female*

1 3.3.279, '’Tis destiny unshunnable, like death'.
2 2.1.231–3, 'very nature will instruct her in it and compel her to some second choice'.
3 4.3.60–1, 'Dost thou in conscience think . . . That there be women do abuse their husbands . . .?'
4 3.3.348–9, 'I had been happy if the general camp . . . had tasted her sweet body'.
5 4.1.46–7, 'many worthy and chaste dames even thus, / All guiltless, meet reproach'.
6 5.2.342, 'Of one that loved not wisely, but too well'.
7 1.3.49, 'Valiant Othello' (It. *molto valoroso*; Fr. *fort vaillant*).
8 1.1.27, 'of whom his eyes had seen the proof' (Iago).
9 1.3.129, 'Her father loved me' (It. *caro a que signori*; Fr. *aymé des seigneurs*).
10 2.1.61–2, 'a maid / That paragons description'.

appetite but by the Moor's good qualities, fell in love with him,[1] and *he, vanquished by the Lady's beauty and noble mind,*[2] *likewise was enamoured of her.*[3] So propitious was their mutual love that, *although the Lady's relatives did all they could to make her take another husband,*[4] they were united in marriage and lived together in such concord and tranquillity while they remained in Venice, that never a word passed between them that was not loving.

It happened that the Venetian lords made a change in the forces that they used to maintain in Cyprus; and they chose the Moor as *Commandant*[5] of the soldiers whom they sent there. Although he was pleased by the honour offered him (for such high rank and dignity is given only to noble and loyal men who have proved themselves most valiant), yet his happiness was lessened when he considered the length and dangers of the voyage, thinking that Disdemona would be much troubled by it. The Lady, who had no other happiness on earth but the Moor, and was very pleased with the recognition of his merits that her husband had received from so noble and powerful a Republic, could hardly wait for the hour when he would set off with his men, and *she would accompany him*[6] to that honourable post. It grieved her greatly to see the Moor troubled; and, not knowing the reason for it, one day while they were dining together she said to him: 'Why is it, my Moor, that after being given such an honourable rank by the Signoria, you are so melancholy?'

The Moor said to Disdemona: 'The love I bear you spoils my pleasure at the honour I have received, because I see that one of two things must happen: either I must take you with me in peril

1 1.3.262–3, 'not / To please the palate of my appetite' (Othello).

2 1.3.253, 'I saw Othello's visage in his mind'; 266, 'to be free and bounteous to her mind'.

3 1.3.168–9, 'She loved me . . . And I loved her'.

4 Brabantio in Act 1; 4.2.127, 'Hath she forsook so many noble matches?'

5 1.2.53, 'Come, captain' (It. *capitano*; Fr. *capitaine* and *chef*).

6 1.3.260, 'Let me go with him.'

by sea, or, so as not to cause you this hardship, *I must leave you in Venice.*[1] The first alternative must inevitably weigh heavily on me, since every fatigue you endured and *every danger we met would give me extreme anxiety.*[2] The second, having to leave you behind, would be hateful to me, since, *parting from you I should be leaving my very life behind.*[3]

'Alas, husband,' said Disdemona, hearing this, 'What thoughts are these passing through your mind? Why do you let such ideas perturb you? *I want to come with you wherever you go, even if it meant walking through fire*[4] in my shift instead of, as it will be, crossing the water with you in a safe, well-furnished galley. *If there really are to be dangers and fatigues, I wish to share them with you;*[4] and I should consider myself very little beloved if, rather than have my company on the sea, you were to leave me in Venice, or persuaded yourself that I would rather stay here in safety than be in the same danger as yourself. *Get ready then for the voyage in the cheerfulness*[5] that *befits the high rank you hold.*'[6]

Then *the Moor joyously threw his arms round his wife's neck and said, with a loving kiss: 'God keep us long in this love, my dear wife!'*[7] Shortly afterwards, having donned his armour and made all ready for the journey, he embarked in the galley with his lady and all his train; then, hoisting sail, they set off, and with a sea of the utmost tranquillity arrived safely in Cyprus.

The Moor had in his company an Ensign of handsome presence but *the most scoundrelly nature in the world.*[8] He was

1 1.3.256, 'if I be left behind'.
2 2.1.2; 46, 'I have lost him on a dangerous sea'; 16, 'never did like molestation view' (It. *estrema molestia*).
3 1.3.295, 'My life upon her faith.'
4 1.3.168, 'She loved me for the dangers I had passed'; 249, 'That I did love the Moor to live with him'.
5 1.3.233, 'A natural and prompt alacrity' (It. *allegrezza*).
6 1.3.240, 'As levels with her breeding' (of Desdemona).
7 2.1.180; 191–3, 'But that our loves and comforts should increase'.
8 4.2.141–2, 'abused by some most villainous knave, / Some base notorious knave'.

in high favour with the Moor, who had no suspicion of his wickedness; for although he had *the basest of minds, he so cloaked the vileness hidden in his heart*[1] with *high sounding and noble words, and by his manner, that he showed himself in the likeness of a Hector or an Achilles.*[2] This false man had likewise taken to Cyprus his wife, a fair and honest young woman. Being an Italian she was much loved by the Moor's wife, and spent the greater part of the day with her.

In the same company there was also *a Corporal who was very dear to the Moor.*[3] This man went frequently to the Moor's house and *often dined with him and his wife.*[4] The Lady, knowing him so well liked by her husband, gave him proofs of the greatest kindness, and this was much appreciated by the Moor.

The wicked Ensign, taking no account of the faith he had pledged to his wife, and of the friendship, loyalty and obligations he owed the Moor, *fell ardently in love with Disdemona*,[5] and bent all his thoughts to see if he could manage *to enjoy her*;[6] but he did not dare openly show his passion, fearing that if the Moor perceived it *he might straightway kill him.*[7] He sought therefore in various ways, as deviously as he could, to make the Lady aware that he desired her. But she, whose every thought was for the Moor, never gave a thought to the Ensign or anybody else. And all the things he did to arouse her feelings for him had no more effect than if he had not tried them. Whereupon *he imagined that this was because she was in love with the*

1 3.3.110–11, 'some monster in thy thought / Too hideous to be shown'; 3.3.139, 'Utter my thoughts? Why, say they are vile and false?'
2 1.1.12–13, 'a bombast circumstance'; 2.1.221–2, 'bragging . . . prating' (of Othello).
3 3.1.49, 'he protests he loves you'; 3.3.48.
4 3.3.58, 'Tomorrow dinner then?'
5 2.1.289, 'Now I do love her too'.
6 1.3.358, 'thou shalt enjoy her'.
7 3.3.362ff.

Corporal;[1] and he wondered how he might remove the latter from her sight. Not only did he turn his mind to this, but *the love which he had felt for the Lady now changed to the bitterest hate*[2] and he gave himself up to studying how to bring it about that, once the Corporal were killed, if he himself could not enjoy the Lady, then the Moor should not have her either. *Turning over in his mind divers schemes, all wicked and treacherous, in the end he determined to accuse her of adultery, and to make her husband believe that the Corporal was the adulterer.*[3] But knowing the singular love of the Moor for Disdemona, and his friendship for the Corporal, he recognized that, unless he could deceive the Moor with some clever trick, it would be impossible to make him believe either charge. Wherefore he set himself to wait *until time and place opened a way for him*[4] to start his wicked enterprise.

Not long afterwards *the Moor deprived the Corporal of his rank for having drawn his sword and wounded a soldier while on guard-duty.*[5] Disdemona was grieved by this and tried many times to reconcile the Moor with him. Whereupon the Moor told the rascally Ensign that his wife importuned him so much for the Corporal that he feared he would be obliged to reinstate him. The evil man saw in this a hint for setting in train the deceits he had planned, and said: 'Perhaps Disdemona has good cause to look on him so favourably!' *'Why is that?' asked the Moor.*[6] 'I do not wish', said the Ensign, 'to come between man and wife, but *if you keep your eyes open you will see for yourself.*'[7] *Nor for all the Moor's inquiries would the Ensign go*

1 2.1.231; 285, 'That she loves him, 'tis apt'.

2 3.3.448–9, 'All my fond love thus do I blow to heaven . . . 'Tis gone' (Othello) (It. *acerbissimo odio*: cf. 1.3.349–50, 'acerb as coloquintida').

3 1.3.391; 2.1.310.

4 3.3.249, 'Leave it to time'; 2.3.294–5, 'the time, the place'.

5 2.3.147ff., 239.

6 3.3.179, 'why is this?'

7 3.3.200, 'Look to your wife, observe her well'.

beyond this:[1] nonetheless his words left such a sharp thorn in the Moor's mind, that he gave himself up to *pondering intensely what they could mean*.[2] He became quite melancholy, and one day, when his wife was trying to soften his anger towards the Corporal, *begging him not to condemn to oblivion the loyal service and friendship of many years just for one small fault*,[3] especially since the Corporal had been reconciled to the man he had struck, *the Moor burst out in anger*[4] and said to her, 'There must be a very powerful reason why you take such trouble for this fellow, for he is not your brother, nor even a kinsman, yet you have him so much at heart!'

The lady, all courtesy and modesty, replied: 'I should not like you to be angry with me. Nothing else makes me do it but sorrow to see you deprived of so dear a friend as you have shown that the Corporal was to you. *He has not committed so serious an offence*[5] as to deserve such hostility. *But you Moors are so hot by nature*[6] that any little thing moves you to anger and revenge.'

Still more enraged by these words the Moor answered: 'Anyone who does not believe that may easily have proof of it! *I shall take such revenge* for any wrongs done to me *as will more than satisfy me*!'[7] The lady was terrified by these words, and seeing her husband *angry with her, quite against his habit*[8] she said humbly: '*Only a very good purpose made me speak to you about this*[9] but rather than have you angry with me *I shall never say another word on the subject*.'[10]

1 3.3.262, 362ff.
2 3.3.111, 'Thou dost mean something'; 157, 'What dost thou mean?'
3 3.3.18, 'My general will forget my love and service'; 64–6, 'his trespass . . . is not, almost, a fault'.
4 3.4.133, 'Is my lord angry?'
5 3.4.116, 'If my offence be of such mortal kind'.
6 3.4.30–1, 'the sun where he was born / Drew all such humours from him'.
7 3.3.446, 'my revenge'; 393, 'Would I were satisfied!'
8 3.4.125, 'My lord is not my lord, nor should I know him'.
9 3.3.76–80.
10 5.2.301, 'From this time forth I never will speak word' (Iago).

The Moor, however, *seeing the earnestness with which his wife had again pleaded for the Corporal,*[1] guessed that the Ensign's words had been intended to suggest that Disdemona was in love with the Corporal, and he went in deep depression to the scoundrel and *urged him to speak more openly.*[2] The Ensign, intent on injuring this unfortunate lady, after *pretending not to wish to say anything*[3] that might displease the Moor, appeared to be overcome by his entreaties and said: '*I must confess that it grieves me greatly*[4] to have to tell you something that must be in the highest degree painful to you; but since you wish me to tell you, and the regard that I must have of your honour as my master spurs me on, *I shall not fail in my duty*[5] to answer your request. You must know therefore that it is hard for your Lady to see the Corporal in disgrace for the simple reason that she takes her pleasure with him whenever he comes to your house. *The woman has come to dislike your blackness.*'[6]

These words struck the Moor's heart to its core;[7] but in order to learn more (although he believed what the Ensign had said to be true, through the suspicion already sown in his mind) he said, with a fierce look: '*I do not know what holds me back from cutting out that outrageous tongue of yours*[8] which has *dared to speak such insults against my Lady*!'[9] Then the Ensign: 'Captain,' he said, '*I did not expect any other reward*[10]

1 3.3.54; 3.4.89ff.
2 3.3.135–6, 'give thy worst of thoughts / The worst of words'.
3 3.3.147.
4 2.3.173, 'Honest Iago, that look'st dead with grieving'.
5 3.3.137; 197, 'To show the love and duty that I bear you'.
6 (Lit., to *tire* of your blackness; Fr., 'qui est déia ennuyée de vostre taint noir') 1.3.350–1, 'She must change . . . sated with his body'; 3.3.267, 'Haply for I am black'.
7 (It. *passorono il cuore*; Fr. *transpercèrent le coeur*) 1.3.219–20, 'But words are words . . . That the bruised heart was pierced through the ear'.
8 2.3.217, 'I had rather have this tongue cut from my mouth' (Iago).
9 3.3.362–6.
10 3.3.382, 'I thank you for this profit'.

for my loving service; but since my duty and my care for your honour have carried me so far, I repeat that the matter stands exactly as you have just heard it, and if your Lady, with a false show of love for you, has so blinded your eyes that you have not seen what you ought to have seen, that does not mean that I am not speaking the truth. For this Corporal has told me all, like *one whose happiness does not seem complete until he has made someone else acquainted with it.*'[1] And he added: 'If I had not feared your wrath, *I should*, when he told me, *have given him the punishment he deserved by killing him.*[2] But since letting you know *what concerns you more than anyone else*[3] brings me so undeserved a reward, *I wish that I had kept silent*,[4] for by doing so I should not have fallen into your displeasure.'

Then the Moor, in the utmost anguish, said, '*If you do not make me see with my own eyes*[5] what you have told me, be assured, I shall make you realize that *it would have been better for you had you been born dumb.*'[6] 'To prove it would have been easy', replied the villain, 'when he used to come to your house; but now when, not as it should have been, but for the most trivial cause, you have driven him away, *it cannot but be difficult for me*,[7] for although I fancy that he still enjoys Disdemona whenever you give him the opportunity, *he must do it much more cautiously than he did before*,[8] now that he knows you have turned against him. Yet I do not lose hope of being able to show you what you do not wish to believe.' And with these words they parted.

1 4.1.25–9, 'knaves . . . [who] cannot choose / But they must blab'.
2 1.2.3–10.
3 4.1.195–6, 'if it touch not you it comes near nobody' (It. *appartiene*; Fr., 'ce qui vous touche plus qu'à aucun autre').
4 3.3.395, 'I do repent me that I put it to you.'
5 3.3.363, 'give me the ocular proof' (It. *vedere co gl'occhi*; Fr. *voir*).
6 3.3.365, 'Thou hadst been better have been born a dog'.
7 3.3.400–5, 'It were a tedious difficulty . . . To bring them to that prospect.'
8 3.3.422, '. . . "Let us be wary, let us hide our loves"'.

The wretched Moor, *as if struck by the sharpest of darts,*[1] went home to wait for the day when the Ensign would make him see that which must make him miserable for ever. But no less trouble did the Ensign suffer by his knowledge of the Lady's chastity, for *it did not seem possible to find a way*[2] of making the Moor believe what he had falsely told him, till, his thoughts twisting and turning in all directions, the scoundrel thought of a new piece of mischief.

The Moor's wife often went, as I have said, to the house of the Ensign's wife, and stayed with her a good part of the day; wherefore seeing that she sometimes carried with her *a handkerchief embroidered most delicately in the Moorish fashion,*[3] *which the Moor had given her and which was treasured by the Lady and her husband too,*[4] the Ensign planned to take it from her secretly, and thereby prepare her final ruin. He had a little girl of three years old, much loved by Disdemona. One day, when the unfortunate Lady had gone to pass some time at the villain's house, he took the child in his arms and carried her to the Lady, who took her and pressed her to her breast. The deceiver, who had great sleight of hand, lifted the handkerchief from her girdle so warily that she did not notice it; and he took his leave of her in great joy.

Disdemona, knowing nothing of it, went back home and, being occupied with other thoughts, did not miss the handkerchief. But a few days later, she looked for it, and not finding it she became afraid that the Moor might ask for it, as he often did. The wicked Ensign, seizing a suitable opportunity, *went to the Corporal's room,*[5] and with cunning malice *left the handkerchief* at the head of his bed. The Corporal did not notice

1 4.1.267–9, '[whom] shot . . . nor dart . . . Could . . . pierce?'

2 3.3.405, 'It is impossible you should see this'.

3 3.3.300, 'I'll have the work ta'en out' (It., 'il qual pannicello era lauorata alla moresca'; Fr., 'vn mouchoir . . . ouuré à la Moresque').

4 3.3.297–300; 3.4.54; 5.2.48.

5 3.3.324; 3.4.188.

it till the next morning when, getting out of bed, he put his foot upon the handkerchief, which had fallen to the floor. *Not being able to imagine how it had come into his house, and knowing that it was Disdemona's,*[1] he determined to give it back to her. So he waited till the Moor had gone out, then went to the back door and knocked. *Fortune, it seems, had conspired with the Ensign*[2] to bring about the death of the unhappy lady; for just then the Moor came home, and hearing a knock on the door went to the window and shouted angrily: 'Who is knocking?' The Corporal, hearing the Moor's voice and fearing that he might come down and attack him, *fled without answering*.[3] The Moor ran down the stairs, and opening the outside door went out into the street and looked around, but could see nobody. Then returning full of evil passion, *he asked his wife who had knocked*[4] on the door below.

The Lady replied truthfully that she did not know. The Moor then said, '*It looked to me like the Corporal*.'[5] 'I do not know', she said, 'whether it was he or somebody else.' The Moor restrained his fury, though he was consumed with rage. He did not want to do anything before consulting the Ensign, to whom he went at once and told him what had occurred, praying him to find out from the Corporal all that he could about it. Delighted with what had happened, the Ensign promised to do so. Accordingly *he spoke to the Corporal one day while the Moor was standing where he could see them as they talked;*[6] *and chatting of quite other matters than the Lady, he laughed heartily*[7] and, displaying great surprise, he moved his head about and gestured with his hands, acting as if he were listening

1 3.4.187–8, 'whose is it?' – 'I know not'.
2 5.2.223–4, 'that handkerchief . . . I found by fortune'.
3 3.3.30–40.
4 3.3.37, 'Was not that Cassio?'
5 3.3.40, 'I do believe 'twas he.'
6 4.1.75, 93ff.
7 4.1.118, 169.

to marvels. *As soon as the Moor saw them separate he went to the Ensign to learn what the other had told him*;[1] and the Ensign, after making him entreat him for a long time, finally declared: '*He has hidden nothing from me. He tells me that he has enjoyed your wife every time you have given them the chance by your absence.*[2] And on the last occasion *she gave him the handkerchief which you gave her as a present when you married her.*'[3] The Moor thanked the Ensign and it seemed obvious to him that *if he found that the Lady no longer had the handkerchief, then all must be as the Ensign claimed.*[4]

Wherefore one day *after dinner*,[5] while chatting with the Lady on various matters, *he asked her for the handkerchief. The unhappy woman*,[6] who had greatly feared this, grew red in the face at the request, and to hide her blushes (which the Moor well noted), she ran to the chest, pretending to look for it. After much search, *'I do not know', she said, 'why I cannot find it;*[7] perhaps you have had it?' 'If I had had it,' said he, 'why should I ask for it? But you will look more successfully another time.'

Leaving her *the Moor began to think how he might kill his wife*,[8] and the Corporal too, in such a way that he would not be blamed for it. And since he was obsessed with this, day and night, *the Lady inevitably noticed that he was not the same towards her as he was formerly*.[9] Many times she said to him, '*What is the matter with you?*[10] What is troubling you? Whereas

1 4.1.29, 168.
2 3.3.341, 'her stolen hours of lust'.
3 3.4.66–7, 'when my fate would have me wive, / To give it her'; 4.1.174.
4 3.3.443–4, 'If it be that, or any that was hers, / It speaks against her with the other proofs.'
5 3.3.284–5, 'Your dinner . . . attend[s]'; 3.4.52, 'Lend me thy handkerchief.'
6 3.4.103, 'I am most unhappy in the loss of it'.
7 3.4.85, 'It is not lost'.
8 3.3.391–2, 'If there be cords or knives, / Poison, or fire'; 4.1.168; 179, 'she shall not live'.
9 3.4.125–6, 'My lord is not my lord'; 4.1.268, 'He is much changed.'
10 4.2.100, 'what's the matter with my lord?'

you used to be the gayest of men, *you are now the most melancholy man alive!*'[1]

The Moor invented various excuses,[2] but she was not at all satisfied, and *although she knew no act of hers which could have so perturbed the Moor*,[3] she nevertheless feared that *through the abundance of lovemaking which he had with her he might have become tired of her*.[4] Sometimes she would say to the Ensign's wife, '*I do not know what to make of the Moor. He used to be all love towards me*[5] but in the last few days *he has become quite another man*;[6] and I fear greatly that I shall be a warning to young girls not to marry against their parents' wishes; and Italian ladies will learn by my example *not to tie themselves to a man whom Nature, Heaven, and manner of life separate from us*.[7] But because I know that he is very friendly with your husband, and confides in him, *I beg you, if you have learned anything from him which you can tell me, that you will not fail to help me*.'[8] She wept bitterly as she spoke.

The Ensign's wife, who knew everything (for *her husband had wished to use her as an instrument in causing the Lady's death*,[9] but she had never been willing to consent), *did not dare, for fear of her husband, to tell her anything*.[10] She said only: '*Take care not to give your husband any reason for suspicion, and try your hardest to make him realize your love*

1 4.2.43, 'why do you weep?'
2 3.3.288.
3 3.4.158, 'I never gave him cause'.
4 1.3.351–2, 'when she is sated with his body she will find the error of her choice' (Iago).
5 4.2.153, 'I know not how I lost him.'
6 3.4.125–6, 'My lord is not my lord'.
7 3.3.233–5, 'Not to affect many proposed matches / Of her own clime, complexion and degree, / Whereto we see, in all things, nature tends' (Iago).
8 4.2.151, 'What shall I do to win my lord again?'
9 3.3.296–7, 'My wayward husband hath a hundred times / Wooed me to steal it'; 5.2.225–7.
10 3.4.24, 'I know not, madam'.

and loyalty.'[1] 'That indeed I do,' said Disdemona, 'but it does not help.'

In the meantime *the Moor sought in every way to get more proof*[2] of that which he did not wish to discover, and prayed the Ensign to contrive to let him see the handkerchief in the Corporal's possession; and although that was difficult for the villain, he promised nonetheless to make every effort to give him this testimony.

The Corporal had a woman at home who worked the most wonderful embroidery on lawn, and seeing the handkerchief and learning that it belonged to the Moor's wife, and that it was to be returned to her, *she began to make a similar one*[3] before it went back. While she was doing so, the Ensign noticed that she was working near a window where she could be seen by whoever passed by on the street. *So he brought the Moor and made him see her*,[4] and the latter *now regarded it as certain*[5] that the most virtuous Lady was indeed an adulteress. *He arranged with the Ensign to kill her and the Corporal and they discussed how it might be done. The Moor begged the Ensign to kill the Corporal*,[6] promising to remain eternally grateful to him. *The Ensign refused to undertake such a thing*,[7] as being too difficult and dangerous, for the Corporal was as skilful as he was courageous; but after much entreaty, and *being given a large sum of money*,[8] he was persuaded to say that he would tempt Fortune.

1 3.4.29, 'Is he not jealous?'; 3.4.100; 4.2.12, 'I durst, my lord, to wager she is honest'.
2 3.3.389, 'I'll have some proof.'
3 3.4.180, 'Take me this work out'; 190, 'I'd have it copied' (Fr., 'se mit à en faire vn semblable, *& en tirer le patron*'. The words in italics (= and take out the pattern) are not found in the Italian original).
4 4.1.156, 'By heaven, that should be my handkerchief!'
5 4.1.74, 'O, thou art wise, 'tis certain.'
6 3.3.475ff., 'let me hear thee say / That Cassio's not alive . . .' – 'But let her live.' – 'Damn her, lewd minx'; 4.1.198ff.
7 4.1.209 (Iago offers to kill Cassio).
8 3.3.472–3, 'I greet thy love . . . with acceptance bounteous'; 1.3.382, 'Thus do I ever make my fool my purse'.

Soon after they had resolved on this, *the Corporal, issuing one dark night from the house of a courtesan with whom he used to amuse himself, was accosted by the Ensign, sword in hand,*[1] who directed a blow at his legs to make him fall down; and *he cut the right leg entirely through, so that the wretched man fell.*[2] The Ensign was immediately on him to finish him off, but the Corporal, who was valiant and used to blood and death, had drawn his sword, and wounded as he was he set about defending himself, while *shouting in a loud voice: 'I am being murdered!'*[3]

At that *the Ensign, hearing people come running*, including some of the soldiers who were quartered thereabouts, *began to flee, so as not to be caught there; then, turning back he pretended to have run up on hearing the noise.*[4] Mingling with the others, and seeing the leg cut off, he judged that if the Corporal were not already dead, he soon would die of the wound, and although he rejoiced inwardly, *he outwardly grieved for the Corporal*[5] *as if he had been his own brother.*[6]

In the morning, news of the affray was spread throughout the city and reached the ears of Disdemona; whereupon, being tender-hearted and not thinking that evil would come to her by it, *she showed the utmost sorrow at the occurrence.*[7] On this *the Moor put the worst possible construction.*[8] Seeking out the Ensign, he said to him: '*Do you know, my imbecile of a wife is in such grief about the Corporal's accident that she is nearly out of her mind!*'[8] 'How could you expect anything else?' said the other, 'since he is her very life and soul?'

1 4.2.235, 'He sups tonight with a harlotry'; 5.1.1ff., 'Wear thy good rapier bare'.
2 5.1.24ff.; 71, 'My leg is cut in two'.
3 5.1.27, 'Help, ho! murder! murder!'
4 5.1.26 SD; 45 SD; 48, 'Whose noise is this . . .?'
5 5.1.56, 'O me, lieutenant!'
6 5.1.71, 'How is't, brother?'
7 5.2.72, 'my fear interprets'; 75, 'Alas, he is betrayed, and I undone'.
8 5.2.76, 'Out, strumpet, weep'st thou for him to my face?'

'Soul indeed!' replied the Moor, 'I'll drag the soul from her body,[1] for *I couldn't think myself a man*[2] if I didn't *rid the world of such a wicked creature.*'[3]

They were *discussing whether the Lady should perish by poison or the dagger,*[4] and not deciding on either of them, when the Ensign said: 'A method has come into my head that will satisfy you and that nobody will suspect. It is this: the house where you are staying is very old, and the ceiling of your room has many cracks in it. I suggest that we beat Disdemona with a stocking filled with sand until she dies. Thus there will not appear on her any sign of the blows. When she is dead, we shall make part of the ceiling fall; and we'll break the Lady's head, making it seem that a rafter has injured it in falling, and killed her. In this way nobody will feel any suspicion of you, for everyone will think that she died accidentally.'

The cruel plan pleased the Moor,[5] and they waited for a suitable opportunity. One night the Moor concealed the Ensign in a closet which opened off the bedchamber, and when the husband and wife were in bed, the Ensign, in accordance with their plan, made some sort of noise. Hearing it the Moor said to his wife:

> '*Did you hear that noise?*'
> 'Yes, I heard it', she replied.
> 'Get up', said the Moor, 'and see what it is.'[6]

The unfortunate Disdemona got out of bed, and as soon as she was near the closet, the Ensign came out and, being strong and muscular, he gave her a frightful blow in the small of her back, which made the Lady fall down at once, scarcely able to draw

1 5.2.50, 'Sweet soul, take heed'.
2 4.1.65, 'Good sir, be a man'; 89–90, 'I shall say you're . . . nothing of a man'.
3 5.2.6, 'Yet she must die, else she'll betray more men'.
4 3.3.391–2, 'If there be cords or knives, / Poison . . .'; 4.1.202.
5 4.1.207, 'the justice of it pleases'; 5.2.247, 'she loved thee, cruel Moor'.
6 5.2.85, 'What noise is this?'

her breath. With the little voice she had *she called on the Moor to help her.*[1] But he, jumping out of bed, said to her, '*You wicked woman,*[2] you are having the reward of your infidelity. This is how women are treated who, pretending to love their husbands, put horns on their heads.'

The wretched Lady, hearing this and feeling herself near to death (for the Ensign had given her another blow), *called on Divine Justice to witness to her fidelity, since earthly justice failed;*[3] and *as she called on God to help her, a third blow struck her, and she lay still,*[4] slain by the impious Ensign. Then, placing her in the bed, and breaking her skull, he and the Moor made the ceiling fall as they had previously planned, and *the Moor began to call for help,*[5] that the house was falling. *Hearing his cries the neighbours ran in and found the bed, and the Lady dead*[6] under the rafters – which made everyone grieve, *for they knew what a good life she had led.*[6]

Next day Disdemona was buried, amid the universal mourning of the people. But God, the just observer of men's hearts, *did not intend such vile wickedness to go without proper punishment.*[7] He ordained that *the Moor, who had loved the Lady more than his life,*[8] on finding himself deprived of her should *feel such longing that he went about like one beside himself, searching for her in every part of the house.*[9] Realizing now that the Ensign was the cause of his losing his Lady and all joy in life, he held the villain in such abhorrence that he could not bear even to see him;

1 5.2.119, 'Help, help, ho, help!' (Emilia).
2 5.2.63, 'O perjured woman'.
3 4.2.82, 'By heaven, you do me wrong'; 88, 'What, not a whore?' – 'No, as I shall be saved'; 5.2.16–17, 'that dost almost persuade / Justice to break her sword!'
4 5.2.83, 'O Lord! Lord! Lord! [(*He*) *smothers her*.]'
5 5.2.162 (Emilia calls for help); 163 SD.
6 5.2.197, 'thou hast killed the sweetest innocent'.
7 5.2.365, 'To you . . . Remains the censure of this hellish villain'.
8 1.3.295, 'My life upon her faith'; 3.3.90, 'perdition catch my soul / But I do love thee'.
9 5.2.18, 'I will kill thee / And love thee after'; 97, 'O insupportable, O heavy hour!'

and if he had not been afraid of the inviolable justice of the Venetian lords, he would have slain him openly. Not being able to do this with safety, *he took away his rank and would not have him in his company, whereupon such a bitter hatred sprang up between them that no greater or more deadly feud could be imagined.*[1]

The Ensign, that worst of all scoundrels, therefore set all his mind to injuring the Moor, and seeking out the Corporal, who had now recovered and went about with a wooden leg instead of the one that had been cut off, he said to him, 'It is time you got your revenge for the leg you lost. If you will come to Venice with me, I shall tell you who the miscreant was, for here I dare not tell you, for many reasons; and I am willing to bear witness for you in court.'

The Corporal who felt himself deeply wronged but did not know the real truth, thanked the Ensign and came with him to Venice. When they arrived there the Ensign told him that it was the Moor who had cut off his leg because of a suspicion he had formed that he was Disdemona's lover, and that for the same reason he had murdered her, and afterwards made it known that the fallen ceiling had killed her. Hearing this, the Corporal accused the Moor to *the Signoria*,[2] both of cutting off his leg and of causing the Lady's death, and called as witness the Ensign, who said that both accusations were true, for the Moor had approached him and tried to induce him to commit both crimes; and that, having then killed his wife through the bestial jealousy that he had conceived in his mind, he had told him how he had killed her.

When the Signoria learned of the cruelty inflicted by *the Barbarian*[3] upon a citizen of Venice, *they ordered the Moor to*

1 (This loss of rank perhaps suggested Iago's hatred when he is not promoted:) 1.1.5; 1.3.385, 'I hate the Moor'.
2 1.2.18, 'the signiory' (= the Signoria).
3 1.3.356, 'an erring Barbarian'.

be apprehended in Cyprus and to be brought to Venice,[1] where with many tortures they tried to discover the truth. But enduring with great steadfastness of mind every torment, he denied everything so firmly that nothing could be extorted from him. Although by his constancy he escaped death, he was, however, after many days in prison, condemned to perpetual exile, in which he was finally slain by Disdemona's relatives, as he richly deserved.

The Ensign returned to his own country; and not giving up his accustomed behaviour, he accused one of his companions, saying that the latter had sought to have him murder one of his enemies, who was a nobleman. The accused man was arrested and put to the torture, and when he denied that what his accuser said was true, *the Ensign too was tortured*, to compare their stories; and *he was tortured so fiercely that his inner organs were ruptured.*[2] Afterwards he was let out of prison and taken home, where he died miserably. Thus did God avenge the innocence of Disdemona. *And all these events were told after his death by the Ensign's wife, who knew the facts*[3] as I have told them to you.

[Story 8 is (as usual) prefaced by a linking passage commenting on the tale just heard:]

It appeared marvellous to everybody that such malignity could have been discovered in a human heart; and the fate of *the unhappy Lady*[4] was lamented, with some blame for *her father, who had given her a name of unlucky augury.*[5] And the party decided that since a name is the first gift of a father to his child, he ought to bestow one that is grand and fortunate, as if he wished to foretell success and greatness. *No less*

1 5.2.328–35, 'You shall close prisoner rest'.
2 5.2.302, 'Torments will ope your lips'; 367.
3 5.2.180ff.
4 1.1.161, 'O unhappy girl!'
5 Desdemona = (Greek) 'unfortunate'; 5.2.339, 'these unlucky deeds'.

was the Moor blamed, who had believed too foolishly.[1] But all praised God because the criminals had had suitable punishment.

No doubt Shakespeare's departures from Cinthio were carefully considered. Some were dictated by the exigencies of staging (Disdemona's death, the Ensign's 3-year-old daughter). Others resulted from Shakespeare's wish to compress and concentrate (the double time scheme, the accelerated ending) – the very opposite, be it noted, of what we find in *Hamlet* and *King Lear*. But Shakespeare's greatest effort went into his characterization, converting Cinthio's stereotype men and women, who exist only as plot mechanisms, into individuals interesting in themselves. Shakespeare's imagination also seized on many details, some of them barely hinted at by Cinthio, and conjured gold out of dross (the threat from 'the Turk', the imagery of sea and water, a generalized sexual antagonism). The handkerchief becomes a crucial exhibit in the play's treatment of 'chance', and also brings with it glimpses of the Egyptian and sibyl, and of Othello's father and mother (3.4.57ff.). One can usually see good reasons for Shakespeare's changes (the development of Brabantio and the addition of Roderigo), or at any rate reasons (the addition of the Clown: the clown actor, a popular performer, had to have a part). Now and then, though, we may feel that Shakespeare might have tried harder to break free from Cinthio, as in the eavesdropping episode (4.1.93ff.). Readers will find it rewarding to compare the play and Cinthio in greater detail.

Apart from Cinthio, many other writers and 'sources' contributed to *Othello*. (I am not convinced that Shakespeare read Bandello in Italian, as has been suggested, since there are

1 5.2.340, 'Nothing extenuate'; 342, 'one that loved not wisely, but too well'; 159–60, 'O gull, O dolt, / As ignorant as dirt!'

English sources for Desdemona's revival after being smothered.)[1] These are mentioned at various points in the introduction and commentary, and can be traced with the help of the index: John Leo, Pliny, Lewis Lewkenor (the translator of Contarini), Lyly, Marlowe, *Arden of Faversham, A Warning for Fair Women, Every Man in His Humour, Every Man out of His Humour*, Terence, Plautus, Ovid, Rabelais, the Bible, popular ballads, songs and proverbs, and the scenic form and characters in Shakespeare's own earlier plays, notably *Titus Andronicus, Much Ado* and *Twelfth Night*.[2] Anyone who thinks of *Othello* as a short story blown up beyond its capacity should keep in mind that Shakespeare packed into it much miscellaneous reading as well as something not far removed from research, his perusal of very recent books on the Mediterranean world, on north Africa and on Venice.

1 See Shaheen, as on p. 375 n. 1.
2 See also Bullough, 195ff., for other possible sources and analogues.

APPENDIX 4

Edward Pudsey's Extracts from *Othello*

Edward Pudsey, gentleman, from Tewkesbury, Gloucestershire, recorded extracts from several plays in notebooks which have survived. Most of the plays belonged to Shakespeare's company, and some of the extracts could have been written down during or just after a performance. Pudsey included passages from *The Merchant of Venice, Much Ado, Titus Andronicus, Romeo and Juliet, Richard 2, Richard 3* and *Hamlet*, and also from Jonson's *Every Man out of His Humour* and from a play called *Irus*. These were published by Richard Savage as *Shakespearean Extracts from 'Edward Pudsey's Booke'* (1888).[1]

Savage did not know Pudsey's will, which has now been printed.[2] The will, dated 8 January 1610, actually referred to his notebooks; administration was granted to his widow on 17 November 1613. Pudsey therefore could have quoted from the published versions of some plays, especially when his longer extracts are close to the quartos.[3] The extracts from *Romeo and Juliet* and *Hamlet*, on the other hand, two plays each of which reached print in two different quarto versions, could have been jotted down during a performance, for in these extracts he sometimes agrees with Q1 and sometimes with Q2 of the same play.

The extracts published by Savage were taken from papers now housed in the Bodleian Library (MS. Eng. poet. d. 3), but

1 Stratford-upon-Avon Note Books, no. 1 (printed and published at Stratford-on-Avon by John Smith; London: Simpkin and Marshall). See also Peter Beal, *Index of English Literary Manuscripts*, vol. 1, part 2 (1980), 449.

2 See *Playhouse Wills 1558–1642: An Edition of Wills by Shakespeare and His Contemporaries in the London Theatre*, ed. E. A. J. Honigmann and Susan Brock (Manchester, 1993), 92–4.

3 For instance, see Savage, *Shakespearean Extracts*, 46 (*Much Ado*).

some leaves from Pudsey's notebooks found their way into the Shakespeare Birthplace Trust Record Office in Stratford-upon-Avon (MS. ER 82). The Stratford leaves contain short extracts from *Othello*, a play not printed until after Pudsey's death, and so transmit the earliest bits of text of the play now known. While we cannot tell whether Pudsey wrote them down in the theatre or later, they look like approximations, attempts to keep track of ideas rather than to record the exact words of the play.

I am grateful to Mairi McDonald of the Birthplace Trust for checking my transcription. I have added numbers in square brackets at the beginning of each of the four lines, have expanded contractions and included alternative and doubtful readings, also in square brackets.

> [1] Dangerous to tell where a soldier lyes. [for] yf I shold say he lodge theer I lyed ther [or 'the^{e}r']
>
> [2] Shee y^{t} is free of her tonng [or 'toung'] ys as frank of her lipps. An ey y^{t} offe^{r}s p[ar]le to p[ro]uocac[i]o[n]
>
> [3] An equalitye of p[er]fections fit in mariage for when ye act ys past theere wilbe
>
> [4] a dulnes much needing ye help of beauty youth loue and such lyke to p[re]uent loathing
>
> [In margin, before line 3] A fit matc^{h}

Compare (1) and 3.4.1–13, (2) and 2.1.100–2, 2.3.21–2, (3) and 2.1.224ff., (4) and 2.1.224–31.

APPENDIX 5

Musical Settings for Songs in *Othello*

Musical adviser: Helen Wilcox

All musical settings are reproduced from F. W. Sternfeld, *Music in Shakespearean Tragedy* (1963), by permission. Note that the wording in the settings may not be the same as that in this edition. A comprehensive listing of all musical settings, incidental music and operas associated with Shakespeare's plays may be found in *A Shakespeare Music Catalogue*, edited by Bryan N. S. Gooch and David Thatcher, 6 vols (Oxford, 1991).

'*And let me the cannikin clink, clink*' (2.3.65–9)

Reproduced from Sternfeld, 146.

'King Stephen was and a worthy peer' (2.3.85–92)

See notes on pp. 340–1. Reproduced from Sternfeld, 149.

Willow Song (4.3.39–50)

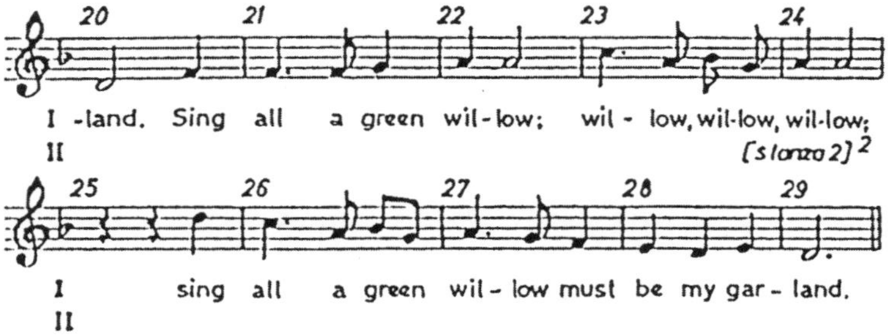
20 21 22 23 24
I -land. Sing all a green wil-low: wil - low, wil-low, wil-low;
II
[stanza 2] 2
25 26 27 28 29
I sing all a green wil - low must be my gar - land.
II

1. [stanza 2, bar 16, singing interrupted:]
   Lay by these.

2 [stanza 2, bar 24, singing interrupted:]
   Prithee, hie thee; he'll come anon.

3 [stanza 3, bar 6, singing stops here:]
   Nay, that's not next. Hark! who is't that knocks? It is the wind.

4 [stanza 4, bar 14, singing stops here:]
   So get thee gone; good night. Mine eyes do itch. Doth that bode weeping?

See notes on pp. 295, 344–5. Reproduced from Sternfeld, 43–4.

ABBREVIATIONS AND REFERENCES

Unless otherwise stated, the place of publication is London.

ABBREVIATIONS

ABBREVIATIONS USED IN NOTES

*	precedes commentary notes involving readings that are not found in either Q or F
as	substantively as in the edition cited (i.e. ignoring accidentals of spelling and punctuation)
cont.	continued
Fc	corrected state of F
Fr.	French
Fu	uncorrected state of F
It.	Italian
Lat.	Latin
lit.	literally
LN	longer note(s)
n.d.	no date
om.	omitted
opp.	opposite
Qc	corrected state of Q
Qu	uncorrected state of Q
SD	stage direction
SP	speech prefix
SR	Stationers' Register (see Arber)
subst.	substantially
this edn	a reading adopted for the first time in this edition
TLN	through line numbering in *The First Folio of Shakespeare*, ed. Charlton Hinman, Norton Facsimile (1968)
t.n.	textual notes at the foot of the page

SHAKESPEARE'S WORKS AND WORKS PARTLY BY SHAKESPEARE

AC	*Antony and Cleopatra*
AW	*All's Well That Ends Well*

AYL	*As You Like It*
CE	*The Comedy of Errors*
Cor	*Coriolanus*
Cym	*Cymbeline*
E3	*Edward III*
Ham	*Hamlet*
1H4	*King Henry IV Part 1*
2H4	*King Henry IV Part 2*
H5	*King Henry V*
1H6	*King Henry VI Part 1*
2H6	*King Henry VI Part 2*
3H6	*King Henry VI Part 3*
H8	*King Henry VIII*
JC	*Julius Caesar*
KJ	*King John*
KL	*King Lear*
LLL	*Love's Labour's Lost*
Luc	*The Rape of Lucrece*
MA	*Much Ado About Nothing*
Mac	*Macbeth*
MM	*Measure for Measure*
MND	*A Midsummer Night's Dream*
MV	*The Merchant of Venice*
MW	*The Merry Wives of Windsor*
Oth	*Othello*
Per	*Pericles*
PP	*The Passionate Pilgrim*
R2	*King Richard II*
R3	*King Richard III*
RJ	*Romeo and Juliet*
Son	*Sonnets*
STM	*Sir Thomas More*
TC	*Troilus and Cressida*
Tem	*The Tempest*
TGV	*The Two Gentlemen of Verona*
Tim	*Timon of Athens*
Tit	*Titus Andronicus*
TN	*Twelfth Night*
TNK	*The Two Noble Kinsmen*
TS	*The Taming of the Shrew*
VA	*Venus and Adonis*
WT	*The Winter's Tale*

REFERENCES

EDITIONS OF SHAKESPEARE

Alexander	*William Shakespeare: The Complete Works,* ed. Peter Alexander (1951)
Ard^1	*Othello*, ed. H. C. Hart, Arden Shakespeare (1903)
Ard^2	*Othello*, ed. M. R. Ridley, Arden Shakespeare, 7th edn (1958)
Bevington	*Othello*, ed. David Bevington, Bantam edn (1988)
Cam	*Othello*, ed. W. G. Clark, J. Glover and W. A. Wright, The Cambridge Shakespeare, 9 vols (Cambridge and London, 1863–6); revised W.A. Wright (1891–3)
Cam^2	*Othello*, ed. Alice Walker and John Dover Wilson, The New Shakespeare (Cambridge, 1957)
Cam^3	*Othello*, ed. Norman Sanders, The New Cambridge Shakespeare (Cambridge, 1984)
Capell	*Mr. William Shakespeare: His Comedies, Histories and Tragedies,* ed. Edward Capell, 10 vols (1767–8). For Capell's annotations see his *Notes and Various Readings to Shakespeare*, 3 vols (1779–83)
Collier	*The Works of William Shakespeare*, ed. John Payne Collier, 8 vols (1842–4)
Collier^2	*The Works of William Shakespeare*, ed. John Payne Collier, 8 vols (1853)
Dyce	*The Works of William Shakespeare*, ed. Alexander Dyce, 6 vols (1857)
F	*Mr. William Shakespeares Comedies, Histories, and Tragedies*, The First Folio (1623)
F2	*Mr. William Shakespeares Comedies, Histories and Tragedies*, The Second Folio (1632)
F3	*Mr. William Shakespeares Comedies, Histories and Tragedies*, The Third Folio (1663)
Folger	*Othello*, ed. Barbara A. Mowat and Paul Werstine, The New Folger Library Shakespeare (New York, 1993)
Furness	*Othello*, ed. Horace Howard Furness, New Variorum Shakespeare (Philadelphia, 1886; repr. New York, 1963)
Hanmer	*The Works of Shakespeare*, ed. Thomas Hanmer, 6 vols (Oxford, 1743–4)
Hart	See Ard^1

Johnson	*The Plays of William Shakespeare*, ed. Samuel Johnson, 8 vols (1765)
Kittredge	*Othello*, ed. George Lyman Kittredge (Boston, 1941)
Knight	*The Pictorial Edition of the Works of Shakespeare*, ed. Charles Knight, 8 vols (1838–43)
Malone	*The Plays and Poems of William Shakespeare*, ed. Edmond Malone, 10 vols (1790)
Muir	*Othello*, ed. Kenneth Muir, New Penguin Shakespeare (Harmondsworth, 1968)
Pope	*The Works of Shakespear*, ed. Alexander Pope, 6 vols (1723–5)
Pope^{2}	*The Works of Shakespear*, ed. Alexander Pope, 8 vols (1728)
Q	William Shakespeare, *Othello*, The First Quarto (1622)
Q2	William Shakespeare, *Othello*, The Second Quarto (1630)
Q3	William Shakespeare, *Othello*, The Third Quarto (1655)
Ridley	See Ard^{2}
Riv	*The Riverside Shakespeare*, ed. G. Blakemore Evans (Boston, 1974; rev. edn 1997)
Rowe	*The Works of Mr. William Shakespear*, ed. Nicholas Rowe, 6 vols (1709)
Rowe^{2}	*The Works of Mr. William Shakespear*, ed. Nicholas Rowe, 6 vols (1709)
Rowe^{3}	*The Works of Mr. William Shakespear*, ed. Nicholas Rowe, 8 vols (1714)
Sanders	See Cam^{3}
Sisson	William Shakespeare, *The Complete Works*, ed. C. J. Sisson (n.d.)
Steevens	*The Plays of William Shakespeare*, ed. Samuel Johnson and George Steevens, 10 vols (1773)
Theobald	*The Works of Shakespeare*, ed. Lewis Theobald, 7 vols (1733)
Var	*Othello*, ed. H.H. Furness, New Variorum Edition (Philadelphia, 1886)
Walker	See Cam^{2}
Warburton	*The Works of Shakespeare*, ed. William Warburton, 8 vols (1747)
Wilson *Titus*	*Titus Andronicus*, ed. John Dover Wilson, The New Shakespeare (Cambridge, 1948)

OTHER WORKS

Abbott	*E. A. Abbott, A Shakespearian Grammar*, 2nd edn (1870, etc.)
Adamson	Jane Adamson, *'Othello' as Tragedy: Some Problems of Judgment and Feeling* (Cambridge, 1980)
Aebischer	Pascale Aebischer, *Shakespeare's Violated Bodies: Stage and Screen Performance* (Cambridge, 2004)
Andreas	James Andreas, '*Othello*'s African American Progeny', *SAR* 57 (1992), 39–57
Arber	*A Transcript of the Registers of the Company of Stationers of London, AD JSS4-1640*, ed. Edward Arber, 5 vols (1875, etc.)
Ashcroft	Peggy Ashcroft, 'Playing Shakespeare', *SS* 40 (1988), 11–19
AT	*American Theatre*
Ath	*Athenaeum*
Barthelemy	Anthony Barthelemy, *Black Face, Maligned Race: The Representation of Blacks in English Drama from Shakespeare to Southerne* (Baton Rouge, LA, 1987)
Battersby	John Battersby, 'The Drama of Staging "Othello" in Johannesburg', *NYT* (26 October 1987)
Bible	Quotations from the Bible are from the 'Bishops' Bible' (1568, etc.), with modernized spelling, except when otherwise indicated
Bland	Sheila Rose Bland, 'How I Would Direct *Othello*', in *Othello: New Essays by Black Writers*, ed. Mythili Kaul (Washington, D.C., 1996), 29–41
Boose, 'Let'	Lynda Boose, '"Let it be Hid": The Pornographic Aesthetic of Shakespeare's *Othello*', in *Othello: New Casebooks*, ed. Lena Cowen Orlin (Basingstoke, 2004), 22–48
Boose, 'Othello'	Lynda Boose, 'Othello's Handkerchief: "The Recognizance and Pledge of Love"', *ELR* 5 (1975), 360–74
Bradley	A. C. Bradley, *Shakespearean Tragedy: Lectures on 'Hamlet', 'Othello', 'King Lear', and 'Macbeth'* (1904) (1991)
Bradshaw	Graham Bradshaw, *Misrepresentatiom: Shakespeare and the Materialists* (1993)
Bristol	Michael Bristol, 'Charivari and the Comedy of Abjection in *Othello*', *RD* 21 (1990): 3–21

Brown	Mark Brown, 'RSC casts its first black Iago for next year's Stratford-staged Othello', *The Guardian* (3 September 2014)
Bullough	Geoffrey Bullough, *Narrative and Dramatic Sources of Shakespeare*, 8 vols (1957–75), vol. 7 (1973)
Burton	Jonathan Burton, *Traffic and Turning: Islam and English Drama 1579–1624* (Newark, NJ, 2005)
Calderwood	James L. Calderwood, *The Properties of 'Othello'* (Amherst, 1989)
Callaghan, *Shakespeare*	Dympna Callaghan, *Shakespeare Without Women: Representing Gender and Race on the Renaissance Stage* (2000)
Callaghan, *Women*	Dympna Callaghan, *Women and Gender in Renaissance Tragedy* (Atlantic Highlands, NJ, 1989)
Carlisle	Carol Jones Carlisle, *Shakespeare from the Greenroom* (Chapel Hill, NC, 1969)
Chambers, *Elizabethan Stage*	E. K. Chambers, *The Elizabethan Stage*, 4 vols (Oxford, 1923)
Chambers, *William Shakespeare*	E. K. Chambers, *William Shakespeare: A Study of Facts and Problems*, 2 vols (Oxford, 1930)
Chew	Samuel C. Chew, *The Crescent and the Rose: Islam and England during the Renaissance* (Oxford, 1937, repr. New York, 1965)
Clinton	Catherine Clinton, 'Fanny Kemble's Journal: A Woman Confronts Slavery on a Georgia Plantation', *Frontiers* 9 (1987), 74–9
Coleridge	Samuel Taylor Coleridge, 'Notes on Some Other Plays of Shakespeare, section IV' (1818), in *Lectures and Notes on Shakespeare and Other English Poets*, volume 1 (1908)
Cornwall	Barry Cornwall, *The Life of Edmund Kean in Two Volumes* (1835)
Coryate	Thomas Coryate, *Coryat's Crudities* (1611)
Courtney	Krystyna Kujawinska Courtney, 'Ira Aldridge, Shakespeare, and Color-Conscious Performances in Nineteenth-Century Europe', in *Colorblind Shakespeare: New Perspectives on Race and Performance*, ed. Ayanna Thompson (New York, 2006), 103–22

Crowther	Bosley Crowther, '*Othello* (1965): The Screen: Minstrel Show "Othello": Radical Makeup Marks Olivier's Interpretation', *NYT* (2 February 1966)
Daileader	Celia Daileader, 'Casting Black Actors: Beyond Othellophilia', in *Shakespeare and Race*, eds. Catherine M.S. Alexander and Stanley Wells (Cambridge, 2000), 177–202
Dekker	*The Dramatic Works of Thomas Dekker*, ed. Fredson Bowers, 4 vols (Cambridge, 1953–8)
Demeter	Jason Demeter, '"This is a Theatre of Assault": Amiri Baraka's *Dutchman* and a Civil Rights *Othello*', *Selected Papers of the Ohio Valley Shakespeare Conference* 1 (2007): http://ideaexchange.uakron.edu/spovsc/vol1/iss2007/
Dent	R. W. Dent, *Shakespeare's Proverbial Language: An Index* (1981)
Dowling	Maurice Dowling, *Othello Travestie: An Operatic Burletta* (1834) in *Nineteenth Century Shakespeare Burlesques, Volume II*, ed. Stanley Wells (Wilmington, DE, 1978)
Drakakis	John Drakakis, 'Introduction', *The Merchant of Venice*, Arden3 (2010), 1–159
E.F.R.	E. F. R. 'Portrait Gallery (No. VIII): Mr. and Miss Vandenhoff', *Tallis's Dramatic Magazine* (April 1851)
Elie	Rudolph Elie, Jr. 'Robeson Gives "Othello" Great Power, Starring in Revival with White Troupe', *Variety* (12 August 1942)
Eliot	T.S. Eliot, *Selected Essays* (New York, 1950)
Elliott	Martin Elliott, *Shakespeare's Invention of Othello: A Study in Early Modern English* (1988)
ELN	*English Language Notes*
ELR	*English Literary Renaissance*
ES	*English Studies*
Erickson	Peter Erickson, *Citing Shakespeare: The Reinterpretation of Race in Contemporary Art and Literature* (New York, 2007)
Everett, '"Spanish" Othello'	Barbara Everett, '"Spanish" Othello: the making of Shakespeare's Moor', *SS*, 35 (1982), 101–12
Faucit	Helen Faucit, Lady Martin, *On Some of Shakespeare's Female Characters* (Edinburgh, 1891)
Fernández	José Ramón Díaz Fernández, 'Othello On Screen: A Comprehensive Film Bibliography', file:///C:/

	Users/athompson/Downloads/Comprehensive_ film-bibliography_Othello.pdf
Gentleman	Francis Gentleman, *Dramatic Censor, or Critical Companion, Volume the First* (1770)
Granville	*Lord Granville Leveson Gower (First Earl Granville) Private Correspondence 1781 to 1821*, ed. Castalia Countess Granville (New York, 1916)
Greenblatt	Stephen Greenblatt, *Renaissance Self-Fashioning: From More to Shakespeare* (Chicago, 1980)
Greg	W W Greg, *The Shakesprare First Folio: Its Bibliographical and Textual History* (Oxford, 1955)
Grehan	Helena Grehan, 'TheatreWorks' *Desdemona*: Fusing Technology and Tradition', *TDR* 45 (2001), 113–25
Hankey	Julie Hankey, *Othello- William Shakespeare*, Bristol Classical Press: Plays in Performance (1987)
Haraway	Donna J. Haraway, *When Species Meet* (Minneapolis, MN, 2008)
Harding	Jason Harding, 'T. S. Eliot's Shakespeare', *Essays in Criticism* 62 (2012), 160–77
Hatchuel and Vienne-Guerrin	*Shakespeare on Screen: 'Othello'*, eds. Sarah Hatchuel and Nathalie Vienne-Guerrin (Cambridge, 2015)
Hawkins	Frederick William Hawkins, *The Life of Edmund Kean: From Published and Original Sources* (1869)
Hazlitt	William Hazlitt, *London Magazine* VI (June 1820), reprinted in *The Collected Works of William Hazlitt*, volume 8, eds. A. R. Waller and Arnold Glover (1903)
Heilman	R. B. Heilman, *Magic in the Web: Action and Language in 'Othello'* (Lexington, Kentucky, 1956)
Hewlett	James Hewlett, 'Matthews', *National Advocate* (8 May 1824)
Higgins	Chester Higgins, 'Othello: Noble Black', *Jet Magazine* (17 March 1966)
Hill	Errol Hill, *Shakespeare in Sable: A History of Black Shakespearean Actors* (Amherst, MA, 1984)
HLQ	*Huntington Library Quarterly*
Homilies	*Certain Sermons or Homilies* appointed to be read in churches in the rime of the late Queen Elizabeth (Oxford, 1844)

Honigmann, 'Date of *Othello*'	E. A. J. Honigmann, 'The First Quarto of *Hamlet and the date of Othello', RES*, 44 (1993), 211–19
Honigmann, *Seven Tragedies*	E. A. J. Honigmann, *Shakespeare: Seven Tragedies. The Dramatist's Manipulation of Response* (1976)
Honigmann, *Shakespeare*	E. A. J. Honigmann, *Shakespeare: Seven Tragedies Revisited: The Dramatist's Manipulation of Response* (Basingstoke, 2002)
Honigmann, *Stability*	E. A. J. Honigmann, *The Stability of Shakespeare's Text* (1965)
Honigmann, 'Stage direction'	E. A. J. Honigmann, 'Re-enter the stage direction: Shakespeare and some contemporaries', *SS*, 29 (1976), 117–25
Honigmann, *Texts*	E. A. J. Honigmann, *The Texts of 'Othello' and Shakesperian Revision* (1996)
Hulme	Hilda M. Hulme, *Explorations in Shakespeare's Language* (1962)
Hunter	G. K. Hunter, *Dramatic Identities and Cultural Tradition: Studies in Shakespeare and His Contemporaries* (Liverpool, 1978)
Jackson	C. Bernard Jackson, *Iago: A Play in Two Acts* (Los Angeles, 1979)
James	Henry James, 'Tommaso Salvini: In Boston, 1883', in *The Scenic Art* (New York, 1957), 168–85
Jennings	Caleen Sinnette Jennings, *Playing Juliet/Casting Othello* (Woodstock, IL, 1999)
Johnson	Samuel Johnson, *Johnson on Shakespeare*, ed. Walter Raleigh (1908)
Jonson	*Ben Jonson*, ed. C. H. Herford and Percy and Evelyn Simpson, 11 vols (Oxford, 1925–52)
Jones, E.	Eldred Jones, *Othello's Countrymen: The African in English Renaissance Drama* (Oxford, 1965)
Jones, L.	LeRoi Jones (aka Amiri Baraka), 'The Revolutionary Theatre', *The Liberator* (July 1965), 4–6
Jones and Niven	James Earl Jones and Penelope Niven, *James Earl Jones: Voices and Silences* (New York, 1993)
Karim-Cooper	Farah Karim-Cooper, *Cosmetics in Shakespearean and Renaissance Drama* (Edinburgh, 2006)
Kastan	David Scott Kastan, *A Will to Believe: Shakespeare and Religion* (Oxford, 2014)
Kaul	Mythili Kaul, 'Preface', in *Othello: New Essays by Black Writers*, ed. Mythili Kaul (Washington DC, 1996), 1–19

Kemble, *Records*	Fanny Kemble, *Records of Later Life* (1882) (New York, 2015)
Kemble, 'Salvini'	Fanny Kemble, 'Salvini's Othello', *Temple Bar Magazine* 71 (July 1884)
Knolles	Richard Knolles, *The General History of the Turks* (1603)
Kolin	Philip C. Kolin, 'Blackness Made Visible: A Survey of *Othello* in Criticism, on Stage, and on Screen', in *Othello: New Critical Essays*, ed. Philip C. Kolin (New York, 2002), 1–87
Leavis	F. R. Leavis, 'Diabolic Intellect and the Noble Hero: A Note on *Othello*', *Scrutiny* (December 1937), 259–83
Lennox	Charlotte Lennox, *Shakespear Illustrated: or the Novels and Histories on which the Plays of Shakespear are Founded, Collected and Translated from the Original Authors: With Critical Remarks: In two volumes. By the Author of the Female Quixote*, 3 vols (1753–4)
Lester	Adrian Lester, Interview with Ayanna Thompson (13 September 2013)
Lewes	George Henry Lewes, *On Actors and the Art of Acting* (1875)
Lindfors	Bernth Lindfors, 'The Signifying Flunkey: Ira Aldridge as Mungo', *Literary Griot* 5 (Fall 1993), 1–11
Lyly	*The Complete Works of John Lyly*, ed. R. Warwick Bond, 3 vols (Oxford, 1902)
MacDonald	Joyce Green MacDonald, 'Acting Black: *Othello*, *Othello* Burlesques, and the Performance of Blackness', *TJ* 46 (1994), 231–49
Mack	Maynard Mack, *Everybody's Shakespeare* (1993)
Malone	Edmund Malone, *Historical Account of the Rise and Progress of the English Stage, and of the Economy and Usages of the Ancient Theatres in England* (1800)
Mandeville	Sir John Mandeville, *The Book of Marvels and Travels* (c. 1371) trans. Anthony Bale (Oxford, 2012)
Mares	Francis Hugh Mares, 'The Origin of the Figure Called "the Vice" in Tudor Drama', *HLQ* 22 (1958), 11–29
Marlowe	*The Complete Works of Christopher Marlowe*, ed. Fredson Bowers, 2 vols (Cambridge, 1973)

Martial	*The Epigrams of Martial*, Bohn's Classical Library (1907)
Memoir	*Memoir and Theatrical Career of Ira Aldridge: African Roscius* (1848)
MIT	MIT's Global Shakespeares open access website: http://globalshakespeares.mit.edu/#
Molà	Lucy Molà, *The Silk Industry of Renaissance Venice* (Baltimore, 2000)
Montaigne	*The Essayes*, tr. John Florio, Everyman's Library, 3 vols (1910)
Morrison	Toni Morrison, Speech given at '*Desdemona*: Dialogues Across Histories, Continents, Cultures', UC Berkeley (28 October 2011): https://www.youtube.com/watch?v=79K_hMW102g
Morrison and Traoré	Toni Morrison and lyrics by Rokia Traoré, *Desdemona* (2012)
MSR	Malone Society Reprints
Muir	Kenneth Muir, *The Sources of Shakespeare's Plays* (1977)
National Theatre	National Theatre Online, 'Emilia and Desdemona: Women in Othello': http://www.nationaltheatre.org.uk/video/emilia-and-desdemona-women-in-othello
Neill	Michael Neill, 'Unproper Beds: Race, Adultery, and the Hideous in *Othello*', *SQ* 40 (1989), 383–412
N&Q	*Notes and Queries*
Noble	Richmond Noble, *Shakespeare's Biblical Knowledge and Use of the Book of Common Prayer* (1935)
NYT	*New York Times*
OED	*Oxford English Dictionary*, 3rd edn (Oxford, 2002)
Okri	Ben Okri, 'Leaping Out of Shakespeare's Terror: Five Meditations on *Othello*', in *A Way of Being Free* (London, 1997), 71–87
Olivier	Laurence Olivier, *On Acting* (1986)
Pao	Angela Pao, 'Ocular Revisions: Re-casting *Othello* in Text and Performance', in *Colorblind Shakespeare: New Perspectives on Race and Performance*, ed. Ayanna Thompson (New York, 2006), 27–45
Partridge	Eric Partridge, *Shakespeare's Bawdy* (1947, repr. 1961)
Pechter	Edward Pechter, *Othello and Interpretive Traditions* (Iowa City, 1999)

PG	*Providence Gazette*
Pliny	Pliny the Elder, *The Historie of the World*, trans. Philemon Holland (1601)
Potter	Lois Potter, *Shakespeare in Performance: 'Othello'* (Manchester, 2002)
PQ	*Philological Quarterly*
Quarshie	Hugh Quarshie, *Second Thoughts about 'Othello'* (Chipping Camden, 1999)
Raber	Karen Raber, *Animal Bodies, Renaissance Culture* (Philadelphia, PA, 2013)
RD	*Renaissance Drama*
Rosenberg	Marvin Rosenberg, *The Masks of Othello: The Search for the Identity of Othello, Iago, and Desdemona by Three Centuries of Actors and Critics* (Berkeley, CA, 1961)
RQ	*Renaissance Quarterly*
Rymer	Thomas Rymer, *A Short View of Tragedy* (1693) in *The Critical Works of Thomas Rymer*, ed. Curt Zimanksy (New Haven, 1956)
SAR	*South Atlantic Review*
SB	*Shakespeare Bulletin*
Sears, *Harlem*	Djanet Sears, *Harlem Duet* (Winnipeg, 1997)
Sears, 'Notes'	Djanet Sears, "Notes of a Coloured Girl: 32 Short Reasons Why I Write for the Theatre", in *Harlem Duet* (Winnipeg, 1997), 11–15
Seeff	Adele Seeff, '*Othello* at the Market Place', *SB* 27 (2009), 377–98
Sellars	Peter Sellars, "Foreword", in Toni Morrison, *Desdemona, Lyrics by Rokia Traoré* (2012), 7–11
Sen, '*Desdemona*'	Ong Keng Sen, '*Desdemona* Program Notes', in *Telstra Adelaide Festival Program Notes* (March 2000)
Sen, 'On'	Ong Keng Sen, 'On *Desdemona*: In Response', *TDR* 45 (2001), 118
Shafer	Jack Shafer, 'Who You Calling "Arab"?' *Slate Magazine* (17 February 2004)
Shattuck	Charles H. Shattuck, *William Charles Macready's 'King John': A Facsimile Prompt-Book* (Urbana, IL, 1962)
Shaw	George Bernard Shaw, 'Preface: Better than Shakespear' in *Three Plays for Puritans* (Chicago, IL, 1901)

Sher	Antony Sher, 'Iago', in *Performing Shakespeare's Tragedies Today: The Actor's Perspective*, ed. Michael Dobson (Cambridge, 2006), 57–69
Sisson	C. J. Sisson, *New Readings in Shakespeare*, 2 vols (Cambridge, 1956)
Smith, 'Othello'	Ian Smith, 'Othello's Black Handkerchief', *SQ* 64.1 (2013): 1–25
Smith, *Race*	Ian Smith, *Race and Rhetoric in the Renaissance: Barbarian Errors* (New York, 2009)
Smith, 'White'	Ian Smith, 'White Skin, Black Masks: Racial Cross-Dressing on the Early Modern Stage', *RD* 32 (2003), 33–67
Snow	Edward A. Snow, 'Sexual Anxiety and the Male Order of Things in *Othello*', *ELR* 10 (1980), 384–412
Snyder	Susan Snyder, *The Comic Matrix of Shakespeare's Tragedies* (Princeton, NJ, 1979)
Spencer	Hazelton Spencer, *Shakespeare Improved: The Restoration Versions in Quarto and on the Stage* (Cambridge, MA, 1927)
Sprague	Arthur Colby Sprague, *Shakespeare and the Actors: The Stage Business in his Plays (1660–1905)* (Cambridge, Massachusetts, 1945)
SQ	*Shakespeare Quarterly*
SRP	*Saturday Review of Politics*
SS	*Shakespeare Survey*
SSt	*Shakespeare Studies*
Stendhal	Stendhal, *Racine and Shakespeare* (1823), trans. Guy Daniels (New York, 1962)
Stern	Tiffany Stern, *Documents of Performance in Early Modern England* (Cambridge, 2009)
Sternfeld	F. N. Sternfeld, *Music in Shakespearean Tragedy* (1963)
Sugg	Richard Sugg, *Mummies, Cannibals, and Vampires: The History of Corpse Medicine from the Renaissance to the Victorians* (New York, 2011)
Taylor and Nance	Gary Taylor and John V. Nance, 'Imitation or Collaboration? Marlowe and the Early Shakespeare Canon', *SS* 60 (2015), 32–47
TDR	*The Drama Review*
Terry, *Four*	Ellen Terry, *Four Lectures on Shakespeare*, ed. Christopher St. John (New York, 1969)
Terry, *Story*	Ellen Terry, *The Story of My Life: Recollections and Reflections* (New York, 1908)

Texts	See Honigmann, *Texts*
Thompson, An	Ann Thompson, 'Charlotte Lennox and her Challenge to the Orthodoxies of Shakespeare Criticism', in *Challenging Orthodoxies: The Social and Cultural Worlds of Early Modern Women*, eds Sigrun Haud and Melinda S. Zook (Surrey, 2014), 147–61
Thompson, Ay, *Passing*	Ayanna Thompson, *Passing Strange: Shakespeare, Race, and Contemporary America* (Oxford, 2011)
Thompson, Ay, 'Two'	Ayanna Thompson, 'Two Actors on Shakespeare, Race, and Performance: A Conversation between Harry J. Lennix and Laurence Fishburne', *SB* 27 (2009), 41–56
Thompson and Turchi	Ayanna Thompson and Laura Turchi, *Teaching Shakespeare with Purpose: A Student-Centred Approach* (2016)
Tilley	Morris Palmer Tilley, *A Dictionary of the Proverbs in England in the Sixteenth and Seventeenth Centuries* (Ann Arbor, MI, 1950)
Tillotson	Geoffrey Tillotson, '*Othello* and *The Alchemist* at Oxford in 1610', *TLS* (20 July 1933)
TJ	*Theatre Journal*
TLS	*Times Literary Supplement*
Towes	John Ranken Towes, *Sixty Years of the Theatre: An Old Critic's Memories* (New York, 1916)
Tynan	Kenneth Tynan, *'Othello': The National Theatre Production* (New York, 1966)
van Gelder	Robert van Gelder, 'Robeson Remembers: An Interview with the Star of "Othello," Partly about His Past', *NYT* 16 (January 1944)
Vaughan, *Othello*	Virginia Mason Vaughan, *Othello: A Contextual History* (Cambridge, 1994)
Vaughan, *Performing*	Virginia Mason Vaughan, *Performing Blackness on English Stages, 1500–1800* (Cambridge, 2005)
Vickers	Brian Vickers, *Shakespeare, Co-Author: A Historical Study of Five Collaborative Plays* (Oxford, 2002)
Vitkus, *Piracy*	Daniel Vitkus, ed., *Piracy, Slavery, and Redemption: Barbary Captivity Narratives from Early Modern England* (New York, 2001)
Vitkus, *Turning*	Daniel Vitkus, *Turning Turk: English Theater and the Multicultural Mediterranean 1570–1630* (New York, 2003)
Vogel	Paula Vogel, *Desdemona, a play about a handkerchief* (New York, 1994)

Walton	J. K. Walton, *The Quarto Copy for the First Folio of Shakespeare* (Dublin, 1971)
Webster	Margaret Webster, *Don't Put Your Daughter on the Stage* (New York, 1972)
Weinert-Kendt	Rob Weinert-Kendt, 'Bill Pullman Plays Othello as a Stranger in a Strange Land (Norway)', *AT* (5 February 2015).
White	Shane White, *Stories of Freedom in Black New York* (Cambridge, MA, 2002)
Wilson *Othello*	John Dover Wilson, 'Introduction', *Othello*, eds. Alice Walker and John Dover Wilson (1957) (Cambridge, 1969), ix–lxix
Wotton	Logan Pearsall Smith, *The Life and Letters of Sir Henry Wotton*, 2 vols (Oxford, 1907, repr. 1966)
Young	Julian Charles Young, *A Memoir of Charles Mayne Young, tragedian, with extracts from his son's journal* (1871)

INDEX

This index covers the Introduction, Commentary and Appendices. It omits Honigmann, *Texts; Othello*; William Shakespeare; and all *OED* entries except those listed as Shakespeare's coinages or 'first here' or 'first recorded' in a particular year.